STUDIES IN THE HISTORY
OF BOOKBINDING

Studies in the History of Bookbinding

Mirjam M. Foot

Scolar Press

Published by
SCOLAR PRESS
Gower House
Croft Road
Aldershot
Hants GU11 3HR
England

Ashgate Publishing Company
Old Post Road
Brookfield
Vermont 05036
USA

British Library Cataloguing-in-Publication Data
Foot, Mirjam M.
Studies in the History of Bookbinding
I. Title
686.309

reprinted 1994

ISBN 0 85967 935 7

Phototypeset in 10 point Garamond by Intype, London
and printed in Great Britain at the University Press, Cambridge.

Contents

Illustrations

Introduction

This book consists of articles on the history of bookbinding and related subjects, written over the past twelve years. Not all that I have written during this period has been included. Book reviews, introductions to catalogues and catalogue entries have been omitted; unpublished lectures have been shelved for a possible future occasion, and several articles on the Henry Davis Gift to the British Library have not been reprinted for the simple reason that their substance has been treated in the two published volumes of *The Henry Davis Gift* (London, 1978, 1983), or will be dealt with in the third volume.

All articles collected here have been published previously or are currently in the press. The date directly underneath the title of each article is that of its first publication (or, for 1, 62 and 64, that of writing), and a note at the foot of the first page of each article indicates where it first appeared.

Several articles have been updated and two have been substantially rewritten. They have been grouped under seven headings and range from such general topics as bookbinding as a subject for study and the need to preserve the book in all its aspects, to more detailed descriptions of individual bindings (from the fifteenth to the twentieth century), and discussions of binders, the binding trade, collectors and collections.

The balance is heavily weighted in favour of gold-tooled bindings, showing an early liking for the splendid products of the sixteenth, seventeenth and eighteenth centuries. Gradually my preference has shifted towards the earlier periods. Over recent years I have become more interested in the study of binding structures and binding techniques and, most recently, in exploring the relation between the history of bookbinding and that of book production, the booktrade, and—more generally—the history of the book and its place in the history of society at large.

Collecting and re-reading one's own articles is a sobering experience. Drawing up a balance sheet of areas investigated in some depth, surfaces barely scratched and territories left unexplored is a salutary and healthy exercise, and I see this book less as an *apologia pro vita mea* than an account of time spent and an indication of what to pursue next.

Mirjam Foot
London, June 1990

Acknowledgements

Many of the articles in this book were first printed in *The Book Collector* and I am grateful to Mr Nicolas Barker for permission to reprint them here.

I am also grateful to Miss Robin Myers and Dr Michael Harris, to the Designer Bookbinders, the Cambridge University Press, the Association Internationale de Bibliophilie, The Library of Congress, to Dr C. de Hamel and Mr R. A. Linenthal, to Dr G. A. M. Janssens, Dr F. G. A. M. Aarts and Rodopi, to Mr N. Israel, Dr Nicholas Pickwood, to the Institute of Paper Conservation, Mr Guy Petherbridge, and to the Society of Bookbinders and Book Restorers.

I am grateful to the following for permission to reproduce photographs of bindings in their collection: the British Library Board; the Society of Antiquaries of London; the Bodleian Library, Oxford; the Librarian of the New University of Ulster, Coleraine; the Herzog August Bibliothek, Wolfenbüttel; Monsieur Henri Schiller; the Syndics of Cambridge University; the Library of Congress; the Archbishop of Canterbury; the Master and Fellows of Magdelene College, Cambridge; the Dean and Chapter of Westminister Abbey; the National Trust.

I am most grateful to the staff of British Library Reproductions; Ms Nicolette Hallet and Mr Michael Falter for their excellent photographs.

I am indebted to Mr David Way for all his help and advice and—as always—to my husband for his never-failing support.

MMF

Part I
WHY BOOKBINDING?

There is no greater conversation killer than an admission to an overriding interest in the history of bookbinding. This usually elicits a nervous little cough, a flat 'how fascinating' and a hasty change of subject. Even among fellow-historians and bibliographers, bookbinding is considered an eccentric subject, out on a limb, not part of the mainstream of cultural or socio-historical research, not even a particularly significant part of the history of the booktrade. Admittedly, most of the published literature has not done much to place the history of bookbinding in a wider historical context, but if one reads carefully and between the lines, it becomes clear that the history of bookbinding touches on, and in some instances invades, a number of other areas of study, such as religion, art, sociology, history of scholarship, patronage, collecting, market forces, readership and education, as well as forming part of the study of book production and booktrade.

The first article that follows was an attempt at showing, originally in the space of a 50-minute lecture, what the study of bookbinding can contribute to the history of the book, its use and its readership. Although it leans for its examples rather heavily on work done by others, especially C. H. Roberts and T. C. Skeat, and C. de Hamel, as well as on work published by myself elsewhere, I have nevertheless included it here as it uses these examples to a different purpose.

The second article discusses an aspect of the economics of the booktrade. Two versions of this paper were published, the first in G. Colin (ed.), *De libris compactis miscellanea*, Brussels (for the Bibliotheca Wittockiana), 1984. The second, slightly amended version appeared in R. Myers and M. Harris (eds.), *Economics of the British Booktrade 1605–1939*, Publishing History, Occasional Series I, Cambridge, 1985. The latter version has been used here.

1 Bookbinding and the History of Books

(1987)*

One can study the history of bookbinding in a variety of ways. In the nineteenth and in the first three-quarters of the present century, the history of bookbinding was virtually synonymous with the history of binding decoration. With the exception of Mlle de Regemorter who studied the construction of Coptic and Anglo-Saxon bindings in the 1940s, 1950s and 1960s,[1] most scholars who devoted themselves to the history of binding were primarily interested in the styles and designs that embellish the covers and in the tools used to effect these designs. In England, the late Graham Pollard became interested in binding structure during the 1950s and published interesting articles on the lacing-in patterns of Anglo-Saxon and early medieval bindings, on medieval binding structures, and on changes in the technique of bookbinding between 1550 and 1830.[2] Other binding historians, such as Jean Vézin in France, Guy Petherbridge and Gulnar Bosch in the US, Roger Powell, Bernard Middleton, Chris Clarkson, and Nicholas Pickwood in Great Britain, and Janos Szirmai in the Netherlands have followed this trend and have produced very good work on the history of binding techniques.

A descriptive study of contemporary binding technique is — of course — nothing new, and one has but to glance at the chronological table in Pollard and Potter's excellent *Early Bookbinding Manuals* (Oxford, 1984) to see that references to bookbinding as a craft have been traced as far back as the sixth century AD. A tenth-century Oriental craftsman, Abū Ja'far al-Naḥḥās, was the first to describe in any detail how to bind books,[3] and this kind of 'trade' literature has continued over the centuries until the present day.

A different way of looking at the history of binding concentrates on the binder and his role in society. Not much work has been done in this field, as most historians of the booktrade seem to have concerned themselves mainly with scribes, or printers and publishers, rather than with binders. Paul Christianson has done some work on binders in medieval England[4] and Ellic Howe's delightful book on *The London Bookbinders*,

* Based on a lecture given at the William Andrews Clark Memorial Library, University of California, L.A., in 1987. To be published by the British Library.

2

1780–1806 (London, 1950)[5] looks at the economic and social position of these craftsmen at the end of the eighteenth and the beginning of the nineteenth centuries. In the introduction to his *List of London Book-binders, 1648–1815* (London, 1950) he again touches on these themes. The publisher, John Dunton, in his *Life and Errors* (London, 1705) wrote biographical sketches of seventeen bookbinders at work during his lifetime and from these one can catch a glimpse of their social standing. They appear a pious assembly, 'true sons of the Church', 'keeping close to the private and public duties of Divine Worship'; politically sound (e.g. R. Baldwin who 'was a true lover of King William, always voted on the right side'); 'tender Husband[s]', 'kind Father[s]', 'dutiful Son[s]', judicious, honest and industrious, in short, pillars of society. This is not the impression created in John Jaffray's manuscript volumes relating to the binding trade in the period from 1786 to 1820,[6] where they come across as a quarrelsome lot, fond of strong drink and not averse to a brawl. Dibdin, whose colourful descriptions of books and their producers are an unfailing source of amusement, hints, for example, at the social status of Charles Lewis, the leading London binder of the early nineteenth century, who went about with 'tassels to his half-boots',[7] a flamboyancy of style which some of his patrons evidently thought unbecoming for a tradesman. From other sources concerning the booktrade, both archival and printed, one can get a picture of the bookbinder as one of the humbler members of the trade, not very highly regarded, although evidently a number of binders prospered and added publishing and bookselling to their binding business, thus becoming employers and businessmen, rather than crafts-men.

Yet another approach to the history of bookbinding is that which shows how the binding as a physical object, its form, its construction, as well as its decoration, can teach us something about the history of the book in general, its development, its use and its readership. Potentially this is a gigantic subject, only three aspects of which I will try and develop here. The first is *how use and readership can dictate the form and construction of the book and vice versa,* and for this we turn to antiquity and look at the development from scroll to codex.

In the West, the most important development in the history of books before the age of printing was the change from scroll to codex. The codex can be defined as a collection of sheets of any material, folded and fastened together at the back or spine and usually protected by covers. There has been very little doubt that the physical origin of the codex is to be found in the writing tablet. When the change from scroll to codex took place, why, and in what circles the codex was first used has been the subject of a debate that has not yet reached its final conclusion.[8]

Scrolls or rolls were long strips of leather or papyrus, the papyrus strips being made of individual sheets glued together. They were inscribed in columns, usually on one side only, and rolled up for storage. When stored the rolls might simply be tied with tapes, or they might have leather wrappers or cylindrical boxes. They might have a wooden or bone roller attached to one end to facilitate rolling and unrolling.

Writing tablets were commonly formed of two or more pieces of wood, held together either by a clasp or by strings passed through pierced holes. The centre of the tablet was usually hollowed out to receive wax (though writing with ink or chalk directly onto wood is not unknown). There is epigraphic evidence that the ancient Greeks used writing tablets of this kind and they are mentioned in Homer, Sophocles and Euripides. In later Greece they were used for any writing of an impermanent nature, such as letters, bills, school exercises, memoranda or author's first drafts. Pliny the younger describes how his uncle compiled his *Natural History*: a slave would take down on wax tablets the author's thoughts, but the final version would be written on rolls, filled on both sides.

Already in the fifth century BC tablets of several leaves were in use, but the nature of the material would set a limit to their number and no specimen surviving from antiquity has more than ten leaves. The Latin word for more than one tablet or for multi-leaved tablets was codex, whether the material was wood (as was usually the case) or ivory. Seneca, Cato and Cicero all used the term, and the latter frequently describes tablets used for business or legal purposes as such. But the word codex did not, until much later, mean a book.

The poet Martial, writing in or near 85 AD, described literary publications in codex form (without using the term), but they were still curiosities, and for at least 200 years more, pagan literature continued to be written on rolls. The earliest use of the word codex for a book dates from the third century AD and it was first used by a Christian writer. This is significant, as it is the Christian literature that was first found in codex form. The earliest surviving fragments of the Christian Bible, dating from the second century, are in this form. It is not until the fourth century, roughly at the time when the Roman Empire became officially Christian, that we find the codex form normally used for non-Christian literature.

The wooden tablets were gradually replaced by pieces of parchment or papyrus. The earliest evidence for a parchment diptych, two leaves of equal size held together by a leather thong, is a deed of registration, written in the last century BC or the first century AD. Both Horace and Persius refer to writing on parchment leaves (*membranae*) and later authors refer to their use for letters, accounts and legal documents. When Quintillian, *c.* 90 AD, writes about *membranae* as the best way for students to take notes, we have reached a stage in the history of the codex where it is more than a tablet but less than a book.

There are arguments in favour of the practicality of the codex form *vis-à-vis* the roll, and Martial points out the convenience to the traveller and the way the codex saves space in a library. It was also cheaper and more compact, as in a codex both sides of the parchment were used, while usually only one side of the roll was covered in writing. For reference use or for finding a specific passage, it has advantages over the roll for the reader, as everyone knows who has ever used a microfilm.[9] All the same, the transition from papyrus or leather roll to parchment codex as the normal form for a book was not a single step. The question whether the parchment codex antedates the papyrus codex is—still—wide open. The format and material are not essentially linked. The slow growth in the use of parchment may be explained by the fact that special skills were required to produce a good quality article. Equally, the yield per animal slaughtered would not have been very great.

All this does not explain why it is that the earliest surviving biblical and other Christian manuscripts are in codex form. In 1954 C. H. Roberts put forward the hypothesis that St Peter's auditors in Rome would have been using parchment notebooks and that St Mark as the first evangelist might have used such notebooks, which were then transmitted to Alexandria, where papyrus was the normal writing material.[10] In 1983 Roberts and Skeat rejected this as implausible because neither St Mark's Gospel nor the Church of Alexandria were so influential in early centuries as to be likely to impose a new pattern of book production on other cities. They suggested instead that the earliest Christian communities, such as those in Antioch and Jerusalem, borrowed the Jewish custom of writing rabbinic sayings on tablets of papyrus. According to Jewish law, oral law (i.e. rabbinic sayings) could not be formally published; formal publication meant having been written on rolls. Instead, they were recorded in 'unpublished' ephemeral form on tablets, and the early Christians were writing the sayings of Jesus down in the same way. A contributing factor may have been the wish of the early Christians to emphasize the break with the pagan cultural tradition; pagan literature was written on rolls, like the formal Jewish law, while the new Christian literature was to be written on tablets or notebooks. Whatever the reason, the surviving evidence bears out the fact that for Christian literature the codex was the preferred format. For pagan literature the codex was practically unknown in the first century, little used in the second century, while its use increased during the third century and in the beginning of the fourth century, and gradually became the normal form during the latter century. It is striking that the tendency to use the codex more and more runs parallel with the Christianization of the Roman Empire.

The second aspect which I would like to develop is *how the spread of learning and the increase in readership, and hence the increase in book production, can be demonstrated in the changes in styles and techniques of bookbinding.*

Let us go to France in the twelfth century, where the development of the Cathedral schools stimulated the booktrade and gave rise to new developments in decorated leather bindings. Prior to this, very few European decorated leather bindings are known. Apart from the seventh-century Anglo-Saxon binding of the Stonyhurst Gospels, and three eighth- or ninth-century bindings now at Fulda,[11] there are no other known European decorated leather bindings until the twelfth century. These earliest Romanesque bindings were made in France and they mostly cover glossed books of the Bible. Christopher de Hamel[12] has shown that they were made in monasteries in Paris, where the manuscripts themselves were produced. These bindings differ from the run-of-the-mill undecorated medieval bindings, not only in the fact that they are embellished with stamps, but also in that they are made of tanned brown leather instead of the white tawed leather of which most plainer bindings are made. Like the plainer bindings they also had clasps. These clasps were made of leather thongs, attached to the outer edge of the upper board, with pierced metal finials that fitted over pins, protruding from nearly half-way across the lower cover. This tells us something about the storage of these books. They could not have fitted side by side in a book chest, as the protruding pin in the lower cover would have damaged the book next to it. These books were therefore meant to be either held in the hand or displayed on a lectern or desk with the lower cover uppermost. Likewise, the use of ornamental stamps indicates that these books were not purely for reading but that they were in themselves ornamental objects. Why were they made at all? G. D. Hobson believed that these books were prepared by the stationers for sale and that their decorated bindings might be intended to attract potential customers.[13] De Hamel questioned this explanation and put forward as an alternative version that these books may have been the cheaper copies of the jewelled or metal bindings made for use in churches. De Hamel suggests that these glossed books of the Bible were essentially privately-owned manuscripts. They were produced in schools where masters gave lectures on the sacred text. These schools were monasteries and religious houses with traditional associations with students and scholarship. Here the masters made the gloss available for copying; they also provided the blank vellum, the exemplars, and—when the book was finished—a cheap and decorative binding.

In addition, the Cistercian belief that an excess of ornamentation was wrong and distracted from the sacred text, clashing with the ancient tradition that it was almost a religious duty to embellish the sacred page, and that monochrome impressed ornamentation was perhaps in order, may have had its influence, especially if we consider that the earliest examples of French Romanesque bindings were presented to the monastery of Clairvaux by Prince Henry, son of King Louis VI, a personal friend of St Bernard. Why then did the production of these stamped bindings virtually stop in Paris in the early thirteenth century, not to be revived until the end of the middle ages? Around 1200 we see the appearance in Paris of the professional stationer, the entrepreneur who controlled the exemplar, but who did not himself make the parchment, nor write the text, nor paint the initials, nor make the binding. He simply arranged for these matters to be done by different craftsmen and scribes, and sold the result. The settlement in Paris of these lay craftsmen meant that the close link between the owner of the exemplar, the scribe and the binder no longer existed. It is interesting that this change in production and publishing pattern resulted in a change of finished product. We now find law books and complete Bibles, but the individual books of the Bible with their glosses in stamped bindings, part of the standard library of the Parisian student during the last quarter of the twelfth century, disappear in the early thirteenth century.

The technique of decorating leather bindings with engraved tools appears to have re-emerged in Paris in the 1370s, but a revival on any scale of stamped bindings on the Continent of Europe goes hand in hand with the monastic revival of the first half of the fifteenth century. The reform movement among the Italian Benedictine Abbeys spread rapidly all over Europe. The two major religious reform movements in Germany were those of the Benedictine monasteries, centralized in the Bursfeld Congregation, and of the Canons Regular of St Augustine. In the Netherlands, it was the Windesheim Congregation and the Brotherhood of the Common Life whose influence on the history of learning and on book production was considerable. The monastic reform, with its return to the strict observance of the rules of the religious orders and its emphasis on study, on reading and on writing, stimulated the formation of monastic libraries and necessitated the binding of books. The Brotherhood of the Common Life especially, made a profession of binding books. These bindings were decorated with blind lines and blind tools and many examples from the fifteenth century, especially from Germany and the Netherlands, but also from Italy and Spain, have survived. Fewer French and English bindings of this period are still in existence. In France, the destruction of monastic libraries at the time of the Revolution was thorough, but earlier, during the seventeenth and eighteenth centuries, many old books had been lovingly rebound. In England the destruction, first at the suppression of the monasteries under Henry VIII and then by the Puritans of Cromwell's time, made sure that very few monastic bindings survived.

The increase in book production after the invention of printing caused an increase in the production of blind-tooled bindings. Soon a cheaper and quicker way of binding decoration was developed at the end of the fifteenth century with the introduction first of rolls and then of panels.

These changes in the styles of binding were not limited to decoration only. A number of changes took place in the construction of books, mostly as a result of the need to speed up production and to cut the cost of binding. Late medieval manuscript books are no different in form and construction from printed books. The main difference in book production after the invention of printing was the possibility of producing, comparatively easily and comparatively quickly, duplicate copies of the same text. This led to an increase in the number of books available, which in turn led to an increased demand for the binder's skill. As is well known, up to the beginning of the nineteenth century, books were as a rule sold unbound in sheets. No publisher, printer or bookseller would go to the expense of having large numbers of books bound without being sure that he could sell them. There are, of course, exceptions to this and certain types of books, such as school books, popular editions of the classics and certain religious or devotional books, sold sufficiently well for a publisher to have a considerable quantity ready bound in stock.

But with the greater availability of books, the demands made on the binding trade, even by the private owners, increased and with them increased the need for the binders to speed up their production and to cut their costs. This can be demonstrated in the change to cheaper materials and to less time-consuming practices from the beginning of the sixteenth century onwards, accelerating after the industrial revolution in the second half of the eighteenth century, and culminating in the gradual mechanization of binding processes in the 1820s and 1830s.[14] To give a few examples: in the middle ages most binding boards were made of wood and, from the tenth century onwards, most volumes were sewn on split or double leather or vellum thongs with a fairly complicated sewing pattern, and formidable methods of lacing the thongs into the boards. By the middle of the sixteenth century boards were, as a rule, made of pasted sheets of waste or low-quality paper or—a little later—of paper shavings; by that time the practice of sewing on single thongs or cords (made of rope or hemp) was well established, and lacing-in patterns had become noticeably simpler. During the sixteenth century recessed cords came into use, thereby reducing the actual sewing time (as the thread would simply be passed over the cord instead of circling round it), and we find that not all cords are laced in. Often only the first, middle and last cords are laced in, the rest being simply cut off. The sewing process itself was further speeded up by sewing two or more sections at a time, a common practice for trade bindings in the seventeenth century and later. Most manuscripts and early printed books had proper headbands. The top of the spine leather can be folded over and sewn through. Headbands were usually sewn over separate cores, sometimes elaborately plaited, always laced in and with the sewing thread tied down in the centre of each section. Already in the sixteenth century we find false headbands being used: a simple strip of alum-tawed leather, folded over a core and sewn, or strips of vellum over-sewn along the width of the spine (but not tied down) and either stuck onto the backs of the sections with the ends laced in, or stuck onto the boards. For cheap work, pulpboard was used as well as pasteboard in the seventeenth and eighteenth centuries, to be replaced by strawboard in the nineteenth century.

The search for cheaper covering materials goes back a long way. Already in the fourteenth century we find limp vellum used for account books, and limp vellum bindings for school books and classical texts were popular, especially in the Low Countries and Germany, but also in Spain and Italy, in the sixteenth and seventeenth centuries. Attempts at using sheepskin, rather than the more expensive calf, came in for censure from the Stationers' Company in London in the seventeenth century. Paper covers for thin pamphlets were used all over Europe, and in the eighteenth century we find canvas used instead of leather to cover school books, to be followed by the various kinds of book cloth in the nineteenth century. Cutting production cost and time sometimes resulted in sewing as many as six sections at a time, in less lacing in, and in the development (at the very end of the eighteenth century) of sewing on tapes that were then inserted into split boards. We find more and more false headbands, simply made of rolled paper, oversewn with silk, and stuck on the outside of the top and tail of the spine or, simpler still, made of strips of coloured linen or calico, rolled round a piece of string and stuck down.

The introduction of casing in the mid- to late 1820s meant that the cases could be made simultaneously with the book being sewn, rounded and backed, thereby again speeding up production as well as laying open the way to mechanization. There are many more examples, but it should by now be clear that an increase of readership and an increase of book production compelled the binders to look for cheaper materials and speedier processes, thereby altering, and in most instances weakening, the traditional structure of the hand-bound book.

The third aspect to be considered is *how the existence of trade bindings, their structure, and consequently their price, reflect the demands of the reading public.*

I mentioned above that publishers or booksellers would have copies of certain types of saleable books ready bound in stock. What kinds of books they were I have already indicated, but we can be more precise. There is evidence from the seventeenth and eighteenth centuries that the bookbinders of London and Westminster, and also those of the city of Dublin, agreed among themselves on set prices for binding specified kinds of books in certain ways. These prices were published and presented to the booksellers or, in the seventeenth century in London, to the Master, Wardens and Assistants of the Stationers' Company. Nine such published documents still survive, five dating from the seventeenth century and four from the eighteenth century.[15] They take the form of broadsheets, printed in two or three columns. The categories into which the entries are divided either reflect various standard styles of binding or—more commonly— sizes and types of books. The first price list dates from 1619. The various binding styles include 'crosse-bound' or *dos-à-dos* bindings, two small books bound together back to back, sharing one cover, a fairly common feature at the end of the sixteenth century and still current in the 1620s and 1630s. Usually one finds the New Testament at one end and the Anglican Prayer-book and the Psalms in metre at the other. There are a number of decorative styles such as 'Gilt ouer', which for the smaller formats may well refer to decoration in gold with the impression of a single large block; 'gilt, edges and corners', i.e. decorated with corner tools or corner blocks and with gilt edges; 'fillets' and 'ouills', both common during this period. There are also entries for 'Bookes [in] sheepes leather' which are cheaper than the others which are bound in calf, and for 'Bookes in hard bords', presumably books that have been sewn and laced-in in boards but not covered, ready for the professional embroiderers to fit their embroidered covers on.

The 1646 price list is arranged by type of book, an arrangement that remains more or less standard for the rest of the century. The last half-column is devoted to 'Sheeps Leather' binding. Under each heading, indicating kind and size of the books (e.g. 'Bibles in follio', 'Bookes in quarto Lattine', 'Bookes in Octavo English', *etc.*), the various binding styles are indicated. We find again 'Gilt over', 'Corners', 'Edges', 'Fillets' and 'Ovills', but a distinction is made between 'Gilt over' and 'Small tooles ordinary'. The latter way of decorating is more expensive and refers to the application of small hand tools. There is also 'Chequer', slightly more expensive than 'Gilt over', but cheaper than 'Small tooles', which refers to an all-over pattern made with one or two repeating tools. Cheaper still are 'Rolles'.

The sizes of the books are indicated by format (folio, quarto, octavo, *etc.*) but also by paper and type sizes (e.g. 'Crown' and 'pot' for paper sizes and 8° 'Minnion', as distinct from 8°, referring to a type size between non-pareil and brevier). Under each size there are examples of what must have been popular books. Apart from Bibles and Prayer-books, which merit categories of their own, we find under 'Bookes in Lattine' such frequently-read authors as Aristotle, Plutarch, Erasmus, Grotius and Vossius. Books in English include various herbals, such as those by Gerrard and Parkinson, Foxe's *Book of Martyrs*, Lancelot Andrewes's *Sermons*

(1641), Josephus's *History*, and—in smaller formats—Rider's Dictionary, Diodati's *Annotations on the Bible* (4°, 1643) and Henry Scudder, *The Christians Daily Walke* (12mo, 1642). The 1669 list is again divided into Bibles and service books in various sizes, and books in Latin and in English. We find the same binding styles as before. Among the non-liturgical books we find editions of classical authors such as Aristotle, Plutarch, Virgil, Horace and Homer, both in Latin and in English translations; dictionaries (Polyglott Lexicon, Cotgrave's Dictionary); history books (Davila, *The Historie of the Civill Warres of France*, London, 1647, 1648; Th. Fuller, *The Historie of the Holy Warre*); devotional works (R. Baxter's *The Saints Everlasting Rest*, 1669; Jeremy Taylor, *The Rule and Exercises of Holy Living* and *Holy Dying*, Allestree's works); and school books (e.g. *Corderius's School-Colloquies*, grammars and primers).

The same pattern is repeated in the 1695 list. The titles of the books are usually given in an abbreviated form (e.g. 'Hales's Contemplations' [Sir Matthew Hale, *Contemplations Moral and Divine*, London, 1695], 'Lake of the Sacrament' [Edward Lake, *Officium Eucharisticum*, London, 1690], 'Burnet's Abridgment' [Gilbert Burnet, *The Abridgment of the History of the Reformation of the Church of England*, London, 1683]). They were obviously very well-known, popular books for which there was a steady market and which, consequently, could be held in stock ready bound. The fact that these well-known titles were used as examples is borne out by the frequent addition in the lists of the words 'or the like'.

The earliest eighteenth-century list to survive, a 1743 Dublin price list, reverts to the pattern of the 1619 list in that it has been arranged according to style or method of binding. Under each heading the prices are quoted for the various sizes. We find 'Gilt Back only' (with gold-tooling on the spine), 'Books Filleted on the Back only with a Tool added thereto' (calling to mind the frequently found flat spines decorated with a double fillet, evenly spaced to suggest bands, with a small tool in each compartment). There are also categories of 'Books bound in Vellum plain' and 'Forril' (vellum made from unsplit sheepskin), which could be had in yellow or green. The heading 'Russia Bands' refers to a form of stationery binding with two or three Russia leather bands across the spine, extending about half way down the sides.[16] As well as 'Plain Sheep', we find 'Grains', charged for by the hundred. This refers to the grain split or outer split of a sheepskin, the cheapest available leather. Under this heading are entries for 'Testaments Saw'd' and 'Grammars ditto', which indicate an early form of perfect binding. The backs of the sections were sawn in, the cords pressed into the grooves and the whole was glued up without any sewing. This was a very cheap and very unstable way of holding a book together, bearing out what I have said earlier about the trade binders' efforts at finding cheaper and quicker methods to bind the ever-increasing numbers of books for sale.

In the 1744 list, bindings are charged for entirely according to size and one could order them in sheep or calf, plain or with edges (probably marbled, sprinkled or even gilt edges) and 'Letterd' (on the spine). In the last London list of the century, published in 1760, the bindings are also priced according to size and many titles of available books are mentioned. The same pattern of classical texts, reference works (atlases, dictionaries), school books and devotional works can be seen, but we now also find travel books (Harrison's *Voyages*, *The Universal Traveller*, Sloane's *Voyage to the Islands . . . and Jamaica*), books on architecture (Gibbs's *Architecture*, Ware's *Architecture*), and what one may call 'leisure reading' (e.g. two translations of Don Quixote [Smollett and Jarvise], Pope's works, Milton's *Paradise Lost* and *Paradise Regain'd*, *Rasselas*, and *Tristram Shandy*, both just published,[17] and even the *Miss's Magazine* and the *Young Lady's Magazine* [in sheep for 5*d* per volume]). It is interesting to see such a clear indication of the broadening of the reading public in the second half of the eighteenth century.

One could move on from the humble trade bindings discussed above to the expression of luxury, of power even, that can be seen in the splendid bindings made to glorify the Word of God, or in the presentation bindings for the high and mighty. Binding patronage reflects the importance attached to books as embodiments of knowledge, but also as objects of art. However, even the run-of-the-mill trade binding, its form, its structure and its decoration, can tell us a certain amount about the development of the book, its use and its readers. In the scroll and the earliest manifestation of the codex, we saw how form and structure were closely linked to use and to readership. The two occurrences of blind-tooled decoration on tanned leather bindings followed increases in book production as a result of a spread of learning. Increases in book production also caused changes in binding techniques born out of the need to bind more books more quickly and more cheaply, while from the kind of books that were bound for the booksellers' stock and that were given these cheaper treatments, one can infer a changing and growing readership.

In the eighteenth and nineteenth centuries bookbinding was classified among the 'useful arts'. It is more than that: it is a mirror which reflects the history of the book and, if one looks closely, the history of society at large.

1. e.g. B. de Regemorter, 'La Reliure des manuscrits de S. Cuthbert et de S. Boniface', *Scriptorium*, III (1949), pp. 45–51. Id., 'La Reliure des manuscrits

gnostiques découverts à Nag Hamadi', *Scriptorium*, xiv (1960), pp. 225–34. Id., 'Ethiopian Bookbindings', *The Library*, 5th series, xvii (1962), pp. 85–88.

2.   G. Pollard, 'Some Anglo-Saxon Bookbindings', *The Book Collector*, xxiv (1975), pp. 130–59. Id., 'The Construction of English Twelfth-Century Bindings', *The Library*, 5th series, xvii (1962) pp. 1–22. Id., 'Changes in the Style of Bookbinding, 1550–1830', *The Library*, 5th series, xi (1956), pp. 71–94.

3.   G. Bosch, J. Carswell and G. Petherbridge, *Islamic Bindings and Bookmaking*, Chicago, 1981, pp. 2–3.

4.   C. P. Christianson, 'Early London Bookbinders and Parchmeners', *The Book Collector*, xxxii (1985), pp. 41–54. Id., 'Evidence for the study of London's late medieval manuscript book trade' in J. Griffiths and D. Pearsall (eds.), *Book Production and Publishing in Britain, 1375–1475*, Cambridge, 1989. Id., *A Directory of London Stationers and Book Artisans, 1300–1500*, New York, 1990.

5.   Reprinted: Merrion Press and Desmond Zwemmer, London, 1988 [89]. See also: E. Howe and J. Child, *The Society of London Bookbinders, 1780–1951*, London, 1952.

6.   Referred to by E. Howe in his *London Bookbinders, 1780–1806*, London, 1950; a typescript of the fourth of a series of manuscript volumes relating to 'The Art and Trade of Bookbinding', compiled by John Jaffray, dated 1864 (London *c.* 1945) is at the British Library (667.r.19).

7.   T. F. Dibdin, *The Bibliographical Decameron*, London, 1817, vol. II, p. 522.

8.   C. H. Roberts and T. C. Skeat, *The Birth of the Codex*, Oxford, 1983, 2nd ed., 1987 (and for information below).

9.   See also M. Gullick, 'Old Books for New', *Fine Print*, xii, 4 (October 1986), pp. 205–8, who argues that the roll as a book form was perfectly adequate for those who used it. I agree that the reasons for the change from roll to codex were probably religious and political, rather than purely practical.

10.   C. H. Roberts, 'The Codex', *Proceedings of the British Academy*, xl (1954), pp. 169–204.

11.   T. J. Brown (ed.). *The Stonyhurst Gospel of Saint John*, Oxford, 1969, pp. 13–23, 45–55. B. de Regemorter, 'La Reliure des manuscrits de S. Cuthbert et de S. Boniface', *Scriptorium*, iii, (1949), pp. 45–51. D. M. Wilson, 'An Anglo-Saxon Bookbinding at Fulda', *Antiquaries Journal*, xli (1961), pp. 199–217.

12.   C. de Hamel, *Glossed Books of the Bible and the Origins of the Paris Booktrade*, Woodbridge, 1984.

13.   G. D. Hobson, *English Binding before 1500*, Cambridge, 1929. See also: Id., 'Further Notes on Romanesque Bindings', *The Library*, series 4, xv (1934–5), pp. 161–211. Id., 'Some Early Bindings and Binders' Tools', *The Library*, series 4, xix (1938–9), pp. 214–33.

14.   For change in and development of binding structures in England, see: B. C. Middleton, *A History of English Craft Bookbinding Technique*, 2nd ed., London, 1978.

15.   M. M. Foot, 'Some Bookbinders' Price Lists of the Seventeenth and Eighteenth Centuries', in G. Colin (ed.), *De Libris compactis miscellanea*, Brussels, 1984, pp. 273–319: See below, pp. 15–67. A fourth eighteenth-century price list: 'A Regulation of Prices Agreed to by *The Company of Bookbinders* of the City of Dublin . . . 1791', was discovered by Miss M. Pollard (in private ownership).

16. See [H. Parry], *The Art of Bookbinding*, London, 1818, pp. 44–46, frontis-piece.
17. S. Johnson, [Rasselas] *The Prince of Abissinia*, 1st ed., London, 1759., L. Stern, *Tristram Shandy*, vols 1, 2, 1st ed., York, 1760 [1759]. The other seven vols were published between 1761 and 1767.

2 Some Bookbinders' Price Lists of the Seventeenth and Eighteenth Centuries

(1985)*

In his *List of London Bookbinders 1648–1815*, published by the Bibliographical Society in 1950 (pp. xxiv, xxxviii), Ellic Howe mentions the existence of four seventeenth-century bookbinders' price lists. The revised *Short-Title Catalogue of Books*[1] has brought to light a comparable list (7154.3), and the memorandum book of James Coghlan discovered and discussed by H.M. Nixon in the *Journal of the Printing Historical Society*, VI (1970) contains three more binders' price lists dating from the eighteenth century.[2] This seems a good opportunity to publish these lists in full, to show how they differ as well as what they have in common, to try to interpret the headings and descriptions — not always perfectly lucid for a twentieth-century reader — and to identify a few of the books listed as examples.

Before embarking on the lists themselves, or on the books and binding styles set out there, I want to point out that these lists cannot be used to establish the original binding price for a specific seventeenth- or eighteenth-century book. They are lists of prices agreed by the bookbinders amongst themselves or, at a later date, between the bookbinders and the booksellers of London and Westminster, in an attempt at establishing a common price for trade bindings. Fine binding is a different subject altogether and the price, dependent on materials used, time taken, and possibly also on the status of the binder, would vary from volume to volume and might even have been negotiable. There must have been a great many more lists than the eight or nine we know now. But as these lists were ephemeral publications, broadsheets to be discarded as soon as a more up-to-date version had been published, it would not be surprising if the majority had perished. One or two references to other lists exist, and more may well turn up in future.

The prices quoted in the seventeenth-century lists are for books bound in calf, unless otherwise specified. Though Turkey leather had been in use in England since the second half of the sixteenth century, it did not become popular much before the Restoration to the throne of Charles II,

* Publishing History, Occasional Series I: R. Myers and M. Harris (eds.), *Economics of the British Booktrade 1605–1939*, Cambridge, 1985.

and it seems to have been used for bespoke work rather than for trade bindings. Morocco was seldom employed before 1721, and Russia leather, though first mentioned as having been used for binding books *c*.1700, was not in common use much before 1730.[3]

The earliest known list, the only surviving copy of which is now in the library of the Society of Antiquaries in London (Lemon 171), is headed 'A generall note of the prises for binding of all sorts of bookes' and is 'Imprinted at London. 1619' (see Fig. 2.1 and Price List 1). It is a broadsheet printed in three columns and, unlike the majority of the lists, the main categories reflect various styles of binding. Within each category the books are priced according to size. The most confusing aspect of this list is the terminology used in the headings. Phrases such as 'Bookes crosse-gilt ouer', 'All sorts of crosse-bound edges', and 'Bookes crosse-fillets' only become intelligible if one realizes that 'crosse' or 'crosse-bound' refers to what we now call *dos-à-dos* bindings: two small books bound together, back to back, sharing one cover. Usually one finds the New Testament at one end and the Anglican Prayer-book and the Psalms in metre at the other. It will be noted that whenever 'crosse' or 'crosse-bound' occurs in a heading, only books in small format are listed and each time at least two titles are mentioned. If 'crosse' means *dos-à-dos*, 'one way' must apply to the more usual single-bound book. 'Gilt ouer' refers to the all-over decoration of the covers in gold, achieved either with small tools or with blocks. In this list no distinction is made between 'Gilt ouer' and 'Small tooles', but a design of corner and centre pieces with or without a semis of small tools is quite common at the time. For the smaller formats 'Gilt ouer' may easily refer to decoration in gold with the impression of a single large block, a popular way to produce cheaply expensive-looking trade bindings.[4] 'Gilt, edges and corners' refers to gilding the edges of the leaves and to the use of corner blocks or corner tools on the covers. 'Fillets' are created by running a brass wheel engraved with either one or two lines along the edges of the covers, or slightly further in, to form a panel. Both one-line and two-line fillets are commonly found on trade bindings of the seventeenth century, either used blind or with gold leaf. 'Ouills' are oval centre blocks, also quite common during this period, and 'sheepes leather' speaks for itself. The latter was used only for smaller formats, however, and the Stationers' Company had in fact forbidden the use of sheepskin for large books.[5] 'Bookes in hard bords' is more puzzling than it sounds, unless it means just that: books sewn and laced-in in boards, but not covered. Considering that the term is applied only to Foxe's *Book of Martyrs* and to Bibles, Prayer-books and Psalters, and considering that this is the golden age of embroidered binding, these may have been provided for the professional embroiderers or for the ladies who occupied their spare time with needlework. Both would require their books in plain boards round which the embroidered covers could be sewn once they were finished.

The majority of the books mentioned in this list are Bibles, Books of Common Prayer and Psalm Books, in all formats from folio to 32°. Psalm Books in 8° and 16° are specified with the word 'Middleborow', perhaps referring to the Middleburg editions of *The Psalmes of David in meeter, with the prose* [which appears in the margin of the Geneva version], printed by R. Schilders, the 8° edition in 1602 (STC 2507.5) and the 16° in 1599 (STC 2499.9). Nicolas Temperley has argued[6] that the term was used in general for any edition of the English version of the metrical psalms with prose psalms in the margin, based on these Middleburg editions. He also points out that the word 'Psalmes' was commonly used for the metrical version while 'Psalter' was used for the prose version, hence the combination of 'Psalter and Psalmes' in the list. A distinction is also made between a 'Church Bible', the Authorized version printed in black letter, and a 'Romane Bible', the Geneva version in Roman letter which was noticeably smaller. Most of the other books on the list can be identified with the help of the *Short-Title Catalogue of Books . . . 1475–1640* (revised edition, vol. 2, London, 1976, vol. 1, 1986), A.F. Allison and V.F. Goldschmidt, *Titles of English Books*, vol. 1: *1475–1640* (London, 1976), R. Watt's *Bibliotheca Britannica* (London, 1824), and the British Library's Catalogue of Printed Books.[7] It seems pointless to clutter this discussion with long lists of titles — which would become singularly tiresome in the description of some of the later price lists which consist almost entirely of titles — the more so as one cannot be certain that the latest available edition of a particular book is the one quoted for. I have therefore limited myself to the identification (in footnotes to the individual price lists) of one or two books in each category. These are meant as examples of the kind of book for which a standard price could be established and which in turn could serve as a guideline for other books, not listed. The frequency with which the phrase 'or the like' occurs shows that this was precisely the purpose the bookbinders had in mind.

Price List 2 is of a slightly different character. Unlike the others it is not an 'agreed' list of prices for binding, agreed between the bookbinders and the booksellers, but it is a statement of 'Bookes as they are sold bound' issued by Thomas Downes, the King's Printer for Ireland in or shortly after 1620. It gives the prices for various kinds and sizes of books, bound, decorated ('Bust'), with bosses, with clasps or with fillets, as charged in London and in Dublin. This is the only list where bosses and clasps are mentioned. The only known copy of this list (STC 7154.3), a half-sheet folio, is held at the Society of Antiquaries and is hidden in a volume of Proclamations concerning Ireland (1572–1670).[8] Unlike the other lists, the prices include the cost of the actual book as well as that of the binding, and those charged 'At London' are consistently lower than those charged 'At Dublin'.

A copy of the next list, a broadsheet in three columns entitled 'A Generall note of the prises for binding all sortes of bookes', 'Printed at London 1646', is among the Thomason Tracts at the British Library (669.f.10(60)), and has a note in George Thomason's hand indicating that he acquired it on 18 June [1646] (Fig. 2.2 and Price List 3). Unlike the 1619 list, this list is arranged by type of book, an arrangement which remains more or less standard for the rest of the century. The last half column is devoted to 'Sheeps Leather' binding. Under each heading, indicating the kind and size of the book, the various binding styles are listed. *Dos-à-dos* bindings have gone out of fashion and do not occur on the list, nor do books in boards, though embroidered bindings were still produced.[9] 'Gilt over', 'Corners', 'Edges', 'Fillets', and 'Ovills' we have met before, but a distinction is made here between 'Gilt over' and 'Small tooles ordinary'. As the latter way of decorating is more expensive, it strengthens the interpretation of 'Gilt over' as decorated either with a block (for the small formats) or with corner and centre pieces, which are quicker to apply than a number of small hand tools. 'Chequer', slightly more expensive than 'Gilt over' (but cheaper than 'Small tooles'), indicates an all-over pattern made with one or two repeating tools,[10] while 'Rolles' refers to decorating the covers with an engraved brass wheel or roll.

A difference in sewing technique, one more expensive than the other, is indicated by 'double lac'd' and 'single lac'd', referring most probably to sewing on raised bands for which four or five cords were used and sewing on sawn-in or recessed bands for which two thongs or cords were sufficient. In this and more frequently in the later lists, sizes are distinguished not only by format but also by paper and type sizes. Here only 'Crown' (15 × 20 in.) and 'pot' (12½ × 15½ in.) paper are noted and a distinction is also made between 'Bibles in Octavo' and 'Bibles in 8 Minnion'.[11] This seems to be an early use of the term 'minion', a type size between nonpareil and brevier which is not mentioned in Moxon.[12] The *Oxford English Dictionary* records as the earliest use of minion, James Howell's *Vocabulary* of 1659 (section L1).

There remains one expression on this list which used to baffle me. Among the prices quoted for 'Sheeps Leather' one of the cheapest is 'All other bookes 8 & 12 guttard'. As the gutter is the inner (spine) margin of the book, the only suggestion I can make is that it refers to 'stabbed' bindings. The practice of stabbing books, a much quicker but also — especially for small formats with a narrow gutter — a much weaker method of holding the sections together than the conventional sewing on thongs or cords on a sewing frame, was restricted by the Stationers'

Company to a set maximum number of leaves per format, but it was widely adopted for school books and popular works of limited size.[13]

An indication that these lists were issued more frequently than the small number of surviving copies would lead one to believe, is a reference in Courtbook C of the Stationers' Company:

> At a Court held at Stationers' Hall on the sixth of August 1649 ... many Bookbinders came and extended a peticion w[i]th a paper of the prizes of binding bookes w[hi]ch they desired might be confirmed by the table. Whereupon the Court declared their willingnesse to helpe them & have desired Mr Robinson and Mr Thrale to yuse the paper and confer with such of them as they shall choose for that and other matters w[hi]ch they desire to make knowne & remedied & then, upon their request the Court will endeavour to give them satisfaction.

The 'table' referred to must have been one of these price lists, almost certainly very similar to the ones we have seen, and indeed on the next list it is spelled out in the title (Price List 4):

> A General Note of the Prices of Binding all sorts of Books; Agreed on by the Book-binders, whose Names are under-written. As it was presented to the Master, Wardens, and Assistants of the Worshipful Company of Stationers, *August*, the *2d*, 1669.

This broadsheet is in four columns, and was 'Licensed, *September* 23. 1669. [by] Roger L'Estrange'. The list, formerly in the library of the Marquess of Bute, acquired by Francis Edwards, Ltd. and presented to the library of Harvard University by Mr Curt H. Reisinger, was edited by W.A. Jackson and a facsimile was presented as a keepsake to members of the Bibliographical Society of America in 1951. The publication of this list enabled the British Library to discover that it possessed a complete copy, but cut up and preserved in two different volumes of the Bagford collection (Harl. 5915 [items 378–83] and Harl. 5960 [item 26], both now in the Department of Printed Books).

Like the 1646 list, this list is arranged by type of book, with the prices for binding in sheep together at the end and subdivided according to size. Under each heading the different binding styles are quoted for and we meet again such specifications as 'Gilt Edges', 'Fillets', 'Ovals', and 'Rolls'. A new distinction is that between 'Edges Extraordinary' and 'Edges Ordinary', made here for the first time and still occurring on the 1695 list. This could refer to gilt edges in both cases, while the covers are left 'ordinary' or plain, or 'extraodinary', i.e. decorated with a lot of gold tooling as in the modern 'extra' binding. It could also possibly refer to the decoration of the edges themselves. The practice of painting edges under the gold started *c.*1650 and it is possible that 'extraordinary' refers to painted and gilt. As gauffering the edges seems to have gone out of fashion by this date, it is less likely to mean that. However, with painted edges we move somewhat outside the realm of trade bindings, and it is more likely that 'ordinary', if it refers to the edges, means coloured or sprinkled, a quite common way of decorating edges during the seventeenth century, while 'extraordinary' may mean gilt or even marbled, a novelty at the time.

'Marble Fillets' we find here for the first time. The practice of marbling leather had only recently been introduced in England, and an early marbled calf binding, covering a tract volume bound by Samuel Mearne for Cor. Pigeon in 1655, was illustrated as plate 1 by H.M. Nixon in his *English Restoration Bookbindings* (1974). On the 1669 list 'Marble Fillets' on a folio cost 8s. or 10s. It is interesting to see that six years later Samuel Mearne charged £3 per volume for large paper copies of the *Book of Common Prayer* supplied to the Chapel Royal in 'marble leather'. This is not just another example of Mearne being excessively expensive — though as he suffered much from non-payment of royal bills, his prices may well not have reflected those of the trade. In this case the book itself was included in the price and, in addition to fillets, the binding was decorated with the cypher of Charles II at the corners of the panel.

Paper sizes are given again: we find 'Fools-Cap' (13½ × 16¾ in.) as well as 'Crown' and 'Pot', and a distinction is made between 'Bibles in Octavo, Brevere' (brevier, the larger type size) and 'Bibles in Octavo, Nonperil' (nonpareil, the smaller size).

The most notable feature of this 'Note of the Prices' is the list of 82 bookbinders 'whose Names are under-written'. Of these eighteen (marked 'a') were booksellers as well as bookbinders; five (marked 'b') were possibly booksellers as well as binders; 45 (marked 'c') were bookbinders who can be identified from the Stationers' Company's records; and fourteen (marked 'd') are known only from this list.[14] Further information on those men can be found in Ellic Howe's *List of London Bookbinders*.

The last list of the seventeenth century,

A General Note of the Prices of Binding All Sorts of Books in Calves-Leather: Agreed on by the Book-Binders, *Freemen* of the City of *London*, And by them Presented to the Master, Wardens and Assistants of the Worshipful Company of *Stationers*, at a Court holden *March*, 1694/5

exists in two copies (Fig. 2.3 and Price List 5), both among the Bagford fragments in the British Library. One is a broadsheet in three columns 'London: Printed, and are to be Sold by *John Whitlock* near *Stationers-Hall*. 1695', (Harl. 5910 [item 115] kept in the Department of Printed Books), and the other is a not quite accurate and later manuscript copy, (Harl. 5910 [fols. 135–7], in the Department of Manuscripts). The Court meeting referred to in the title took place at Stationers' Hall on Monday, 4 March 1694/5 and during this meeting 'A Peticion of severall Bookbinders representing the lowe condition they were brought to by the lownesse of prices and dearness of Lether was exhibited at this Court being their Approbacion to a table of Rates therewith presented'.[15] Like the earlier lists, the books have been arranged by size, but now the secular titles come first, grouped according to size and language, and the last few lines of the list are devoted to 'The antient allow'd Rate of Binding *Bibles* in *Calf*. In this section only the familiar styles 'Gilt Edges', 'Edges Extraordinary', 'Edges Ordinary', 'Fillets', and 'Ovals' are specified and the prices are the same as those for 1669. The main portion of the list gives the titles *'or the like'* for which binding prices are quoted, followed by generalizations such as '*All Fools Cap thick*', '*All middle siz'd*' or even '*All others*'. The paper sizes specified here include '*Demy*' (17½ × 22 in.) and '*Fools Cap*'.

The source for the three eighteenth-century price lists described here is James Coghlan's memorandum book. On pp. 9–11 he mounted a cut-up list (Price List 6), a broadsheet in three columns, 'Printed by Edward Bate, in *George's Lane* near *Dame's Street*', headed:

> Whereas the BOOKBINDERS of the City of *Dublin* at a Meeting the 15th Day of *September* 1743, then held, did Unanimously Agree, that from and after the 29th of the said Month no Books are to be Bound, Paper Gilt or Black'd, for Booksellers, under the following Prices.

This is the earliest surviving evidence of the Dublin bookbinders combining forces to establish a minimum rate of pay for various types of work. When, in the Spring of 1766, a controversy arose between the binders and booksellers of Dublin about a proposed increase in the price of binding amounting to about nine per cent, the 'former Regulations in the year 1743' were recalled. Two years later, on 25 April 1768, a third price increase was published.[16]

This 1743 list resembles the 1619 price list in that it has been arranged according to style or method of binding. Under each heading the prices are quoted for the various sizes, expressed in formats and paper sizes. Very few actual titles are mentioned. The prices 'For the Gilt Work' are on the whole comparable with those for 'Edges Ordinary' on the 1669 and 1695 London price lists[17] and suggest therefore a certain amount, but not a great deal, of gold tooling. 'Gilt Back only', i.e. with gold tooling on the spine, is a great deal cheaper, and cheaper still are 'Books Filleted on the Back only with a Tool added thereto', calling to mind the frequently encountered flat spines decorated with double fillets, evenly spaced to suggest bands, with a small tool in each compartment. 'Vellum plain' speaks for itself, and 'Forril', vellum made from unsplit sheepskin, is divided into 'yellow' (i.e. natural) and 'green'. On p. 43 of his memorandum book James Coghlan tells us how to make 'Green for Velum' by adding 'Viniger' to 'Brass fileings Desolved in Oyl of Viteral' [oil of vitriol: concentrated sulphuric acid], and on p. 63 he gives another 'Approved Recept' 'To Green Velum, or Foral':

> a Little Vardigrace [verdigris] to half pint of Viniger Best Sort. Take Care Not to put to Much Vardigrace in a Quarter pound is Sufficient to put in a pint & half of Best Viniger. NB: Finding Did not Strike my Velum I put a Little pot ashes [potash: a crude form of potassium carbonate] (viteril [vitriol: a sulphate of iron] answers Better) in it & Used it hot Doing it over Several times it Did.

On the list 'Russia Bands' is placed between 'Books bound in Vellum plain' and 'Forril', and as only large sizes are mentioned it probably does not refer, as I thought at first, to books sewn on cords and bound in Russia leather — an aromatic, diced, usually reddish-brown leather made from calf or cow-hide — but to a form of stationery binding with two or three Russia leather bands sewn across the spine, extending about half way down the sides, as described and illustrated in [H. Parry], *The Art of Bookbinding*.[18] There are separate categories for 'Books bound in Calve's Leather and Letter'd only' [with the title on the spine], for books in 'Plain Sheep' and for 'Books bound in Sheep Banded'. The latter probably refers to sewing on raised cords or bands, a more expensive procedure than either stabbing or sewing on recessed cords.[19]

'Gilt Paper and Black', charged for by the ream, is more likely to refer to gilding or blackening the edges of the paper than to gilding or embossing and colouring black whole sheets. Though funeral services and the like were usually stitched in black paper wrappers, embossed or gilt paper was not yet all that common in England at this date. Metallic-varnish paper or embossed paper was made in London from the early 1690s, but it seems improbable to me that it was produced in quantity in Dublin in the 1740s, the more so as most of the embossed paper that was used at the time was imported from Germany.[20] It is just possible that these prices were sales prices for black and (imported) embossed paper. Robert Dossie describes a method 'of gilding proper for the edges of books and paper', suggesting that the edges of whole sheets were gilt.[21] Similarly, in the 1813 London *Bookbinders' Price-Book* there is a section at the end on 'Gilding and Blacking Paper and Cards', also priced per ream or per pack, and in Parry's *Art of Bookbinding* of 1818, at the end of the chapter on stationery binding, instructions are given for gilding paper and black-edge paper. The gilding here clearly refers to the edges of the paper, while black-edge paper may be notepaper with a black rim along the edges. John Arnett[22] gives a recipe for blackening the edges of a book with ivory black, lamp black or antimony, mixed with a little paste, and we know that James Coghlan considered '½ lb of Antimoney' among the 'Nessesary Utentils in the Arts of Bookbinding'.[23] Ruling paper for account books or for ledgers was also considered part of a binder's metier and Coghlan, who had acquired a 12-inch ruler and a 'Founting' pen for this task, gives several recipes for red and black ink. Red ink can be made from '3 pints of Stale Bear (rather than vineger) 4 oz of Brazel Dust. Some people puts allom [alum] in it tho Butt 1 oz: in this quantety. Simmer these for one Hour together, then Str[ain] it and Bottel it up for Use. Cork it' (p. 32). While the 'Best Recept for Makeing Black Ink for Sail' (p. 33) reads as follows:

> Boyl a pound of Logwood and a Quarter of an ounce of allum in five Quarts of water (ale Measure) when the Coulor is is pretty Strong which you may try with a pen, put in half a pound of Galls [gall nuts, containing tannic acid], and let them Simmer allso, trying as Before, then put in 6 ounces of Copras [copperas: ferrous sulphate] & the Same Quantety of Gum Arabeck Let them Steep All Night and then Simmer it ove[r] a Gentle fire Let it Cool & Strain it off for Use.

In the margin he added 'I should have said Simmer for it Must Not Boyl' and again 'NB: it Should Not Boyl at all'.

The remaining two categories, 'Grains' and 'Lacquerd Work', deal with books by the hundred. 'Grains' refers to the grain split or outer split of a sheepskin, the cheapest available leather. 'Testaments Saw'd' (and 'Grammars ditto') indicate an early form of 'perfect binding'. The backs of the sections were sawn in, the cords pressed into the grooves, and the whole was glued up without any previous sewing: a very cheap and very unstable way of holding the book together.[24] 'Lacquerd Work', as we know it from Persian bindings of the seventeenth, eighteenth and nineteenth centuries, seems out of place on a trade list, and it may refer to varnished bindings, though I am not sure whether varnish was used on bindings as early as the first half of the eighteenth century. As described by Arnett (p. 137), varnishing seems quite a complicated operation and would warrant the price of £2.10s for a hundred Prayer-books better than the less labour-intensive habit, fairly common in the seventeenth and eighteenth centuries, of polishing the covers with a polishing iron over one or two coats of glaire. At a guess it may even refer to marbling the leather, several recipies for which are given by Coghlan, such as the one on p. 42: 'Brown for Books Viz What We Call the Prusian Marble on Leather Books Viz Pot ash Steepd or Mixd With Water flung on after the Sperits of Vitriol [a distilled essence of vitriol]'. Another one among his 'Aproved Recepts' (p. 63) reads:

> My Brown for Books is Bound in Calf is Pot Ashes Soked & Weekned with Water thro'd on the Book Standing on its fore Edges Make the Run or Prussion Marble ... Oyl of Vitirol is Also Used in My Marblee Weekned with Water a Litle Coppris [copperas] in Water is Also What I Marble & Sprinkle with Very Light.

Certainly marbled and sprinkled covers were very popular at the time.

A large variety of paper sizes is mentioned in this list, including for bound books: 'Imperial' (22 × 30 in.), 'Super-Royal' (19¼ × 27½ in.), 'Royal' (19¼ × 24 in.), 'Medium' (18 × 23 in.), 'Demy' (17½ × 22 in.), and 'Propatria' (a watermark most commonly used in eighteenth-century Britain in Foolscap paper: 13½ × 16¾ in.). The paper sizes for writing paper are 'Demy' (15½ × 20 in.), 'Post' (15¼ × 19½ in.), and again 'Propatria' (writing Foolscap: 13½ × 16¾ in.).

One year later, on 14 May 1744, the 'Bookbinders of the Citys of London & Westminster & the libertys thereof' addressed themselves to the booksellers with the statement that 'In Consideration of the exorbitant prices that Leather now Bears. . . . By an Absolute Necessity are Obliged to Come to the following Resolutions in Regard to the Undermentioned prices for the Different sizes of Books' (Price List 7). This price list was copied by James Coghlan on pp. 13–15 of his memorandum book and no printed copy has yet been found. The list starts with prices for binding and lettering books of different sizes indicated by format and paper size. Then follows a section of books bound in calf with or without decorated edges, also priced according to format, paper and type sizes, with a few titles mentioned as examples, followed by 'Sheep Binders prices' per hundred, where mainly individual titles are given. The 'Sowing & Folding *Prices*' are quoted per 'Alphabett', i.e. for the quires A–Z, or per hundred sheets, and a distinction is made between sewing each section separately or all-along ('Sowing only one Sheet at a time'), sewing two-on ('Sowing only two Sheets at a time'), and 'Common Sowing' which may well mean six-on or more. 'Black or Gilt Paper' and 'Ruleing Paper' we have met before. The prices for 'Black or Gilt Paper' given here, however, are noticeably lower than those charged in Dublin the previous year. The paper sizes indicating the sizes of bound books mentioned on this list are 'Royal', 'Demy', 'Crown' (15 × 20 in.), 'Fools Cap' and 'medium'; the sizes for 'Black or Gilt Paper', probably referring to writing paper, are 'post' and 'Fools Cap'; and 'Ruleing Paper' includes 'Pott' (12½ × 15½ in.). The type sizes listed are 'Brevier', 'minion', 'Nonpariel', 'pica' and 'Long primer'.

A copy of the last list to be discussed here (Price List 8) addressed 'To the BOOKSELLERS of London and Westminster', establishing 'The Prices for BINDING agreed on the 2d of *June*, 1760', was found folded and tipped-in on p. 16 of Coghlan's memorandum book. It is printed in two columns and under each heading indicating the sizes, a list of titles is given as examples, followed by the remark '*All Books on the same Paper and Thickness, the like Price*'. The paper sizes are familiar. Binding styles are indicated summarily and consist of 'plain Calf', 'Calf', 'Sheep, Rolled' and 'Red Sheep, Rolled'; we encounter 'half bound' here for the first time. Coghlan bought six small calf skins and a pared sheepskin at one shilling each, while red basil, 'sheep skin tanned, used for common bindings', as

Arnett puts it (p. 203), cost him ten pence. Bibles and Books of Common Prayer, also arranged by size, are grouped together at the end.

In an attempt to see whether the bookbinders kept to the standard prices quoted in the lists, I looked through a large number of bills for binding work done for Raylton in the 1720s and 1730s.[25] I compared these with the London price list for 1744, and notwithstanding the fact that only relatively few titles are mentioned in this list, the comparable entries showed that the prices paid earlier by Raylton were either the same as or slightly lower than those indicated in 1744. I also looked through a quantity of bills of work done for George Hawkins, the bookseller, dating from the 1740s, 1750s and 1760s.[26] Not all bills specified in sufficient detail the materials used and the style of binding, and several posts obviously included the price of the books themselves. But a number of bills for binding only (such as those of Wm. Cook, of 1760) quoted the same titles, bound and decorated in the same way as those mentioned in the 1760 list, charging the same price.

In 1787 James Fraser, a master bookbinder, tried to persuade the binders and journeymen to work at piece rates instead of for a settled weekly wage. In an 'Address to the Master and Journeymen Bookbinders of *London* and *Westminster*'[27] he breaks down into components the process of binding in calf, lettering (on morocco lettering pieces), and colouring or gilding the edges, of a 12° book of 18 sheets, a crown 8° of 23 sheets, and an 8° of 36 sheets. The cost of the actual work and the materials comes to 'Better than 6d¾', 'Better than 7d¾' and 'About 11d½' for these three sizes respectively. He also lists the overheads (rent, coal, candles, wear and tear, and an errand boy), and gives the fair market price for a 12° in calf, lettered, at 1s, that for a crown 8° at 1s. 1d and that for an 8° at 1s. 4d, a rise of about 4d per volume since 1760 (though the 1760 list does not specify any treatment of the edges). In order to put this in perspective, it may be interesting to note that in 1750 or 1760 a forwarder's wages were 10s. 6d per week. When Jock McKinlay came to London to work as a journeyman, around 1760, he was paid 9s, but he was 'a shocking bad workman'.[28] Finishers were paid more, though according to Laban 'There were very few Finishers then, little or no finishing, except the lettering being required', a statement not borne out by the earlier price lists but pertinent in the light of the 1760 list. In 1786 the rates ranged from 15s to 18s per week for a 12½ hour day; a finisher got 21s and an extremely competent finisher might rise to 24s. This meant that in order to break even and earn his minimum wage, a forwarder in 1760 had to bind at least ten books a week. For a competent craftsman this would not present any difficulties, a state of affairs that prompted R. Pratt, a binder who worked at Buckingham House, to remark that from 1760 to 1780 'Bookbinding was as well paid a Trade as any other'.

A generall note of the prises for binding of all sorts of bookes.

Gilt ouer one way.
Folio.

Bibles folio Roman, or the like	11 s. — 0 d.
Com. and Psalmes: or the like	7 s. — 0 d.

In 4°.

Bibles 4°, or the like	5 s. — 6 d.
Com, and Psalmes, or the like	3 s. — 6 d.

In 8°.

Bibles 8°, or the like	2 s. — 8 d.
Com. Test. & Psalmes, or the like	2 s. — 0
Com. and Psalmes, or the like	2 s. — 0
Psal. 8° Middleborow, or the like	2 s. — 0

In 12°.

Bibles in 12°, or the like	2 s. — 8 d.
Com. and Psalmes in 12°,	1 s. — 8 d.
Practice of piety, and the like,	1 s. — 4 d.
Helpe to	1 s. — 2 d.

Test. Psalmes 16°. Middleborow,	1 s. — 2 d.
Psalmes 16° Middleborow,	1 s. — 0 d.
Psalmes 16° common, or the like,	0 — 10 d.

In 24°.

Com. Test. Psal. 24°, or of that sort,	1 s. — 2 d.

In 32°.

Psalmes 32°, Rom. and English, one with another,	0 — 8 d.

Bookes crosse-gilt ouer.
In 24°.

Com. Test. Psalmes 24° crosse-guilt,	1 s. — 8 d.
Test. Psalmes 16° crosse-guilt,	1 s. — 8 d.

In 32°.

Psalter and Psalmes 32,	1 s. — 4 d.

Bookes of all sorts gilt, edges and corners.

Church Bible corners in folio,	15 s. — 0
Bible folio Romane, or the like,	8 s. — 6 d.
Com. and Psal. folio, or the like,	6 s. — 0

In 4.

Bible 4. great Rom.	4 s. — 0
Bible 4, or the like,	3 s. — 8 d.
Com. and Psalmes 4, or the like,	2 s. — 6 d.

In 8.

Bible 8, or the like,	2 s. — 4 d.
Com. Test. Psalmes, or the like,	2 s. — 4 d.
Psalmes 8. Middleborow, or the like,	1 s. — 8 d.

In 12.

Bibles in 12, or the like,	2 s. — 4 d.
Test. Psalmes 12, or the like,	2 s. — 2 d.
Sanctuaries, or the like,	1 s. — 2 d.

In 16.

Test. Psalmes 16. Middleborow, or the like,	1 s. — 0

In 24.

Com. Test. & Psalmes, or such other,	1 s. — 0

In 32.

Psalmes in 32,	0 — 8 d.

Bookes edges and fillets.

Bibles folio large,	10 s. — 0
Bibles folio Roman, or the like,	6 s. — 0
Com. and Psalmes, or the like,	4 s. — 6 d.

In 4.

Bibles 4 Rom. great letter,	3 s. — 4 d.
Bibles 4 English,	3 s. — 0
Com. Psalmes 4, or such like,	2 s. — 0

In 8.

Bibles 8 or the like,	1 s. — 10 d.
Com. Test. Psalmes,	1 s. — 10 d.
Psalmes 8 Middleborow, or the like,	1 s. — 6 d.

In 12.

Bibles in 12,	1 s. — 10 d.
Sanctuaries, Dauids Key, and Practice of Piety, and the like,	1 s. — 0
Helpe to Deuotion, or the like,	1 s. — 0

In 16.

Test. Psal. 16 Middleborow edges,	1 s. — 0
Psalmes 16. Middleborow edges,	0 — 10 d.
Psalmes 16 Com. or the like,	0 — 8 d.

In 24.

Com. Test. Psalmes 24 edges,	0 — 11 d.
Test. Psalmes 24. or the like,	0 — 10 d.

In 32.

Psalmes 32, or the like,	0 — 7 d.

All sorts of crosse-bound edges.
In 16.

Test. Psal. 16 Middleborow, or the like,	1 s. — 6 d.

In 24.

Test. Com. and Psalmes 24, or the like,	1 s. — 6 d.

In 32.

Prayers and Psalmes 32 crosse,	1 s. — 2 d.

Bookes folio fillets.

Martyrs two volumes,	12 s. — 0
Church-Bible,	6 s. — 0
Romane Bible,	3 s. — 4 d.
Raleighs History,	3 s. — 4 d.
Perkins, or the like,	2 s. — 8 d.
All folio's like Babingtons,	2 s. — 6 d.
All folio's, like Com. & Psalmes,	2 s. — 4 d.

In 4.

Bibles in 4, large Romane,	2 s. — 0
Bibles 4. and such like,	1 s. — 10 d.
Com. & Psalmes, & the like,	1 s. — 2 d.

In 8.

Bibles 8. or the like,	1 s. — 2 d.
Com. Test. and Psalmes, & the like,	1 s. — 2 d.
Test. Psalmes, and Psalmes,	1 s. — 0
All bookes like the Plaine mans path-way,	0 — 9 d.

In 12.

Bible 12, or the like,	1 s. — 0
Practice of piety, or the like,	0 — 8 d.

In 16.

Test. Psalmes 16 Middleborow,	0 — 7 d.
Psalmes 16 Middleborow,	0 — 6 d.
Psalmes 16 Com. or the like,	0 — 5 d.

In 24.

Com. Test. and Psalmes, or the like,	0 — 7 d.

In 32.

Psalmes in 32, or the like,	0 — 5 d.

Bookes crosse-fillets.
In 16.

Test. Psalmes 16, Middleborow,	1 s. — 0

In 24.

Com. Test. Psalmes in 24 crosse,	0 — 11 d.

In 32.

Psalter and psalmes in 32,	0 — 9 d.

Bookes in ouills.

Camden with maps,	4 s. — 6 d.
Church-Bible,	5 s. — 0
Raleighs histories,	2 s. — 6 d.

Imprinted at LONDON. 1619.

Plutarch, or the like,	2 s. — 4 d.
Bible folio Romane,	2 s. — 2 d.
Perkins, and the lik,	5 s. — 6 d.
Purchas, and the like,	1 s. — 8 d.
Commines, and the like,	1 s. — 6 d.

In 4.

Bible in 4, and the like,	1 s. — 2 d.
Smiths sermons, and the like,	0 — 10 d.

In 8.

Bibles in 8, and the like,	0 — 8 d.
All sorts of Test. psalmes 8,	0 — 6 d.
All lattin bookes large,	0 — 8 d.
All lattin bookes small,	0 — 6 d.

In 12.

Bibles in 12.	0 — 8 d.
Test. Psalmes in 12, or the like,	0 — 6 d.
All Latin bookes in 16,	0 — 5 d.
All Latin bookes in 24,	0 — 4 d.

Law-bookes.

Statutes at large,	2 s. — 6 d.
Rastall Abridgement, folio,	1 s. — 8 d.
Poultons Abridgement, folio,	1 s. — 6 d.
Daltons Iustice, folio,	1 s. — 4 d.
Wests Presidents in 4,	1 s. — 0
Iustice of peace, in 8,	0 — 6 d.

Bookes sheepes leather.

Test. in 8, or the like,	0 — 4 d.
Grammers, or the like,	0 — 2 d. ob.
Silua, or the like,	0 — 4 d.

In 16.

Tullies Orations, or the like,	0 — 3 d.
Psalmes in 16 common,	0 — 2 d.

In 32.

Psalmes in 32,	0 — 2 d.

Bookes in hard bords.

Martyrs,	7 s. — 0
Bible folio large,	4 s. — 6 d.
Bible folio small,	3 s. — 8 d.
Bible med.um,	2 s. — 0

In 4.

Bible in 4,	1 s. — 2 d.
Test. Com. psalmes in 4,	1 s. — 2 d.
Com. booke and psalmes in 4,	0 — 9 d.

In 8.

Bible 8,	0 — 8 d.
Com. Test. psalmes in 8,	0 — 7 d.
Psalter, Test. and psalmes,	0 — 7 d.
Test. psal 8vo	0 — 6 d.
Com. and psalmes in 16, Com.	0 — 4 d.

All sorts of Latin bookes, in folio and quarto.

Bibliotheca patrum,	3 s. — 6 d.
Tastatus, and the like,	3 s. — 0
Tremellius bible,	2 s. — 4 d.
Gorron, or the like,	2 s. — 0
Stella on Luke, or the like,	1 s. — 8 d.
Piscator in 4,	1 s. — 4 d.
Tremellius bible in 4, or the like,	1 s. — 2 d.
Dictionarium poet cum,	1 s. — 0
All other small quarto's,	0 — 10 d.

FINIS.

Fig. 2.1   List of binding prices 'Imprinted at LONDON. 1619.'

Price List 1

A generall note of the prises for binding of all sorts of bookes.

Gilt ouer one way.
Folio.
Bibles folio Roman, or the like ⸻⸻⸻ 11s.– 0d.
Com. and Psalmes: or the like ⸻⸻⸻ 7s.– 0d.

In 4ᵗᵒ.
Bibles 4ᵗᵒ, or the like ⸻⸻⸻ 5s.– 6d.
Com. and Psalmes, or the like ⸻⸻⸻ 3s.– 6d.

In 8°.
Bibles 8°, or th[e lik]e, ⸻⸻⸻ 2s.– 8d.
Com. Test. & P[sal]mes, or the like, ⸻⸻ 2s.– 6d.
Com. and Psalmes, or the like, ⸻⸻⸻ 2s.– 0
Psal. 8° Middleborow, or the like, ⸻⸻ 2s.– 0

In 12°.
Bibles in 12°, or the like ⸻⸻⸻ 2s.– 8d.
Com. and Psalmes in 12°, ⸻⸻⸻ 1s.– 8d.
Practice of Piety, and the like, ⸻⸻⸻ 1s.– 4d.[1]
Helpe to D[evotion,] ⸻⸻⸻ 1s.– 2d.[2]

[*In* 1]6°.
Test. Psalmes 16°. Middleborow, ⸻⸻ 1s.– 2d.
Psalmes 16° Middleborow, ⸻⸻⸻ 1s.– 0d.
Psalmes 16° common, or the like, ⸻⸻ 0 –10d.

In 24ᵗᵒ.
Com. Test. Psal. 24°, or of that sort, ⸻⸻ 1s.– 2d.

In 32°.
psalmes 32°, Rom. and English, one with another, ⸻ 0 – 8d.

Bookes crosse-gilt ouer.
In 24°.
Com. Test. Psalmes 24° crosse-guilt, ⸻⸻ 1s.– 8d.
Test. Psalmes 16° crosse-guilt, ⸻⸻⸻ 1s.– 8d.

In 32.
Psalter and Psalmes 32, ⸻⸻⸻ 1s.– 4d.

Bookes of all sorts gilt, edges and corners.
Church Bible corners in folio, ⸻⸻⸻ 15s.– 0

Bible folio Romane, or the like, —————————— 8s.– 6d.
Com. and Psal. folio, or the like, —————————— 6s.– 0

In 4.
Bible 4. great Rom. ———————————————— 4s.– 0
Bible 4, or the like, —————————————————— 3s.– 8d.
Com. and Psalmes 4, or the like, ———————————— 2s.– 6d.

In 8.
Bible 8, or the like, —————————————————— 2s.– 4d.
Com. Test. Psalmes, or the like, —————————— 2s.– 4d.
Psalmes 8. Middleborow, or the like, ———————— 1s.– 8d.

In 12.
Bibles in 12, or the like, ———————————————— 2s.– 4d.
Test. Psalmes 12, or the like, —————————————— 2s.– 2d.
Sanctuaries, or the like, —————————————————— 1s.– 2d.[3]

In 16.
Test. Psalmes 16. Middleborow, or the like, —————— 1s.– 0

In 24.
Com. Test. & Psalmes, or such other, ————————— 1s.– 0

In 32.
Psalmes in 32, ——————————————————————— 0 – 8d.

Bookes edges and fillets.
Bibles folio large, —————————————————————10s.– 0
Bibles folio Roman. or the like, —————————————— 6s.– 6d.
Com. and Psalmes, or the like, —————————————— 4s.– 6d.

In 4.
Bibles 4 Rom. great letter, ———————————————— 3s.– 4d.
Bibles 4 English, ——————————————————————— 3s.– 0
Com. Psalmes 4, or such like, —————————————— 2s.– 0

In 8.
Bibles 8 or the like, ———————————————————— 1s.–10d.
Com. Test. Psalmes, ————————————————————— 1s.–10d.
Psalmes 8 Middleborow, or the like, ————————— 1s.– 6d.

In 12.
Bibles in 12, ————————————————————————— 1s.–10d.
Sanctuaries, Dauids Key,[4] and ⎫
Practice of Piety, and the like, ⎬ ——————————— 1s.– 0
Helpe to Deuotion, or the like, ————————————— 0 –10d.

In 16.
Test. Psal. 16 Middleborow edges, ——————————— 1*s.*– 0.
Psalmes 16. Middleborow edges, ——————————— 0 –10*d.*
Psalmes 16 Com. or the like, ——————————— 0 – 8*d.*

In 24.
Com. Test. Psalmes 24 edges, ——————————— 0 –11*d.*
Test. Psalmes 24. or the like, ——————————— 0 –10*d.*

In 32.
Psalmes 32, or the like, ——————————— 0 – 7*d.*

All sorts of crosse-bound edges.
In 16.
Test. Psal. 16 Middleborow, or the like, ——————————— 1*s.*– 6*d.*

In 24.
Test. Com. and Psalmes 24, or the like, ——————————— 1*s.*– 6*d.*

In 32.
Prayers and Psalmes 32 crosse, ——————————— 1*s.*– 2*d.*

Bookes folio fillets.
Martyrs two volumes, ———————————12*s.*– 0
Church-Bible, ——————————— 6*s.*– 0
Romane Bible, ——————————— 3*s.*– 4*d.*
Raleighs History, ——————————— 3*s.*– 6*d.*[5]
Perkins, or the like, ——————————— 2*s.*– 8*d.*
All folio's like Babingtons, ——————————— 2*s.*– 6*d.*[6]
All folio's, like Com. & Psalmes, ——————————— 2*s.*– 4*d.*

In 4.
Bibles in 4, large Romane, ——————————— 2*s.*– 0
Bibles 4. and such like, ——————————— 1*s.*–10*d.*
Com. & Psalmes, & the like, ——————————— 1*s.*– 2*d.*

In 8.
Bibles 8, or the like, ——————————— 1*s.*– 2*d.*
Com. Test. and Psalmes, & the like, ——————————— 1*s.*– 2*d.*
Test. Psalter, and Psalmes, ——————————— 1*s.*– 0
All bookes like the Plaine mans path-way, ——————————— 9*d.*[7]

In 12.
Bible 12, or the like, ——————————— 1*s.*– 2*d.*
Practice of piety, or the like, ——————————— 8*d.*

In 16.
Test. Psalmes 16 Middleborow, —————————————— 7*d*.
Psalmes 16 Middleborow, —————————————— 6*d*.
Psalmes 16 Com. or the like, —————————————— 5*d*.

In 24.
Com. Test. and Psalmes, or the like, —————————— 7*d*.

In 32.
Psalmes in 32, or the like, —————————————— 5*d*.

Bookes crosse-fillets.
In 16.
Test. Psalmes 16, Middleborow, —————————— 1*s*.– 0

In 24.
Com. Test. Psalmes in 24 crosse, —————————— 0 –11*d*.

In 32.
Psalter and psalmes in 32, —————————————— 9*d*.

Bookes in ouills.
Camden with maps, —————————————————— 4*s*.– 6*d*.
Church-Bible, ————————————————————— [5*s*.] [in ms]
Raleighs histories, ————————————————— 2*s*.– 6*d*.
Plutarch, or the like, ———————————————— 2*s*.– 4*d*.
Bible folio Romane, ————————————————— 2*s*.– 2*d*.
Perkins, and the like, ———————————————— 5*s*.– 6*d*.[8]
Purchas, and the like, ———————————————— 1*s*.– 8*d*.[9]
Commines, and the like, ——————————————— 1*s*.– 6*d*.

In 4.
Bible in 4, and the like, ——————————————— 1*s*.– 2*d*.
Smiths sermons, and the like, ————————————— 0 –10*d*.

In 8.
Bibles in 8, and the like, ——————————————— 0 – 8*d*.
                                        [altered in ms to 9*d*.]
All sorts of Test. psalmes [8] [4 deleted, 8 in ms] ————— 0 – 6*d*.
All lattin bookes large, ——————————————— 0 – 8*d*.
All lattin bookes small, ——————————————— 0 – 6*d*.

In 12.
Bibles in 12. ————————————————————— 0 – 8*d*.
Test. Psalmes in 12, or the like, ————————————— 0 – 6*d*.
All Latin bookes in 16, ——————————————— 0 – 5*d*.
All Latin bookes in 24, ——————————————— 0 – 4*d*.

Law-bookes.

Statutes at large,	2s.– 6d.
Rastall Abridgement, folio,	1s.– 8d.
Poultons Abridgement, folio,	1s.– 6d.
Daltons Iustice, folio,	1s.– 4d.[10]
Wests Presidents in 4,	1s.– 0[11]
Iustice of peace, in 8,	0 – 6d.

Bookes sheepes leather.

Test. in 8, or the like,	0 – 4d.
Grammers, or the like,	0 – 2d.ob.
	[obulus = half penny]
Silua, or the like,	0 – 4d.[12]

In 16.

Tullies Orations, or the like,	0 – 3d.
Psalmes in 16 common,	0 – 2d.

In 32.

Psalmes in 32,	0 – 2d.

Bookes in hard bords.

Martyrs,	7s.– 0[13]
Bible folio large,	4s.– 6d.
Bible folio small,	3s.– 8d.
Bible medium,	2s.– 0

In 4.

Bible in 4,	1s.– 2d.
Test. Com. psalmes in 4,	1s.– 0
Com. booke and psalmes in 4,	0 – 9d.

In 8.

Bible 8,	0 – 8d.
Com. Tes. psalmes in 8,	0 – 7d.
Psalter, Test. and psalmes,	0 – 7d.
[In 16 deleted; whole entry in ms:- Test psal 8ᵗᵒ	0 – 6d.]
Com. and psalmes in 16, Com.	0 – 4d.

All sorts of Latin bookes, in folio and quarto.

Bibliotheca patrum,	3s.– 6d.
Tastatus, and the like,	3s.– 0

Tremellius bible, ————————————————————— 2s.– 4d.
Gorron, or the like, ——————————————— [2]s.– 0
                                    [1 altered in ms to 2]
Stella on Luke, or the like, ————————————— 1s.– 8d.[14]
Piscator in 4, ————————————————————— 1s.– 4d.
Tremellius bible in 4, or the like, ————————— 1s.– 2d.
Dictionarium poeticum, ——————————————— 1s.– 0
All other small quarto's, ——————————————— 0 –10d.

FINIS

Imprinted at LONDON. 1619.

Notes to Price List 1

1. Lewis Bayly, *The Practise of Pietie*, 12°, London, 1619.
2. Samuel Hieron, *A Helpe unto Devotion*, 12°, London, 1618.
3. either: John Hitchcock, *A Sanctuary for Honest Men*, 12°, London, 1617 or: Sir John Hayward, *The Sanctuarie of a Troubled Soule*, 12°, London, 1618.
4. Richard Middleton, *The Key of David*, 12°, London, 1619.
5. Sir Walter Raleigh, *The History of the World*, fol. London, 1617.
6. Gervase Babington, *Workes* (4 parts), fol. London, 1615.
7. Arthur Dent, *The Plaine Mans Path-way to Heaven*, 8°, London, 1619.
8. William Perkins, *Works* (3 vols), fol. London-Cambridge, 1616–18.
9. Samuel Purchas, *Purchas his Pilgrimage*, fol. London, 1617.
10. Michael Dalton, *The Countrey Justice*, fol. London, 1619.
11. William West, *Simboleography . . . with divers presidents*, 4to, London, 1615, 1618.
12. Simon Pelegromius, *Synonymorum Sylva*, 8°, London, 1619.
13. John Foxe, *Book of Martyrs* (2 vols), fol. London, 1610.
14. Didacus Stella, *In . . . Evangelium secundum Lucam enarrationum tomus primus/secundus* (2 vols), fol. Antwerp, 1608.

A Generall note of the priſes for binding all ſortes of bookes

Bibles in follio *London* or the like.

	li	s	d
Gilt over, or double lac'd	0	11	0
Corners, or ſingle lac'd	0	8	0
Edges and Fillets	0	6	6
Fillets	0	3	6
Ovills	0	2	6

Bibles in quarto great Roman or the like

Small tooles ordinary	0	8	0
Gilt over, or double lac'd	0	5	6
Chequer	0	5	10
Corners, or ſingle lac'd	0	3	8
Gilt edges	0	3	0
Fillets	0	2	0
Ovills	0	1	4

Bibles in quarto ſmale or the like

Smale tooles ordin.	0	8	0
Gilt over, or double lac'd	0	5	4
Corners or ſingle lac'd	0	3	6
Gilt edges	0	2	10
Fillets	0	1	10
Ovills	0	1	2

Bibles in 8 Minnion or the like.

Smale tooles ordina.	0	5	0
Gilt over, or double lac'd	0	3	0
Corners or ſingle lac'd	0	2	6
Chequer	0	3	2
Gilt edges	0	2	0
Fillets	0	1	3
Ovills	0	0	10

Bibles in Octavo or the like

Smale tooles ordinary	0	4	6
Chequer	0	2	10
Gilt over or double lac'd	0	2	8
Corners or ſingle lac'd	0	2	4
Edges gilt	0	1	10
Fillets	0	1	2
Ovills	0	0	9

Bibles in 12 or all other ſmale Bibles.

Smale tooles ordinary	0	4	0
Chequer	0	2	8
Gilt over or double lac'd	0	2	6
Corners or ſingle lac'd	0	2	0
Gilt edges	0	1	8
Fillets	0	1	0
Ovills	0	0	8

Teſtament and Pſalmes in 24 or the like

Gilt over	0	1	0
Gilt Edges	0	0	9
Fillets	0	0	6

Pſalmes in 8 Middleborough or the like.

Gilt over, or lac'd	0	2	4
Gilt Edges	0	1	6
Fillets	0	0	10
Ovills	0	0	8

Pſalmes in 24 or the like

Gilt over, or lac'd	0	0	9
Gilt Edges	0	0	7
Fillets	0	0	5

Pſalmes in 32 or the like

Gilt over	0	0	9
Gilt Edges	0	0	7
Fillets	0	0	5

Bookes in Folio lattine.

Atlas major 3 voll. or the like fillets	1	10	0
Lyra 6 voll large, Ariſt. Opera 2 voll, Plutarchi Opera 2 voll. or the like. — Fillets a voll.	0	5	6
— Rolls	0	4	0
Hutteri heb. Biblia, Buxtorph. heb. Biblia, Buxtorph. Concord. or the like. — Rolles a voll.	0	3	6
Montanus Biblia Ent., Eraſmi Epit. 1 vol., Mendz. in Reg. 1 vol., Grotius in vet. Teſt. or the like. — Fillets	0	4	4
— Rolles	0	3	0
Gerrard. Harm. Mathew Paris., Scapula Lex. Eſtius in Epiſt. or the like.	0	2	6
Gerrardi Loci Com. 4 vol., Grot. in vet Teſt. 3 vol., Sibelii Opera 5 vol. or the like. — Rolles	0	2	0

Bookes in quarto Lattine.

Sculteti Medulla., Mellificium Hiſtoricum., Voſſii Gram. Hiſpan: Biblia. or the like. — Rolles	0	1	4
All Latine bookes 4 if large paper	0	1	0
If thick at	0	1	2
All latine bookes 4 pot paper rolles	0	0	10
If thick at	0	1	0

Bookes in 8 12 & 24

Buxtorphi Lexicon, Paſſoris Lexicon, Lumbard in Senten. or the like. — Rolles	0	0	8
All thinne latine bookes 8 rolles	0	0	7
All latine bookes 12 & 16 rolles	0	0	5
All bookes 24 & 32 Fillets	0	0	5

Bookes in follio Engliſh

Atlas 2 voll. or the like in Fillets	1	0	0
Iſaackſons Chron. or the like. Rolles	0	3	0
Gerrards Herball, Parkinſons Herball and the like. — Fillets	0	4	4
— Rolles	0	3	0
Booke of Martyrs or the like, fil.	0	12	0
Rolles.	0	8	0
Newmans Con. Turkiſh Hiſt. Rawleighs Hiſtory, Andrews Sermons, or the like. — Rolles	0	2	6
Annotations. Survey of London. Joſephus Hiſt: Perkins Workes 3 vol. or the like. — Rolles	0	2	0
Sands Ovid. Bakers Chron: or the like. — Rolles	0	1	10
Hackwells Apol: Cotgraves Dictionary. Hierons Works. Boyſes Workes, or the like. — Rol.	0	1	8
Canterburies Doome. Hookers Policie. Pembles Workes. Feild of the Church. or the like. — Rolles	0	1	6
Daltons Juſtice, Henry the 7. Holy State. Holy War or the like. — Rolles	0	1	4

Bookes in 4 Engliſh

Riders Dictionary, Piſcator in N: Teſt. or the like. — Rolles	0	1	4
Weſts Preſidents, Thomas Dict., Diodates Notes or the like. — Rolles	0	1	2
Goodwins W: Caryls Workes. or the like. — Rolles	0	1	2
Weymes workes 4 vol., Wills and Teſtam., Crittica Sacra. or the like. — Rolles	0	1	0
All ſmale 4 pot paper, Rolles	0	0	10

Bookes in Octavo Engliſh

Souls Conflict. Records Arethmat: or the like. — Rolles	0	0	7

Bookes in 12 Engliſh.

Scudders daily Walke, Mirour of Martyrs, Practice of Piety or the like. — Rolles	0	0	5

Sheeps Leather

All ſmale Follio pot paper	0	0	10
All thinne Crown, in quarto at	0	0	7
All thick pot paper in quarto at	0	0	6
All thinne pot paper in quarto at	0	0	5
Hunts Arethmaticke 8, Records Arethmaticke 8, Smetius 8, Large Teſtaments 8 and the like.	0	0	4
All thinne Crown, one with another	0	0	3 ob
Teſtaments in 8 and 12, Virgill. 8, Quarles Poems 8 and the like.	0	0	3 ob
All other bookes 8 & 12 guttard	0	0	3
All ſortes of ſmale bookes, as Gramers Pſalters & the like	0	0	2 ob
Pſalter Teſtament pſalmes in 8	0	0	7
Teſtament Pſalmes 8	0	0	6
Teſtament Pſalmes 12	0	0	5
All ſortes of thinne bookes ſheeps Leather fillets. as Grammers, Pſalters, ſmale 12. 24 and 32.	0	0	4
Primers gilt the Groſſe	1	0	0
Primers plaine the Groſſe	0	10	0

Printed at London 1646.

FINIS

Fig. 2.2 List of binding prices 'Printed at London 1646.'

Price List 2

Bookes as they are sold bound,

	At London.			At Dublin.		
	li.	sh.	d.	li.	sh.	d.
Church Bible in *folio* Bost, Bust, and Claspt	1	12	00	2	00	00
Communion and Psalmes *folio* bound	0	07	00	0	09	00
Bible in *12°* with Psalmes & Geneal. in fill.	0	06	06	0	08	00
Bible in *fol.* Roman old with notes fill.	1	00	00	1	04	00
Bible in *folio* median with Psalmes and Genealog. fill.	1	00	00	1	04	00
Bible in *quarto* great Rom. new, with Psal. & Geneal. fill.	0	14	06	0	18	00
Bible in *quarto* small Rom. with fillets	0	11	06	0	13	04
Bible in *quarto* new Engl. with Psal. & Geneal. fill.	0	11	06	0	13	04
Bible in *octavo* Psal. & Geneal. fillets with Service	0	07	00	0	08	06
Testament and Psalmes in *quarto* fill.	0	05	06	0	06	08
Testament and Psal. in *octavo* boords clasp.	0	02	06	0	03	00
Communion Booke and Psalmes *quarto* fill.	0	04	00	0	05	00
Communion Booke and Psalmes *oct.* clasp.	0	02	08	0	03	04
Communion Booke and Psalmes *16°* claspt	0	01	10	0	02	04
Ciceronis Officia *octavo* sheepes leather,	0	01	00	0	01	04
Ciceronis Sententiæ in *duodecimo* bound	0	01	00	0	01	04
Ovidij Metamorphosis *oct.* bound	0	01	00	0	01	04
Ovidij Epistolæ *octavo* bound	0	01	00	0	01	04
Pallingenius in *octavo* bound[1]	0	01	02	0	01	06
Setoni Dialectica in *octavo* bound[2]	0	01	00	0	01	06
Aphthonius in *octavo*	0	01	00	0	01	04
Salustij Historia in *octavo* bound	0	01	00	0	01	04
Æsopi Fabulæ in *oct.* bound	0	00	07	0	00	10

Item	£	s	d		£	s	d
[…] (cut off)	0	…	…		0	…	…
Castaleonis Dialogi *oct.* bound	0	01	02		0	00	10
Terentius *octo* bound	0	01	[0]0		0	00	09
Primmers plaine	0	00	04		0	00	04
Other small Schoole-bookes.							
Corderius in *octavo*	0	00	04		0	00	04
Isocratis ad Demonicum in *oct.*³	0	00	06		0	00	04
Nowelli Catechismus medius.	0	00	06		0	00	04
Ovidius de Tristibus	0	00	06		0	00	04
Sturmij Epistolæ *octavo*	0	00	04		0	00	04
Vivis Exercitationes Ling. Lat.⁴	0	00	06		0	00	04
Catones in *octavo*	0	00	04		0	00	03
Epitome Colloquiorum Erasmi⁵	0	00	04		0	00	03

With all other Priviledged Bookes according to these differences in their prizes.

Notes to Price List 2

1. Marcellus Palingenius, *Zodiacus Vitae … opus*, 8°, London, 1616.
2. Joannes Setonus, *Dialectica*, 8°, London, 1617.
3. Isocrates, *Oratio ad Demonicum*, 8°, Louvain, 1551 (?).
4. Joannes Ludovicus Vives, *Linguæ Latinæ exercitatio*, 8°, London [? 1612] or Edinburgh, 1620.
5. Desiderius Erasmus, *Epitome Colloquiorum*, 8°, London, 1608.

Price List 3

A Generall note of the prises for binding all sortes of bookes

Bibles in follio *London* or the like.

	li	s	d
Gilt over, or double lac'd	0	11	0
Corners, or single lac'd	0	8	0
Edges and Fillets	0	6	6
Fillets	0	3	6
Ovills	0	2	6

Bibles in quarto great Roman or the like

Small tooles ordinary	0	8	0
Gilt over, or double lac'd	0	5	6
Chequer	0	5	10
Corners, or single lac'd	0	3	8
Gilt edges	0	3	0
Fillets	0	2	0
Ovills	0	1	4

Bibles in quarto smale or the like

Smale tooles ordin.	0	8	0
Gilt over, or double lac'd	0	5	4
Corners or single lac'd	0	3	6
Gilt edges	0	2	10
Fillets	0	1	10
Ovills	0	1	2

Bibles in 8 Minnion or the like.

Smale tooles ordina.	0	5	0
Gilt over, or double lac'd	0	3	0
Corners or single lac'd	0	2	6
Chequer	0	3	2
Gilt edges	0	2	0
Fillets	0	1	3
Ovills	0	0	10

Bibles in Octavo or the like

Smale tooles ordinary	0	4	6
Chequer	0	2	10
Gilt over or double lac'd	0	2	8
Corners or single lac'd	0	2	4

Edges gilt	0	1	10
Fillets	0	1	2
Ovills	0	0	9

Bibles in 12 or all other smale Bibles.

Smale tooles ordinary	0	4	0
Chequer	0	2	8
Gilt over or double lac'd	0	2	6
Corners or single lac'd	0	2	0
Gilt edges	0	1	8
Fillets	0	1	0
Ovills	0	0	8

Testament and Psalmes in 24 or the like

Gilt over	0	1	0
Gilt Edges	0	0	9
Fillets	0	0	6

Psalmes in 8 Middleborough or the like.

Gilt over, or lac'd	0	2	4
Gilt Edges	0	1	6
Fillets	0	0	10
Ovills	0	0	8

Psalmes in 24 or the like

Gilt over, ot [sic] lac'd	0	0	9
Gilt Edges	0	0	7
Fillets	0	0	5

Psalmes in 32 or the like

Gilt over	0	0	9
Gilt Edges	0	0	7
Fillets	0	0	5

Bookes in Folio lattine.

Atlas major 3 voll. or the like fillets	1	10	0

Lyra 6 voll large Arist. Opera 2 voll Plutarchi Opera 2 voll. or the like.	} Fillets a voll.	0	5	6
	Rolls	0	4	0
Hutteri heb. Biblia Buxtorph. heb. Biblia Buxtorph. Concord. or the like	} Rolles a voll.	0	3	6

Montanus Biblia Ent.					
Erasmi Epit. 1 vol.	}	Fillets	0	4	4
Mendz. in Reg. 1 vol.	}	Rolles	0	3	0
Grotius in vet. Test.					
or the like.					
Gerrard. Harm. Mathew Paris.					
Scapula Lex.[1] Estius in Epist. or the like. }			0	2	6
Gerrardi Loci Com.					
4 vol.					
Grot. in vet Test. 3 vol.	Rolles		0	2	0
Sibelii Opera 5 vol.					
or the like.					

Bookes in quarto Lattine.					
Sculteti Medulla.[2]					
Mellificium Historicum.					
Vossii Gram. Hispan:	Rolles		0	1	4
Biblia. or the like.					
All Latine bookes 4 if large paper			0	1	0
If thick at _____			0	1	2
All latine bookes 4 pot paper rolles			0	0	10
If thick at _____			0	1	0

Bookes in 8 12 & 24					
Buxtorphi Lexicon[3]					
Passoris Lexicon	Rolles _____		0	0	8
Lumbard in Senten.					
or the like.					
All thinne latine bookes					
8 rolles			0	0	7
All latine bookes 12 &					
16 rolles			0	0	5
All bookes 24 & 32	Fillets _____		0	0	5

Bookes in follio English					
Atlas 2 voll. or the like in Fillets			1	0	0
Isaacksons Chron.[4]					
or the like.	Rolles		0	3	0
Gerrards Herball	Fillets _____		0	4	4
Parkinsons Herball	Rolles _____		0	3	0
and the like.					
Booke of Martyrs or the like, fil.			0	12	0
Rolles. _____			0	8	0

Newmans Con. Turkish Hist. Rawleighs History Andrews Sermons,[5] or the like.	Rolles	0	2	6
Annotations. Survey of London. Josephus Hist: Perkins Workes 3 vol. or the like.	Rolles	0	2	0
Sands Ovid. Bakers Chron:[6] or the like.	Rolles	0	1	10
Hackwells Apol: Cotgraves Dictionary. Hierons Works. Boyses Workes. or the like.	Rol.	0	1	8
Canterburies Doome.[7] Hookers Policie. Pembles Workes. Feild of the Church. or the like.	Rolles	0	1	6
Daltons justice Henry the 7. Holy State.[8] Holy War. or the like.	Rolles ————	0	1	4
Bookes in 4 English Riders Dictionary[9] Piscator in N: Test. or the like.	Rolles ————	0	1	4
Wests Presidents Thomas Dict. Diodates Notes[10] or the like.	Rolles ————	0	1	2
Goodwins W: Caryls Workes. or the like.	Rolles	0	1	2
Weymes workes 4 vol. Wills and Testam. Crittica Sacra. or the like.	Rolles	0	1	0
All smale 4 pot paper,	Rolles	0	0	10
Bookes in Octavo English Souls Conflict.[11] Records Arethmat: or the like.	Rolles	0	0	7

Bookes in 12 English.
Scudders daily Walke[12]
Mirour of Martyrs   } Rolles   0   0   5
Practice of Piety or the
like.

Sheeps Leather
All smale Follio pot paper   0   0   10
All thinne Crown, in quarto at   0   0   7
All thick pot paper in quarto at   0   0   6
All thinne pot paper in quarto at   0   0   5
Hunts Arethmaticke 8
Records Arethmaticke 8[13]
Smetius 8   0   0   4
Large Testaments 8 and the like.

All thinne Crown, one with another   0   0   3[ob]
Testaments in 8 and 12
Virgill. 8   0   0   3[ob]
Quarles Poems 8[14] and the like.
All other bookes 8 & 12 guttard   0   0   3
All sortes of smale bookes, as
Gramers Psalters & the like   0   0   2[ob]
Psalter Testament psalmes in 8   0   0   7
Testament Psalmes 8 —————————————   0   0   6
Testament Psalmes 12 ————————————   0   0   5
All sortes of thinne bookes
sheeps Leather fillets. as
Grammers, Psalters, smale   0   0   4
12. 24 and 32.
Primers gilt the Grosse ————————————   1   0   0
Primers plaine the Grosse ———————————   0   10   0

Printed at London 1646.
FINIS

Notes to Price List 3

1. Johannes Scapula, *Lexicon Graeco-Latinum*, fol. London, 1637.
2. Abraham Scultetus, *Medulla Theologiæ Patrum Syntagma*, 4°, Francfurt, 1634.
3. Johannes Buxtorfius, the elder, *Lexicon Hebraicum et Chaldaicum*, 8°, London, 1646.
4. Henry Isaacson, *Saturni Ephemerides, sive Tabula Historico-chronologica*, fol. London, 1633.

5. Lancelot Andrewes, *XCVI Sermons*, fol. London, 1641.
6. Sir Richard Baker, *A Chronicle of the Kings of England*, fol. London, 1643.
7. William Prynne, *Canterburies Doome*, fol. London, 1646.
8. Thomas Fuller, *The Holy State*, fol. Cambridge, 1642.
9. John Rider, *Rider's Dictionarie*, 4°, London, 1640.
10. Giovanni Diodati, *Pious Annotations, upon the Holy Bible*, 4°, London, 1643.
11. Richard Sibbes, *The Soules Conflict with it selfe*, 8°, London, 1636.
12. Henry Scudder, *The Christians Daily Walke*, 12°, London, 1642.
13. Robert Record, *The Ground of Arts. Teaching . . . Arithmeticke*, 8°, London [1646].
14. Francis Quarles, *Divine Poems*, 8°, London, 1642.

Price List 4

A General Note of the Prices of Binding all sorts of Books;

Agreed on by the Book-binders, whose Names are under-written. As it was presented to the Master, Wardens, and Assistants of the Worshipful Company of Stationers, *August*, the *2d*, 1669.

Ogilby's Bibles in Folio, or the like.

	l.	*s.*	*d.*
Gilt Edges in one Volumn	01	00	00
Fillets only	00	12	00
Plain Ovals	00	08	00

Bibles in small Folio, London, or the like.

Edges and Fillets	00	06	06
Fillets	00	03	06
Ovals	00	02	06

Bibles in Quarto, Cambridg, or the like.

Edges Extraordinary	00	05	00
Edges Ordinary	00	03	06
Fillets	00	02	06
Ovals	00	01	06

Bibles in Octavo, Brevere, or the like.

Edges Extraordinary	00	03	06
Edges Ordinary	00	02	04
Fillets	00	01	06
Ovals	00	01	00

Bibles in Octavo, Nonperil, or the like.

Edges Extraordinary	00	02	10
Edges Ordinary	00	01	10
Fillets	00	01	02
Ovals	00	00	10

Bibles in 12.

Edges Extraordinary	00	02	06
Edges Ordinary	00	01	06
Fillets	00	01	00
Ovals	00	00	08

Bibles in 24.

Edges Extraordinary	00	02	06
Edges Ordinary	00	01	06
Fillets	00	01	00
Ovals.	00	00	08

Service-Book, Testament, and Psalms, Brevere, Octavo.

Edges Extraordinary	00	02	10
Edges Ordinary	00	01	10
Fillets	00	01	02
Ovals	00	00	10

Service Brevere in 12. & Psalms, or otherwise.

Edges Extraordinary	00	01	08
Edges Ordinary	00	01	02
Fillets	00	00	09
Ovals	00	00	06

Service in 24. With Psalms, &c.

Edges Extraordinary	00	01	02
Edges Ordinary	00	00	10
Fillets	00	00	08
Plain	00	00	06

Books in Folio, Latin.

	l.	*s.*	*d.*
Atlas Major, 3 *Vol.* or the like, Rolls	1	10	00
Aristot. 2 *Vol.* Rolls	0	11	00
Lexicon Poliglott, or the like, 2 Vol.	0	12	00
Item, in one Vol. Rolles	0	08	00
Plutarchi Opera, 2 Vol. or the like, Rolls	0	08	00

	l.	s.	d.
Lipsius in Senecam			
Lipsius in Jacitum [sic] } or the like	0	03	06
Buxtorph. Heb. Bib.			
Corpus Juris Civ. one Vol.	0	04	00
In 2 Vol. or the like	0	06	00
Critici Sacri, 9 Vol.[1] or the like, Rolles	1	10	00
Scapulae Lexicon, Grotius in Vet. Test. or the like	0	03	00
Ravanella. S. 3 Vol.	0	09	00
Estius in Epist. or the like, one Vol.	0	02	06
Brennius in Bib. Gerrardi Loci Com. } 4 Vol. or the like	0	08	00

Books in Quarto, Latin.

	l.	s.	d.
Sculteti Medulla			
Mellificium Hist. } Rolls	0	01	04
Vosii Gram.[2] or the like			
All Latin Books in Quarto, Large & thick	0	01	02
If not thick	0	01	00
All Latin Books, Pot-paper, Rolls, Thick,	0	01	00
If not thick	0	00	10

Books in 8. 12. and 24.

	l.	s.	d.
Screvelius's Lexicon,[3] Octo. large	0	00	10
Virgil, Horatius vel } Rolls *Paterculius*, and the like	0	00	10
All thick Octo. Latin, Rolls	0	00	08
All thin Octo.	0	00	07
All Twelves and Sixteens	0	00	06
All Twenty fours	0	00	05

Books in Folio, English.

	l.	s.	d.
Ogilby's China, Virgil, all his other Books, or the like, in single Vol. Marble Fillets	0	08	00
Æsop compleat in one, *Iliads* and *Odysses*[4] in one, or the like, Marble Fillets	0	10	00
The same Books plain	0	07	00
The same Books single	0	05	00
	l.	s.	d.
Kings Works, or the like	0	03	06
Hammond on N. Testament			
Poultons Stat. or the like, Rolls	0	03	00

Davila's Hist.[5] *Rawleighs* Hist.	or the like	0	03	00
Plutarchs Lives *Heylins* Cosmog.	or the like	0	02	06
Cotgraves Dict. *Bakers* Chronicle,		0	02	00
Taylors Cases of Conscience,	Rolls			
Life of Christ,	Rolls	0	01	10
Hammond on Psalmes *Spotwood* Hist, or the like		0	01	08
Cassandra, or the like		0	01	06

Small Folio.

Fullers Holy War[6] *Hubbards* Reports *Baccalin*, and the like All Pot Folio's small	0	01	04

Books in Quarto, English.

Goldman, or the like, Rolls	0	01	06
Hughs Grand Abridgment, being 3 Vol. Rolls	0	04	00
Wests Presidents. *Thomas* Dict. or the like	0	01	02
Carills twelfth part, or the like	0	01	00
Baxters Saints Rest[7]	0	01	02
Baxters Reasons, Rolls. And all such English Quarto's thick	0	01	00
All small Pot-paper Quarto's Rolls	0	00	10

Books in Octavo, English.

All large Octo. *Decay of Piety*, or the like	0	00	09
Taylors Living and Dying,[8] or the like	0	00	08
All thin Crown Octavo's	0	00	07
All Pot Octavo's, *Quarles* Poems, &c	0	00	06

Books in 12. and 24.

All large Twelves	0	00	06
All small Twelves and Twenty-four's	0	00	05

Sheeps Leather, Folio's.

Ottaman Empire, or the like, Rolls	0	01	02
Noyes Reports,[9] or the like, Rolls	0	01	00
All thick Pot Folio's	0	01	00
All thin Pot	0	00	10

	s.[sic].	s.	d.
Large Quarto, Sheep.			
Placita Redivia, or the like, Rolls	0	00	10
All thin Crown Rolls	0	00	09
All Fools-Cap, or the like, Rolls	0	00	08
Quarto's Pot-paper, Sheep.			
Stillingfleets Origines Sacra,[10] or the like, rolls	0	00	08
All thick Pot	0	00	06
All thin Pot	0	00	05
Octavo's Large.			
Decay of Piety, or the like	0	00	05
Gent. Callings,[11] or the like	0	00	04
Records Arithm. *Erasmus* Colloq.			
Testaments Octo. Rom. or the like	0	00	04
All thin Crown, and all Fools-Cap	0	00	03½
Octavo Pot.			
Test. Octo. Com. *Quarles* Poems.			
Randolphs Poems. *Hools* Corderius,[12]			
or the like	0	00	03
All thin Pot	0	00	02½
Large Twelves.			
Present State of Eng. Pr. of Piety, or the like	0	00	03
Meads almost a Christ.[13] Ac. of Com. the like	0	00	02½
Redemption of Time, or the like	0	00	02
Pot Twelves.			
Baxters Call.[14] Doct. Bible, or the like	0	00	02½
Twenty-four's.			
Practice of Piety, or the like	0	00	03
Gerrards Meditat, Crums of Comf.[15] or the like	0	00	02½
All thin Twenty-four's	0	00	02
All sorts of Thin Books, Sheeps-Leather Fillets,			
As Grammars, Psalters	0	00	04
Small 12s, 24s, and 32s.			
Primmers Gilt, the Gross	1	00	00
Primmers Plain, the Gross	0	10	00

Thomas Hunt.[c]
Samuel Mearn.[a]
Thomas Raw.[a]
George Eversden.[a]
George Calvert.[a]
William Richardson.[c]
Edward Powel.[a]
Robert Cutler.[a]
Hilliam Harris.[c]
William Rands.[a]
Humphry Toy.[c]
William Branch.[c]
Edward Gough.[b]
Francis Hyarne.[c]
Henry Evans.[c]
Joseph Moore.[a]
John Downs.[d]
William Sherington.[c]
Robert Deevs.[c]
Thomas Hodyson.[b]
Thomas Cooper.[d]
William Terry.[c]
Joseph Cater.[c]
John Homersham.[d]
Nathan Brookes.[c]
Edward Eccleston.[b]
Christopher Lingerd.[c]
Stephen Cope.[c]

Richard Oliffe.[d]
Thomas Allsop.[a]
William Potter.[d]
Thomas Lammas.[c]
William Redmayne.[c]
Peter Scarlet.[d]
Robert Smith.[c]
John Fletcher.[c]
Thomas Kequick.[c]
Richard Dew.[c]
John Bishop.[c]
Walter Dunn.[c]
William Mason.[c]
John Mendey.[c]
William Stephens.[c]
William Willis.[c]
Walter Davis.[a]
Martin Barnham.[d]
Langlie Curtis.[a]
Robert Cox.[c]
Jonathan Adams.[d]
Richard Littleton.[d]
John Hewet.[c]
John Shepherd.[c]
Richard Barnes.[c]
William Baker.[c]
Thomas Hartley.[b]
Samuel Freeman.[c]

William Curtis.[c]
William Veery.[d]
Samuel Cook.[c]
Joshua Mitchel.[a]
Joshua Conuiers.[a]
Samuel Sprint.[a]
John Grover.[c]
Wiliam Charles.[c]
Richard Sympson.[a]
William Hilliard.[d]
Richard Janua.[a]
Gregory Pool.[c]
George Bale.[c]
William Bishop.[c]
Adam Winch.[c]
Thomas Brown.[a]
James Parkhurst.[c]
John Shrimton.[c]
John Spicer.[a]
Richard Hewes.[b]
Robert Finnis.[d]
John Major.[c]
Nathaniel Oldfield.[c]
Daniel Barber.[c]
James Hatton.[d]
William Goff.[d]

Licensed, *September* 23. 1669. ROGER L'ESTRANGE.

Key

[a] Bookseller and bookbinder.
[b] Possibly bookseller; certainly bookbinder.
[c] Bookbinder found elsewhere in Stationers' Company records.
[d] Bookbinder known only from this list.

Notes to Price List 4

1. John Pearson, *Critici Sacri*, 9 vols, fol. London, 1660.
2. Gerardus Vossius, *De arte grammatica libri*, 4°, Amsterdam, 1662.
3. Cornelius Schrevelius, *Lexicon Manuale Graeco-Latinum*, 8°, London, 1663.
4. Homer, *Iliad*, fol. London, 1669; Homer, *Odyssey*, fol. London, 1665: price quoted for 'in one', i.e. bound together, and for 'single'.

5. Enrico Caterino Davila, *The Historie of the Civill Warres of France*, fol. London, 1647, 1648.
6. Thomas Fuller, *The Historie of the Holy Warre*, fol. [Cambridge] 1651.
7. Richard Baxter, *The Saints Everlasting Rest*, 4°, London, 1669.
8. Jeremy Taylor, *The Rule and Exercises of Holy Living*, 8°, London, 1663; Idem, *The Rule and Exercises of Holy Dying*, 8°, London, 1655.
9. Sir William Noye, *Reports and Cases*, fol. London, 1669.
10. Edward Stillingfleet, *Origines sacrae*, 4°, London, 1666.
11. [? Richard Allestree], *The Gentleman's Calling*, 8°, London, 1668.
12. Charles Hoole, [ed], *Maturinus Corderius's School Colloquies*, 8°, London, 1657.
13. Matthew Mead, *The Almost Christian Discovered*, 12°, London, 1664.
14. Richard Baxter, *A Call to the Unconverted*, 12°, London, 1663.
15. Michael Sparke, *The Crums of Comfort*, 24°, London [? 1650], and part: London, 1652.

A General Note of the Prices of Binding

All Sorts of

BOOKS in CALVES-LEATHER:

Agreed on by the

BOOK-BINDERS,

Freemen of the City of *London,*

And by them Presented to the Master, Wardens and Assistants of the Worshipful Company of *Stationers,* at a Court holden *March,* 169⅘.

Books in Folio, Latin.

	l.	s.	d.
Lexicon Polyglotton *in Two Vol.* or the like }	00	15	00
Grotii Opera, *in 4 Vol. or the like*	00	14	00
Eusebius, *&c. in 3 Vol.*	00	12	00
Euripides	00	02	09
M. T. Ciceronis Opera *in 2 Vol.*	00	06	06
Limborch Theolog.	00	02	06

Quarto, Latin.

	l.	s.	d.
Cambridge Dictionary, *or the like*	00	02	00
All thin Quarto Demy	00	01	06
All Fools Cap thick	00	01	06
All Fools Cap thin	00	01	04

Octavo, Latin.

	l.	s.	d.
All Variorum's *thick*	00	01	02
All thin	00	01	00
Coles Dictionary	00	01	00
All middle siz'd	00	00	09
All Fools Cap	00	00	08
Cambridge Phrases	00	01	02

Twelves, Latin.

	l.	s.	d.
Gradus ad Parnassum	00	00	08
Ovidii Metamorphosis	00	00	08
All thin Twelves Large	00	00	07
All Small	00	00	06
Comp. Prayer Latin	00	00	08

Twenty Fours, Latin.

	l.	s.	d.
Ovidii Opera, *or the like*	00	00	07
All others	00	00	06

Folio, English.

	l.	s.	d.
Camden's Britannia *large*	00	12	00
Camden *small*	00	06	00
Clark on the Bible	00	04	00
Josephus	00	03	06
Hammond's Works 4 Vol.	00	14	00
Geograph. Dictionary	00	04	06
Manton's Works 4 Vol.	00	15	00
Bp. Reynold's Works	00	04	00
Bp. Taylor's Life of Christ	00	03	00
Duty of Man's Works	00	03	00
Baker's Chronicle	00	02	09
Dryden's Juvenal	00	02	04

Folio, Fools Cap.

	l.	s.	d.
Burnet's Theory *complete*	00	02	04
Oxford Com. Prayer	00	02	06
Laud's Life Fol.	00	02	04
Watson's Body of Divinity	00	02	00
L'Estrange's Esop	00	02	00
Burnet's History of the Reformation, *in 2 Vol. with Cuts*	00	05	06
Prince Arthur	00	02	00
Pearson on the Creed	00	02	00
Brown's Works	00	02	00
Acts for One Session of Parl. *large*	00	02	06
The same Small	00	01	00

Quarto, English.

	l.	s.	d.
Complete Clerk	00	01	06
Baxter's Saints Rest	00	01	00
Dr. Sherlock of the Trinity	00	01	02
Bp. Patrick on Genesis	00	01	04

Octavo *Large,* English.

	l.	s.	d.
Burnet's Abridgment	00	00	10
Gibson's Anatomy	00	01	00
Duty of Man	00	00	10
Plutarch's Morals 5 Vol.	00	04	02
Plutarch's Lives 5 Vol.	00	05	00
Dr. Sherlock of Death	00	00	09
Lock of Education	00	00	08
Terence *in English*	00	00	10
Jure Maritimo	00	01	00
Salmon's Dispensatory	00	01	00
Peche's Storehouse	00	01	00
Parson's Counsellor	00	00	10
Wingate's Abridgment	00	00	10
Hales's Contemplations	00	00	10
Dr. Scott's Christian Life 3 Vol.	00	02	06

All Fools Cap Octavo's.

	l.	s.	d.
Allen's Persuasive, *&c. in 4 Vol.*	00	03	04
Peche's Herbal	00	00	08
Pia Desideria	00	00	08
Chamberlain's State of England	00	00	08

All Large Twelves.

	l.	s.	d.
New State of England	00	00	08
Duty of Man	00	00	08
Devout Christian	00	00	08
Busbequius Epist. English	00	00	08

All thin Twelves.

	l.	s.	d.
Lake of the Sacrament	00	00	07
Devout Communicant	00	00	07
All small Twelves and Twenty Fours	00	00	06

The antient allow'd Rate of Binding Bibles in Calf.

Ogilby's Bibles Folio, or the like.

	l.	s.	d.
Gilt Edges	01	00	00
Fillets only	00	12	00
Plain	00	08	00

Bibles Quarto, Cambridge or the like.

	l.	s.	d.
Edges Extraordinary	00	05	00
Edges Ordinary	00	03	06
Fillets	00	02	06

Bibles Octavo, Brevere.

	l.	s.	d.
Edges Extraordinary	00	03	06
Edges Ordinary	00	02	04
Fillets	00	01	06

Bibles Octavo, Nonpareil.

	l.	s.	d.
Edges Extraordinary	00	02	10
Edges Ordinary	00	01	10
Fillets	00	01	02

Bibles Twelves and Twenty Fours.

	l.	s.	d.
Edges Extraordinary	00	02	06
Edges Ordinary	00	01	06
Fillets	00	01	00
Ovals	00	00	08

LONDON: Printed, and are to be Sold by *John Whitlock* near *Stationers-Hall.* 1695.

Fig. 2.3   List of binding prices 'LONDON: Printed, and are to be Sold by *John Whitlock* near *Stationers-Hall.* 1695.'

Price List 5

A General Note of the Prices of Binding All Sorts of BOOKS in
CALVES-LEATHER:

Agreed on by the BOOK-BINDERS, *Freemen* of the City of *London*,
And by them Presented to the Master, Wardens and Assistants of the
Worshipful Company of *Stationers*, at a Court holden *March*, 1694/5.

Books in **Folio**, Latin.

	l.	*s.*	*d.*
Lexicon Polyglotton *in Two Vol. or the like*	00	15	00
Grotii Opera, *in 4 Vol. or the like*	00	14	00
Eusebius, &c. *in 3 Vol.*	00	12	00
Euripides	00	02	09
M.T. Ciceronis Opera *in 2 Vol.*	00	06	06
Limborch Theolog.[1]	00	02	06

Quarto, Latin.

Cambridge Dictionary, *or the like*	00	02	00
All thin Quarto Demy	00	01	06
All Fools Cap thick	00	01	06
All Fools Cap thin	00	01	04

Octavo, Latin.

All Variorum's *thick*	00	01	02
All thin	00	01	00
Coles Dictionary[2]	00	01	00
All middle siz'd	00	00	09
All Fools Cap	00	00	08
Cambridge Phrases	00	01	02

Twelves, Latin.

Gradus ad Parnassum[3]	00	00	08
Ovidii Metamorphosis	00	00	08
All thin Twelves *Large*	00	00	07
All Small	00	00	06
Comp. Prayer *Latin*	00	00	08

Twenty Fours, Latin.

Ovidii Opera,[4] *or the like*	00	00	07
All others	00	00	06

Folio, English.	*l.*	*s.*	*d.*
Camden's Britannia *large*	00	12	00
Camden *small*	00	06	00
Clark on the Bible	00	04	00
Josephus	00	03	06
Hammond's Works 4 *Vol.*[5]	00	14	00
Geograph. Dictionary	00	04	06
Manton's Works 4 *Vol.*	00	15	00
Bp. Reynold's Works	00	04	00
Bp. Taylor's Life of Christ[6]	00	03	00
Duty of Man's Works	00	03	00
Baker's Chronicle	00	02	09
Dryden's Juvenal	00	02	04

Folio, Fools Cap.			
Burnet's Theory *complete*[7]	00	02	04
Oxford Com. Prayer	00	02	06
Laud's Life *Fol.*	00	02	04
Watson's Body of Divinity	00	02	00
L'Estrange's Esop	00	02	00
Burnet's History of the Reformation, *in* 2 *Vol.* with Cuts[8]	00	05	06
Prince Arthur	00	02	00
Pearson on the Creed	00	02	00
Brown's Works	00	02	00
Acts for One Session of Parl. *large*	00	02	06
The same *Small*	00	02	00

Quarto, English.			
Complete Clerk	00	01	06
Baxter's Saints Rest	00	01	06
Dr. Sherlock of the Trinity[9]	00	01	02
Bp. Patrick on Genesis	00	01	04

Octavo *Large*, English.	*l.*	*s.*	*d.*
Burnet's Abridgment[10]	00	00	10
Gibson's Anatomy	00	01	02
Duty of Man	00	00	10
Plutarch's Morals 5 *Vol.*	00	04	02
Plutarch's Lives 5 *Vol.*	00	05	00
Dr. Sherlock of Death	00	00	09
Lock of Education	00	00	08
Terence *in English*	00	00	10

Jure Maritimo	00	01	00
Salmon's Dispensatory	00	01	00
Peche's Storehouse	00	01	00
Parson's Counsellor	00	00	10
Wingate's Abridgment	00	00	10
Hales's Contemplations[11]	00	00	10
Dr. Scott's Christian Life 3 *Vol.*	00	02	06

All Fools Cap **Octavo's.**

Allen's Persuasive, *&c. in* 4 *Vol.*	00	03	04
Peche's Herbal[12]	00	00	08
Pia Desideria	00	00	08
Chamberlain's State of *England*	00	00	08

All Large **Twelves.**

New State of *England*	00	00	08
Duty of Man[13]	00	00	08
Devout Christian	00	00	08
Busbequius Epist. English	00	00	08

All thin **Twelves.**

Lake of the Sacrament[14]	00	00	07
Devout Communicant	00	00	07

All small Twelves *and* Twenty Fours	00	00	06

The antient allow'd Rate of Binding *Bibles* in *Calf.*

Ogilby's Bibles **Folio,** or the like.

Gilt Edges	01	00	00
Fillets only	00	12	00
Plain	00	08	00

Bibles **Quarto,** *Cambridge* or the like.

Edges Extraordinary	00	05	00
Edges Ordinary	00	03	06
Fillets	00	02	06

Bibles **Octavo,** Brevere.

Edges Extraordinary	00	03	06
Edges Ordinary	00	02	04
Fillets	00	01	06

Bibles **Octavo**, Nonpareil.			
Edges Extraordinary	00	02	10
Edges Ordinary	00	01	10
Fillets	00	01	02

Bibles **Twelves** and **Twenty Fours**.			
Edges Extraordinary	00	02	06
Edges Ordinary	00	01	06
Fillets	00	01	00
Ovals	00	00	08

LONDON: Printed, and are to be Sold by *John Whitlock* near *Stationers-Hall*. 1695.

Notes to Price List 5

1. Philippus a Limborch, *Theologia Christiana*, fol. Amsterdam, 1695.
2. Elisha Coles, *A Dictionary English-Latin*, 8°, London, 1692.
3. *Gradus ad Parnassum*, 12°, London, 1691.
4. Publius Ovidius Naso, *Opera*, 24°, Amsterdam [1674].
5. Henry Hammond, *Works* (4 vols), fol. London, 1684.
6. Jeremy Taylor, *Antiquitates Christianæ; or the History of the Life ... of ... Jesus*, fol. London, 1684.
7. Thomas Burnet, *The Theory of the Earth*, fol. London, 1690.
8. Gilbert Burnet, *The History of the Reformation of the Church of England* (2 vols with plates), fol. London, 1681, 1683.
9. William Sherlock, *A Vindication of the Doctrine of the Holy ... Trinity*, 4°, London, 1694.
10. Gilbert Burnet, *The Abridgment of the History of the Reformation of the Church of England*, 8°, London, 1683.
11. Sir Matthew Hale, *Contemplations Moral and Divine*, 8°, London, 1695.
12. John Pechey, *The Compleat Herbal*, 8°, London, 1694.
13. [Richard Allestree], *The Whole Duty of Man*, 12°, London, 1695.
14. Edward Lake, *Officium Eucharisticum*, 12°, London, 1690.

Price List 6

Whereas the BOOKBINDERS of the City of *Dublin* at a Meeting the 15th Day of *September* 1743, then held, did Unanimously Agree, that from and after the 29th of the said Month no Books are to be Bound, Paper Gilt or Black'd, for Boooksellers, under the following Prices.

N.B. By unanimous Consent, it was the Day aforesaid further Resolved, That all Octavos shall be charg'd Ten Pence, Twelves Eight Pence (at least) and so in Proportion for Books of Larger Size, as rated underneath, to all Gentlemen, Authors or others.

For the GILT WORK.

	l.	s.	d.
Imperial Folio Bible	1	2	9
Super-Royal	0	18	0
Royal Folio ditto	0	16	3
Medium	0	14	0
Demy Folio ditto	0	10	0
Propatria, or Paper of that Size	0	8	0
Bibles, Quarto, with Cuts	0	6	6
Ditto without	0	5	0
Bibles, large Octavo	0	2	6
Ditto large Twelves	0	1	6
Ditto smaller Twelves	0	1	4
Ditto Eighteens	0	1	2
Royal Folio Common-Prayers	0	10	0
Medium ditto	0	6	6
Common-Prayers Quarto	0	3	6
Ditto Octavo	0	1	10
Ditto large Twelves	0	1	4
Ditto the next Size Twelves	0	1	2
Ditto the long Lines Twelve	0	1	0
Ditto the short Lines Fine Paper	0	0	10
Ditto the common Sort	0	0	9
Ditto Twenty-fours	0	0	10

Books bound in VELLUM plain.
FOLIOS.

	l.	s.	d.
Imperial	0	6	6
Super-Royal	0	5	6
Royal	0	4	6
Medium	0	3	6
Demy	0	2	6
Propatria	0	2	0
Pocket Books Demy	0	0	9
Ditto Propatria	0	0	7

RUSSIA BANDS.

	l.	s.	d.
Imperial	0	16	0
Super-Royal	0	14	0
Royal	0	12	0

Medium		0	10	0
Demy		0	8	0

FORRIL.

	s.	d.			
Medium Fol.					
yellow	1	9	green	2	0
Demy Fol.					
ditto	1	4	ditto	1	6
Propatria Fol.					
ditto	0	10	ditto	0	11
Pocket Books common Size				0	0	3

Quartos, long or broad, the one half
Price of Folio's, in either Vellum or Forril.

Books GILT BACK only.

	l.	s.	d.
Imperial Folio	0	2	0
Super-Royal ditto	0	2	0
Royal ditto	0	2	0
Quartos of the above Sizes each	0	1	0
Medium Folios, and under that Size	0	1	6
Quartos Medium and under that Size	0	0	10
Royal Octavo	0	0	7
Medium ditto	0	0	5
Twelves of all Sizes	0	0	4

GILT Paper and BLACK.

Demy in Quarto the Rheam	0	9	0
Thick Post ditto the Rheam	0	7	0
Thin Post ditto the Rheam	0	4	6
Propatria Folio the Rheam	0	5	0
Ditto Quarto the Rheam	0	5	0
Post Paper Octavo the Rheam	0	6	0

Books bound in Calve's Leather and Letter'd only.
FOLIOS.

Imperial	0	8	0
Super-Royal	0	6	6
Royal	0	5	0
Medium	0	3	6
Demy	0	2	10
Propatria	0	2	4

QUARTOS.

Imperial ————————————————	0	4	0
Super-Royal ————————————————	0	3	3
— Ditto Musick twelve Sheets	0	2	0
Royal ————————————————	0	2	6
Medium ————————————————	0	1	9
Demy ————————————————	0	1	5
Propatria ————————————————	0	1	2

OCTAVOS.

Royal ————————————————	0	1	2
Medium ————————————————	0	0	9

TWELVES.

Without Distinction ————————————	0	0	7

  N.B. All Dictionaries, such as *Coles, Boyer, Bailey, Dyche, Schrevelius*'s Lexicon, and all Octavo Bibles, bound plain are to be Ten-pence, and no Quarter Book of any Sort whatsoever to be allowed.

GRAINS.

Testaments Saw'd per 100	0	12	6
Grammars ditto per 100	0	10	5
Burton's Books and Psalters per 100	0	8	4
Countess of Morton,[1] and others per 100	0	8	4

LACQUERD WORK.	*l.*	*s.*	*d.*
Common-Prayers and Manuals per Hundred, whereof one Quarter to be Shagreen	2	10	0

In a single Quarter six to be Shagreen.

Books FILLETED on the Back only with a Tool added thereto.

Imperial Folio			
Super-Royal ditto each Book	0	0	6
Royal ditto			
Medium ditto ————————————————	0	0	4
Demy ditto ————————————————	0	0	3
Propatria ditto ————————————————	0	0	3
Quartos of all Sizes ————————————	0	0	2
Octavos Royal, and all under	0	0	1
Twelves of all Sorts each ————————	0	0	1

For lettering the Volume in Black on the second Pannel of Folios and Quartos, each Book	0	0	2
For all Octavos and Twelves ditto	0	0	1
For Filleting and Rolling all Octavos and Twelves each	0	0	3

Books bound in SHEEP Banded.
FOLIOS

Coasting Pilot	0	3	0
Royal	0	2	9
Medium	0	2	6
Demy	0	2	0
Propatria	0	1	8

QUARTOS.

Royal	0	1	4
Medium	0	1	3
Demy	0	1	0
Propatria	0	0	9
Octavo, if Letter'd	0	0	7
Twelves	0	0	4
Testaments of each Sort	0	0	4

Plain SHEEP.

Testaments single 2½d. each, per 100	1	0	10
Grammars ditto 2¼d. each, per 100	0	18	9
Burton's Books and Psalters 2d. each, per 100	0	16	8
Countess of Morton's,[1] and others of or near that Size, 1½d. each	0	12	6

RUL'D PAPER.
All Ruling, except the common Pounds Shillings and Pence on Six penny and Propatria Paper, to be one Penny per Hundred.

Printed by EDWARD BATE, in *George's* Lane near *Dame's Street*.

Note to Price List 6

1. Anne Douglas, Countess of Morton, *The Countess of Morton's Daily Exercise*, 12°, London, 1689.

Price List 7

may 14th 1744.

To the Booksellers of London & Westminster. &c:
Gentlemen
At a Considerable meeting of the Bookbinders of the Citys of London &
Westminster & the libertys thereof
In Consideration of the exorbitant prices that Leather now Bears by the
Scarceness of that Commodity. By an Absolute Necessity [we] are Obliged
to Come to the following Resolutions in Regard to the Undermentioned
prices for the Different sizes of Books. These Gentlemen, we hope may
appear Reasonable to you, haveing Lost by all the work lately Undertaken,
&c.

The Prices are as follows — Viz:

	s	:	*d.*
Royal folio Letter'd	7	:	0:
Demy D°	4	:	0:
Crown D°	3	:	0.
Fools Caps D°	2	:	9.
Chamber's Dict: per Vol. & Books of that size Letterd	4	:	6.
Roy 4to Lett^d	3	:	0.
Demy D°	2	:	0.
Crown D°	1	:	9.

	s.		*d.*
Fools Cap letterd 4^{to}_____	1	:	6
Roy: 8vo plain_____	1	:	2
Demy D°_____	0	:	10
12^{ismo} D°_____	0	:	7

		s.		*d.*
All	Dictionarys or Lexicons 4to	2	:	0
	8vo Ditto_____	1	:	0
	Magazines & Books of y^t Size	1	:	0
	8vo Sheep rould_____	0	:	7
	12^{ismo} D°_____	0	:	5.

NB that Books of all Sizes with Cutts are to be considered.

The Edges Binders Prices in Calves Leather.

	l	:	*s*	:	*d*
Bible Royal Edges_____	0	:	14	:	0
D° plain Royal_____	0	:	7	:	0

Ditto Small fol°:	0	:	3	:	6
Ditto Edges	0	:	7	:	0
Large 4to plain	0	:	2	:	3
D° in Edges	0	:	4	:	6.
Small 4to plain	0	:	1	:	9
D° Edges	0	:	3	:	6
Octavo Brevier plain	0	:	1	:	2
D° Edges	0	:	2	:	0.
minion plain	0	:	0	:	9.
D° Edges	0	:	1	:	2.
Nonpariel plain	0	:	0	:	7.
D° Edges	0	:	0	:	11.

	s	:	d.
Common prayer Royal plain	5	:	6.
folio medium plain	3	:	0.
folio Demy plain	2	:	6.
Ditto Edges	5	:	0—
4to Royal plain	2	:	6—
Small 4to plain	1	:	3—
Ditto Edges	2	:	6—
8vo Large Letter Edges	1	:	6—
8vo pica Edges	1	:	1—
D° with Testament	1	:	6—

	s	:	d.
8vo Ditto plain	0	:	9.
Brevier Edges	0	:	7½
D° with Testament Edges		:	10—
Small 12ismo	0	:	6—
24°. Edges	0	:	5—
D° with Testament	0	:	7½
Bible Nonpariel fine paper			
Cambridge Edges	1	:	0—
D° plain	0	:	8—
Com[m]on prayer Cambridge Brevier	0	:	9—
All Common prayer with Cutts 2 pence More			
All Sacrament Books Black Calf Under the Size			
of the new Week's preparation[1]	0	:	6
Size of the New	0	:	7
All Common prayers in Sheep a halfpenny Less			

Sheep Binders prices p[er] C neat

	l :	s :	d
Oxford Testament	0 :	18 :	0.
Long primer Testament	1 :	6 :	0—
Psalters	0 :	15 :	0.
Lillys Grammers with the Construction	0 :	16 :	0.
Ward's Ditto	0 :	18 :	0—
Dyches Spelling Book[2] and all such	0 :	16 :	0—
Chapman's Book & Accedents	0 :	14 :	0.
All printed Down of 12: Sheets each and Under	0 :	16 :	0.
All above 12 Sheets	0 :	18 :	0.
New Week's preparation	0 :	17 :	0.
Hoppus Meshuring[3]	0 :	18 :	0.
London Spelling, Weald Ditto. Watts Songs London New Meathod &c:	0 :	13 :	0.
New Year's Gift. Mortons Devotion Devout Companion		13 :	0
Common prayer 24°, Old psalms Almo [?] Beza's Testament &c:		16 :	0

Sowing & Folding *Prices*

Folio's 1 farthing an Alphabett F[olding?]
S[ewing?]
4[tos]: & 8[vos]: 1 halfpenny a hundred Sheets.
folding & 12[s]: 1 penny folding 18[s]
1 penny halfpenny a hundred folding —4[tos] 8[vos] 12[s] 18[s] Common Sowing
1 penny p[er] C Sheets: for Sowing only two Sheets at a time three half
pence. & for Sowing only one Sheet at a time 2 pence for Every hundred
Sheets the Sowing —

NB: that the Above is the very full price. Some women will work
Cheeper. —

Black or Gilt Paper		s :	d
Thick post 4[to]		1 :	6—
La thin D°:		1 :	3—
Fools Cap D°		1 :	3—
Small thin 4[to]	P[er] Ream	1 :	0—
Thick Post 8[vo]		1 :	0—
Thin 8[vo]		0 :	10—

	s	:	d
Ruleing Paper			
Folio Pott or Fools Cap p[er] Rm	1	:	0—
4ᵗᵒ D° p[er] Rm_____	2	:	0—
fo°. For foulding & Sowing p[er] D°	0	:	6
4ᵗᵒ p[er] Ditto_____	0	:	10—
NB: that 3 hund & 84 Lines is one q.ʳ			
we Charge or by the thousand_____		:	6—

Notes to Price List 7

1. *The New Week's Preparation for a Worthy Receiving of the Lord's Supper*, 12°, London [1744].
2. Thomas Dyche, *A Guide to the English Tongue*, 12°, London, 1713 (possibly a later edition).
3. Edward Hoppus, *Practical Measuring Made Easy*, 8°, London, 1738.

Price List 8

TO THE BOOKSELLERS of LONDON and WESTMINSTER.
GENTLEMEN,
In Consideration of the great Advance on both Sorts of Leather, the Bookbinders of *London* and *Westminster*, by a general Agreement, have fixed the following Prices for Binding; which the Support of Ourselves and Families will oblige us strictly to observe.

The PRICES for BINDING agreed on the 2d of *June*, 1760.

FOLIO's, Imperial Paper.

	l.	s.	d.
ALBINUS's Tables, Calf, lettered[1]_____	1	2	0
Ditto, half bound, lettered_____	0	11	0
Catesby's Carolina, per Vol. lettered_____	0	16	0
Atlas Maritimus, lettered_____	0	16	0
Palmyra, or Balbec, lettered[2]_____	0	10	0
Heads and Lives of illustrious Persons, gilt and lettered	0	14	0

All Books on the same Paper and Thickness, the like Price.

FOLIO's, Royal Paper.

Campbell's Vitruvius, per Vol. lettered[3]	0	8	0
Religious Ceremonies, per Vol. lettered_____	0	8	0
Gibbs's Architecture, lettered_____	0	7	6
Clarendon, lettered_____	0	7	0

Norden's Travels, per Vol._____	0	8	0

All Books on the same Paper, &c. the like Price.

FOLIO's, Demy.

Harrison's Voyages, per Vol. lettered_____	0	6	3
System of Geography, ditto, lettered_____	0	6	3
Stow's Survey, per Vol. lettered_____	0	6	9
Ware's Architecture, lettered_____	0	6	9
Maitland, per Vol. lettered_____	0	6	9
Rapin with Heads, &c. lettered_____	0	5	3
Statutes at Large, lettered_____	0	5	3
Universal Traveller, lettered_____	0	5	9
Bailey's Dictionary, lettered_____	0	5	9
Chamber's Dictionary, per Vol. lettered_____	0	5	3
James's Dictionary, per Vol. lettered_____	0	5	9
Burkitt with Cuts, lettered_____	0	5	3
— without Cuts, lettered_____	0	4	3
Stackhouse's Bible, per Vol.[4]_____	0	5	3
Sloan's Jamaica, per Vol.[5]_____	0	8	6
Illustration of the Bible_____	0	6	9

All Books on the same Paper, &c. the like Price.

FOLIO's, Crown.

Stackhouse's Body of Divinity, lettered[6]_____	0	3	9
Taylor's Life of Chirst with Cuts_____	0	4	0
Jacob's Law Dictionary, lettered_____	0	3	6
Wood's Conveyancer, lettered_____	0	3	6
Tillotson's Sermons, per Vol. lettered_____	0	3	6
Bion's Instruments_____	0	3	6

All Books on the same Paper, &c. the like Price.

FOLIO's, Fool's-Cap.

Peere Williams's Reports_____	0	3	3
Viner's Abridgment[7]_____	0	3	3
Ludlow's Memoirs_____	0	3	3

All Books on the same Paper, &c. the like Price.

QUARTO's, Royal Paper.

Smollett's Don Quixote, lettered[8]_____	0	3	3
Jarvises' Don Quixote, lettered_____	0	3	6
Pope's Works, lettered_____	0	3	0
Bolingbroke_____	0	3	0

All Books on the same Paper, &c. the like Price.

QUARTO's, Demy.

	l.	s.	d.
Ainsworth's Dictionary, lettered[9]	0	2	9
Boyer's Dictionary, lettered	0	2	6
Cruden's Concordance, lettered	0	2	6
Heister's Surgery, lettered	0	2	6
Addison's Works, per Vol. lettered	0	2	3
Hook's Roman History, per Vol. with Cuts, lettered	0	2	6
Gravesand's Philosophy, per Vol. lettered	0	2	6
Taylor on the Romans, lettered	0	2	3
Philosophical Transactions, lettered	0	2	3
Emerson's Mechanics, lettered[10]	0	2	3

All Books on the same Paper, &c. the like Price.

OCTAVO's, Royal Paper, in plain Calf.

	l.	s.	d.
Clarendon's History, Calf[11]	0	1	3
Molloy's De Jure Maritimo	0	1	3
Owen's Dictionary, in 4 Vols. plain, per Vol.	0	1	9
— in 8 Vols. plain, per Vol.	0	1	6
Ainsworth's Dictionary, plain, in 1 Vol.	0	2	0
— Ditto, in 2 Vols. per Vol.	0	1	6
Robertson's Navigation, per Vol. plain	0	1	3
— in 1 Vol. plain	0	1	6
Shervin's Tables	0	1	3

All Books on the same Paper, &c. the like Price.

OCTAVO's, Demy, Calf.

	l.	s.	d.
Boyer's Dictionary	0	1	2
Bailey's Dictionary	0	1	2
Schrevelius's Lexicon	0	1	2
Magazines	0	1	2
Crouch's and Saxby's Rates	0	1	1
Burn's Justice, per Vol.[12]	0	1	0
Complete Housewife	0	1	0
Smollett's History of England, 11 Vols. plain, per Vol.	0	1	2
Ditto, 7 Vols. with Cuts, per Vol.	0	1	2
New Duty of Man	0	1	1
Peerage of England, per Vol.	0	1	1
Virgil, Delph.	0	1	1
Martin's Philosophy, per Vol.	0	1	1
— Grammar	0	1	1
Prussian Infantry and Cavalry	0	1	1

Bland's Discipline	0	1	0
Gordon's Grammar	0	1	0
Duty of Man	0	1	0
Salmon's Grammar	0	1	1
And all Octavo's, such as Sherlock's Sermons, &c.	0	0	11
Tillotson's Sermons, per Vol.	0	1	0

All Books on the same Paper, &c. the like Price.

Crown OCTAVO's, Calf.

Hervey	0	0	9
Pope's Works, per Vol.	0	0	9
New Duty of Man	0	0	9
Bartlet's Farriery[13]	0	0	9

All Books on the same Paper, &c. the like Price.

Demy TWELVES, Calf.

Nature display'd	0	0	10
Dryden's Virgil[14]	0	0	10
Martin's and Salmon's Gazetters	0	0	10
New Manual	0	0	9
Milton's Paradise Lost and Regain'd	0	0	9
Theobald's Shakespear, per Vol.	0	0	9
Spectators, Tatlers, and Guardian, &c.	0	0	8

All Books on the same Paper, &c. the like Price.

Small TWELVES, Calf.

Rasselas, Shandy, and Pope's Works[15]	0	0	7
Gay's Fables with Cuts	0	0	9

All Books on the same Paper, &c. the like Price.

OCTAVO's, Sheep, Rolled.

Drelincourt on Death[16]	0	0	8
Wingate's Arithmetic	0	0	8
Wild's Surveying	0	0	8

All Books on the same Paper, &c. the like Price.

Large TWELVES and Crown OCTAVO's, Sheep, Rolled.

Salmon's and Martin's Gazetters	0	0	8
New Duty of Man	0	0	7
New Manual	0	0	7
Marshal on Sanctification, &c.[17]	0	0	7
Bartlett's Farriery	0	0	7

All Books on the same Paper, &c. the like Price.

Demy TWELVES, Sheep, Rolled,

Hawney's Measurer	0	0	6
Croxall's Æsop	0	0	6
Beveridge's Thoughts[18]	0	0	6
Harrison's Cookery, &c.	0	0	6

Red Sheep, Rolled.

Letter Writer	0	0	6
Rider and List	0	0	5
Dodsley's Gent. and Baldwin's Journal, &c.	0	0	6
— Lady's	0	0	4½

All Books on the same Paper, &c. the like Price.

Small TWELVES, Sheep, Rolled.

Miss's Magazine	0	0	5
Young Lady's Magazine, per Vol.	0	0	5
Howe's Meditations[19]	0	0	5

All Books on the same Paper, &c. the like Price

BIBLES.

Royal Bible	0	9	0
Medium Bible	0	6	6
Small Folio Bible	0	4	3
Large Quarto Bible	0	2	6
Small Quarto Bible	0	2	0
Octavo Bible	0	1	4
Minnion Bible	0	0	11
Nonpariel Bible	0	0	9
Twenty-fours Bible	0	0	8

COMMON-PRAYERS.

Royal Prayer	0	5	0
Folio Prayer Medium	0	4	0
——————— Demy	0	3	6
Quarto Prayer	0	1	9
Octavo Prayer	0	1	0
Brevier Twelves Prayer	0	0	8
Small Twelves Prayer	0	0	7
Twenty-fours Prayer	0	0	6

Notes to Price List 8

1. Bernardus Siegfried Albinus, *Tables of the Skeleton and Muscles of the Human Body*, fol. London, 1749.
2. Robert Wood, *The Ruins of Palmyra*, fol. London 1753; Idem, *The Ruins of Balbec*, fol. London, 1757.
3. Colin Campbell, *Vitruvius Britannicus*, 3 vols fol. London, 1717–1725.
4. Thomas Stackhouse, *A New History of the Holy Bible*, 2 vols fol. London, 1752.
5. Sir Hans Sloane, *A Voyage to the Islands . . . and Jamaica*, 2 vols fol. London, 1707–1725.
6. Thomas Stackhouse, *A Complete Body of Divinity*, fol. London, 1734.
7. Charles Viner, *A General Abridgment of Law and Equity*, 24 vols fol. Aldershot, 1747–1758.
8. Miguel de Cervantes Saavedra, *The History and Adventures of the Renowned Don Quixote. Translated . . . by T. Smollett*, 4°, London, 1755.
9. Robert Ainsworth, *A Compendious Dictionary of the Latin Tongue*, 4°, London, 1751.
10. William Emerson, *The Principles of Mechanicks*, 4°, London, 1758.
11. Edward Hyde, 1st Earl of Clarendon, *The History of the Rebellion*, 3 vols 8°, Oxford, 1720–1721.
12. Richard Burn, *The Justice of the Peace*, 3 vols 8°, London, 1758.
13. John Bartlet, *The Gentleman's Farriery*, 8°, Eton, 1754.
14. Publius Virgilius Maro, *The Works of Virgil. . . . Translated by Mr Dryden*, 12°, London, 1730.
15. Alexander Pope, *Works*, 12°, London, 1757.
16. Charles Drelincourt, *The Christian's Defence against the Fears of Death*, 8°, London, 1751.
17. Walter Marshall, *The Gospel-Mystery of Sanctification*, 8°, Edinburgh, 1733 (or possibly a later edition).
18. William Beveridge, *Private Thoughts upon Religion*, 2 parts 12°, London, 1752.
19. Charles Howe, *Meditations*, 12°, Dublin, 1754.

Notes to the text

1. A.W. Pollard & G.R. Redgrave, *A Short-Title Catalogue of Books . . . 1475–1640*, London, 1926, (revised edn., vol.ii, London, 1976, vol.i, London, 1986.).
2. At the end of this fascinating article in which Coghlan's binding equipment and stationery stock are described, H.M. Nixon announced a second article intended to deal with the binders' price lists and some of the recipes. He then kindly and generously handed this material over to me and, though it is a disappointment not to have his comments on these lists, it may be useful to put them into perspective by publishing all known lists at the same time. I am also grateful to the editor of the *Journal of the Printing Historical Society* for relinquishing his claim.
    After this article had been published, Miss Mary Pollard discovered a fourth eighteenth-century price list, issued in Dublin in 1791 (private collection).

3. For this and much of the information used throughout this article I am indebted to G. Pollard, 'Changes in the style of bookbinding, 1550–1830', *The Library*, Ser. 5, XI (1956), pp. 71–94, and to Bernard Middleton, *A History of English Craft Bookbinding Technique*, 2nd edn., London, 1978, *passim*. See also Bernard Middleton, 'The Bookbinders case unfolded', *The Library*, Ser. 5, XVII (1962), pp. 66–76, and H.M. Nixon, *Five Centuries of English Bookbinding*, London, 1978, p. 48.

4. H.M. Nixon, *Broxbourne Library: Styles and Designs of Bookbinding*, London, 1956, pp. 126–7; see also pp. 118–20.

5. E. Arber, *A Transcript of the Registers of the Company of Stationers, 1554–1640*, 5 vols, London, 1875, vol.I, p. 100. W.A. Jackson, *Records of the Court of the Stationers' Company 1602–1640*, London, 1957, p. 176.

6. N. Temperley, 'Middleburg Pslams', *Studies in Bibliography*, XXX (1977), pp. 162–70.

7. I am grateful to the President and Council of the Bibliographical Society for making the typescript and proofs of vol.i available for research. For the post-1641 lists, D. Wing, *Short-Title Catalogue of Books . . . 1641–1700*, New York, 1945–51, revised edns of vols i and ii, New York, 1972, 1982 and A.F. Allison and V.F. Goldschmidt, *op. cit.*, vol.2: *1641–1700*, London, 1977 have been used, as well as Watt and the British Library Catalogue.

8. I am very grateful to Mr John Hopkins, Librarian of the Society of Antiquaries, for his help in finding this list.

9. E.g. H.M. Nixon, *op. cit.*, p. 132, pp. 143–4.

10. E.g. G.D. Hobson, *English Bindings 1490–1940 in the Library of J.R. Abbey*, London, 1940, pl.28.

11. The sizes in inches given here and below are the approximate sizes per sheet, and are taken from E.J. Labarre, *Dictionary and Encyclopaedia of Paper and Paper-Making*, Amsterdam, 1952; P. Gaskell, 'Notes on Eighteenth-Century British Paper'. *The Library*, Ser. 5, XII, (1957), pp. 34–42, and *An Alphabetical List of the Names of the Several Species of Writing Papers, Printing Papers . . . with their Size and Value per Ream*, London, 1781 (broadsheet, BL, 510.i.6(7)).

12. J. Moxon, *Mechanick Exercises*, London, 1683–4. See also W. Savage, *A Dictionary of the Art of Printing*, London, 1841, pp. 802–3.

13. D. Foxon, 'Stitched books', *The Book Collector*, XXIV, (1975), pp. 111–24.

14. H.R. Plomer, *A Dictionary of the Booksellers and Printers who were at Work in England . . . 1641–1667*, London, 1907; idem, *A Dictionary of the Printers and Booksellers . . . 1668–1725*, London, 1922. D.F. McKenzie, *Stationers' Company Apprentices 1605–1640*, Charlottesville, Va., 1961; idem, *Stationers' Company Apprentices 1641–1700*, Oxford, 1974.

15. Stationers' Company Court Book F. fol. 218[b].

16. J.W. Phillips, 'The Origin of the publisher's binding in Dublin', *Transactions of the Cambridge Bibliographical Society*, II (1954), pp. 92–4.

17. The price for a Bible, 'Quarto, without Cuts' is 5*s*, the same as that for 'Edges Extraordinary' for the same size Bible in 1669 and 1695.

18. [H. Parry], *The Art of Bookbinding*, London, 1818, pp. 44–6, frontispiece.

19. See A.N.L. Munby, 'Chirms banded bindings', *Transactions of the Cambridge Bibliographical Society*, I (1950), pp. 181–6.

20. R. Dossie, *The Handmaid to the Arts*, London, 1758, vol.i, pp. 392–4 contains a section on how to make embossed and metallic-varnish paper, but the author also complains that 'The manufactures of the gilt and marbled papers

have not been so much cultivated in our own country, as it were to be wished, since very great sums have been always annually paid, both to Germany and Genoa, on this account'.

21. ibid., p. 397.

22. J. Arnett, *Bibliopegia*, London (etc.), 1835, p. 53.

23. H.M. Nixon, 'The memorandum book of James Coghlan', *Journal of the Printing Historical Society*, VI (1970), pp. 39–41. This and quotations concerning Coghlan's binding equipment below are taken from the 'Catalogue' printed in this article. The price lists and the recipes are quoted from the manuscript.

24. I am grateful to Dr Nicholas Pickwoad and to Mr David Foxon for information on these points.

25. I am grateful to Mr Michael Harris for providing me with xerox copies from originals in the Public Record Office C 114/182 PT II.

26. These bills are at the Stationers' Company. I am grateful to Miss Robin Myers for drawing them to my attention.

27. Published in full in E. Howe, *The London Bookbinders 1780–1806*, London, 1950, appendix iii.

28. ibid., p. 9 for this and the information and quotations below; and J. Jaffray, *A Collection of Manuscripts Relating to the Art and Trade of Bookbinding*, 4 (1864), (not published). A typescript of this is in the British Library (667.r.19), pp. 190–1, 216–7, 224–5.

Part II
BOOKBINDING: A DEAD CRAFT?

History is a constantly moving process; it does not stop at any given date but is made hourly; it is 'an unending dialogue between the present and the past'.* Contemporary bookbinding is not a phenomenon that only functions here and now; it is a continuation of, sometimes a reaction to, what went on before. Contemporary craftsmen and artists are not always aware of this. Some explicitly deny all interest in the past, not wanting to be contaminated by it. Others, *per contra*, are grateful to find their roots in a long and honourable tradition. Binders who are also restorers have a strong practical need to come to grips with past techniques and materials.

In the same way, not all binding historians are interested in the present. The past is safer, easier to understand and therefore easier to control. The wilder manifestations of contemporary book-art are outside their comprehension and are consequently ignored. Although I cannot claim actually to like a number of the more *outré* productions, where the book is no longer recognizable as a book, and although I doubt whether some 'book works' are in fact bookbindings at all, I try and look at them in an historical perspective and as an expression of the mind and emotions of a contemporary artist. The majority of contemporary bookbindings, however, are perfectly accessible, even to the untrained eye, and many are exquisitely beautiful.

One of the more attractive aspects of contemporary design binding is the way it is determined by the book it contains. There are examples of historical bindings where the design relates to the text, but these are the exception rather than the rule, whereas most contemporary binders—at least those working in Europe and the United States—conceive the binding as a direct result of the text, its subject and style, and the way it has been produced. All this is reflected, not only in the design, but also in the materials and technique used for the binding.

In Great Britain, the society of Designer Bookbinders has done a great deal to promote this philosophy. It has done much to present binding as an art form to a wider public; it encourages young craftsmen to strive for technical perfection, and it frequently attains the very high standards it

---

* E. H. Carr, *What is History?*, London, 1961, p. 24.

has set. It has also proved quite conclusively, and continues to prove, that bookbinding is not a dead craft, that it flourishes and develops and that, though based on and rooted in a long-standing tradition, it manifests itself as a remarkably contemporary art form.

A man who did much to encourage bookbinding students was Thomas Harrison, in whose memory a bookbinding competition was founded which, under a different name, still takes place. A brief record of the Thomas Harrison Memorial Competition is followed by an account of ten years' acquisition activity in the field of modern binding by the British Library. Three individual twentieth-century binders are also discussed.

3 A Binding by Paul Kersten, 1900

(1987)*

Paul Kersten, the pioneer of modern German bookbinding, is better known in Germany than in this country. His work has been well illustrated in German trade journals and both his 60th and his 70th birthdays gave rise to short appreciations of Kersten as craftsman, artist, teacher and writer.[1]

He was born on 18 March 1865. He learnt the craft at his grandfather's bindery in Glauchau and at the school for hand finishing at Gera. He worked in Berlin in the shops of W. Collin and C. W. Vogt and Son, and in Mülhausen with Jenner. From 1894 to 1896 he travelled to Bucharest and Stockholm. Back in Germany, he worked in the bindery of H. Sperling for whom he made about 70 bindings that made a great impression at the Sächsisch-Thüringische exhibition in Leipzig in 1897. The binding decoration reflected the contents of the book, an unusual feature in Germany at that time.

From 1898 to 1901 the Bundpapierfabrik A.G. of Aschaffenburg employed him to design decorated paper.[2] He then became director of a factory making writing materials in Erlangen and for six months he worked on his own in Breslau. However, he did not like the business side of life and in 1904 he went to Berlin where he became manager of the bindery of Lüderitz and Bauer. He found his vocation in teaching. For many years he taught several bookbinding and art classes in Berlin where he also had his own atelier. He both designed and executed his own bindings, as well as designing publishers' bindings, and in 1897–8 he designed a collection of modern finishing tools.

He collected a remarkable library of binding literature and wrote several books and a host of articles about the technique of bookbinding, binding decoration, history of binding and decorated paper. The best known are perhaps *Moderne Entwürfe für Bucheinbände* (2 volumes, Halle, [1904–06]) and *Der exakte Bucheinband* that went into four editions between 1909 and 1923. He died in Berlin in November 1943.

---

* English and Foreign Bookbindings 43, *The Book Collector*, xxxvi, pp. 531–2.

1. F. A. Schmidt-Künsemüller, *Bibliographie zur Geschichte der Einbandkunst* Wiesbaden, 1987, lists 52 items altogether.
2. M. M. Foot, 'The Olga Hirsch Collection of Decorated Papers', *The British Library Journal*, VII (1981), p. 25 and fig. 9; reprinted below as article 46.

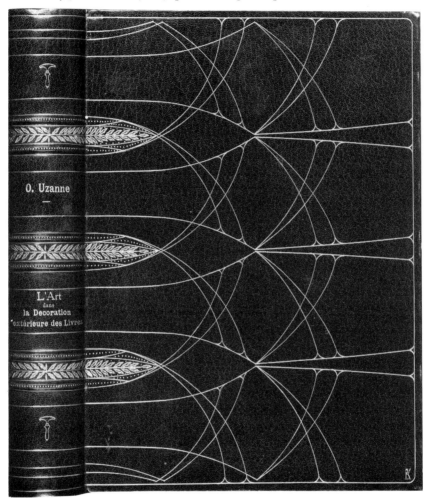

Fig. 3.1   O. Uzanne, *L'art dans la decoration exterieure des livres*, Paris, 1898.
Green morocco, tooled in gold. 275 × 200 × 42 mm.
British Library, C.183.a.4.

4 A Binding by W. T. Walker, 1909

(1984)*

In 1981 the British Library received by donation two bindings made at the beginning of the present century by Walter Thomas Walker (1876–1965) which are typical products of their time. The binder shows himself an able pupil of Francis Sangorski who is best known for his jewelled bindings in what Howard M. Nixon once called 'the everything bar the kitchen stove style'.[1] Francis Sangorski drowned off Selsey Bill on 1 July 1912 and so shared the fate of his most lavish binding, on Omar Khayam's *Rubaiyat*, which went down with the Titanic. He taught W. T. Walker at the Northampton Polytechnic Institute at Clerkenwell from 1908 till 1912. Prior to this, in April 1896, the nineteen-year-old Walker, a student at the People's Palace, had been awarded an evening exhibition in science and technology.

The binding illustrated was awarded the first prize in the examination of the City and Guilds of London Institute in 1909; the Prince of Wales presented Walker on this occasion with a silver medal. The binding is a typical examination piece, showing that the candidate could produce chamfered boards, was proficient in onlaying, inlaying and tooling in gold, could fit neat leather joints and doublures, and knew how to sew headbands and cope with silk end-leaves.

In March 1912 both Sangorski and John Williams, head of the Artistic Crafts Department at the Northampton Institute, recommended him for the vacant appointment of Binding Clerk in the Stationery Office.[2]

The second binding, which is undated, is a little more restrained in design. It is made of green goatskin with red onlays and gold-tooled floral sprays, and it covers F. E. Hulme, *Familiar Wild Flowers*, London [?1897] (British Library, C. 129.m.19).

1. H. M. Nixon, *Five Centuries of English Bookbinding*, London, 1978, p. 216.
2. Information from correspondence, donated together with the bindings, the medal and the patterns for the binding illustrated by the binder's niece, Miss W. K. Booker.

---

* English and Foreign Bookbindings 28, *The Book Collector*, XXXIII, pp. 66–7.

Fig. 4.1 *The Gallery of Modern British Artists*, London, n.d.
Brown goatskin onlaid in green and red and tooled in gold;
inlaid and gold-tooled doublures. 242 × 184 × 22 mm.
British Library, C.129.m.20.

5 The Thomas Harrison Memorial Competition 1955–1975: A Record

(1975)*

When in 1975 Designer Bookbinders assumed the responsibility for organizing and financing the bookbinding competition, a yearly event to give all those outside the hallowed circle of Fellows the opportunity to show their work, I was asked to write a brief account of its immediate predecessor, the Thomas Harrison Memorial Competition. Now, eighteen years later, the competition still continues, some years more successfully than others. Although some of the rules have been changed—a set book has been introduced and prizes have been awarded in a differing range of categories—the basic aims, to promote craft bookbinding and to encourage young craftsmen to devote their time, talents and attention to achieving the highest technical and artistic standards, still remain. The man in whose memory this all started would have given his approval.

Thomas Harrison MBE, FRSA was born in 1876 in Kirby Lonsdale, Westmorland, the son of a stonemason. He was apprenticed as a finisher to Fazakerley's at Liverpool; after he was made free he studied art and design at the Liverpool College of Art where he distinguished himself and won City & Guilds awards. He came to London and worked as a journeyman finisher in several West End shops including Zaehnsdorf. Later he became manager there and at H. T. Wood, whose proprietor he eventually became, and where his drive raised the firm's old reputation for high quality bindings. His first book *The Bookbinding Craft and Industry* came out in 1926. The slump of the 1930s caused Wood's collapse and the firm went into liquidation. Harrison left the West End and from about 1934 became technical adviser to Nevetts. In 1939 he set up on his own in Colindale and worked with the help of Miss Florence Wilson until his death in 1955. He taught at the Northampton Polytechnic and at the London School of Printing and during the war at the Sutton School of Art. His *Bookbinding for Printers* was published in 1949. He had great influence on his pupils. His shop was always open to everyone and all who listened to him talking about the 'mechanics' of leather binding came under his spell. He lived for his craft and liked to talk about the technique

* *Designer Bookbinders Review*, VI (1975), pp. 10–18 (this article has been shortened).

of fine binding. He had a passion for thoroughness and always insisted on the highest standards of craftsmanship. He was much loved, and his death left a void in the lives of all who knew him.

As a memorial to Harrison, H. A. (Roger) de Coverly started a fund to finance an annual award for craft bookbinding, to be competed for by students, craftsmen and apprentices. Under the presidency of Sir Robert Leighton, a Memorial Committee was established to administer the fund. Its chairman was Dr Desmond Flower, its Honorary Secretary and Honorary Treasurer were H. A. de Coverly and F. G. Marshall, and its other members were G. Glover, Kenneth Hobson, Ellic Howe and James Moran. In 1957 F. Neale joined the Committee, later to be replaced by W. J. Bull and R. Riley, and in 1971 B. Maggs and H. M. Nixon were elected to it. The death of Sir Robert Leighton in 1959 left the presidency vacant.

An appeal was launched in 1955 and the response was so generous that, when the first competition was held in 1957, the Committee was able to enlarge the original scheme by including a special class for younger craftsmen together with an open award. The first exhibition of entries was mounted at the galleries of the Times Bookshop Company in Wigmore Street, alongside an exhibition of nineteen bindings by Thomas Harrison, dating from *c.* 1901 until shortly before his death, and 24 examples of 'Historic English Bindings', ranging from a 1526 *Heroides*, decorated with the arms of Katherine of Aragon and Henry VIII, to a 1955 inlaid binding by Sangorski & Sutcliffe.

For the next two years the exhibitions were held at the Times Bookshop. This company covered the expenses of the exhibitions and gave the opening party, to which the press was invited. In 1960, when the number of entries had risen from 47 to 81, the exhibition took place at the National Book League in Albemarle Street, where it remained—first downstairs and later upstairs—a yearly event, except for 1967, until 1974. The terms for accommodation at Albemarle Street were generous; special terms for printing were obtained, and the arranging, judging and manning of the exhibitions were done voluntarily. However, the Memorial Committee had henceforth to cover all expenses, helped by several generous donations.

Only one entry was allowed per craftsman; these had to be made a year to 18 months prior to the exhibition and were divided into three classes according to the age of the competitors: Class A up to the age of 26, Class B up to the age of 21 and Class C open for anyone over 26. They were judged by an independent panel of judges, appointed by the Committee. In 1960 J. B. Corderoy initiated an extra prize in Class B for the most competent forwarding and in 1962 an open award for the best flexible binding was offered by Mrs N. F. Clogstoun and H. A. de Coverly. More special prizes were awarded during later years, such as that for the most successful design, and in 1965 Miss Elizabeth Greenhill started a prize for the best woman binder, which was changed in 1972 to an award for finishing. Some bindings were 'highly commended'. The 1966 catalogue stated that in any one year a total of nine prizes might be awarded; this maximum dropped to a total of seven in 1969. However, the maximum was only occasionally reached and in some years no major award was announced or no prize awarded at all in a particular class.

In 1957 a covenant was started, which produced a modest income for seven years; after that the fund, which was registered as a charity and therefore exempt from income tax, was run on a yearly hand-to-mouth basis. In 1959 it received a grant of £250 from The Pilgrim Trust; in 1971, £50 from the Arts Council, and in 1973 the Crafts Advisory Committee contributed £75. Prize money was largely donated by Major J. R. Abbey, M. Breslauer, J. B. Corderoy (and after his death by his colleagues at Camberwell in his memory), Mrs N. F. Clogstoun, H. A. de Coverly, Dr D. Flower, who also covered a deficit in 1970, K. Hobson, Miss Elizabeth Greenhill, H. M. Nixon, Designer Bookbinders (regularly since 1970) and others. By 1966 the original fund was exhausted. H. A. de Coverly advanced the costs for that year, but the illness and subsequent resignation of the Treasurer and the unsettled accounts were reasons for forgoing the competition in 1967. This caused great concern and elicited many protests. At a committee meeting in 1968 D. Flower and K. Hobson offered to cover the cost of some of the awards on a modified basis and, with the help of the by then established donations, it seemed possible to continue the yearly competitions. H. A. de Coverly undertook to act as Treasurer as well as Secretary. Subscriptions from teachers at the London College of Printing and elsewhere, and donations from booksellers and bookbinders kept the fund afloat until 1974. As costs increased some of the money designated for prizes had to go towards covering exhibition expenses. Showcases, which had hitherto been provided free of charge, had to be hired from 1970.

Financial difficulties were not the only worries. Syllabus reforms in technical and art colleges, indicating a move away from pure craftsmanship, caused the number of entries to fall from between 65 and 78 during the first five years of the 1960s, to 22 in 1974. Standards of technique dwindled as well. During the late 1960s and early 1970s the judges complained disappointedly of carelessness and lack of finesse, lack of appreciation of detail and neglect of the finer technical points, of ambitious designs unsupported by basic craftsmanship; lack of continuity in the design of the covers and that of the spine was commented on several times. However, appreciation of originality of concept and high standards of technique in the winning entries were expressed as well, and on some occasions bindings from the competitions were bought by the British Museum and the Victoria & Albert Museum.

The appearance of the catalogues seemed to mirror the general decline. The death in 1973 of Roger de Coverly, who had been the driving force behind the competitions and their main organizer, was a heavy blow, and following the resignation of the new Honorary Secretary, Mrs J. Carr Griffiths and the chairman, Dr D. Flower, the Thomas Harrison Memorial Committee was dissolved in December 1974.

6 Modern Bookbindings Acquired by the British Library, 1974–1983

(1984)*

The British Library's collection of twentieth-century bookbindings has not received much publicity, overshadowed as it is by the unrivalled collections of bindings from the past. When Howard M. Nixon wrote about the English and foreign bookbindings added to the Department of Printed Books between 1963 and 1974[1] most emphasis was given—and rightly so—to the acquisition of older material, though the six handsome twentieth-century French bindings bequeathed to the Library by Major Abbey merited and got an illustration each.

The following note on twentieth-century bindings acquired by the British Library during the last ten years may help to redress the balance.

The earliest is a gold-tooled dark green morocco binding made by Sarah Prideaux in 1902, covering John Addington Symonds, *Walt Whitman, a study* (London, 1893), presented by Mrs Christopher Webb through the Friends of the National Libraries in May 1976 (C.143.b.9: Fig 6.1).

Miss Winifred K. Booker, a niece of the binder Walter Thomas Walker, gave two examples of her uncle's work. One of them, an elaborately tooled and onlaid brown morocco binding in the Sangorski tradition, won him the first prize in the examination of the City and Guilds of London Institute in 1909. The silver medal which the Prince of Wales presented to him on that occasion was well deserved. The binding covers *The Gallery of Modern British Artists* (London, n.d.) (C.129.m.20).[2]

Though it is difficult to judge the lasting value of contemporary art, it cannot be denied that contemporary binding design in Britain has developed to a remarkable extent over the past quarter-century. The craftsmanship of the best British hand bookbinders is impeccable, and original and even exciting work has emerged over recent years.

Although excellent work is also done abroad, the Library has in the first instance concentrated its efforts on acquiring examples from the work of post-war English binders. Several of these were already represented in the collections, though some with early work only, different in concept and execution from later developments, and the Library still lacks examples

* *The British Library Journal*, x (1984), pp. 68–82.

Fig 6.1   J. A. Symonds, *Walt Whitman*, London, 1893, bound by Sarah
Prideaux in 1902.
British Library, C.143.b.9.

of the work of several binders who have proved their worth. The acquisition of modern bookbindings is in no way a closed subject.

One of the first bindings commissioned by the British Library covers
a copy of *X Sermons preached by . . . John Donne . . . chosen by Geoffrey
Keynes* (London, 1923). It was made by William Matthews during the
spring and early summer of 1976. A linear design on black goatskin

Fig. 6.2 J. Donne, *X Sermons*, London, 1923, bound by William
Matthews in 1976.
British Library, C.144.d.8.

Fig. 6.3   R. Graves, *At the Gate*, London, 1974, bound by Sally Lou
Smith in 1976.
British Library, C.109.q.7.

displays the brilliant gold tooling for which Matthews was justly famous
(C.144.d.8: Fig 6.2). In a letter of 8 December 1976, Matthews called it
'perhaps my best binding'. He died, aged 79, on Good Friday of the
following year.[3]

At the same time as William Matthews was approached, Sally Lou Smith
was asked to bind a book for the Library's collections. She chose Nikolay
Gogol's *The Overcoat, From Tales of Petersburg*, printed in Verona by
the Officina Bodoni in 1975, and covered it in dark brown goatskin with
crumpled onlays in grey and black, tooled in blind to an abstract design.
The brown goatskin doublures are tooled in gold (C.129.g.7). This very
attractive binding was finished in 1978, two years after her binding for
Robert Graves, *At the Gate. Poems* (London, 1974), made of dark brown
goatskin decorated with crumpled onlays of orange, brown and grey
goatskin and smooth onlays in brown and blue, and tooled in gold. The
gold-tooled doublures are of orange goatskin with onlays in dark brown,
brown and grey (C.109.q.7: Fig 6.3).

A third commission with a most felicitous outcome was that of a binding by Sydney Cockerell. His work, like that of William Matthews and Sally Lou Smith, had hitherto been poorly represented in the Library's collections. It was his own wish to bind a music book and a recently published edition of Benjamin Britten's *Death in Venice* (London, 1979) received a natural toned vellum binding, tooled in gold and black to a design reminiscent of Venice by night. The book was forwarded by Desmond Shaw and designed and tooled by Joan Tebutt and Sydney Cockerell (C.183.b.7: Fig 6.4).

Several donations of modern bindings received during the 1960s and early 1970s were mentioned by Howard Nixon.[4] Without doubt the largest and most important of these was part of the generous gift of *c*.800 bookbindings presented by Henry Davis CBE in 1968. Henry Davis was first and foremost a collector of historical bindings, but although his taste in contemporary artefacts was fairly conservative and although, with one exception, no bindings were added to the collection since 1968, several French and English post-war examples deserve a mention.

A wild and elegant bird, onlaid in pink and pale blue on brown goatskin, flying through a web of gold-tooled lines, decorates the covers of Jean Lurçat, *Géographie animale* (Geneva, 1948), bound by Thérèse Moncey (Fig 6.5). The first volume of Proust's autobiographical novel, *Du côté de chez Swann* (Paris, 1914), bound *c.* 1950 by J. Anthoine Legrain in black goatskin, shows a small green onlaid circle, while the author's name and the title are tooled in pink, gold and blind. A delicate little binding of pale green and turquoise calf with onlays of silver-blue, grey-green and dark green snakeskin, tooled in silver by A. Jeanne, was designed by Rose Adler in 1957 for Roger Frène's *Les Nymphes* (Paris, 1921). The most beautiful modern binding in the Gift, a Vergil by Pierre-Lucien Martin, has been described elsewhere.[5] No major collection of bindings would be complete without one by Paul Bonet. With the Davis Gift the Library acquired its first Bonet binding, made in 1962 in green goatskin, onlaid in orange, red and pale blue calf and tooled in gold to a sun-burst design. A second Bonet with a similar design was bequeathed to the Library by Major Abbey in 1970.

The twentieth-century English bindings in Henry Davis's collection have been illustrated in vol. II of *The Henry Davis Gift, A Collection of Bookbindings*.[6] Among these are examples of the work of Elizabeth Mac-Coll, Sybil Pye and Katharine Adams, including the latter's last completed bindings, two huge volumes of Cervantes, *The History of . . . Don-Quixote* (London, 1927–8), bound in 1947 when Katharine Adams was 85, in green goatskin tooled in gold with vine leaves and bunches of grapes. Several bindings by fellows of Designer Bookbinders date from the 1950s and 1960s. The work of Trevor Jones is represented by three examples one of which, on James Joyce, *Finnegans Wake* (London, 1950), is in white

Fig. 6.4   B. Britten, *Death in Venice*, London, 1979, bound by Sydney
Cockerell in 1980.
British Library, C.183.b.7.

Fig. 6.5   J. Lurçat, *Géographie animale*, Geneva, 1948, bound by
Thérèse Moncey.
British Library, Henry Davis Gift.

sheepskin, dyed in a multitude of shades and tooled in black and gold to a design showing a map of Dublin. An orange goatskin binding tooled in black and gold to a geometrical design of lines and squares was made by Jeff Clements c. 1957–8 and covers Saul Steinberg, *The Art of Living* (London, 1952). A binding by Philip Smith, dated 1961, on W. Y. Evans Wentz, *The Tibetan Book of the Dead* (London, 1957), in purple goatskin decorated with multi-coloured feathered onlays, gold- and black-blocking, and embroidery by Dorothy Smith, charts an early stage in the development of this versatile artist. Elizabeth Greenhill bound a copy of Sir John Rothenstein, *British Art since 1900* (London, 1962) in yellow goatskin and decorated it with onlays in various shades of blue, grey, orange, brown and green, and linear gold tooling.

The issue of *The Book Collector* for the Spring of 1975 contained seventeen essays on the history of bookbinding, dedicated to Howard Nixon by his grateful friends and colleagues and presented to him on his retirement from the British Library. Henry Davis, with customary generosity, commissioned Bernard Middleton to bind two copies of this issue, one for presentation to Howard Nixon, the other to be added to his gift to the British Library. The binding is of black goatskin, inlaid in green and onlaid in red, and tooled in blind and gold to a design inspired by the original wrapper, incorporating the names of the contributors to this special number. The green goatskin doublures and end-leaves are onlaid in red and tooled in gold and black.

The fellowship of Designer Bookbinders organizes regular exhibitions at which fellows and members can show their work. During one of these, held at the Waterloo Place Gallery of the Crafts Advisory Committee during the summer of 1974, the Department acquired a copy of Alain Robbe-Grillet, *Jealousy* (Kentfield, California, 1971), bound by Denise Lubett in 1973 in black goatskin, with yellow onlays outlined in blind, showing a design of sharp peaks, inspired by the pen and ink drawings by Michèle Forgeois which illustrate the book (C.109.q.5: Fig 6.6). A second binding by Denise Lubett, on Guillaume de Deguileville, *Geoffrey Chaucer's A.B.C. called La priere de Nostre Dame* (San Francisco, 1967) was made in 1981 of black goatskin and onlaid in red to an arabesque design (C.129.m.12: Fig.6.7). At an exhibition of work by the Designer Bookbinders at Hatchard's in the summer of 1978, the Department bought a copy of John Sparrow's *Lapidaria septima* (Cambridge, 1975) bound by Jeff Clements in brown goatskin with inlays of black and grey goatskin and recessed inlays edged in orange and white (C.129.i.2: Fig 6.8).

The 1970s saw the emergence of a new generation of outstanding young bookbinders, not all of whom are yet represented in the Library's collections. Two examples of David Sellars's work did come to the Library. One, a black goatskin binding with crumpled onlays of yellow goatskin

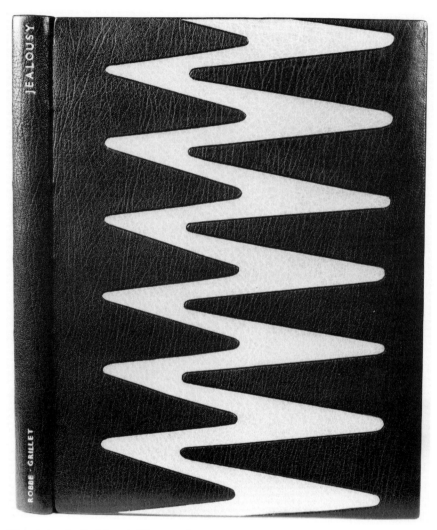

Fig. 6.6 A. Robbe-Grillet, *Jealousy*, Kentfield, Cal., 1971, bound by
Denise Lubett in 1973.
British Library, C.109.q.5.

and sunk inlays in grey, was made in 1975 and covers John Milton's
Paradise Lost and Paradise Regain'd (San Francisco, 1936) (C.144.k.5: Fig
6.9). The other is a very recent acquisition, bought during a Designer
Bookbinders exhibition at Bertram Rota's bookshop in June 1983. It is a
copy of *The Four Gospels* (Leipzig, 1932), bound in 1981 in an impressive,
entirely black binding described by the binder as made of 'natural dyed

Fig. 6.7   G. de Deguileville, *Geoffrey Chaucer's A.B.C.*, San Francisco, 1967, bound by Denise Lubett in 1981. British Library, C.129.m.12.

goatskin [with] suspension of leather dust inlays [and] black suede onlays', tooled to a design of squares, showing a cross in the centre of both covers. It has an ingenious box which consists of four parts slotting into each other (C.183.a.32). On the same occasion the Library acquired a binding by Angela James, made in 1982 for Leonard Clark, *An Intimate Landscape* (London, 1981). The lower part of the white calf binding is decorated with strips of plywood and the upper cover has a cut-out compartment in the shape of a window, framed in wood, revealing a delicately embroidered panel let into the facing end-leaf. The embroidery shows a landscape with a hill, trees, a vegetable garden, and grazing sheep (C.183.b.8: Fig 6.10).

The yearly bookbinding competition at which young aspiring binders have a chance to show their craft, organized under the auspices of Designer Bookbinders, is a good hunting-ground for new talent. In 1976 David Kevin Stevens was awarded the first prize for his binding of St John of the Cross, *Cantique d'amour divin entre Jesus Christ et l'ame devoté* (Paris, 1944), in red goatskin, tooled in gold and black to a design of

Fig. 6.8   J. Sparrow, *Lapidaria septima*, Cambridge, 1975, bound by Jeff
Clements in 1978.
British Library, C.129.i.2.

Fig. 6.9   J. Milton, *Paradise Lost and Paradise Regain'd*, San Francisco,
1936, bound by David Sellars in 1975.
British Library, C.144.k.5.

Fig. 6.10   L. Clark, *An Intimate Landscape*, London, 1981, bound by
Angela James in 1982.
British Library, C.183.b.8.

Fig. 6.11   St John of the Cross, *Cantique d'amour divin*, Paris, 1944,
bound by David Stevens in 1976.
British Library, C.144.e.1.

intertwined bands composed of oval and egg-shaped tools, with gold- and
blind-tooled black goatskin doublures (C.144.e.1: Fig 6.11).

Two more non-British modern bindings deserve a mention: a white and
black box calf binding with orange inlays on the spine, tooled in black
and white to an abstract design on Arthur Rimbaud, *Une Saison en enfer*
(Brussels, 1873), made in 1948 by Rose Adler (C.129.m.13),[7] and an exquis-

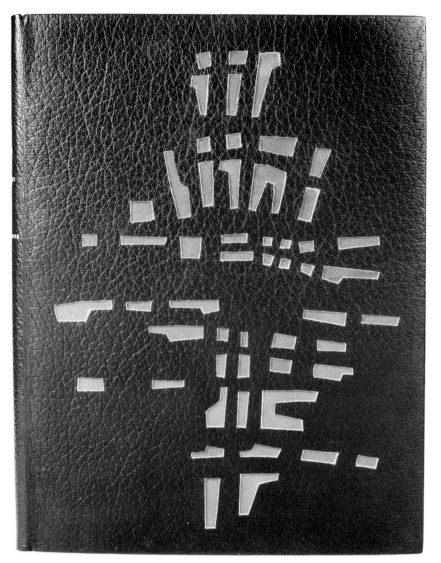

Fig. 6.12 H. Michaux, *Apparitions*, Paris, 1946, bound by Micheline de Bellefroid in 1983.
British Library, C.183.a.33.

ite binding by a Belgian binder whose work deserves to be better known on this side of the Channel. Micheline de Bellefroid designed and executed in 1983 a black goatskin binding with cut-out compartments in olive green calf edged in pale green, for Henri Michaux, *Apparitions* (Paris, 1946).

The gold lettering on the spine was done by Anne Thimmesch (C.183.a.33: Fig. 6.12).

1. H. M. Nixon, 'English Bookbindings added to the Department of Printed Books, 1963 to 1974', *British Library Journal*, I (1975), pp. 181–90. H. M. Nixon, 'Foreign Bookbindings added to the Department of Printed Books from 1963 to 1974', *British Library Journal*, III (1977), pp. 44–55.
2. Illustrated in *The Book Collector*, xxxiii (1984) p. 67, and above, p. 73.
3. See his obituary in *The Times* (14 April 1977).
4. H. M. Nixon, arts. cit.
5. M. M. Foot, 'A Binding by Pierre-Lucien Martin 1961', *The Book Collector*, xxxvi (1987), pp. 244–5; see also below, article 7.
6. M. M. Foot, *The Henry Davis Gift*, vol. II: *A Catalogue of North European Bindings*, London, 1983, nos. 229–50.
7. Illustrated in Martin Breslauer, *Fine Bindings*, Catalogue 104, part 2 (1981), no. 272.

7 A Binding by Pierre-Lucien Martin, 1961
(1987)*

Pierre-Lucien Martin was born at Denault on 3 July 1913. He was a pupil at the École Estienne and worked in various binders' ateliers before joining A. J. Gonon in 1936. In September 1940 he set up his own workshop and after the war he made his first attempts at original design. He produced what he described as 'my first modern binding' in 1946[1] and two years later he won the prize of the Société de la Reliure Originale, of which he became a member in 1951. He took part in a large number of exhibitions, as well as having three shows completely devoted to his work. A fourth took place in the Bibliotheca Wittockiana in Brussels in February and March 1987. He died on 13 September 1985.

He was an artist of remarkable vitality, and the sheer variety of his designs is astonishing. He was very well served by those who executed his ideas. All his bindings have been exquisitely made and the finishing is outstanding. Throughout his career Martin came back periodically to letter forms, but the intertwining letters in roman and italic in contrasting colours seem a feature of the early 1960s. In 1960 and 1961 he bound two copies of Louis Aragon, *Elsa* (Paris, 1959)[2] one in blue the other in pink calf, decorated to the same design showing the title of the book in onlaid interlacing roman and italic letters in much the same way as can be seen on the binding illustrated here.

1. On: P. Eluard, *La Dernière Nuit*, Paris, 1942 (C. Blaizot (ed.) *Pierre-Lucien Martin*, Brussels, 1987, no. 2).
2. *Modern French Bookbindings by members of the Société de la Reliure Originale*, London: Arts Council, 1961, no. 116. C. Blaizot (ed.) *Pierre-Lucien Martin*, Brussels, Bibliotheca Wittockiana, 1987, no. 46.

* English and Foreign Bookbindings 41, *The Book Collector*, xxxvi, pp. 244–5

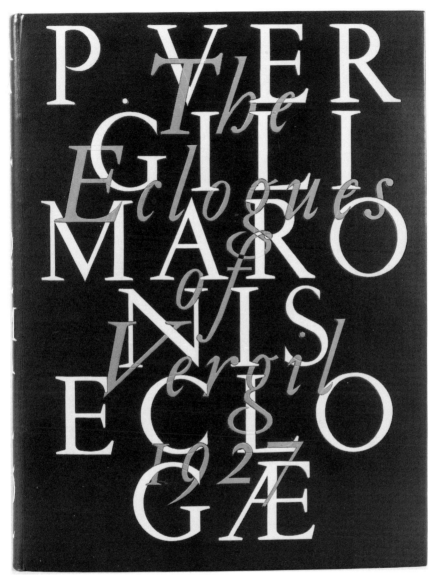

Fig. 7.1   Virgil, *The Eclogues and Georgics in Latin and English*. Vol I:
The Eclogues, London, 1927.
Olive brown calf with onlays in white and fawn. 330 × 250
× 30 mm.
British Library, Henry Davis Gift.

Part III
THE LATE MEDIEVAL TRADITION IN BOOKBINDING

The history of English decorated bookbinding starts with a bang, in that the earliest-known decorated European binding can be attributed with confidence to Northumbria and, with a little less confidence, to the late seventh century AD. Three other early examples of the craft have been dated to the eighth or ninth century. Then follows a gap in our knowledge, about four centuries wide, until we reach the fourth decade of the twelfth century when a number of beautifully tooled tanned leather bindings were produced, first in France, then in England and somewhat later in Germany and Austria. These Romanesque bindings originated in monasteries in Paris, and most of the English and German examples can also be traced back to a monastic origin.

There is some surviving evidence of the production of tooled leather bindings in France during the fourteenth century, but it is not until the monastic revival on the Continent during the first half of the fifteenth century that we encounter a real revival of blind-stamped bindings, particularly in Italy, Germany and the Netherlands. Fewer examples from Spain and France seem to have survived, and English decorated bindings were not produced in any quantity until well after the invention of printing.

Many but certainly not all of these late medieval bindings were made in monasteries. The names of a large number of binders have come down to us from archival sources, but it is extremely difficult to link these names with actual products. We are on firmer ground with those binders who signed their bindings, but they are but few, and even there extreme caution is necessary as so little is known about tool cutters, the movement of tools and the production and movement of panels. Were they engraved, like the small hand tools and rolls?[1] Were they made for individual binders or for publishers or booksellers? Where were they produced and did they travel or were they produced in multiple copies? Were small tools reproduced on order? As long as these, and many more, questions remain unanswered, we cannot but pursue the well-trodden path of recording and identifying individual tools and combinations of tools, of establishing groups of related bindings and of postulating workshops which, for lack of firm evidence, have to be circumscribed and nicknamed. The study of binding techniques could—in theory—lead to the postulation of workshop practices but tends—in practice—to come up against lack of firm evidence and the low survival rate of untouched, unrestored datable and locatable examples.

This Part deals with blind-tooled bindings, produced in monasteries and in lay workshops, in England, the Netherlands and Germany during the fifteenth and early sixteenth centuries. It also shows how treacherous it can be to try and locate bindings on grounds of style and tool design and how easily the North Sea could be crossed.

1. S. Fogelmark, *Flemish and Related Panel-Stamped Bindings*, New York, 1990, argues with conviction that the majority of panels were cast.

8 English Decorated Bookbindings of the Fifteenth Century

(1989)*

The period from 1375 to 1475 is not propitious for the study of decorated English bookbindings. Much earlier, during the second half of the twelfth century and the beginning of the thirteenth, splendidly tooled leather bindings were produced in Winchester, London and probably Durham,[1] and the earliest known European decorated leather binding, which may be as early as the seventh century, comes from Northumbria.[2] There is however a notable gap in the production and survival of tooled leather bindings during the fourteenth and the first half of the fifteenth centuries. It is just possible that the binding covering Stephen Langton, *Super Ecclesiasticum*, a manuscript in Durham Cathedral Library dating from the first half of the thirteenth century, was made in the thirteenth or fourteenth century[3] but, though the tools used to decorate this binding have an archaic look, their arrangement has more in common with that found on bindings made during the second half of the fifteenth century. Another binding in Durham University Library decorated with Romanesque type tools in an unusual arrangement may date from the end of the thirteenth century.[4]

The scarcity of decorated leather bindings dating from before 1450 may be due to the fact that the grandest medieval bindings were made of precious metals or rare fabrics. Practically no English silver-gilt or silver bindings have survived,[5] the majority having been melted down during the Reformation, and most of the fabric bindings of this period have suffered from the ravages of time and moths. Nevertheless, there is a certain amount of documentary evidence for the one-time existence of medieval treasure bindings as well as for textile bindings made during the fourteenth and fifteenth centuries.[6] The only surviving early English embroidered binding, now inlaid in eighteenth-century calf, is that on the fourteenth-century Felbrigge Psalter. The upper cover, which is still remarkably fresh, shows the Annunciation, while the lower cover shows a rather worn representation of the Crucifixion.[7]

Apart from references to and a few remains of what must have been

* J. Griffiths and D. Pearsall (eds.), *Book Production and Publishing in Britain 1375–1475*, Cambridge, 1989, pp. 65–86.

the top end of the market, a fair number of plain leather medieval bindings made for more general use survive, but they are very difficult to date.

There seem to be only minor variations in the way English binders of the fifteenth century chose and handled their materials.[8] Most bindings of the period are sewn on alum-tawed, sometimes on tanned leather thongs; the thongs are laced into the wooden boards, lie in grooves on the inside of the boards and are secured by square or round pegs, sometimes in a staggered pattern.[9] In some cases there are traces of a whitish clay-like substance covering the exposed thongs, presumably used to make an even surface for the vellum paste-downs. The boards themselves are made of wood, usually oak,[10] frequently finished with a slight bevel—sharply bevelled boards, commonly found in Germany and sometimes in the Netherlands, are unusual. Headbands have in many cases not survived. Those that have withstood the wear and tear of use are frequently sewn in white or blue and white thread over an alum-tawed, sometimes a tanned leather core, and are either laced in in tunnels on the inside of the boards and pegged like the thongs, or are brought over the outside of the boards and then disappear into holes in the wood. Sometimes the headbands are covered with the spine leather The boards are often cut flush with the edges of the leaves, though I have equally often found them flush at the fore-edge and with slight protruding squares at the top and tail. Clasps, normally two, are commonly used and have leather thongs, almost invariably hinging on the upper cover.[11] Chain marks, signs of an occasional later addition, occur from time to time, often at the bottom right-hand corner but also in the centre of the top edge of the upper cover. End-leaves are usually of vellum and in many cases the paste-downs, once secured to the inside of the covers, have now been lifted. Neil Ker has shown that manuscript paste-downs were commonly used in Oxford during the late fifteenth and sixteenth centuries.[12] They were already in use there in the 1470s and though they are also on occasion found in bindings produced elsewhere, they seem indeed to turn up most frequently in Oxford bindings.

During the fifteenth century and at the beginning of the sixteenth, the book trade in England was much influenced by imports and immigrants from the Continent. I have tried to show (below pp. 146–163)[13] that the binding trade during this period owed much both to immigrant binders and to the importation of binding designs, tool designs and decorative panels, especially from the Low Countries, while Low Country influences on binding technique are also discernible.

Two binding designs widely used on both sides of the Channel show a frame of intersecting fillets around fillets forming a diamond and a saltire (see Fig. 8.1), or fillets dividing the centre into smaller diamond-shaped

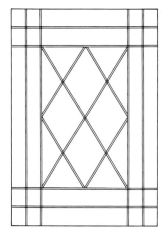

Fig. 8.1   Drawing of binding
design: see also
Oldham, *EBSB*, pl. II,
no. 1; pl. IV.

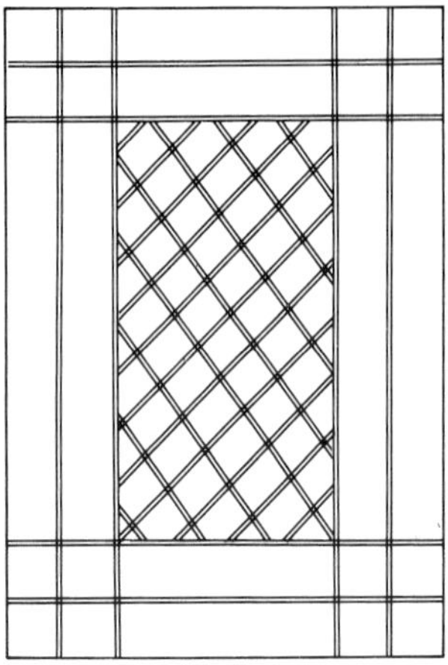

Fig. 8.2   Drawing of binding
design: see also
Oldham, *EBSB*, pl. II,
no. 3; pl. XII.

and triangular compartments (see Fig. 8.2). The design formed by the arrangement of small stamps in rows, frequently found in Oxford and sometimes in London, is also found in France.

The design of the small hand tools used to decorate English bindings of the second half of the fifteenth century equally shows strong Low Country influence. Many of the motifs, such as dragons, fighting cocks, double-headed eagles, various kinds of monsters, pelicans, lambs-and-flags, roses, fleurs-de-lis and pineapples, are found in abundance in the Netherlands as well as in England, and a great deal of attention to detail is necessary in order to distinguish certain types of tools used in both countries.

The surviving tooled leather bindings produced in England during the second half of the fifteenth century have been the subject of study by a number of binding historians. Of these G. D. Hobson, J. B. Oldham and more recently Graham Pollard have been most prolific, and their work has been the starting point for this article.[14]

Though tooled bindings were produced in monasteries in Canterbury, Jervaulx, Tavistock and at Osney Abbey near Oxford, and in towns such as Winchester and possibly also Salisbury, the main centres of bookbinding during the second half of the fifteenth century were London, Oxford and Cambridge.

Fewer than a dozen binderies are known to have started work before 1475 and possibly the earliest of these is that of the Scales binder. He worked in London from the 1450s until after 1481 and his work, which can be divided into two distinct groups, has been discussed in detail by Nicolas Barker.[15] The most characteristic feature of this bindery is that it practised the technique of cutting the leather with a knife to effect part of the design, a habit otherwise unknown in England though popular in German-speaking countries during the fifteenth century. The Scales binder also used 36 decorative stamps (from one of which, a pair of scales, he gets his name), and a total of 20 bindings from his shop are known to have survived: thirteen produced before 1465 and seven between 1466 (or later) and 1481.

A binder of whose work only two examples are now known, who used a square tool with four flowers very similar to that used by the Scales binder, may also have worked in London. He bound a fifteenth-century manuscript of Albertus Magnus, *De caelo et mundo*, now at Pembroke College, Cambridge,[16] and a copy of the Middle English Brut Chronicle, c.1450–75, which was lot 12 in the Bute sale at Sotheby's on 13 July 1983.

A third binder who may have been located in London and who worked before 1474 was christened by Graham Pollard the Sheen binder. Three bindings from this shop are known, decorated with characteristic bird, animal and monster tools arranged in concentric frames.[17]

Another early bindery that arranged its tools in concentric frames, also achieving an all-over style of decoration, was at work possibly between 1460 and 1463 and had strong connections with Salisbury. It bound two manuscripts written by Herman Zurke for Gilbert Kymer, physician to Humphrey, Duke of Gloucester, twice Chancellor of the University of Oxford and treasurer and later Dean of Salisbury cathedral.[18] The Register of Vallis Scholarium at Salisbury and a manuscript volume of Coluccio Salutati's treatises that belonged to William Witham, Dean of the Arches and canon of Wells, were also bound in this shop.[19] The bindings that cover the manuscripts written for Gilbert Kymer are decorated with a set of word-stamps forming the phrases 'mon bien mon/dain', 'ladi help' and 'ih[es]u m[er]cy', as well as with pictorial stamps showing a flower vase, a small dog with an erect tail, a square tool with a double-headed eagle and another depicting a fleur-de-lis. The double-headed eagle and fleur-de-lis tools form the link with the other two bindings of this group, which in turn are also decorated with tools attributed by J. B. Oldham to his binder I.[20] Oldham's binder J,[21] whom he tentatively placed in Salisbury, is said by Graham Pollard (who gave the location of this workshop as uncertain) to have been responsible for four bindings.[22] A fifth binding belongs to this group. It covers a translation (1488) by William Sellyng, prior of Canterbury, of a sermon by St John Chrysostom and other works in an early sixteenth-century manuscript.[23] The tools illustrated by Oldham clearly come from Salisbury MS 99 and though they are extremely similar to those on the other bindings in this group (BL Add. MSS 6173, 15673; Bodley MS Laud Misc. 701 and MS Douce 246), I believe them to be different. It is highly probable that Oldham saw only Salisbury MS 99, and it would be wiser to attribute the other four bindings to a separate unlocated workshop (Fig. 8.3 nos. 1–9).[24] The two other small groups established by J. B. Oldham which may have started work before 1475 are his binders K and L.[25] Binder K arranged his tools in horizontal rows within a frame composed of individual stamps on Burlaeus, *De vita et moribus philosophorum* (Cologne, 1472). The spine of this binding has been lined with strips cut from an English manuscript which makes reference to St Albans and Chelmsford.[26]

Of the work of binder L, only one example also seems to have survived. It covers a collection of religious and other treaties, the last item of which is a suit in the Consistory Court of Exeter between the abbey of Tavistock and others, and Thomas Ralegh, rector of St John's-by-Anthony, 1422–7. The original covers now onlaid on later brown sheep, are decorated in blind with diagonal fillets dividing the covers into diamonds and triangles, filled with rose and fleur-de-lis tools.[27]

A bindery located in Oxford, which may have been at work already during the 1450s, uses six imitation romanesque tools. Strickland Gibson illustrated several examples from this group, as well as detailed drawings of the majority of the tools used to decorate these bindings (Fig. 8.3, nos. 10–15).[28] G. D. Hobson identified 22 bindings belonging to this shop; Graham Pollard and Nicolas Barker have contributed one each, and nine or ten more can now be added.[29] Graham Pollard attributed three bindings from this group to Thomas Hokyns of Oxford, who worked from 1438 to 1465, ten to his successor John More, who worked from 1439 to 1472, and an unspecified number to Thomas Hunt, who worked from 1473 to 1492.[30] Apart from the facts that Thomas Hokyns is recorded as a bookbinder who worked in Oxford when the earliest bindings in this group may have been produced, that at the time of his death in 1465 his goods were in the house of the University Stationer, John More, and that the University Stationer, Thomas Hunt, was still alive when the last bindings of this group may have been made, there is no reason to attribute any bindings in this group to any of these three men. The 34 bindings now known cover manuscripts and books dated between *c.* 1450 and 1489; the tools used to decorate them link them together and indicate that they were the work either of one shop or possibly of two shops of which the second bought or inherited the tools of the first. They display a variety of designs, ranging from all-over and central-block designs to circle and diaper designs. Not too much importance should be attached to a variation in design, as designs, though influenced by habit and fashion, are easy to copy.

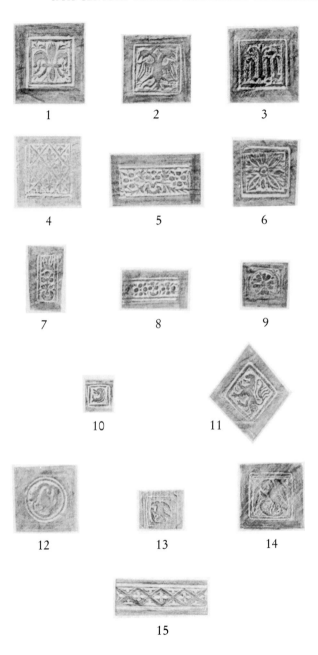

Fig. 8.3   A plate of tools: no. 1–9 unlocated bindery, compare Oldham's binder J; nos. 10–15 previously unrecorded tools from the Oxford quasi-romanesque group.

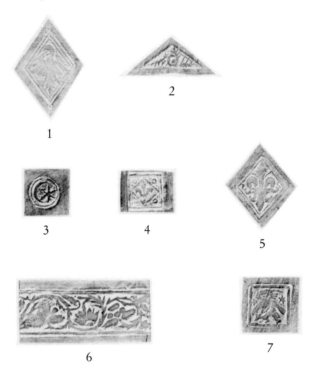

Fig. 8.4   A plate of tools: nos. 1–2 from MS Bodley 460; nos. 3–5
          previously unrecorded tools belonging to the Fishtail binder; no.
          6 previously unrecorded tool belonging to the Demon binder;
          no. 7 previously unrecorded tool belonging to the Lattice
          binder.

It is just possible that the Fishtail binder, who worked in Oxford from
c. 1473 to c. 1500, acquired two tools that occur on bindings of this
Oxford quasi-romanesque group. The large fleur-de-lis that is found on
MS Bodley 460[31] in combination with Gibson tools 10 and possibly 6, as
well as two tools that are neither in Gibson nor in Oldham (Fig. 8.4, nos.
1–2), may be identical with that on BL Add. MS 34807, bound by the
Fishtail binder, though I am not absolutely certain that this is so. A better
case can be made for the curly-tailed monster[32] that occurs on the binding
of Leonardus de Utino, *Sermones quadragesimales de legibus* (Paris, 1477)
in combination with Gibson's tools, 55, 73 and 79.[33]

J. B. Oldham knew thirteen examples of the Fishtail binder's work,
covering manuscripts and books printed between 1473 and 1498.[34] Graham
Pollard mentioned seventeen known bindings and suggested that the Fishtail binder's name was Christopher Coke, a bookbinder recorded in

Oxford from 1484 who died in 1501.[35] I have seen nineteen or twenty examples altogether with the same or possibly a slightly extended range of imprints[36] and three tools can now be added to this shop's decorative material (Fig. 8.4, nos. 3–5).

Two more pre-1475 binderies can be identified: the Demon binder, who worked in Cambridge, possibly between *c.* 1473 and *c.* 1497, and the Winchester Virgin and Child binder, whose bindings cover manuscripts and books with imprints between 1474 and 1497.

In *Bindings in Cambridge Libraries*[37] G. D. Hobson identified nine bindings from a Cambridge binder whom he christened the Demon binder. J. B. Oldham found two more examples[38] and another three, two of which are recent acquisitions by the British Library, can now be added. One covers three incunabula printed between 1488 and 1494 and bound together;[39] the second covers Cicero, *Epistolae ad familiares* (Venice, 1494)[40] and displays a new floral tool not found in Oldham (Fig. 8.4, no. 6). The Virgin and Child binder was discovered and discussed by Neil Ker;[41] Graham Pollard added four to Ker's seven known examples[42] and in 1980 the British Library acquired an anthology of Middle English verse, a Winchester manuscript of *c.* 1487, bound in the same shop.[43]

During the last quarter of the fifteenth century, a variety of binderies emerged that were engaged in the production of decorated leather bindings. A certain amount has been written about these shops and their products, and I propose to present the state of knowledge, bring it up to date where possible and, in a few cases, make some different suggestions.

Some of these shops can be located and most can be given approximate dates for the span of their working life, with the dated manuscripts and the imprints of the books providing at least a *terminus post quem* for the bindings. As was the case for the earlier fifteenth-century bindings, the majority of the bindings that can be located were made in London, Oxford or Cambridge. I have mentioned Salisbury and Winchester as other poss- ible centres; A. I. Doyle has made a good case for a small group of late fifteenth-century bindings to have been produced in or near Durham,[44] and a group of eleven decorated bindings can be assigned to Canterbury. G. D. Hobson published a list of six bindings made there, and J. B. Oldham brought the number up to eleven.[45] The bindings show different designs on each cover, often incorporating one or two circles and chequ- ered areas made by using square or triangular hatched tools side by side with plain ones. Other characteristic stamps depict running hares, stags, flowers and word-stamps forming the phrase 'time deum'. Graham Pollard described how he rediscovered that the binder responsible for this set of bindings was John Kemsyn, who worked for the churchwardens of St Andrews, Canterbury, during the 1480s and 1490s.[46]

The only pre-1500 British binder who signed his bindings with his full name was Patrick Lowes, a Scot, who bound and signed the Haye manuscript, a translation of three medieval French treatises into Scots by 'Gilbert of the Haye, knycht', dated 1456. The binding, which is probably about 30 years later than the manuscript, shows a central-block design built up of round and square tools, depicting roses, animals, including unicorns, and a variety of saints, as well as lamb-and-flag tools, decorative stamps and word-stamps forming the names 'ihesus', 'maria', 'iohannes' and the legend 'patricius lowes me ligavit'. Several of the tools, including the lamb-and-flag tool and a stamp showing a dog fighting a lion, also occur on a binding in Aberdeen University Library.[47]

Notwithstanding the impressive number of names of bookbinders who worked in London during the fourteenth and fifteenth centuries discovered by Paul Christianson,[48] the groups of bindings that can be attributed to London are but a few. I mentioned earlier the Scales and the Sheen binders, as well as the binder of Pembroke MS 204 who may have been a Londoner; for the later part of the fifteenth century only four or possibly five shops can be added. In *Bindings in Cambridge Libraries*, G. D. Hobson discussed the Indulgence binder,[49] so named because of the discovery by Henry Bradshaw of two different indulgences printed by John Lettou that were found lining the quires of a two-volume Latin Bible (Cologne, 1480) in Jesus College, Cambridge. In *Blind Stamped Panels in the English Booktrade*, Hobson listed fifteen bindings from this shop, placed it in London and adopted Bradshaw's suggestion that Lettou may have been the binder.[50] Graham Pollard added two more bindings to the list and attributed the whole group with increasing conviction to Lettou.[51] Recently two other bindings from this shop have come to light, one covering Aegidius Carlerius, *Sporta fragmentorum* (Brussels, 1478), the other Littleton, *Tenores novelli* (c. 1482);[52] close inspection of the latter raises the suspicion that this may have been a remboîtage. Meanwhile, William Ward and Christopher de Hamel have found strips of indulgences printed by Lettou and by Caxton used to strengthen the spines of bindings from the Rood and Hunt binder, who worked in Oxford and to whom I shall return later.[53] The discovery of indulgences printed by two different printers, one working in London, the other in Westminster, in a binding by an Oxford binder shows that such fragments cannot be used as proof either of the place of binding or of the identity of the binder. All we can say at this point is that the unfortunately named Indulgence binder worked from c. 1475 to c. 1480 or possibly c. 1482, and that the location of his shop is still uncertain.

We are on firmer ground with the binder who worked for William Caxton and Wynkyn de Worde. Thirty-nine examples from this shop are now known, covering manuscripts and books printed between [1477] and 1511.

Howard M. Nixon has conclusively proved that, though the bindings can be divided into five groups, they all come from one or possibly from two shops; that the binder or binders worked in close relationship with William Caxton and after his death with his successor Wynkyn de Worde; and that the documentary evidence does not justify the identification with any named individual.[54] Two of the Caxton binder's designs, Nixon's types A and B, show Low Country influence, and two of his tools in particular (the triangular stamp with a dragon and the fleur-de-lis tool) look like straightforward copies of Netherlandish examples. They are indeed so closely similar that Graham Pollard believed them to be identical with those used on two Flemish manuscripts in the Bodleian Library.[55] Close inspection shows small differences, but this type of tool was much in use in the southern Netherlands and particularly in Bruges.[56]

Three more examples from Caxton's bindery have emerged since Nixon wrote his articles. One covers Reuchlin's *Vocabularius* (Basel, 1481) and another St Augustine, *Confessiones* (Cologne, 1482).[57] Both are now in the British Library. A third, a fifteenth-century manuscript *Formula Novitiorum* in English, is at Queens' College, Cambridge (MS 18).

A binder who used a rebus stamp, identified by G. D. Hobson as Henry Cony, worked in London until after 1503. Ten examples of his work are known, covering books printed between 1483 and 1492.[58]

The Crucifer binder, of whose work ten examples are known, covering manuscripts and books dated between [1476] and 1507, worked in London and was probably employed by Richard Pynson,[59] a stationer and printer who also probably owned a bindery. He came to England before 1491. During a long-drawn-out quarrel with Russhe's executors, he was called a bookbinder. He was appointed Printer to the King in 1508 and died in 1530.[60]

On the binding of Lord Newton's copy of the 1487 Sarum *Missal*, one of the Crucifer binder's tools occurs in combination with two tools that belonged to J. B. Oldham's binder A. This binder also bound four other books printed between 1480 and 1488.[61]

One of Pynson's two rose panels (Oldham, *Panels* RO1), both found in combination with the Crucifer binder's square floral tool on the indenture (1503) made between Henry VII and Thomas Silkesteade, prior of Winchester (now at Windsor Castle),[62] also occurs alone or together with one of Pynson's two signed panels (Oldham MISC. 14). As well as the two Rose panels (Oldham RO1 and 2) and the two signed panels (Oldham MISC. 4 and 14), Pynson used a panel depicting St John the Baptist (Oldham ST 18). These panels are found alone or in various combinations on eleven bindings.[63]

There are a few instances of panels being used before 1500. The famous trio of Dutch panels found, together with some tools belonging to the

Indulgence binder, on the first volume of a six-volume set of Vincent of Beauvais's *Works* (c. 1473–8) at Corpus Christi College, Oxford, were discussed with much ingenuity by G. D. Hobson, who attributed the binding to William de Machlinia and dated it c. 1482–7. Graham Pollard suggested that the volume was bound by Pynson in a consciously archaic style as late as c. 1515.[64] As these arguments were to a large extent based on the probably false assumption that John Lettou was the Indulgence binder, the question as to the owner of the panels and the date of their use in England remains unresolved.

It seems likely that the earliest use of a panel in London dates from c. 1494. Howard M. Nixon showed that an animal in foliage panel (Oldham AN 17), which was used on a presentation binding of a [1494] Sarum *Horae* at Lambeth Palace, was also used by Caxton's binder.[65]

It is possible that a small panel depicting St George (Oldham ST 10) which belonged to the Cambridge binder WG and which is found on three books with the imprint dates of 1490, 1491 and 1494,[66] was used earlier than the Caxton binder's panel. Another small panel, this time showing the English Royal arms (Oldham HE 5), may also have been used before 1500. It is found on a book at Westminster Abbey, probably originally a blank book, which now contains some manuscript prayers of Erasmus written some time after the book was bound. This panel belonged to the Half-Stamp binder and there is no reason to believe that it was used before 1495.[67]

With the subject of panel stamps we move decidedly into the sixteenth century, and this is not the place for further discussion.

We must return to London, where the last bindery to be discussed that may have been located there was at work at the very end of the fifteenth century and at the beginning of the sixteenth. It used curious romanesque type tools, like the Oxford quasi-romanesque bindery mentioned above, and it arranged them, at least on one occasion, in a typical romanesque design. Only two examples from this shop are known. One covers Terence, *Vulgaria* [London, c. 1483] and shows the tools arranged in a large circle between two horizontal rows of large stamps (Fig. 8.5);[68] the other is on Marsilio Ficino, *Epistolae* (Venice, 1495). The latter binding has been lined with leaves from a book printed by Pynson in [1501] and is now at Westminster Abbey Library.[69]

To our knowledge of the binders who worked in Cambridge during the end of the fifteenth century and the first decade of the sixteenth, only very little can be added.

J. B. Oldham divided a large group of bindings produced in Cambridge into the work of the Pre-Unicorn binder and that of the Unicorn binder. He attributed to the former five bindings executed between 1480 and 1485.[70] Seven of his ten tools are also found on bindings by the Unicorn

Fig. 8.5   Terence, *Vulgaria* [London, c. 1483].
A London 15th-century binding with quasi-romanesque tools.
British Library IA 55454.

binder whose shop was discovered and described by G. D. Hobson;[71] he knew of 44 examples of his work. J. B. Oldham brought the number up to 73 and Graham Pollard, who did not make any distinction between the Unicorn binder and the Pre-Unicorn binder, stated that 'nearly 100 bindings by the Unicorn binder' are known; they cover books dated from 1478 to 1507.[72] Since Graham Pollard wrote this, the British Library has acquired a copy of M. A. Sabellicus, *Rerum Venetarum decades* (Venice, 1487, IC 21646) from this shop. G. D. Hobson suggested in his Sandars Lectures that the Unicorn binder may be Walter Hatley, University Stationer, who worked in Cambridge from 1484/5 to 1504 or possibly

1508, but Graham Pollard has pointed out that Hatley's dates also coincide with those of another Cambridge binder who goes by the nickname of the Heavy binder.

A bindery that used two stamps very similar to those belonging to the Unicorn binder, and that owned a fleur-de-lis tool found together with tools from the Unicorn bindery on the work of yet another binder, used a signed tool with the monogram WG. The same shop also owned a roll with two monograms WG and IG and two panels signed IG. Oldham has shown that the output of this bindery, which covers books printed between 1478 and 1533, can be divided into three groups, linked either by the WG stamp or by the WG-IG roll, and he has suggested that it was run by two generations, father (WG) and two sons (the elder WG and the younger IG). The first group, which is the only one to contain bindings produced before 1500, covers the period 1478 to 1507 and consists of over 100 bindings.[73]

Three binders who used tools belonging to the Unicorn binder, as well as having other tools in common, are the Lattice binder, the Heavy binder and the Monster binder, but much more research is needed before any firm conclusions can be drawn about these shops. J. B. Oldham suggested[74] that they were three different binders: the Lattice binder, who worked from 1485 to 1511 and who acquired six tools from the Unicorn bindery; the Heavy binder, who worked from 1485 to 1505 and who used the same lattice tool (Oldham 72) as the Lattice binder and the Unicorn binder; and the Monster binder, whose bindings cover books printed between 1481 and 1505, but who seems to have acquired one of his tools from the Heavy binder, two from the Lattice binder and nine from the Unicorn binder. Only the monster tool seems to have been used by no one else. If this is the case, he probably did not start work until c. 1505. Of these binders' work, 44 examples made by the Lattice binder were mentioned by Oldham and Pollard,[75] and two were recently acquired by the British Library, a *Homeliarius Doctorum* (Nuremberg, 1494) with one unrecorded tool (Fig. 8.4, no. 7) and one volume of Gerson's *Opera* (Strasburg, 1494).[76] Seventeen come from the Heavy binder's shop; only four specimens of the Monster binder's output have been recorded.

In addition to an 'unnamed' Cambridge binder of whose work only one book in three volumes is known to exist, J. B. Oldham has made a tentative case for Cambridge as the home of both the Athos binder and the Antwerp binder.[77] The first was active at the end of the fifteenth century, and six examples of his craft are known to have survived; the second produced 22 bindings now known, and he seems to have worked during the last two decades of the century. Recently, the Pierpont Morgan Library acquired a binding by the Antwerp binder covering St Augustine, *Explanatio Psalmorum* [c. 1485?].[78]

In a fascinating lecture delivered to the Bibliographical Society on 15 April 1969,[79] Graham Pollard displayed the results of years of searching the archives of the colleges, the university and the city of Oxford. He found a number of named bookbinders whose activities in the way of binding books, exercising the office of University Stationer, receiving money, hiring houses, owing rent, being sued in court, dining and dying he recorded, and whose dates he linked with those postulated for the work of several binders hitherto only known by nicknames. There are no cast-iron proofs for any of these identifications, but some sound highly probable.

The largest and most interesting of the binderies that worked in Oxford during the last quarter of the fifteenth century is that which for generations has been called the Rood and Hunt bindery.[80] This shop bound books printed by early Oxford printers, among whom was Theodoric Rood, as well as books imported from the Continent which may have been for sale through Thomas Hunt's bookshop.

In 1483 the Louvain printer John of Westfalia and Peter Actors, later the Royal Stationer, called on Thomas Hunt and arranged for him to take a consignment of books on the basis of sale or return. Dr D. E. Rhodes[81] has shown that books of John of Westfalia's press sold well in Oxford, and several of these were bound there at the time by the Rood and Hunt binder. He decorated them either to a central-block design with horizontal rows of stamps or with the stamps arranged in concentric frames, or, less frequently, to a diaper design. The stamps themselves bear a very close resemblance to tools used in the Netherlands and especially to those employed in Louvain by Ludovicus Ravescot, an illuminator, printer and bookbinder who worked from *c.* 1473 until after 1501 and who is known to have bound for John of Westfalia. Another Louvain binder who worked on occasion for the printer Johan Veldener also used tools closely similar in design.[82]

No up-to-date list of bindings by the Rood and Hunt binder has been published. Gibson listed twelve examples (mostly with now obsolete pressmarks).[83] Graham Pollard said that he knew of 23 bindings, covering manuscripts and printed books dated between 1478 and 1482;[84] Christopher de Hamel has identified two more, one an odd volume of Nicholas de Lyra's Bible Gloss (Venice, 1481) at Dunedin, the other a canon law text printed in Padua in 1476 at All Souls.[85] Dr Lotte Hellinga has reported another example on a 1482 Lathbury in the Folger Library in Washington; a copy of Petrus de Alliaco, *De imagine mundi* [Louvain, *c.* 1483] bound in this shop was sold by Christie's on 24 July 1970 (lot 3) and is now in Mr Otto Schaefer's library at Schweinfurt.[86] Pollard pointed out that the dates 1478–1482 fit neither Rood nor Hunt, but do fit a certain Nicholas Bokebynder who lived in Cat Street, was paid for binding in 1478 and

1483, and who seems to have left Oxford by the end of 1483 owing rent and 'taking his tools with him'.[87] There is, alas, one snag. The Rood and Hunt binding at Stonyhurst College covers a copy of Petrus Lombardus, *Sententiarum libri IV*, printed at Basel by Nicolaus Kesler on 8 March 1486, and it cannot have reached Oxford and received its binding until three years after Nicholas Bokebynder appears to have left.

A group of bindings which may be of earlier date than the work of the Rood and Hunt binder is that of Oldham's binder C.[88] Graham Pollard reported but did not list eleven bindings on books printed between 1475 and *c.* 1485.[89] Binder C may be connected with the group of Oxford quasi-romanesque bindings, but as the linking tool is the large fleur-de-lis, and as a number of variants of this tool exist, I am not yet convinced that this is so. Another binder who may have started work in Oxford in the late 1470s is the Floral binder. J. B. Oldham listed 22 examples of this binder's work, and Graham Pollard mentioned 'some thirty books' bound by him with dates ranging from 1476 to 1496, identifying him with Thomas Uffyngton, bookbinder, who appears in the Oxford records between 1479 and 1496.[90]

The Dragon binder was discussed in turn by G. D. Hobson, J. B. Oldham and by Graham Pollard who identified him with Thomas Bedford who bound for Magdalen College in 1487 and who succeeded Christopher Coke as University Stationer. His own successor was appointed in 1507. The 47 examples of the Dragon binder's work cover books with imprints between 1486 and 1506.[91]

The bindings produced by the Fruit and Flower binder cover books printed beteen 1491 and 1512. J. B. Oldham knew seventeen examples from this shop and Graham Pollard more than 40. If Pollard is right in identifying this binder with George Chastellaine (before 1502–13), he falls outside the period covered in this article.[92]

The Half-Stamp binder, who owned a small panel with the English royal arms, also possessed a set of hand stamps, including a hand with a pointing finger and an easily recognizable heart tool. His work, consisting of 23 known bindings, covers books with imprint dates between 1491 and 1511. J. B. Oldham was not certain of his location, but Graham Pollard placed him in Oxford on the basis of the discovery in one of his bindings of several leaves from the accounts for 1459 of an Oxford Stationer.[93]

We are left with three small groups, probably produced in Oxford, which do not seem to connect with any of the groups discussed thus far. In *The Book Collector* for 1975 David Rogers published an Oxford binding on a Boccaccio manuscript of *c.* 1480 and connected it with a binding on J. Nider, *Consolatorium timorate conscientie* (Paris, 1478) [and other works] and with a manuscript of Alexander Hales written in 1477 at All Souls (MS 322).[94] The dolphin tool also occurs on a detached cover which

J. B. Oldham saw in Durham Cathedral in 1951.[95] A second group of four bindings, three with a diaper design and the fourth with a rather clumsily filled panel (all decorated with Gibson's tools 22–26, 38), cover books printed between 1478 and 1487.[96]

A third group of six bindings, two with a central circle design on one cover and a central diamond on the other cover and four with diaper designs, covering manuscripts and books printed in 1482 and 1483, display Gibson's tools 60–71.[97] Seven groups of uncertain location remain to be discussed and there is very little if anything that I can add to the work published by Hobson, Oldham and Pollard.

The Huntsman binder, who owes his name to his most distinctive tool, a finely engraved image of a behatted figure holding a spear and standing among trees, bound one manuscript and books printed between 1477 and 1498. J. B. Oldham listed ten examples, and the British Library acquired a few years ago a 1498 Basel (Froben) Bible in two volumes from this shop.[98]

I have commented below (article 13) on the un-English technical habits of the Lily binder, and the designs of some of his tools also show Low Country influence. J. B. Oldham listed eighteen examples of his work covering books printed between 1481 and 1504. There is a copy of J. Beets, *Expositio decalogi* (Louvain, 1486), bound by him at Cambridge University Library, and Bartolus de Saxoferrato's *Digestum novum* (Venice, 1493) may also have come from this bindery.[99]

Of the work of the Bat binder only three examples were listed by J. B. Oldham, one on a manuscript and two on books printed in 1486 and 1489;[100] a fourth covering Alexander de Villa Dei, *Doctrinale* (Paris, 1489) was sold at Christie's in New York on 8 April 1981 (lot 118).

Oldham's binder E bound books printed between 1486 and 1491, and two examples of his work came to Cambridge University Library with the books from Peterborough Cathedral.[101]

J. B. Oldham recorded ten examples of the work of the Octagonal Rose binder, covering books printed between 1489 and 1496, and Graham Pollard saw eleven bindings from this shop.[102] A larger group of bindings has survived that can be attributed to the Foliaged Staff binder. J. B. Oldham and Graham Pollard both mention 38 examples but do not list them. They are said to cover manuscripts and books printed between 1489 and 1502.[103]

The last group to be mentioned was produced by the Greyhound binder. G. D. Hobson first distinguished this binder; J. B. Oldham listed ten examples of his work and suggested Oxford as a probable place of their production. He seemed to have worked during the 1490s, and Graham Pollard, who placed him among the unlocated binderies, has pointed out that of the ten volumes known to have been bound by him, six were given by Bishop Richard Fox to Corpus Christi College, Oxford.[104]

It will be clear from this survey that, although a great deal of valuable work has been done in the field of fifteenth-century English bookbinding, much more research is needed to establish whether the binderies whose tools seem to link were in fact more than one shop, whether the many small groups are in all cases the products of as many separate establishments, and whether the still uncertain origin of many of the groups of bindings cannot be more firmly determined. Especially, more data are necessary in order to come to any firm conclusions about the identity of the nameless binders. Archive research as carried out by Graham Pollard and Paul Christianson is extremely valuable, but unless an unambiguous fact such as a binder's signature, a contemporary note on the original endleaves or a bill for binding an identifiable book connects the man with the object, identification based on the availability of a name on the one hand and a group of bindings on the other, even with matching dates for both, remains conjectural.

1. G. D. Hobson, *English Binding Before 1500*, Cambridge, 1929; *idem*, 'Further Notes On Romanesque Bindings', *The Library*, 4th series, xv (1934–5), pp. 161–210; *idem*, 'Some Early Bindings and Binders' Tools', *The Library*, 4th series, xix (1938–9), pp. 202–49; H. M. Nixon, 'The Binding of the Winton Domesday', in M. Biddle (ed.), *Winchester in the Early Middle Ages. Winchester Studies* i, Oxford, 1976, pp. 526–40; C. de Hamel, *Glossed Books of the Bible and the Origins of the Paris Booktrade*, Woodbridge, Suffolk, 1984, pp. 64–86; M. M. Foot, 'Bindings', in *English Romanesque Art 1066–1200*. Catalogue of an exhibition at the Hayward Gallery, London, 5 April–8 July 1984, London, 1984, pp. 342–9.

2. T. J. Brown (ed.), *The Stonyhurst Gospel of St John* [with a technical description of the binding by Roger Powell and Peter Waters], Roxburghe Club, 1969.

3. MS A.iii.28: Hobson, *Before 1500*, pp. 34–5, pl. 31; A. I. Doyle, 'Medieval Blind-Stamped Bindings Associated with Durham Cathedral Priory', in G. Colin (ed.), *De libris compactis miscellanea. Studia Bibliothecae Wittockianae*, i, Brussels, 1984. I am most grateful to Dr Doyle for showing me this article in proof.

4. MS Cosin v.ii.8; Hobson, 'Some Early Bindings', pp. 241–2; Doyle, *Wittockiana*.

5. For early examples see P. Needham, *Twelve Centuries of Bookbinding*, New York and London, 1979, pp. 33–8; H. M. Nixon, and M. M. Foot, *The History of Decorated Bookbinding in England*, Oxford, 1992, pp. 18–23.

6. Nixon and Foot, *Op. Cit.*, pp 23–4.

7. BL, MS Sloane 2400; C. Davenport, *English Embroidered Bookbindings*, London, 1899, p. 3.

8. Graham Pollard has written about the construction of medieval bindings and changes in binding techniques in 'Some Anglo-Saxon Bookbindings',

The Book Collector, xxiv (1975), pp. 130–59; 'The Construction of English 12th-Century Bindings', *The Library*, 5th series, xvii (1962), pp. 1–22; 'Describing Medieval Bookbindings', in J. J. G. Alexander and M. T. Gibson (eds.), *Medieval Learning and Literature. Essays presented to R. W. Hunt*, Oxford, 1976, pp. 50–65; 'Changes in the Style of Bookbinding, 1530–1830', *The Library*, 5th series, xi (1956), pp. 71–94. See also B. Middleton, *A History of English Craft Bookbinding Technique*, 2nd edn, London, 1978.

9. I have seen a few cases where pairs of thongs have been laced in to form a large V-shape, alternating with single thongs.

10. For two examples of leather boards see Pollard, 'Construction of English 12th-Century Bindings', p. 13, and J. B. Oldham, *English Blind-Stamped Bindings*, Cambridge, 1952, p. 31 (quoted as Oldham, *EBSB*).

11. Oldham, *EBSB*, p. 8, first noted this habit of English (and French) binders; the clasps on German and Dutch bindings hinge on the lower cover.

12. N. R. Ker, *Early Pastedowns in Oxford Bindings*, Oxford, 1954.

13. First published as: M. M. Foot, 'Influences from the Netherlands on Bookbinding in England during the Late Fifteenth and Early Sixteenth Centuries', *Actes du XIᵉ Congrès International de Bibliophilie*, Brussels, 1979, pp. 39–64 (with literature).

14. Hobson, *Before 1500*; Oldham *EBSB*; G. Pollard, 'The Names of Some English Fifteenth-Century Binders', *The Library*, 5th series, xxv (1970), pp. 193–218 (quoted as Pollard, 1970).

15. N. J. Barker, 'A Register of Writs and the Scales Binder', *The Book Collector*, xxi (1972), pp. 227–44, pp. 356–79. One more can be added: Abridgement of the Book of Assizes, MS. mid-15th century, with one unrecorded tool; acquired by the British Library, 1988, see below, article 9.

16. MS 204; Hobson, *Before 1500*, p. 53, pl. 38.

17. MS Bodley 117, Manchester, John Rylands University Library, MS Lat. 211, Oxford, Magdalen College, MS 145; Pollard, 1970, pp. 201, 211, pl. ii. The binding of Magdalen College, MS Lat. 196 can still not be linked with any known binding or group of bindings.

18. Oxford, Merton College, MS 268 (Hobson, *Before 1500*, pl. 34); Bodley, MS Laud misc. 558.

19. BL, Add. MS 28870 and Manchester, Chetham's Library, Mun. A.3.131 (MS 27929). All four bindings are discussed in Pollard, 1970, pp. 204, 212. It is possible that these bindings were made in Oxford.

20. Oldham, *EBSB*, pl. xxvii, nos. 402–5, p. 31, note 1.

21. *Ibid.*, nos. 406–10, p. 31, note 1.

22. Pollard, 1970, p. 212 (iic). They are: Bodleian, MS Laud misc. 701; Bodleian, MS Douce 246; BL, Add. MS 6173; and Salisbury Cathedral, MS 99.

23. BL, Add. MS 15673.

24. This shop may link with the Crucifer binder and Pynson. The fleur-de-lis tool found on Bodleian, MS Laud Misc. 701 and on MS Douce 246 (Fig. 8.3, no. 1) seems to be identical with the fleur-de-lis tool found on the Indenture at Windsor (see p. 107) and on a Henry VII deed in Bremen Town Library (see J. B. Oldham, *Blind Panels of English Binders*, Cambridge, 1958, RO1. I have not seen this book).

25. Oldham, *EBSB*, pl. xxvii, nos. 411–18, p. 31 note 1.

26. Bodleian, MS 4° B 1 Art. Seld. All tools on this binding are upside down. The book does not appear to have been re-sewn.

27. BL, Add. MS 24057.

28. S. Gibson, *Early Oxford Bindings*, Oxford, 1903, (quoted as Gibson), pls. I, II, III, IV, V, VIII, XII, XIII, XIV, XVII, XXXI; tools 1–18, 27–32, 52–9, 72–81. This bindery (or these binderies) used seven more tools not in Gibson: one is Oldham, *EBSB*, tool 159; for the other six see Fig. 8.3, nos 10–15.

29. Hobson, *Before 1500*, p. 48, pls. 35–6; Pollard, 1970, pl. IV (All Souls MS 82); N. J. Barker, 'Quiring and the Binder', in *Studies in the Book Trade in Honour of Graham Pollard*, Oxford, 1975, p. 15; Bodley, MS Lyell 16 (Barker's attributions of these bindings are based on Pollard's work: see below). The additional attributions are: *Chronica*, MS 15th cent., Lambeth, MS 340; *Liber precum*, MS 15th cent., Lord Middleton, now on deposit in Nottingham University Library, MS MiLM 11; P. Nicolettus, *Summa naturalium*, Venice, 1476, Ripon Cathedral, XVIII.H.9 (I owe this reference to Nicolas Barker); Leonardus de Utino, *Sermones quadragesimales de legibus*, Paris, 1477, Leicester, Wyggeston Hospital; Jacobus de Theramo, *Consolatio peccatorum*, Gouda, 1481, Shrewsbury School, B.III.24 (Oldham, *Shrewsbury School Library Bindings*, Oxford, 1943, pl. 1, quoted as Oldham, *Shrewsbury*); Nicolaus de Lyra, *Super libros Salomonis et Prophetas*, Nuremberg, 1481, Durham Cathedral, Inc.1.f; Magninus (Mediolanensis), *Regimen sanitatis*, Louvain, 1482, Gloucester Cathedral, Sel. 3–21; Michael of Hungary, *Sermones*, MS Oxford, c. 1470–83, Sotheby's, 6th December 1983, lot 64; G. Lyndewode, *Constitutiones Provinciales*, [Oxford, 1483], BL, IC 55322 (Goff L 413, Proctor 9753. I am not sure that this binding belongs to this group; the binding is very worn and the tools are difficult to identify); Antonius de Butrio, *Speculum de Confessione*, [Louvain, after 1483] [and seven other tracts], Lambeth, 1483.3. For MS Bodley 460 see the Fishtail binder (p. 104). I do not think that MS Bodley 95 belongs to this group (see Barker, 'Quiring', p. 24). The tools on this binding are similar to, but not identical with, Gibson, tools 12, 68, 79.

30. Pollard, 1970, pp. 201–3, 212 (Pollard's unidentified group III ii a also belongs to this Oxford quasi-romanesque group). The date of the start of this shop is still uncertain (see Barker, 'Quiring', p. 14).

31. Attributed to the Fishtail binder by Barker, 'Quiring', p. 28.

32. Oldham, *EBSB*, pl. XVIII, no. 159.

33. See note 29 above, list.

34. Oldham, *EBSB*, p. 22, note 4, lists ten examples. See also pls. XVI, XVIII. Thirteen are noted but not listed in J. B. Oldham, 'English Fifteenth-Century Binding' in *Festschrift Ernst Kyriss*, Stuttgart, 1961, p. 170. H. M. Nixon has told me that the date of printing of no. V of Oldham's list (CA 43 in Westminster Abbey Library) is [1498].

35. Pollard, 1970, pp. 210, 213 (IV c 2).

36. As well as the bindings mentioned by Oldham (*EBSB*, p. 22, note 4): T. Valois and N. Trivet, *Commentarius in S. Augustini libros de civitate dei*, MS 15th cent., Bodleian, MS Laud misc. 128; Bartholomeus de Urbino, MS 15th cent., MS Bodley 460 (I am not sure that the attribution of this binding to the Fishtail binder is correct); Theological tracts, MS 15th and early 16th cent., BL, Add. MS 34807; Cicero, *De Senectute* [and other works], Deventer, n.d., CUL Inc. 4.E.4.1 (Oates 3447); Leonardus de Utino, *Sermones*, Paris, 1477, Leicester, Wyggeston Hospital (see above, note 29); Johannes Salesberiensis, *Policraticus* [and other works], Cologne, 1480, Lincoln Cathedral, SS 3.19; Laurentius Valla, *Elegantiae*, Paris, 1491, BL, IA 40179 (BMC VIII, 145); Thomas Aquinas, *Catena aurea super quattuor Evangel-*

istas, Venice, 1493, Reigate Church; *Sermones super orationem dominicam* [and other works], Paris, 1494, BL, IA 40664 [etc.] (BMC VIII, 29; VIII, 27/ 8; VIII, 106). Cato, *Disticha de moribus*, Deventer [between 1492 and 1500], and four other educational works [Cologne, c. 1480]; [Southern Netherlands, not before 1491]; Paris, 1491; [Paris, c. 1478–82], BL, IA 47755 [etc.] (GW 6293; Vouilléme (Köln) 417; Campbell 21; Copinger 5229; Hain 14635).

37.   G. D. Hobson, *Bindings in Cambridge Libraries*, Cambridge, 1929, pl. XIII.

38.   Oldham, *EBSB*, p. 18, note 3, pl. XIV.

39.   Boethius, *De consolatione philosophiae*, Cologne, 1488, IB 3600 (Goff B 783); Boethius, *De disciplina scholarium*, Louvain, 1485, IB 49177a (BMC IX, 143); J. Versor, *Quaestiones super libros Ethicorum Aristotelis*, Cologne, 1494, IB 4880 (Goff v 256).

40.   IB 22910 (BMC v, 443). Dr A. I. Doyle has reported a third binding from this shop in the New York Public Library (MS 121).

41.   N. R. Ker, 'The Virgin and Child Binder, LVL, and William Horman', *The Library*, 5th series, XVII, (1962), pp. 77–85. A. G. Watson (ed.), *Books, Collectors and Libraries*, London, 1985, pp. 100–10.

42.   Pollard, 1970, pp. 208, 213. See also E. Wilson, *The Winchester Anthology: a facsimile of BL. Add. MS 60577*, Cambridge, 1981, p. 7 (with a correction to Pollard's list).

43.   Add. MS 60577.

44.   Doyle, *Wittockiana*.

45.   Hobson, *Before 1500*, pl. 33, p. 15, note 6. Oldham, *EBSB*, p. 24, note 15 (lot 123a in Sotheby's sale on 22 May 1950 is now in the British Library as part of the Henry Davis Gift: see M. M. Foot, *The Henry Davis Gift*, vol. 2, London, 1983, no. 2, pl. xx).

46.   Pollard, 1970, pp. 204–5, 212.

47.   J. H. Stevenson, *The Fifteenth Century Scots Binding of the Haye Manuscript*, Edinburgh, 1904; G. D. Hobson, 'Further Notes on the Binding of the Haye Manuscript', *Papers of the Edinburgh Bibliographical Society*, XIV (1930), pp. 89–97; W. S. Mitchell, 'Scottish Bookbinding' in A. Kent, H. Lancour and J. E. Daily (eds.), *Encyclopedia of Library and Information Science*, vol. 27; *Scientific and Technical Libraries to Slavonic Paleography*, New York and Basel, 1979, pp. 117–19.

48.   P. Christianson, 'Early London Bookbinders and Parchmeners', *The Book Collector*, XXXII (1985), pp. 41–54, and 'Evidence for the Study of London's Late Medieval Manuscript Book Trade', J. Griffiths and D. Pearsall (eds.), *Book Production and Publishing in Britain 1375–1475*, Cambridge, 1989, pp. 87–108. I am most grateful to Dr Christianson for showing me both articles in typescript. See also P. Christianson, *A Directory of London Stationers and Book Artisans, 1300–1500*, New York, 1990.

49.   Hobson, *Cambridge*, pl. IX; *Before 1500*, p. 20.

50.   G. D. Hobson, *Blind-Stamped Panels in the English Book-Trade*, London, 1944, pp. 21–2. See also J. B. Oldham, *Blind Panels of English Binders*, Cambridge, 1958, Rel 2, AN 3, AN 4.

51.   Pollard, 1970, pp. 195, 207, 212, 214, 215.

52.   The first is Bodleian Library, Auct. Q.1.3.10; the other Heritage Bookshop, Catalogue 144, March 1982, item 248, previously sold at Sotheby's, 23 February 1959, lot 57.

53.   [W. Ward in] Sotheby's catalogue, 16 October 1979, lot 253 (this binding is now BL, IB 55317a); C. de Hamel in an unpublished paper read to the

Oxford Bibliographical Society on 1 December 1982. I am very grateful to Dr de Hamel for showing me the typescript of his paper.

54. H. M. Nixon, 'William Caxton and Bookbinding', *Papers Presented to the Caxton International Congress 1976, Journal of the Printing Historical Society*, XI (1976–7), pp. 92–113; 'Caxton, his Contemporaries and Successors', *The Library*, 5th series, XXXI (1976), pp. 305–26.

55. Pollard, 1970, p. 205.

56. Foot, 'Influences', pp. 48–9; see article 13 below.

57. IB 37262A (BMC III, 746) and IA 3941 (BMC I, 241).

58. Hobson, *Before 1500*, p. 23; *English Bindings 1490–1940 in the Library of J. R. Abbey*, London, 1940, p. 185. See also Oldham, *EBSB*, pp. 27–8, pl. XXI, and *Kyriss Festschrift*, p. 164. Pollard, 1970, p. 207 (with further literature), p. 213.

59. M. M. Foot, 'A Binding by the Crucifer Binder, *c.* 1505', English and Foreign Bookbindings 11, *The Book Collector*, XXVIII (1979), pp. 554–5; see below, article 11.

60. H. R. Plomer, 'Two Lawsuits of Richard Pynson', *The Library*, NS X (1909), p. 116; E. G. Duff, *The Printers, Stationers and Bookbinders of Westminster and London from 1476 to 1535*, Cambridge, 1906.

61. Oldham, *EBSB*, pl. XXVI, p. 31, note 1. They are: Westminster Abbey, CC.41(1), [Deventer, ? 1480]; Leicester, Guild Hall 15/59, n.p., 1488; Hereford Cathedral, MS H.2.19, Louvain, 1488; Ushaw College, XVIII. c.5.17, [Basel, 1489/90]. I have only seen J. B. Oldham's rubbings of these bindings. It is possible that the large fleur-de-lis tool found on Leicester Guild Hall 15/59 is that used by binder C. (Oldham, *EBSB*, tool no. 360) who in turn links with the Oxford quasi-romanesque group. However, this is a relatively common tool and the one used by binder A may well be a variant.

62. The fleur-de-lis tool on this binding also occurs on two bindings at the Bodleian Library, MS Laud misc. 701 and MS Douce 246, which belong to the group of four unlocated bindings (see p. 102). Oldham has found this fleur-de-lis together with Pynson's panel RO1 on the binding of a Henry VII deed in Bremen Town Library (see note 24 above).

63. Oldham, *Panels*, RO1, MISC 4, MISC 14 lists nine. One was sold at Christie's, 12 November 1974, lot 149 (previously sold at Sotheby's, 31 May 1960, lot 9) (RO2 and MISC 14) and one is BL, Add. MS 59862 (RO1).

64. Hobson, *Panels*, pp. 19–23; Pollard, 1970, pp. 214–15. Vol. 1 is Oxford, Corpus Christi College, Φ. A.4.1.

65. Nixon, 'William Caxton and Bookbinding', p. 102; Nixon and Foot, *Op. Cit.*, p. 15.

66. Oldham, *Panels*, ST 10; Pollard, 1970, pp. 216–18.

67. Hobson, *Before 1500*, p. 25, pl. 55; Nixon and Foot, *Op. Cit.*, p. 16; see also above, p. 112.

68. BL, IA 55454 (Goff T 111).

69. CC.24 (*STC* 2, 494.9). Hobson, *Before 1500*, p. 24, pl. 54.

70. Oldham, *EBSB*, pp. 18–19, pl. XI.

71. Hobson, *Cambridge*, pls. XIV, XV; *Before 1500*, pp. 21–2, pls. 47–9.

72. Oldham, *Shrewsbury*, pp. 52–5; *idem*, 'Note on Some New Tools Used by the "Unicorn Binder"', *The Library*, 5th series II (1948), pp. 283–4; *idem, EBSB*, p. 17, pl. XI; *idem, Kyriss Festschrift*, pp. 169–72; Pollard, 1970, pp. 208, 212, 213. As Pollard does not list the additional ?27 bindings I am not sure whether the recent BL acquisition (IC 21646; BMC V, 308/9) was

known to him. As this binding once belonged to Major Abbey, he probably did know it.

73. Oldham, *EBSB*, pp. 16–17, pl. x; *idem, Shrewsbury*, pp. 58–64. See also Hobson, *Cambridge*, pp. 46–7; *idem, Before 1500*, pp. 22–3, pl. 51; Pollard, 1970, pp. 208, 213.

74. Oldham, *Shrewsbury*, pp. 7–12; *idem, EBSB*, pp. 18–19, pl. xi.

75. *Ibid.*, p. 18; Pollard, 1970, p. 213.

76. Respectively IB 7480a (BMC ii, 439) and IB 2178a (BMC i, 153).

77. Oldham, *EBSB*, pp. 19–20, pl. xiv; *idem, Kyriss Festschrift*, pp. 172–3. See also Pollard, 1970, p. 213.

78. GW 2908. Dr Doyle reports that Durham Cathedral, Inc. 32–34 are bound by this binder.

79. Printed in *The Library*, 5th series, xxv (1970), pp. 193–218.

80. W. H . J. Weale, *Bookbindings and Rubbings of Bindings in the National Art Library*, 2 vols., London, 1898, 1894; Gibson, nos. 17–20; W. H. J. Weale and L. Taylor, *Early Stamped Bookbindings in the British Museum*, London, 1922; Hobson, *Before 1500*, pl. 37, p. 17.

81. D. E. Rhodes, 'Account of Cataloguing Incunabula in Oxford College Libraries', *Renaissance Quarterly*, xxix (1976), pp. 1–20. See also his *Catalogue of Incunabula in all the Libraries of Oxford University outside the Bodleian*, Oxford, 1982.

82. Foot, 'Influences'.

83. Gibson, nos. 17–20 (with note).

84. Pollard, 1970, pp. 209, 212.

85. In his paper to the Oxford Bibliographical Society (see note 53 above). The All Souls pressmark is SR.58.g.1.

86. I owe this information to Dr de Hamel.

87. Pollard, 1970, p. 209.

88. Oldham, *EBSB*, pl. xxvi, p. 31, note 1. See also my note 61 above.

89. Pollard, 1970, p. 212.

90. Oldham, *EBSB*, p. 22, note 6, pl. xviii; Pollard, 1970, pp. 210, 213.

91. Hobson, *Before 1500*, p. 24, note 1, pl. 52; Oldham, *Shrewsbury*, pp. 46–9; *idem, EBSB*, pp. 21–2, pl. xv; *idem, Kyriss Festschrift*, p. 168; Pollard 1970, pp. 210–11, 213. Dr Doyle has reported one more example at Upholland College, Lancs.

92. Oldham, *EBSB*, p. 23, pls. xvii, xviii; *idem, Kyriss Festschrift*, p. 168; Pollard, 1970, pp. 211, 213.

93. Oldham, *Shrewsbury*, pp. 36–8; *idem, EBSB*, pp. 29–30, pls. xxiv, xxv; Pollard, 1970, pp. 196, 213.

94. D. Rogers, 'An Unpublished Early Oxford Binding', *The Book Collector*, xxiv (1975), pp. 65–9.

95. Inc.4A. J. Duns Scotus, *Quaestiones super libro quarto sententiarum*, Strassburg, 1474.

96. M. M. Foot, 'An Oxford Binding, *c.* 1480. English and Foreign Bookbindings 30', *The Book Collector*, xxxiii (1984), pp. 332–3; see article 10.

97. Littleton, *Tenores novelli*, MS 15th cent., Cambridge, St John's College, C.13 (Gibson, no. 24); *Summa Theologiae*, 4 vols., Nuremberg, 1482, Oxford, Brasenose College, UB/S.I.16; Lathbury, Oxford, 1482, BL, IB 55317 (Proctor 9749); Bertachinus, *Repertorium iuris*, Nuremberg, 1483, 2 vols. (ii, iii) Oxford, New College, Founders Library, A.9.5.6; Peter

Carmelianus, MS in or after 1486, BL, Add. MS 33736; *Biblia*, [Nuremberg, 1487], Worcester Cathedral, Inc. 8.

98. Oldham, *EBSB*, p. 30, note 7, pl. xxv; BL, IB 37895a (BMC iii, 791/2).
99. Oldham, *EBSB*, p. 29, note 5, pl. xxiii. CUL Inc. 3.F.2.8 (3284) (Oates 3814); BL, IC 21428 (Goff B 220) (the binding is very worn).
100. Oldham, *EBSB*, p. 28, note 7, pls. xxii, xxiii.
101. Oldham, *EBSB*, p. 31, note 1, pl. xxvi. CUL Pet.Q.2.7 (Oates 3093.5 and 3093.7); CUL Pet.G.1.12 (Oates, 4007.2, 249.5, 3779.5 and 1118.5). To the remaining groups of binders whom Oldham (*EBSB*, p. 31, note 1) simply indicated by a letter, i.e. binders B, D, F, G and H and who worked during the 1480s and 1490s, I have at present nothing to add.
102. Oldham, *Shrewsbury*, p. 56; *EBSB*, p. 30, note 5, pl. xxv; Pollard, 1970, p. 213.
103. Oldham, *EBSB*, p. 30, pl. xxvi; Pollard, 1970, p. 213.
104. Hobson, *Cambridge*, pl. xv (p. 49); *Before 1500*, p. 24, pl. 53; Oldham, *EBSB*, p. 21, note 3, pl. xv; Pollard, 1970, p. 213.

9 A Binding by the Scales Binder, 1456–65

(1990)*

The main centres of English bookbinding during the second half of the fifteenth century were London, Oxford and Cambridge. Although a fair number of plain leather bindings of this period have survived, fewer than a dozen binderies producing tooled leather bindings are known to have started work before 1475. Possibly the earliest of these is that of the Scales binder. He worked in London from the 1450s until after 1481 and his work, noted by M. R. James, was first systematically described by G. D. Hobson.[1] Hobson identified twelve bindings from this binder, whom he named after one of his most characteristic tools, a pair of scales. J. B. Oldham[2] and Graham Pollard[3] also discussed this binder's work, but the most detailed account was published by Nicolas Barker[4] who identified seven more examples and observed that the tools used to decorate the bindings fall into two groups. The first group consists of twelve bindings, all covering manuscripts, none of which is demonstrably later than 1465. The second group of seven bindings covers two undated manuscripts and five printed books dated between 1466 and 1481.

A recently discovered example of this binder's work belongs to Barker's first group. It covers the abridgement of the Book of Assizes in French, compiled in the mid-fifteenth century. The manuscript (now BL Add. MS 65194) is written on paper in eight quires of fourteen folios with a final quire of eight folios. The vellum end-leaves consist of a pair of conjugate manuscript leaves plus one blank leaf at each end. The pair of manuscript leaves at the end contains a copy of an entry on the King's Bench roll for Hilary 34 Henry VI,[5] so that the binding cannot be earlier than 1456.

The manuscript is sewn with thin cord on four split alum-tawed thongs, and the inner fold of each quire has been strengthened with a thin strip of paper. The backs of the quires have been lined with vellum between the thongs and there are remnants of leather headbands, tied down with sewing thread in the centre of each quire. The boards are made up of vellum leaves, plain and manuscript, pasted together and covered with brown calf. There are remnants of leather ties. The covers are tooled in

* The British Library Journal, XVI (1990), pp. 103–6.

Fig. 9.1a   Abridgement of the Book of Assizes, MS mid-15th century.
Blind-tooled brown calf. 198 × 135 × 40 mm.
British Library, Add. MS 65194.

Fig. 9.1b   Abridgement of the Book of Assizes, MS mid-15th century.
Lower cover.

blind to a panel design. A border of rectangular tools surrounds a central panel, filled on the upper cover with rows of tools, while on the lower cover the central compartment has been decorated with a knife, showing on a cross-hatched ground the initial b, almost certainly that of the original owner of the binding. This feature of cut-leather decoration is one of the characteristics of the Scales binder's work, a technique otherwise unknown in England, though popular in German-speaking countries during the fifteenth century. The rectangular tool that has been used to form the border on the lower cover does not occur on any of the previously-known bindings from this shop.

Nicolas Barker drew attention to the Scales binder's unusual habit of signing the quires of a number of books he bound.[6] The manuscript discussed here has catchwords, written in the lower inner margin of the verso of the last folio of each quire, probably by the scribe of the text. Following the catchword is an oblique stroke, after which comes, slightly lower down, the quire number in roman numerals, sometimes preceded or followed by a dot. The roman numerals are almost always in a darker ink and the shape of the v is distinct from that of the scribal v. It is therefore likely that these signatures were added by the binder.

Unlike so many bindings of this period, this binding has not been restored and it looks remarkably fresh with clear impressions of the tools. The British Library has been particularly fortunate to acquire it and owes a debt of gratitude to the Pilgrim Trust and the Friends of the National Libraries who enabled it to do so.

1. G. D. Hobson, *Bindings in Cambridge Libraries*, Cambridge, 1929, pp. 14–25; *English Binding before 1500*, Cambridge, 1929, pp. 17–18.
2. J. B. Oldham, *English Blind-stamped Bindings*, Cambridge, 1952, p. 25; 'English fifteenth-century binding' in *Festschrift Ernst Kyriss*, Stuttgart, 1961, pp. 164–5.
3. G. Pollard, 'The Names of some English fifteenth-century binders', *The Library*, 5th series, xxv (1970), pp. 193–218.
4. N. J. Barker, 'Collector's piece IV. A Register of Writs and the Scales Binder', *The Book Collector*, xxi (1972), pp. 227–44, 356–79.
5. I am grateful to my colleague Andrew Prescott for identifying the text of the manuscript and the text of the end-leaves.
6. N. J. Barker, art. cit., p. 368. See also N. J. Barker, 'Quiring and the binder' in *Studies in the Book Trade in Honour of Graham Pollard*, Oxford, 1975, pp. 11–31.

10 An Oxford Binding, c. 1480
(1984)*

The fifth item in a list of books circulating among the Fellows of All Souls College, Oxford, in the early sixteenth century[1] is volume 2 of Duns Scotus, *Quaestiones in quattuor libros sententiarum*, Venice, 1478 (now All Souls, L.R.3.h.II), bound in brown calf over wooden boards, tooled in blind to a panel design, with fillets, a square stamp showing a squirrel and a round stamp depicting a dove (or a raven) with a palm branch in its beak surrounded by the legend S[igillum] ST VINCEN[T]. The volume is sewn on four split alum-tawed thongs; the binding has brass studs at the corners of the panel and in the centre, as well as traces of two pairs of clasps, hinging on the upper cover; and there are vellum manuscript pastedowns and end-leaves. The squirrel stamp, which has been put in sideways (a usage common in Germany and Flanders, but also found in London and Oxford) occurs on three other bindings, all with vellum manuscript paste-downs or end-leaves. One covers Walter Burley, *Expositio super artem veterem Porphyrii et Aristotelis*, Venice, n.d., with a late fifteenth-century English ownership inscription.[2] One is on Leonardus Aretinus' translation of Aristotle's *Ethica*, Oxford, 1479, and has on the first leaf in a contemporary hand entries of payments received from the Prior of Osney.[3] The third covers three works by St John Chrysostom printed in Cologne in and c. 1487,[4] with two late fifteenth-century manuscript additions, and with an early sixteenth-century English ownership note. A floral branch tool used on this binding belonged to the Fishtail binder.[5]

Though St Vincent is not a Saint most readily associated with an English monastery,[6] the position of the clasps, the early English notes, the presence of manuscript pastedowns and end-leaves, and the link with the Fishtail binder suggest that these bindings were made in England, probably in or near Oxford.

---

1. N. R. Ker, *Records of All Souls College Library 1437–1600*, Oxford, 1971, pp. 100, 156.

---

* English and Foreign Bookbindings 30, *The Book Collector*, XXXIII, pp. 332–3.

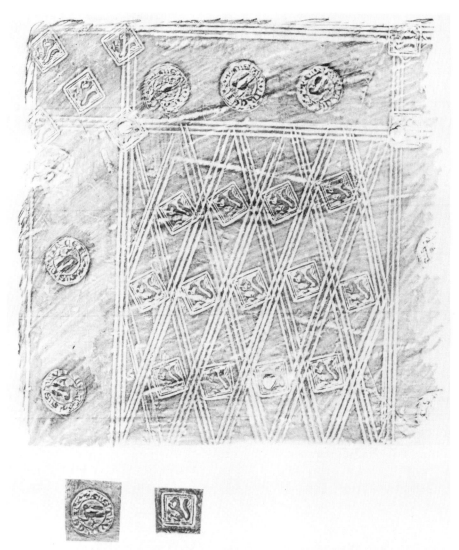

Fig. 10.1   Duns Scotus, *Quaestiones in quattuor libros sententiarum*,
Venice, 1478.
Brown calf, tooled in blind. 310 × 195 × 45 mm.
All Souls College, Oxford, L.R.3.h.II.
Rubbing of part of the binding and the tools.

2. British Library, IB 19997 (BMC v, 206).
3. S. Gibson, *Early Oxford Bindings*, London, 1903, no. 9.
4. *Homiliae super Matthaeum*, 1487 (BMC i, 228); *Epistola ad Cyriacum*, n.d. [*c.* 1487] (BMC i, 228–9); *Sermones de patientia in Job*, 1487 (BMC i, 227–8). King's Lynn Public Library.
5. J. B. Oldham, *English Blind-Stamped Bindings*, Cambridge, 1952, pl. xviii, no. 162.
6. I have not been able to find a monastery dedicated to St Vincent. F. Arnold-Forster, *Studies in Church Dedications*, London, 1899, lists five pre-Reformation churches dedicated to St Vincent, Martyr. Mr Anthony Hobson has suggested (letter, d.d.7.12.1984) that the seal may have belonged to an individual St[ephen] Vincent, who has not been traced.

11 A Binding by the Crucifer Binder, c. 1505

(1979)*

J. B. Oldham listed in his *English Blind-Stamped Bindings* five bindings by the Crucifer binder, four on manuscripts and one covering a 1476 Venice Thomas Aquinas.[1] Graham Pollard[2] mentioned a New Year's gift to Henry VII on 1 January 1500 bound by the same binder; H. M. Nixon discovered another binding by this binder, covering a Sarum *Missal* printed for Caxton in 1487, belonging to Lord Newton,[3] which connects the Crucifer binder with Oldham's binder A. Three more bindings from this shop can now be added. One covers the earliest Book of Ordinances of the Goldsmiths' Company written between 1478 and 1483, with additional material dated 1505 and 1507. The composition of the manuscript and the presence of binder's signatures suggest that the book was bound after the manuscript had been completed. The second is illustrated here and covers an Indenture between Henry VII and Richard [Chetham], Prior of Leeds in Kent, sealed on 20 April 1505. The third is on a very similar Indenture made between Henry VII and Thomas Silkesteade, Prior of Winchester, sealed on 12 June 1503. It is now at Windsor Castle and is bound in brown calf decorated with the Crucifer binder's square floral tool, a large fleur-de-lis and two of Pynson's rose panels (RO. 1–2).[4] This binding combined with the knowledge that the Crucifer binder was active in 1499 and was still at work as late as 1507 strongly suggests that Pynson employed this binder, or had his own bindery. Pynson, who had arrived in England before 1491 and was called a bookbinder during his quarrel with John Russhe's executors,[5] used one of these rose panels (RO.1) together with his signed panel, probably for the first time on *Abbreviamentum Statutorum*, printed by himself in 1499, using some of his own printer's waste as pastedowns.[6]

1. Formerly at St Albans School, sold at Sotheby's, 19 November 1974, 186.
2. *The Library*, 5th series, xxv (1970), p. 200.
3. *Journal of the Printing Historical Society*, xi (1976–7), p. 106.

---

*English and Foreign Bookbindings 11, *The Book Collector*, xxviii, pp. 554–5.

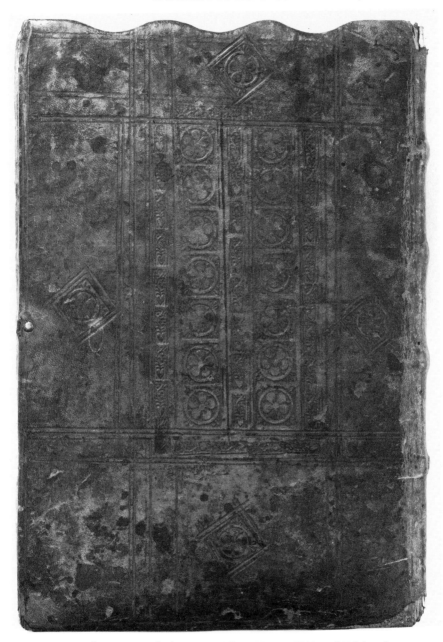

Fig. 11.1   Indenture made between King Henry VII and Richard
[Chetham], Prior of Leeds, sealed on 20 April 1505.
Lower cover: Brown calf, blind tooled. 277 × 191 × 19 mm.
British Library, Henry Davis Gift.

4. This is almost certainly the binding rubbed by Weale and referred to by Oldham (*EBSB*, p. 28).
5. *The Library*, NS x, 1909, p. 116.
6. These two panels decorate a 1501 Maideston, sold at Sotheby's, 31 May 1960, 9.

12 Monasteries and Dragons.

A selection of Dutch and Flemish bindings of the late fifteenth and early sixteenth centuries in the British Library, Cambridge University Library and the Bodleian Library, Oxford

(1980)*

The British Library in London does not seem the most obvious place to study late fifteenth- and early sixteenth-century bookbindings from the Netherlands, and if one considers the amount of valuable work which has been done in the countries of their origin by Prosper Verheyden, Luc Indestege, and A. Hulshof and M. J. Schretlen, to mention but a very few, it may even seem preposterous to embark upon such a venture. However, if one casts one's net a little wider to include Cambridge University Library and the Bodleian Library at Oxford,[1] the catch turns out to be big and varied enough to warrant display. It is so large and of such variety indeed that it is only possible to mention here a relatively small proportion of all the bindings found and I have confined myself to those with an early monastic provenance and to those made—in most cases signed—by known binders.

The diversity of the Netherlandish[2] bindings of this period manifests itself mainly in the way they are decorated. The way they are constructed is, if not uniform, at least based on one model. Almost all of them are sewn on thongs, either of vellum or of tawed leather, which are laced in grooves into the wooden boards and pegged with round or square pegs. The boards are covered in calf or hide or occasionally in sheepskin, and the headbands are sometimes made of plaited leather but more often covered with the spine leather. Metal bosses are used from time to time on large books and metal clasps are often found, almost always with the hinges on the lower cover. The paste-downs, by now often lifted, and the end-leaves are frequently made of plain vellum or of parts of vellum manuscripts. The edges are as a rule left plain. The designs are effected either with the impression of one or more panels, or with fillets and small tools. The usual pattern is one of intersecting fillets which form a rectangle,

* *Hellinga. Festschrift/Feestbundel/Mélanges*, Amsterdam, N. Israel, 1980, pp. 193–204.

divided by a saltire—with or without a diamond or a cross or both—into compartments; these are either left empty or filled with decorative tools. A cross-hatched pattern is less common.

Several books are bound in vellum; some have a flap covering the fore-edge and reaching half way across the upper cover; some are sewn on thongs and a few are stitched through the folds of the sections and through the spine. An interesting open-backed Deventer binding of c.1487, now in the Bodleian Library, was illustrated and described by H. M. Nixon in his *Broxbourne Library. Styles and Designs of Bookbindings* (London, 1956), no. 9. Professor W. G. Hellinga drew attention to a *Blaffert en register van de losrenten en lijfrenten der stad Gouda* (Gouda [after 1489]): BL, IB. 47421, BMC IX, 40) in a limp vellum binding in which fragments of printer's waste were found that belonged to the Collaciebroeders at Gouda.[3] One book, a copy of Gerardus Zutphaniensis, *De spiritualibus ascensionibus* (Deventer, n.d.: CUL, Inc. 6.E.4.1 [2926], Oates 3439) belonged to the Brothers of the Common Life of the Hieronymushuis at Utrecht and is bound in a piece of blind-tooled calf taken from a larger book.

A contemporary monastic provenance as such does not, of course, mean that the book was bound in that monastery. A number of monasteries are known to have had their own binderies and if the same tools occur on several bindings with the same monastic provenance, it may be reasonable to assume that they were made there. In a number of cases the bindings were left plain or were decorated with fillets only or with a very few small and commonly used floral or star-shaped tools; in others the condition of the binding was such that accurate observation and identification of the tools was impossible. Several books in this category did belong to various monasteries. A plain brown calf binding on a Louvain *Herbarius* (CUL, Inc. 4.F.2.7. [3273], Oates 3804) was in the possession of the Fratres Cruciferi;[4] bindings decorated with fillets only belonged to the nuns of St Mary Magdalen at Utrecht,[5] to the nuns of the convent of St Ursula at Schiedam,[6] to the sisters at Heusden,[7] and to the Benedictine Monks at Stavelot,[8] and a 1496 Antwerp *Plenarium* (CUL, Inc. 4.F.6.5. [3443], Oates 3983) in a badly rubbed blind-tooled brown calf binding also comes from the convent of St Mary Magdalen at Utrecht.

A fair number of the more elaborately tooled bindings were made by or for the order which has had more influence on the history of books and bookbinding than any other, that of the Windesheim Congregation. A 1495 Schoonhoven *Breviarium Traiectense* (BL, IB. 48701, BMC IX, 104) is bound in brown calf and tooled in blind with a one-headed eagle, a fleur-de-lis, a sacred monogram, a crown of thorns, a mã tool and small decorative tools, all of which are found on Pars I of *Summa Antonini* (Strasburg 1490) which was bound at the Monastery of Nieuwlicht near

Hoorn.[9] From the same bishopric comes a binding from the monastery of the Canons Regular of St Augustine at Utrecht,[10] covering a manuscript Diurnal on vellum (BL, Add. MS 40153). The tools which were used to decorate this binding have been attributed by Hulshof and Schretlen both to the Canons Regular and to the Brothers of the Common Life at the Hieronymushuis.[11] Both institutions are known to have had their own bindery and both binderies seem to have been active during the late fifteenth and early sixteenth centuries, while the Canons Regular seem to have used the heart tool and the fleur-de-lis as early as 1458.

A most unusual panel on a 1484 Cologne *Ars dicendi sive perorandi* (Bodley, Auct. 2.Q.3.33, Fig. 12.1) shows a hunting scene, four medallions with a pelican, a lamb-and-flag, a mounted hunter and two lions, two behatted intertwined dragons and two monsters drinking from a fountain, separated by the legend 'non stant federa metu facta'. A strip along the top reads: 'odium suscitat rixas', and one along the bottom: 'Litem.inferre. caue.'[12] Around the panel are several impressions of a tool that depicts Christ giving a blessing. Prosper Verheyden found this same tool on a manuscript *Actus fratrum predicatorum* with a contemporary ownership inscription of the Windesheimer convent of Korsendonck near Turnhout.[13] Another panel, showing Christ crucified surrounded by the legend 'Jhesum.autam./transiens.per.medium./Illorum.Jbatt./Jhesus.maria.Johes.' and a scroll tool with 'facons' decorate a brown calf binding on several devotional treatises written in Flemish (Bodley, Broxbourne 1794). It was made for or possibly at the Augustinian nunnery of Faconshof at Antwerp.[14]

Two well-known Windesheim monasteries near Brussels that owned binderies are Groenendaal and Rooklooster. A 1501 Basle *Amici Sermones* (Bodley, Broxbourne 1557) was bound at Groenendaal in brown hide tooled in blind with a border roll, small fleurs-de-lis, crowns, pomegranates and flowers, and with a rectangular label lettered 'Gruenendale' on the upper cover.[15] Three bindings now in the British Library and one in the University Library at Cambridge were made at Rooklooster.[16] Jacobus de Voragine, *Sermones de tempore per totum annum* (BL, IB. 49211, BMC IX, 151)[17] and John of Hoveden's *Carmen de passione domini* (CUL, Inc. 6.F.2.8 [3293], Oates 3824), both printed at Louvain, were bound at Rooklooster in brown calf tooled in blind with floral tools and square tools containing the lion of St Mark. These same tools occur on Franciscus de Mayronis, *Sermonum de tempore* (Brussels, n.d.: BL, IB. 49532, BMC, IX, 175) accompanied by a pelican, a cock, a fleur-de-lis and a rectangular strip with 'roedencloester'. A two-volume manuscript *Breviary* (BL, Add. MSS 11863–4) with a Rooklooster provenance is bound in red-dyed leather and decorated with a panel depicting two rows of six creatures in roundels, separated by a hunting scene.[18] Several manuscript tracts of Bonaventura,

Fig. 12.1 *Ars dicendi sive perorandi*. Cologne, 1484.
Blind tooled brown calf. 290 × 202 × 62 mm.
Bodleian Library, Auct. 2.Q.3.33

dated 1486–91, bound together with Nicolaus de Hanapis, *Biblia Pauperum* (Antwerp 1491: CUL, Add. 6453 [and] Inc. F.6.3 [3430], Oates 3968) in brown calf decorated with fillets and small heart-shaped and floral tools come from Bethleem, the monastery of the Canons Regular of St Augustine near Louvain.[19] Another binding with the same provenance was made by Ludovicus Ravescot, a binder to whom I shall return presently, and covers Johannes Herolt's *Sermones discipuli de tempore* (Deventer, n.d.: CUL, Inc. 2.E.4.1 [4269], Oates 3456).[20]

Among the books bound by or for other religious orders and communities, which I will mention in their geographical order working roughly south-eastwards, is a 1479 Utrecht Gregorius I, *Homiliae* (Bodley, Inc. e.N.2) in brown calf decorated with a round lamb-and-flag tool which belonged to the Poor Clares at Haarlem.[21] A manuscript *Psalter* (Bodley, Broxbourne, R.961) in brown calf with two impressions of an Image of Pity Panel on each cover comes from the convent of Marienborch at Soest.[22] Another brown calf binding, tooled in blind with two different fleur-de-lis tools and two flower tools covers Raymundus de Sabunde, *Theologia naturalis* (Deventer n.d.: Bodley, Auct. I.Q.3.15) and was once in the possession of the Brothers of the Common Life at Doesburg,[23] and a *Vocabularius utriusque iuris* (Louvain, n.d.: CUL, Inc. 1.F.2.2 [3238], Oates 3768) in brown hide over wood and decorated with a round fleur-de-lis, a rose and a leaf tool, was bound in or for the Premonstratensian abbey of St Mary of Bern near Heusden.[24] A 1484 Louvain Hugo de Prato Florido, *Sermones dominicales* (CUL, Inc. 3.F.2.2 [3249], Oates 3778) in brown calf tooled in blind with a crowned one-headed eagle, a fleuron and a small fleur-de-lis has as provenance 'Nazareth in Waelwijck'.[25] Two bindings are decorated with the same tools as were used by the Brothers of the Common Life at 's-Hertogenbosch,[26] one covers Franciscus de Mayronis, *Sermones* (Brussels, n.d.: Bodley, Auct. Q. sub. fen.II.16), the other Bernardus Parmensis, *Casus longi decretalium* (Louvain, 1484: CUL, Inc. 3.F.2.6 [3269], Oates 3800). This last binding has a square eagle tool as well as two of the fleur-de-lis tools and the leaf tool that were used by the Brothers at 's-Hertogenbosch. Another binding from the immediate neighbourhood comes from the convent of St Sophia;[27] it is made of brown calf, tooled with a small lion and a large double-headed eagle, and covers a 1488 's-Hertogenbosch *Gemmula Vocabulorum* (CUL, Inc. 4.E.12.1 [3130], Oates 3658).

Going further south we find a copy of Bernard of Clairvaux, *Homiliae* (Antwerp [c. 1487] [and other works]: Bodley, Auct. i.Q. inf. 1.11.) bound in blind-tooled brown calf that belonged to Peter Verhoeven, the 'father' of the nuns of the convent of Thabor at Malines.[28] A Missal in Latin on vellum (BL, Add. MS 24075),[29] written and bound at or for the monastery of St Adrian at Grammont is decorated with a roll, pineapple tools and a square lion tool, and a manuscript Old Testament in Flemish in two volumes (BL, Add. MSS 15310–11)[30] was written and bound in 1461 and 1462 for the nuns of St Katherinedael at Hasselt. The Fratres Cruciferi stamped their badge, held by an angel, on the binding of Johannes Beets, *Commentum super decem praeceptis decalogi* (Louvain, 1486: BL, IB.49344, BMC, IX, 165).[31] There has been some argument as to whether the bindings with this badge were made at Huy or at Maastricht, but the examples cited by Prosper Verheyden tip the scale heavily in favour of Maastricht. Also from Maastricht, but from the library of the Beghards there, is a Conradus de Brundelsheim, *Sermones Socci de tempore* (Deventer, 1480: CUL, Inc. 3.E.4.1 [2894], Oates 3423), volume I of which is in brown calf, tooled in blind with stylized trefoils suspended from arches,[32] and other small decorative tools, two of which occur on the binding of a 1495 Delft Nicolaus Salicetus, *Antidotarius animae* (CUL, Inc. 6.E.2.3 [2840], Oates 3367) which is also decorated with two scrolls reading 'ihesus' and 'maria' and a panel with five pairs of animals and birds in roundels. The same panel and the same scrolls turn up on a manuscript Book of Hours in Flemish (BL, Add. MS 24332),[33] which in turn has a round tool with a double-headed eagle, a star and a music tool with MA and two notes.[34] These tools have also been found on other bindings from the Beghards at Maastricht, and the music tool and the star occur on a binding covering a *Martyriologium Viola Sanctorum* (Strasburg, 1516) at the Bodleian Library (Douce MM499).

Two more monasteries are represented, that of the Cistercians of Le Jardinet near Walcourt, Namur, where Ambrosius's *De officiis* (Louvain, n.d.: BL, IA. 49142, BMC IX, 147) was bound in brown calf and decorated in blind with several tools including a lamb-and-flag, a crucifixion, a crown and a square tool of a tree in a garden,[35] and that of the Benedictines at Stavelot. One plain binding from this abbey I mentioned above and two more decorated examples are at the British Library. One covers a two-volume manuscript Smaragdus, *Commentarius in regulam S. Benedicti* on vellum (Add. MSS 16961–2),[36] the other a St Basil, *Opera* (Paris, 1520: C.128.g.6).

Turning from the more or less anonymous monastic binders to those who tooled their name on their products, we encounter three Bruges binders who signed their work: Anthonius de Gavere, Ludovicus Bloc and Jean Guilebert. Anthonius de Gavere, who was active between 1459 and 1505, bound a 1493 Venice *Missale Romanum* (BL, IA. 23359 a)[37] in brown calf and decorated it with four impressions of a panel showing two rows of four birds and animals in foliage surrounded by the legend 'ob. laudem/ xpristi. librum. hunc/recte. ligaui/anthonius. de. gauere'. Luc Indestege[38] knew of ten other binders who used this legend with their own name substituted, among whom are Ludovicus Bloc, Jean Guilebert and Ludovicus Ravescot. The same panel occurs four times on two manuscript *Breviaries* on vellum, one at Oxford (Bodley, Broxbourne R.962) and the other at the British Library (MS Royal 2A.XII).[39] The panels on the latter binding are separated by a strip with music-playing angels and by one showing a piper and four dancing peasants. Prosper Verheyden described five different Flemish versions of this strip,[40] one of which was used by Ludovicus Bloc who worked at Bruges from 1484 to 1529. He used it to separate two impressions of his signed panel depicting two rows of four animals in foliage surrounded by Bloc's version of the 'ob laudem xpristi' legend on the binding of manuscript Prayers in Latin (BL, Eg. 2125).[41] Jean Guilebert, 'die men heet meese', lived and worked in the Frere Strate in Bruges between 1469 and 1489. His wife is mentioned as a widow in 1490. He owned two panels, a smaller one with the 'ob laudem xpristi' legend which is found used together with Anthonius de Gavere's signed panel,[42] and a larger one with his name on a strip between two rows of four pairs of birds and monkeys in vine branches[43] which was used as late as 1538 and occurs *c*.1530 on a binding at the Bodleian Library,[44] together with Joris de Gavere's signed panel. E. P. Goldschmidt's conclusion[45] that there were, therefore, two Jean Guileberts and that the later one worked at Ghent is not necessarily the right one. Prosper Verheyden has shown conclusively[46] that panels were used in the Netherlands as early as the second half of the thirteenth century, and it is well known that panels have a considerably longer life span than small hand tools. An inscription, deleted but visible under ultraviolet light, in a manuscript Book of Hours at the Pierpont Morgan Library decorated with Guilebert's larger panel, which reads, 'Desen bouc heft ghebonde Jan guilbert die men heet meese wonnende in de frere strate'[47] points quite clearly to Jean Guilebert of Bruges as the owner of both panels as well as of a number of small tools some of which occur on the binding of Johannes Gerson's *Opuscula* (Brussels, 1475: Bodley, Auct. I.Q. III.14) which has on the paste-down of the lower cover the inscription 'Johannes meese [me] ligavit'.[48] Fig. 12.2 shows the same triangular dragon tool (1) and the same fleur-de-lis (a) that were used on the binding of Laurentius Valla, *Elegantiae* (Louvain, n.d.: CUL, SSS. 40. 16 [3165], Oates 3694).[49] The rayed rosette which is found on the Gerson also occurs on a 1508 manuscript *Missale ad usum . . . Tornacensis* (Bodley, Broxbourne 1105),[50] and the rayed rosette and the fleur-de-lis found on both the Gerson and the Valla also turn up on Josephus, *Antiquitates Judaeorum* (n.p. nd.: Queens' College, Cambridge),[51] which in turn has a triangular dragon tool (4) which was used on the binding of a 1477 Nuremberg *Biblia Latina* (BL, IC. 7159, BMC II, 414–5).[52] This binding is also decorated with a slightly larger fleur-de-lis (e) and with a briquet tool,[53] both different from the fleur-de-lis (c)

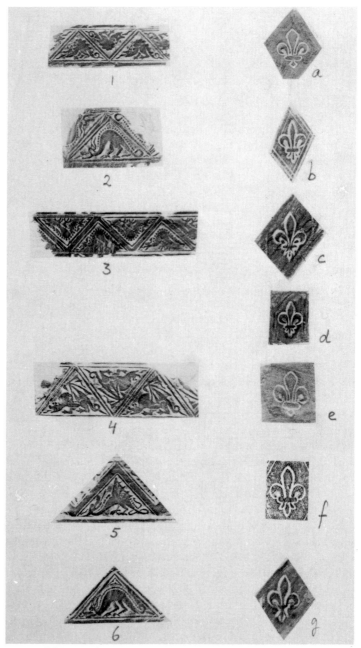

Fig. 12.2   Rubbings of some of the dragon and fleur-de-lis tools used in the Netherlands during the late fifteenth and early sixteenth centuries

and the briquet which occur on a volume of moral and religious treatises in French written by David Aubert in 1475 and bought by Margaret of York, Duchess of Burgundy (Bodley, MS. Douce 365).[54] The dragon (5) found on this last binding, however, is the same as that on a binding at the University Library at Utrecht[55] which has a briquet tool that may be identical with that on the 1477 Bible.

We have here ten bindings, all on books written or printed during the later part of the fifteenth century or during the very beginning of the sixteenth, all connected by one or more tools, on which five different dragons, six different fleurs-de-lis, and at least three different briquet tools are found: a tangled situation which will need a great deal more research before it can be unravelled. To sow yet more confusion, a 1480 Gouda St Jerome, *Vanden leven der heiligher vaderen* (Bodley, Broxbourne R.102) in brown calf is tooled with a triangular dragon tool (6) and a fleur-de-lis (g), both closely similar to those on the 1508 manuscript Tournai Missal.

Having been led astray by dragons and fleurs-de-lis, I must return to the signed bindings. Ludovicus Ravescot,[56] an illuminator, printer and bookbinder at Louvain worked from *c.*1473 until after 1501. He bound for Johannes de Westfalia, whose 'portrait' he used on the bindings for this well-known printer, publisher and bookseller, and for William Schevez, Archbishop of St Andrews, who visited Louvain in 1491.[57] Goldschmidt's solution of the rebus tool, which attributes the bindings with the portrait of Johannes de Westfalia to Ravescot, still seems preferable to other guesses, especially considering that the tools which occur on the binding of the copy of *Fasciculus Temporum*, printed by Johan Veldener at Louvain in 1476, now in the Koninklijke Bibliotheek at The Hague and illustrated in J. W. Holtrop, *Monuments typographiques* (The Hague, 1857, pl. 130) which has a tool with Veldener's name, are similar to, but not identical with, those on the 'rebus' bindings.[58]

Luc Indestege's discovery of a signed panel confirms that Ludovicus rather than Johannes Ravescot was the binder. Of the many known examples of his work, I would like to mention here the binding of a 1486 Venice Lucanus, *Pharsalia* (Bodley, Broxbourne 784),[59] two bindings in the British Library, both covering works by Justinian I; one is a *Volumen de tortis* (Venice, 1492) in the Henry Davis Gift,[60] the other a 1493/4 Venice *Codex* (IC. 21425, BMC v, 327), and one in Cambridge University Library (Inc. 2.E.4.1 [4269], Oates 3456) covering Johannes Herolt, *Sermones discipuli de tempore* (Deventer, n.d.).[61] A brown calf binding tooled in blind with vine branches, fleurs-de-lis, small eagle tools, rosettes and round tools depicting a unicorn covers the works of Prudentius in Latin and other works, all printed at Deventer in the early 1490s (CUL, Inc.

4.E.4.3. [4082], Oates 3523).[62] An inscription on the vellum paste-down led Sir Stephen Gaselee to attribute this binding to the printer and book-dealer Richard Pafraet of Deventer. The tools that decorate this binding have not been found on any other binding covering books printed by Pafraet and, as there is no evidence that Pafraet had a binder's shop, it seems safer to attribute this binding to a binder who worked for Pafraet rather than to the printer himself. Johannes de Wouda, a member of a family of bookbinders and copyists at Antwerp,[63] who was probably the son of Jan van Wouw who was a member of the St Luke's Guild in 1453 and who died in the early 1490s, signed the panel with the crowned double-headed eagle that occurs on a volume of five religious works printed between 1494 and 1500 (Bodley, Broxbourne 1514).[64] A Ghent bookseller and bookbinder who signed his panels was Victor van Crombrugghe who worked during the beginning of the sixteenth century until his death in 1518; thereafter his widow continued the business. He used a panel depicting the Scourging at the Pillar, an Image of Pity panel and a strip with a double-headed eagle, a wyvern, a wolf and a stag on Augurellus, *Iambicus libri, Sermonum libri, Carminum libri* (Venice, 1505: BL, Henry Davis Gift).[65] Jan Tijs who worked at Malines from c.1508 until c.1537 signed an Annunciation panel that decorates the binding of Johannes Gerson, *Dialogus de perfectione cordis* (Paris [?1495]: Bodley, Broxbourne 1541).[66] A pair of empty covers in the Henry Davis Gift to the British Library are decorated with several small tools that were used at Utrecht c.1500, including a head of Christ, a lamb-and-flag, two different eagle tools, a fleur-de-lis, a rose and a running dog.[67] It also has a binder's mark with the name henrick houtegen [?]. The same collection contains two bindings by Jan Ryckaert of Ghent who worked from c.1511 until 1546;[68] one is on a copy of Francisco Mario Grapaldi, *De partibus aedium* (Parma, 1506),[69] the other on two works by Isaac and Johannes Tzetzes printed at Basle. Other bindings by him in the British Library cover a manuscript *Cartularium Abbatiae S. Bavonis* (Add. MS 16952),[70] a manuscript *Querelle entre le Duc d'Austrie . . . et le Roy de France* (Add. MS 17717),[71] a 1528 Paris St John Chrysostom (C.66.c.9) and a 1540 Venice Johannes Staphyleus (C.66.c.13). Another example is at Cambridge University Library and covers a 1517 Paris Geoffrey of Monmouth, *Britannie utriusque regum et principum origo* (Rel d. 51.14).

The panels with the IB and IP monograms and the panels signed by Jacobus Clercx de Ghele of which I found several examples would take me too far into the sixteenth century; nor is there room here to discuss the considerable number of blind-tooled bindings that can be attributed to particular places. These and the large number of unattributed panel-stamped bindings and the wealth of bindings decorated with small tools found at the British Library, at Bodley and at Cambridge University

Library whet the appetite for a thorough search in the various other universities, colleges and private and public libraries throughout the country.

1. I am most grateful to Mr J. C. T. Oates and Mr D. McKitterick of Cambridge University Library, and to Mr R. J. Roberts and Mr P. Morgan of the Bodleian Library for facilitating my research and for all their help.
2. I have not included bindings from Westphalia and the Rhineland but have limited myself to the area called the Netherlands during the reign of Charles V. See H. D. Darby and H. Fullard (eds.), *The New Cambridge Modern History*, vol. xiv: Atlas, Cambridge, 1970, map 150a.
3. L. and W. Hellinga, *The fifteenth-century printing types of the Low Countries*, Amsterdam, 1966, vol. i, pp. 86–7.
4. Their location is not named. The Fratres Cruciferi had binderies at their houses at Huy, Namur and Maastricht.
5. Laurent, *Somme le roi* Delft, 1478: Bodley, Auct. 7. Q.7.64. H. F. van Heussen, *Kerkelijke Historie en Oudheden der Zeven Vereenigde Provincien*, Vol. II, *De Historie van het Utrechtsche Bisdom*, Leiden, 1726, p. 106.
6. Two Books of Hours in Dutch, Delft, 1480 [and] Delft, 1484: CUL, Inc. 5.E.2.2. [2815] (Oates 3342, 3350). R. C. H. Römer, *Geschiedkundig overzigt van de kloosters en abdijen . . . van Holland en Zeeland*, Leiden, 1854, vol. i, pp. 575–83.
7. *Sermones Sensati*, Gouda, 1482: CUL, Inc. 3.E.3.1 [2871] (Oates 3400). Van Heussen, *op. cit.*, p. 377.
8. *Gemma Vocabulorum*, Deventer, 1498: CUL, Inc. 5.E.44 [3040] (Oates 3576).
9. P. Verheyden, 'Noord-Hollandse Boekbanden', *Het Boek*, xxxi (1952–4), pp. 207–10, pl. 3. J. G. R. Acquoy, *Het klooster te Windesheim en zijn invloed*, Utrecht, 1875–80, vol. iii, p. 24.
10. Acquoy, *op. cit.*, vol. iii, p. 18. A. Hulshof, 'Een en ander over de bibliotheek van het Regulierenklooster te Utrecht', *Tijdschrift voor boek- en bibliotheekwezen*, viii (1910), pp. 17–48.
11. A. Hulshof and M. J. Schretlen, *De kunst der oude boekbinders*, Utrecht, 1921, pl. I, 4, 8 pl. III, 3, 10, 11. G. H. M. Delprat, *Verhandeling over de Broederschap van G. Groote*, Arnhem, 1856, pp. 151–2.
12. W. H. J. Weale, *Bookbindings and rubbings of bindings in the National Art Library, South Kensington Museum*, London, 1898–94, vol. ii, R.320 (quoted as 'Weale').
13. A letter from P. Verheyden dated 18 June 1932. Royal Library Brussels, MS 2740. Acquoy, *op. cit.*, vol. iii, pp. 30–33.
14. E. P. Goldschmidt, *Gothic and Renaissance bookbindings*, London, 1928, no. 63, pl. XXVI (exhibited at the *Wereldtentoonstelling voor koloniën, zeevaart en oud-vlaamsche kunst*, dl. v: *Boekbanden*, Antwerp, 1930, no. 12 (quoted as 'Antwerp 1930'). Acquoy, *op. cit.*, vol. iii, pp. 219–23.
15. Goldschmidt, *op. cit.*, no. 87, pl. CV. Acquoy, *op. cit.*, vol. iii, p. 14. For other bindings from this monastery see—among others—Weale, R.339; Antwerp 1930, nos. 215–20; P. Verheyden, 'La Reliure Flamande', *Trésors de l'art Flamand. Mémorial de l'exposition d'art Flamand ancien à Anvers*, vol. ii, Paris, 1932, pl. C, 181 (quoted as 'Trésors'); P. Verheyden, 'La Reliure

en Brabant', *Mémorial de l'exposition d'art ancien à Bruxelles*, Brussels, 1935, pl. IV-V.

16. Acquoy, *op. cit.*, vol. III, pp. 16–18.
17. W. H. J. Weale and L. Taylor, *Early stamped bookbindings in the British Museum*, London, 1922, no. 142, pl. XI, 3.
18. P. Verheyden, art. cit. (*Mémorial . . . Bruxelles*, 1935), pl. III, (2). A fifth example with a Rooklooster provenance, BL, IB. 49520 (BMC IX, 174) has been rebound.
19. Acquoy, *op. cit.*, vol. III, pp. 56–9. Vicomte de Ghellinck Vaernewijck, 'La Reliure Flamande au XVe siècle', *Annales de l'Académie Royale d'Archéologie de Belgique*, Antwerp, 1901–2, pp. 405–6. See also: Antwerp 1930, nos. 203–3; *Gothieke en Renaissance boekbanden . . . tentoongesteld in het Museum Plantin-Moretus*, Antwerp, 1938, no. 8 (quoted as 'Plantin-Moretus 1938').
20. Possibly: G. D. Hobson, *Bindings in Cambridge Libraries*, Cambridge, 1929, p. 34, list no. III.
21. Römer, *op. cit.*, vol. I, pp. 522–3. P. Verheyden, art. cit. (*Het Boek*, 1952–4), p. 200.
22. Weale, R.389. Van Heussen, *op. cit.*, p. 217.
23. Delprat, *op. cit.*, pp. 131–6. Acquoy, *op. cit.*, vol. II, pp. 135–6.
24. Römer, *op. cit*, vol. I, pp. 70–75.
25. F. B. Gramaye, *Taxandria*, Brussels, 1610, p. 142. Römer, *op. cit.*, vol. I, p. 411.
26. P. Verheyden, 'Boekbanden uit 's-Hertogenbosch', *Het Boek*, XXI (1933), pp. 209–39, pl. 7, 8, 12. Delprat, *op. cit.*, pp. 126–31.
27. P. Verheyden, art. cit. (*Het Boek*, 1933), pp. 236, 238.
28. P. Verheyden, 'De paneelstempel Onze-Lieve-Vrouw-ten-Troon', *De Gulden Passer*, XXIV (1946), p. 30, pl. 5.
29. Weale, R.365, vol. I, p. lxi.
30. Weale, R.337, vol. I, p. lxv. Weale-Taylor, *op. cit.*, nos. 57–8. J. Brassinne, *La Reliure Mosane*, Liège, 1912, 32, vol. II, pl. CVII, CVIII.
31. Rebound in the nineteenth century, but with one original cover retained. Weale-Taylor, *op. cit.*, no. 373. Brassinne, *op. cit.*, vol. II. pl. XCVII, see also pl. XCVI, vol. I, pp. 19–21, pl. XXI; P. Verheyden, 'Boekbanden uit Maastricht', *Het Boek*, XXII (1933–4), p. 137, pl. II, pp. 169–72; Le Vicomte de Jonghe d'Ardoyne (*et al.*), *Armorial Belge du Bibliophile*, Brussels, 1930, p. 405.
32. Hulshof and Schretlen, *op. cit.*, pl. VIII, 3.
33. Weale, R.288,379. P. Verheyden, art. cit. (*Het Boek*, 1933–4), p. 137, pl. 5, see also pp. 152–6, pl. 6.
34. Hulshof and Schretlen, *op. cit.*, pl. VIII, 13, 11, 7, but not 14, 15. Brassinne, *op. cit.*, vol. II, pl. CIX.
35. Weale-Taylor, *op. cit.*, no. 262. Brassinne, *op. cit.*, vol. II, pl. LXXXIX.
36. Weale, R.357. Weale-Taylor, *op. cit.*, no. 268. Brassinne, *op. cit.*, vol. I, p. 14, vol. II. pl. LXXXIII, see also vol. I, pl. II-V, vol. II, pl. LXXIX, LXXX; Goldschmidt, *op. cit.*, no. 90, pl. XXXVIII.
37. Weale, R.311, see also vol. I, p. liv. vol. II, R. 310–13; Vicomte de Ghellinck Vaernewijck, art. cit., pp. 412–13; L. Gruel, *Manuel historique et bibliographique de l'amateur de reliures*, Paris, 1887–1905, vol. II, pp. 85–7, pl. opp. p. 86; Antwerp 1930, no. 168. P. Verheyden, 'De paneelstempel van Wouter van Duffel', *De Gulden Passer*, XV (1937), p. 19; Plantin-Moretus 1938,

no. 18; L. Indestege, 'Schmuckformen auf flämischen Einbände', *Gutenberg-Jahrbuch* (1958), p. 275.

38. L. Indestege, art. cit. (*Gutenberg-Jahrbuch*, 1958), p. 275; Id., 'New light on Ludovicus Ravescot', *Quaerendo*, 1 (1971), p. 17.

39. Weale, R. 312. P. Verheyden, 'De boerendans op Vlaamsche Boekbanden', *De Gulden Passer*, xx (1942), p. 221, pl. 4.

40. P. Verheyden, art. cit. (*Gulden Passer*, 1942), pp. 209–37. See also Weale, R. 419–20; P. Verheyden, 'Banden met blinddruk bewaard in het museum Plantin-Moretus', *Tijdschrift voor boek- en bibliotheekwezen* IV (1906), pp. 34 (pl. 4), 36 (pl. 5); Antwerp 1930, nos. 238, 243, 250, 251; Plantin-Moretus 1938, nos. 28–30, 38; *Boekbanden uit vijf eeuwen. Catalogus*, Ghent, 1961, nos. 33 (pl. IX), 40 (pl. XII) (quoted as 'Ghent 1961'). For another English variant see J. B. Oldham, *English blind-stamped bindings*, Cambridge, 1952, pl. XXVIII, XXXVI.

41. Weale, R.376, Vicomte de Ghellinck Vaernewijck, art. cit., p. 412. P. Verheyden, art. cit. (*Gulden Passer*, 1942), p. 223, see also pl. 6. See also Goldschmidt, *op. cit.*, no. 107, pl. XLII (Antwerp 1930, no. 169); L. Indestege, 'De Boekband in de Zuiderlijke Nederlanden tijdens de 16e eeuw', *De Gulden Passer*, XXXIV (1956), pl. 1 (opp. p. 48); L. Indestege, art. cit., (*Gutenberg-Jahrbuch*, 1958), p. 275.

42. Gruel, *op. cit.*, vol. II, pp. 89–90. P. Verheyden, art. cit. (*Gulden Passer*, 1937), p. 19.

43. Weale, R.308–9, see also vol. I, pp. liv-v.

44. S. Gibson. *Some notable Bodleian bindings*, Oxford, 1901–4, pl. 14. See also L. Indestege, art. cit. (*Gutenberg-Jahrbuch*, 1958), p. 273, pl. 1.

45. Goldschmidt, *op. cit.*, no. 120.

46. P. Verheyden, art. cit. (*Gulden Passer*, 1937), pp. 1–36.

47. P. Needham, *Twelve centuries of bookbindings*, New York, 1979, no. 25, n. 9, to whom I owe this clinching argument confirming a hitherto unsubstantiated suspicion.

48. Hobson, *op. cit.*, pl. X, p. 28, list, no. 1.

49. Ibid., list, no. III.

50. Ibid, list, no. VII. Nixon, *op. cit.*, no. 12. The fleur-de-lis (b) is different and the dragon tool (2) on this binding is the same as that on Ghent 1961, pl. XL, 14 and on no. 20 (pl. VII). This binding has yet another fleur-de-lis tool (c) and a different briquet. The fleur-de-lis is the same as that on a Bruges MS. Raoul Le Fèvre [*c.* 1470], sold at Sotheby's, 13.7.1977, 60, which has a dragon (3) that is also found on a Cologne *De pollutionibus nocturnis* by Johannes Gerson (BL, IA. 2728, BMC I, 180–1; Weale-Taylor, *op. cit.*, no. 73), with yet another fleur-de-lis tool (d).

51. Hobson, *op. cit.*, pl. X.

52. Ibid., list, no. IV. Weale-Taylor, *op. cit.*, no. 160, pl. XII, 4–6.

53. Very closely similar to and possibly identical with that on Hulshof and Schretlen, *op. cit.*, pl. IX, 14.

54. Hobson, *op. cit.*, p. 29, list no. VIII (Hobson suggests the tools are the same).

55. Hulshof and Schretlen, *op. cit.*, p. 15, pl. IX, 13,15, with yet another fleur-de-lis (f).

56. Goldschmidt, *op. cit.*, nos. 25–6, pl. XII, CI. Hobson, *op. cit.*, pl. XII. R. Juchhoff, 'Johann Veldener in Löwen als Buchdrucker und Buchbinder', *Gutenberg-Jahrbuch*, 1933, pp. 43–8. L. Indestege, art. cit. (*Gulden Passer*,

1956), p. 49. L. and W. Hellinga, *op. cit.*, vol. I, pp. 62–3. L. Indestege, art. cit. (*Quaerendo*, 1971), pp. 16–18.

57. G. H. Bushnell, 'Portrait of a Bibliophile IV, William Schevez, Archbishop of St Andrews, d. 1497', *The Book Collector*, IX (1960), pp. 19–29.

58. See the angle of the pelican's right wing and the inclination of her head; see also the tufts of hair on the heads of the eagle and the position of its claws in relation to its wings. The double-headed eagle, the pelican and the garden tool look very closely similar to those attributed to Maastricht by Hulshof and Schretlen, *op. cit.*, pl. VI, 12, 14, 16.

59. Hobson, *op. cit.*, p. 34, list. no. VII.

60. Goldschmidt, *op. cit.*, no. 26. M. M. Foot, *The Henry Davis Gift*, vol. 2, London, 1983, no. 287.

61. Possibly Hobson, *op. cit.*, p. 34, list no. III. This binding was once in the possession of the Bethleem monastery near Louvain. For other Ravescot bindings see, among others, Weale, R.356; P. Verheyden, art. cit. (*Mémorial . . . Bruxelles*, 1935), pl. XI; Plantin-Moretus 1938, nos 5–6; Maggs Bros., Cat. 890 (1964), pl. XXXII.

62. Weale, R.325. Sir S. Gaselee, *A list of early printed books*, Cambridge, 1920, no. 207. M. E. Kronenberg, 'Catalogus van vroege drukken, in het bezit van Stephen Gaselee', *Het Boek*, x (1921), pl. opp. p. 74, p. 76.

63. P. Verheyden, art. cit. (*Tijdschrift voor boek- en bibliotheekwezen*, 1906), pp. 54–5, 77. P. Verheyden, 'De vijftiende-eeuwse boekbinder(s) Jan van Wouw te Antwerpen', *Baekelmans ter eere* (Antwerp, 1945), pp. 95–106. L. Indestege, art. cit. (*Gulden Passer*, 1956), pp. 50–51.

64. Goldschmidt, *op. cit.*, no. 119, pl. XLVII (Antwerp 1930, no. 23). P. Verheyden, art. cit. (*Baekelmans ter eere*, 1945), p. 98. L. Indestege, 'Een onbekend paneelstempel van de Antwerpse binder Jan van Wouw', *De Gulden Passer*, XXXV (1957), pp. 121–2, No. II. See also Gruel, *op. cit.*, vol. II, p. 173; P. Verheyden, 'Boekbanden met blinddruk . . . te Mechelen', *Bulletin du cercle archéologique, littéraire et artistique de Malines*, XV (1905), p. 259.

65. Weale, R.381, 382, vol. I, p. lx. Goldschmidt, *op. cit.*, no. 70 (Antwerp 1930, no. 141, Plantin-Moretus 1938, no. 20). M. M. Foot, *op. cit.*, no. 289.

66. Weale, R. 410. P. Bergmans, 'Reliures de Jan Tijs', *Inventaire archéologique de Gand* (1903), p. 313. Gruel, *op. cit.*, vol. II, p. 157. P. Verheyden, 'De Boekbinder Jan Tijs te Mechelen', *Bulletin du cercle archéologique, littéraire et artistique de Malines*, XXII (1912), pp. 114–23, pl. 1. *Trésors*, pl. XCIX, 178. Antwerp 1930, no. 130. Ghent 1961, nos. 136–7, pl. XX. See also: P. Verheyden, 'Nog een band van Jan Tijs', *Mechlinia* (November 1921), pp. 97–100. L. Indestege, art. cit. (*Gulden Passer*, 1956), p. 51. L. Indestege, art. cit. (*Gutenberg-Jahrbuch*, 1958), p. 281.

67. Hulshof and Schretlen, *op. cit.*, pl. IV, 4, 5, 7, 13, 15. M. M. Foot, *op. cit.*, no. 288.

68. G. Caullet, 'Le Relieur au monogramme I.R.: Jan Ryckaert, de Gand', in: *Revue des bibliothèques et archives de Belgique* (1906), pp. 162–75. Hulshof and Schretlen, *op. cit.*, pl. IX, 1–6. M. E. Kronenberg, 'Vervolging van kettersche boeken in de Nederlanden', *Het Boek*, XVI (1927), p. 169. Goldschmidt, *op. cit.* nos. 142–5, pl. LIV, CVI. Antwerp 1930, nos. 152–5. Plantin-Moretus 1938, nos. 25–6. M. Jaarsma, *Het schoone boek*, Bussum, 1950, pl. 6. Ghent 1961, p. 43, nos. 70–81, pl. XVII. See also below n. 69–71. M. M. Foot, *op. cit.*, 291, 292.

69. Goldschmidt, *op. cit.*, no. 145, pl. LIV.
70. Weale, R.363.
71. Weale, R.364.

13 Influences from the Netherlands on Bookbinding in England during the late fifteenth and early sixteenth centuries

(1979)*

If one compares bookbindings made in the Low Countries at the end of the fifteenth century and during the beginning of the sixteenth with those made in England during the same period, similarities—especially in binding and tool design—are obvious. A few binders who worked in England used binding techniques that owe more to Continental than to English habits. Low-Country influence on the decorative aspects of English bookbinding is more obvious, and the reason for this influence can be found in the development of the booktrade.

During the fourteenth and early fifteenth centuries the booktrade on the whole was far from vigorous. This seems particularly to have been the case in England, but also on the Continent, until the monastic revival in Italy and Germany early in the fifteenth century, and especially the foundation of the Windesheim Congregation in Holland at the end of the fourteenth century, contributed to the revival of learning and of book production. The invention of printing gave another boost to the booktrade, and in its wake came an increase in output of decorated leather bindings.

In England there was still no brisk trade in books. In his Sandars Lectures, delivered at Cambridge in 1959,[1] Graham Pollard characterized the English booktrade during the second half of the fifteenth century as a 'bespoke trade'. For practically any book that was wanted, a text might have to be found and would then have to be copied and bound. The stationers carried little stock, and that mainly limited to second-hand books, school books and service books.

Demand exceeded supply and gradually more and more printed books were imported from abroad. Already in the 1460s there are isolated examples of printed books being imported into England; these imports increased during the 1470s.[2] Caxton's *Recuyell of the Histories of Troy*,

* *Actes du XIe Congrès International de Bibliophilie*, Brussels, 1979, pp. 39–64.

printed in Bruges at the end of 1473 or during the first months of 1474, may have been meant for the English market as well as for the English retinue at the court of Margaret, Duchess of Burgundy, and the English colony of merchants there.[3] The *Sarum Breviary*, printed in the southern Netherlands *c.* 1475 was definitely meant for sale in England.

At the end of 1477 printed books were classed as general merchandise for purposes of duty (no duty had been payable on the import of manuscripts). By 1479/80 England had been discovered as a potential market for printed books and a brisk trade developed.

Several scholars from Plomer onwards[4] have studied the customs rolls of the Port of London from which it is abundantly clear that a great many printed books were imported. For example, during 1480 over 1200 volumes are mentioned. The earliest consignments came from Germany, the Low Countries and Italy (in English, Flemish, Dutch and occasionally Venetian ships); the rolls show that from 1490/91 imports from France also became more numerous.

Initially these imports were encouraged. When in January 1484 an act was passed to regulate and restrict the conditions under which foreigners could carry on business or trade in England, a proviso was added to the effect that

> this act or any parcel thereof . . . shall not extend, or be in prejudice, disturbance, damage or impediment to any artificer or merchant stranger, of what nation or country he be, or shall be of, for bringing into this realm, or selling by retail or otherwise, any books written or printed, or for inhabiting within this said realm for the same intent, or any scrivener, alluminor, binder or printer of such books, which he hath or shall have to sell by way of merchandise, or for their dwelling within this said realm for the exercise of the said occupations. . . . [5]

It is clear from this proviso that not only the import of books was exempted from the usual restrictions, but the immigration of stationers from abroad was welcomed.

This was exactly what was happening. As well as the many imported service books, classical texts, non-English literature and books printed abroad for the English market, printers, publishers, booksellers and bookbinders came to England, establishing themselves mainly in London, Oxford and Cambridge. In London only the freemen were allowed to keep open shop within the walls and to sell by retail. Aliens had to sell their books wholesale or establish a shop in one of the liberties, or do the round of the country fairs. There is evidence that books were sold at country fairs, and that they were sold bound.

If one takes into account the weight of a bound book (bound in wooden boards) and remembers that in certain cases books were imported on a basis of sale or return—and what sensible businessman would go to the expense of having a book bound that he was not sure of selling?—it seems most probable that as a rule books were imported in sheets. The fact that they were shipped in tuns or barrels confirms this. However, chests, boxes and baskets of books are also mentioned, and a number of books must have come in bound, otherwise there would have been no need to forbid the import of foreign-bound books in 1534. From the existence of a substantial number of foreign-printed books in early English bindings, it seems that these books sold well and were bound fairly soon after their arrival, probably on the instigation of the retail bookseller.

It has been the more or less accepted view regarding the elaborately decorated bindings of the later sixteenth and seventeenth centuries that the buyer, especially if he was a collector of taste, would buy a book in sheets and have it bound to order by one of the fashionable binders of the time. There is certainly a fair amount of evidence that this was indeed the case.

In the late fifteenth century and during the beginning of the sixteenth, it seems as if the big stationers were instrumental in getting the books they sold bound, either by their own bindery on the premises or by a craftsman nearby. The sheer size of the output of such 'binders' (or rather stationers) as John Reynes, Garrett Godfrey and Nicholas Spierinck suggests that they did not bind themselves, but either employed a number of men on the premises or used a bindery elsewhere which they issued with their signed panels and rolls to be used on the bindings of the books they published and/or sold. The same pattern can be seen earlier with books published by Caxton at Westminster and those associated with Theodoric Rood and Thomas Hunt at Oxford. In both cases *one* binder seems to have been most frequently employed and, in Caxton's case, had access to the printer's waste.

At the same time there were also a number of small binderies at work in London, Oxford and Cambridge, but there is as yet too little evidence to determine whether they worked for the publishers or mainly for individual clients.

For the first 40 years after the introduction of printing into England, the booktrade seems by and large to have been in the hands of foreigners. Among the names of those who imported books on any scale in addition to Caxton are Henry Frankenberg, who lived in London at least by 1482, and his partner Bernard van Stondo; Peter Actors, who came from Savoy and was appointed royal stationer in 1485; Martinus in't Hoffe, merchant of Cologne; Andreas Stork; Andreas Ruwe, a native of Frankfurt, and 'Johannis de Aquisgrano', Jan van Aken, who was shown by Juchhoff[6] to be the same man as the Louvain printer John of Westfalia. He and Peter Actors called on Thomas Hunt of Oxford in 1483 and arranged for him to take a consignment of books on the basis of sale or return. I will come back to this agreement in a moment and show how a distinct Louvain influence can be discerned in the design of the tools used by the binder who worked for Thomas Hunt and Theodoric Rood.

Among the early sixteenth-century importers were Frederick Egmont, a stationer from the Netherlands who worked first in London and from 1502 in Paris; Francis Birckman, who had come from Cologne; John Bienayse, a Paris and Rouen bookseller; Wynkyn de Worde, a native of Alsace who worked with and later succeeded Caxton; William Facques; Joyce Pilgrim; Michael Morin, who came from Paris, and Nicholas Speryng or Spierinck who probably came from Antwerp but had settled in Cambridge before 1514. In 1485 Peter Actors was appointed stationer to King Henry VII and was given 'license to import, so often as he likes, from parts beyond the sea, books printed and not printed into the port of the city of London, and other ports and places within the kingdom of England, and to dispose of the same by sale or otherwise without paying customs etc. thereon and without rendering any accompt thereof'.[7] Two foreigners succeeded him: William Facques, a Norman who assumed the title of Printer to the King in 1503; and Richard Pynson, also a Norman by birth, in 1508.

By the turn of the century the established printers and stationers, whether natives or denizens, began seriously to feel foreign competition. The Stationers' Company, which had existed since 1403, bestirred itself and there were endless riots and disorders arising out of troubles between the established stationers, concentrated in London, and foreign competitors. Actions brought in the Star Chamber bear witness to the frequent attacks by native workmen on foreigners, such as an action brought by Pynson and others against Henry Squire and his companions in 1500. The position of aliens was far from easy. They paid high taxes, could not hold land, were not allowed to keep foreign apprentices or employ foreign workmen and suffered from various other disadvantages. Their position could be improved and secured either by naturalization, for which an act of Parliament was needed, or by denization. Once naturalized a foreigner obtained all rights and privileges of a native Englishman. As a denizen he obtained the privilege of living and trading like a native, but he remained subject to heavy taxes levied on aliens and he was seriously handicapped in inheriting or bequeathing real property.[8] Since freedom of the City was a jealously guarded privilege and by no means easy to obtain, strangers and denizens settled in the liberties, such as St Martin's le Grand, Blackfriars, Southwark and Westminster. St Paul's Churchyard, though not a liberty, seems to have become the great resort of the stationers.

While the going was still good for the stationers, and while both the importation of books and the immigration of foreign stationers were tolerated and even encouraged during the last three decades of the fifteenth and the first two of the sixteenth centuries, aliens dominated the English booktrade.

A fair amount of work has been done on foreign printers and booksellers who lived and worked in England. E. Gordon Duff,[9] G. D. Hobson[10] and J. B. Oldham[11] among others have studied the work of the immigrant binders, although they largely limited themselves to the owners of panels and rolls. According to J. B. Oldham most panels used in England were imported from abroad, the majority from the Netherlands; importation of rolls and stamps was less common. There is a certain amount of evidence to suggest the importation of panels from the Netherlands, and an even larger amount of material to show the influence of Netherlandish design on English panels. I think Oldham is right in believing that the majority of the small hand tools and rolls used in England were cut here, but there is again sufficient evidence, at least for a substantial number of stamps, of strong Low-Country influence on the design of the tools as well as on the design of the bindings.

Both Hobson and Oldham did a great deal of work on the panels that were used in England and there is no need to repeat that here. The small hand tools that were used by a number of binders who worked in London, Oxford and Cambridge have been less frequently discussed. That some of these binders came from the Low Countries or were at least influenced by Netherlandish examples is noticeable not only from the design of their bindings and their tools, but from the way they treated their boards, headbands and clasps and from the way they used their tools. Plaited headbands such as occur on bindings from the Low Countries were unusual in England. The Greyhound binder, who possibly worked in Oxford or London in the 1490s, occasionally used them, and pink plaited headbands are found on bindings by the Lily binder. This last binder who was active in the 1480s till at least 1504 also used sharply bevelled boards, not at all common in England but a known feature on Netherlandish bindings. He also put metal shoes on the edges of the boards, again a habit more common in the Low Countries than in England, and he even occasionally broke J. B. Oldham's strictest rule by putting his clasps on his bindings with the hinges on the lower cover. Three binders who occasionally put tools on the spines of their bindings, a German rather than an English habit, are the Unicorn binder who worked in Cambridge c. 1478–1507, the Indulgence binder (c. 1475–1482) and the Fruit and Flower binder who worked in Oxford c. 1491–1512. Several German and Flemish binders were in the habit of putting a square stamp in sideways. The characteristic Lion-of-St Mark stamp, used on Rooklooster bindings, is often found that way up, and three English binders—the man who worked for Caxton, the Antwerp binder (1477–98) and the London Scales binder (1450s–after 1481) occasionally did the same.

Two binding designs were widely used both in the Netherlands and in England, that which shows a frame of intersecting fillets around diagonal fillets forming diamonds and triangles with a stamp in each, and that of a frame of intersecting fillets around a diamond and a saltire. The design that used small square stamps in rows in the centre is also found on both sides of the sea, but perhaps less frequently.

There is a remarkably close connection in the design of many of the small hand tools used in the Netherlands and in England. Caxton's binder is a good example. H. M. Nixon has convincingly shown[12] that the binder who worked both for Caxton and for Wynkyn de Worde, though he worked in different styles, was one man. Two of his designs in particular, Nixon's types A and B, show Low Country influence, but his dragons in triangles and his two fleur-de-lis tools especially look straightforward copies of Netherlandish examples. They are indeed so close that they led Graham Pollard to believe them to be identical with those used on two Flemish manuscripts at the Bodleian Library.[13] Close inspection reveals small differences. Figure 13.1 shows a selection of mainly Bruges dragons and fleur-de-lis. The top two (1 and a) were used by Jean Guilebert 'die men heet meese' of Bruges (1469–89) on two bindings. One, on Johannes Gerson's *Opuscula*, Brussels, 1475 (Bodley, Auct. I. Q.III. 14), is signed on the paste-down of the lower cover 'Johannes meese [me] ligavit'; the other covers Laurentius Valla, *Elegantiae*, Louvain, n.d. (CUL, 3694).[14] Dragon number 2 and fleur-de-lis b occur on a manuscript *Missale ad usum . . . Tornacensis* in the Broxbourne Library, now at the Bodleian Library (1105), and dragon 2 and fleur-de-lis c are found together on a fifteenth-century manuscript life of St Coleta in Dutch that was exhibited in Ghent in 1961.[15] Fleur-de-lis c also occurs on a Bruges manuscript of Raoul le Fèvre's *Recueil des histoires de Troie* of *c.* 1470 (sold at Sotheby's, 13.VII.1977,60) in combination with dragon 3, and on a volume of moral and religious treatises in French (Bodley, Ms. Douce 365), written by David Aubert in 1475 and bought by Margaret of York, Duchess of Burgundy, together with dragon 5. Dragon 3 also occurs, together with fleur-de-lis d, on J. Gerson's *De pollutionibus nocturnis*, Cologne, n.d. (BL, IA.2728). Guilebert's fleur-de-lis a is found on Josephus, *Antiquitates Judaeorum*, n.p.n.d. at Queens' College Cambridge, together with dragon number 4. This same dragon also ornaments a 1477 Nuremberg Bible in the British Library (IC.7159), there accompanied by fleur-de-lis e. Dragon 5, who turns up on the moral treatises for Margaret of York, is closest to the one used by Caxton's binder (C).[16] He can also be seen on a binding at the university library at Utrecht[17] together with fleur-de-lis f. The last two, dragon 6 and fleur-de-lis g, occur on a 1480 Gouda St Jerome, *Vanden leven der heiligher vaderen* in the Broxbourne Library (R102). Caxton's binder's fleur-de-lis (C)[18] is closest to fleurs-de-lis c, f and g.

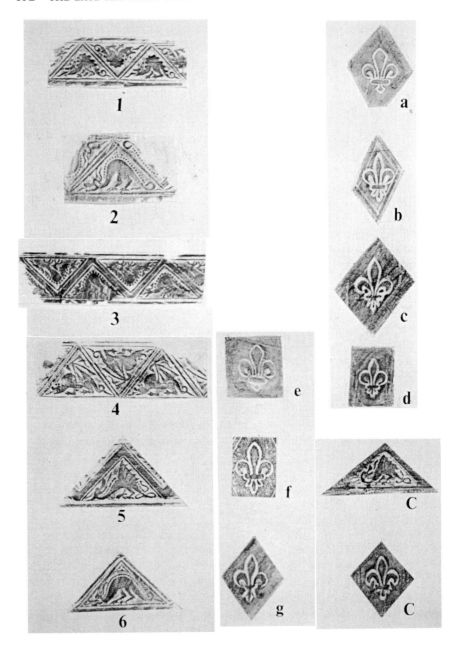

Fig. 13.1 Rubbings of some similiar dragon and fleur-de-lis tools used in the Netherlands (1–6, a-g) and by Caxton's binder (C)

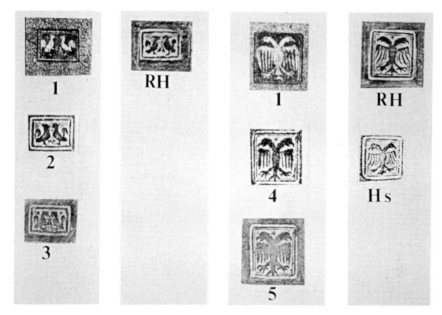

Fig. 13.2   Rubbings of some similar fighting cocks and square eagle
tools used in the Netherlands (1–5) and in England (RH,
Hs)

I mentioned earlier the agreement between John of Westfalia, who was
in partnership with Peter Actors, and Thomas Hunt of Oxford by which
the latter took a consignment of books on the basis of sale or return. Dr
D. E. Rhodes has shown[19] that books from John of Westfalia's press sold
well in Oxford. Several of these were bound there at the time by the
binder who worked for Theodoric Rood and Thomas Hunt, identified by
Graham Pollard as Nicholas Bokebynder.[20]

The bindings by this 'Rood-and-Hunt' binder are all decorated to a
typical Oxford design of horizontal rows of small pictorial stamps, several
of which have close counterparts in the Netherlands and especially in
Louvain in the tools used by Ludovicus Ravescot, an illuminator, printer
and bookbinder who worked there from c. 1473 until after 1501 and who
is known to have bound for John of Westfalia. Another Louvain printer
and publisher, Johan Veldener, employed at least once[21] a binder who
used tools closely similar in design to those used by Ravescot and by the
Rood-and-Hunt binder.

The pair of little cocks in Fig 13.2 (RH) is the tool the Rood-and-Hunt
binder used, while cocks tool no. 1 was used on the binding for Veldener.
Cocks tool no. 2 turns up in Utrecht while no. 3 comes from a Brussels
Joannes de Turrecremata, *Tractatus contra principales errores perfidi macho-*

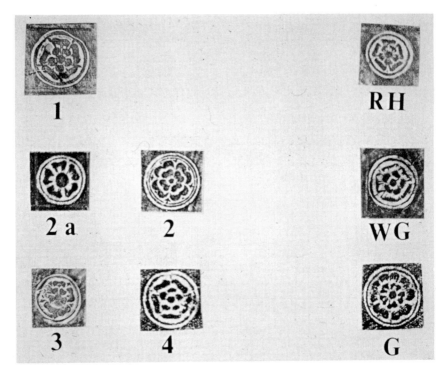

Fig. 13.3   Rubbings of some similar round rose tools used in the
Netherlands (1–4) and in England (RH, WG, G)

meti et turcorum, n.d. (BL, IB.49502) with an early Brussels provenance.
The double-headed eagle in the top right (RH) was used by the Rood-
and-Hunt binder; eagle 1 belonged to Veldener's binder; eagle 4 comes
from Maastricht and eagle 5 belonged to Ravescot.

Another English binder, the s.c. Half-stamp binder who worked in
Oxford between 1491 and ?1511, owned a similar but smaller eagle tool
(Hs) as well as two more tools, a pelican and a lamb-and-flag (Fig 13.5),
which also have Netherlandish counterparts. The Cambridge Demon
binder (1473–97), whom we will meet again, also possessed a similar eagle
tool.[22]

A round rose tool used by the Rood-and-Hunt binder (Fig. 13.3) shows
a strong resemblance with that used by Ravescot (1). Two Utrecht
examples (2a, 2), one of which occurs on a binding made for the Hieronymushuis (2a) and one that may have been used by the Brothers of the
Common Life at 's-Hertogenbosch (3), together with an example from
Maastricht (4) show that this was a far from uncommon tool in the
Netherlands. There are many English variants, two of which are shown

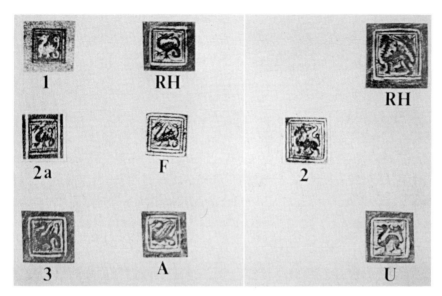

Fig. 13.4   Rubbings of some similar monster tools used in the
Netherlands (1–3) and in England (RH, F, A, U)

here; one turns up on bindings made in Cambridge by WG (1478–1507),
the other on bindings made in London by the Greyhound binder (G).

Two more Rood-and-Hunt tools (RH), a monster biting its curled tail
and a large monster vaguely related to the dromedary, have Netherlandish
models, though perhaps less close ones (Fig. 13.4). Monster 1 again belongs
to Veldener's binder; 2a occurs on a binding made for the Hieronymushuis
and 3 comes from the Brussels Turrecremata. Other English binders who
owned similar curly-tailed monsters, even closer to the Netherlandish
versions in fact than the Rood-and-Hunt tool, are the Fishtail binder (F),
who worked in Oxford between c. 1473 and c. 1500, and the Antwerp
binder (A), who often used a tool depicting the arms of Antwerp, probably
came from that town and worked in England from c. 1477 to 1498. As
well as the Rood-and-Hunt binder, the Cambridge Unicorn binder (U)
owned a dromedary-type monster, while a smaller version was used in
Utrecht (2).

Two different sets of tools (Fig. 13.5) show, if not a close copying of
stamps used in both countries, at least a close relationship in their design.
On the left are Veldener's binder's tool of a pelican in her piety (1),
closely similar to one used by Ravescot (5), a Maastricht example (4), and
one belonging to a Utrecht binder (2a) who seems to have worked both
for the Hieronymushuis and for the Canons Regular of St Augustine
there.[23] Three English binders used a similar design but on a round instead

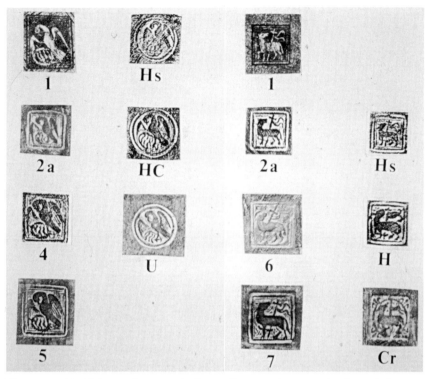

Fig. 13.5   Rubbings of some similar pelican and square lamb-and-flag
tools used in the Netherlands (1–7) and in England, Hs,
HC, U, H, Cr)

of a square tool: the Half-stamp binder (Hs); Henry Cony (HC), a
London binder who was active from *c.* 1490 until after 1503; and the
Unicorn binder (U).

On the right are a lamb-and-flag tool used by Veldener's binder (1),
one from a Utrecht binding made for the Hieronymushuis (2a), one on a
Deventer Johannes de Sancto Geminiano, *Liber de exemplis* (CUL, 3433)
with a Malines provenance (6), and one on a Dutch Bible in two volumes
written between 1460 and 1462 and bound for the nuns of the convent St
Katherinedael at Hasselt (BL, Add. MSS 15310–1) (7). The English variants
were used by the Half-stamp binder (Hs), the Heavy binder (H), who
worked in Cambridge between 1485 and 1505 and who is one of the two
contenders for the name of Walter Hatley[24]—the other claimant being the
Unicorn binder—and the Crucifer binder (Cr) whom I suspect of having
been, or at least of having worked for, Richard Pynson.[25]

Smaller and more purely decorative tools tend to occur in a variety of
places, are easy to copy and therefore seem to be less conclusive (Fig.

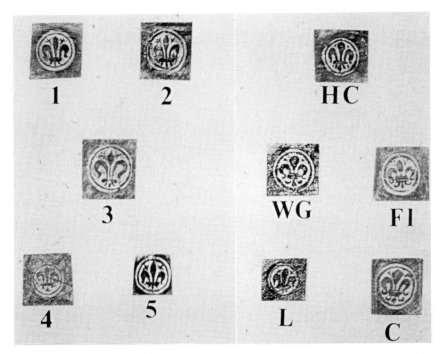

Fig. 13.6   Rubbings of some similar round fleur-de-lis tools used in the Netherlands (1–5) and in England (HC, WG, Fl, L, C)

13.6). The fleur-de-lis is a very common motif and not only on bookbindings, but the small round fleur-de-lis tool with two 'stamina' is quite distinctive and can again be found both in the Netherlands and in England. The Netherlandish examples were used on the Brussels Turrecremata (1), on bindings made for or by the Brothers of the Common Life at 's Hertogenbosch (2), on the binding of a Deventer edition of Filelfo's *Epistolae familiares* (CUL, 3525) (3), on that of a Dutch psalter, Delft, 1480 (Bodley, Auct. M. inf. 1.9) (4), while fleur-de-lis 5 was used in Maastricht. The English tools (on the right) belonged to Henry Cony (HC), to WG (this tool looks like a very close copy of that used on a Louvain binding at the Bodleian that was alas too worn to rub),[26] to the Oxford Floral binder (Fl) (*c.* 1476–96), to Caxton's binder (C) and to the Lily binder (L) on whose Netherlandish binding habits I have already commented.

The Lily binder also owned a fleuron, shown at the bottom of the righthand group in Fig. 13.7, similar to one found on the binding of a 1484 Louvain Hugo de Prato Florido, *Sermones dominicales* (CUL, 3778) that belonged to the monastery Nazareth at Waalwijck (5). Another similar fleuron comes from Maastricht (4), and a different, slightly spikier kind

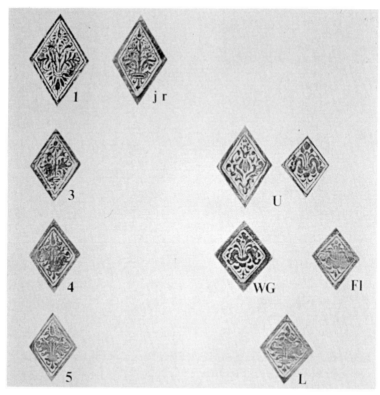

Fig. 13.7   Rubbings of some similar fleuron tools used in the
Netherlands (1–5, jr) and in England (U, WG, Fl, L)

(3) occurs on a sixteenth-century Dutch manuscript *Devote oefening der
heilige sacrament weerdelick te ontfangen* in the Broxbourne library (802);
another taller one (1) comes from Utrecht and may have belonged to
Dirck Claesz Roest, and one (jr) was used by Jan Ryckaert of Ghent (*c.*
1511–1546). The other English versions were used by the Unicorn binder
(U), by WG and by the Floral binder (Fl).

A very common English early-sixteenth-century tool is the so-called
pineapple (Fig. 13.8). J. B. Oldham gives 20 close variants, four of which
are shown here. The top one on the right hand side (JR) belonged to
John Reynes; Ai was used in London on books printed between 1482 and
1520; B9 was used *c.* 1530–32 and A8 occurred *c.* 1510.

However English these tools may seem to any admirer of Oldham, a
number of closely similar ones were used in the Netherlands. Pineapple
1 comes from Maastricht, 2 decorates a binding made for the Croziers
there, and 3 was used in Utrecht. Other examples were found on a
manuscript Missal (BL, Add. MS 24075) that belonged to the monastery

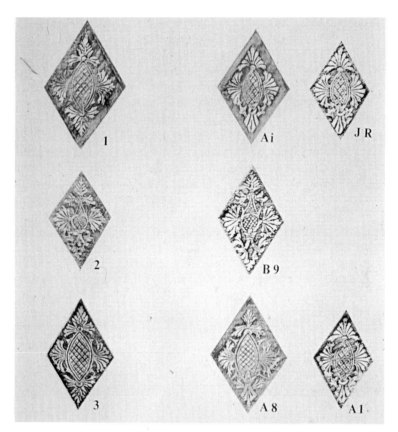

Fig. 13.8   Rubbings of some similar pineapple tools used in the
Netherlands (1–3) and in England (JR, Ai, B9, A8)

of St Adrian near Audenaerde, on a 1475 Louvain J. N. de Milis, *Repertorium juris* (CUL, 3700), and a slightly freer version occurs on a 1490 Alost
edition of Angelus de Clavasio's *Summa de casibus conscientiae* in the
British Library (IB. 49026) which has the arms of Antwerp on the binding.
In most cases the Netherlandish examples seem to be the earlier ones.

I would like to draw a few tentative conclusions, based on the way
these binders worked, on their designs and on the designs of their tools,
and backed by the many instances when named binders from the Low
Countries are known to have come to England and to have worked there.

A case could be made for the Caxton binder being an immigrant from
Bruges and for the Rood-and-Hunt binder having come from Louvain. It
is also possible that Caxton, having himself been familiar with Low-
Country bindings, explained their designs and their tools to a craftsman
at Westminster, and that John of Westfalia produced Louvain samples for

the Rood-and-Hunt binder, who adopted the design of the tools but preferred the Oxford manner of arranging them in horizontal rows.

The Lily binder was almost certainly an immigrant from the Netherlands and the Antwerp binder most probably came from Flanders. There is also a possible case to be made for the Greyhound binder to have immigrated from the Netherlands and for the Bat binder, whom I have not mentioned before, to have come from Cologne. It seems certain that Netherlandish tool design did influence the English tool cutters.

Though the immigrant binders made an invaluable contribution to English binding and tool design, and though the foreign stationers put the English booktrade on the map, they were less and less appreciated by the native members of the booktrade as competition became more severe, and gradually the screw repressing the alien was tightened.

In 1523 an act was passed stating that no alien, whether denizen or not, practising any handicraft, should take any apprentices who were not English born and that he should not keep more than two foreign journeymen.[27] This restriction did not apply in Oxford or Cambridge, but in London where it was already the custom that no freeman of the Stationers' Company took any foreign apprentices, this act more or less blocked the way into the Stationers' Company for any foreigner.

In February 1529 an even more stringent act was passed which decreed 'that no stranger artificer nor a denizen which was not a householder the 15 of February last past shall not set up nor kepe any house, shop or chambre wherein they shall occupy any handy craft within this realm'.[28]

The worst blow came in 1534. On Christmas Day an act came into effect which put the alien printer and bookseller on a level with every other alien craftsman and annulled the protective clause that had been appended to the act of 1484, pointing out that

> sithen the makinge of the sayde provision [i.e. the protective clause], many of thys realme, beinge the kinges naturall subiectes, have given them so diligently to learne and exercise the sayd craft of printynge, that at this day there be within this realme a great numbre conning and expert in the sayde science or crafte of printinge, as able to exercise the sayde crafte in all poyntes, as any straunger in any other realme or countrey. And furthermore where there be a great numbre of the kinges subiectes within thys realme, whyche live by the crafte and misterie of bindinge of bookes, and that there be a great multitude well experte in the same: yet all this not withstandinge there are divers persones, that bringe from beyonde the sea great plentye of printed bookes, not onely in the Latin tongue, but also in our maternall Englishe tongue, some bounde in bordes, some in lether, and some in parchemente, and them sell by retayle, wherby many of the kinges subiectes, beinge binders of bookes and havinge none other facultie wherwyth to get theyr living, be destitute of worke, and lyke to be undone; except some reformacion herein be had. Be it therfore enacted by the kinge our soveraygne lorde, the lordes spirituall and temporall, and the commons in thys present parliament assembled, and by aucthoritie of

the same, that the saide prouiso, made the first yere of the sayde king Richarde the thirde, from the feaste of the Nativitie of our Lorde God next comminge, shalbe voyde and of none effecte

Special protection was given to the native binding trade by stipulating 'that no person or persons, resiant or inhabytant within this realme, after the sayde feaste of Christmas next coming, shal bie to sell againe any printed bookes brought from anye partes out of the kinges obeysance, redye bounden in bourdes, lether, or parchement, upon peine to lose and forfaite for every booke bound out of the sayde kinges obeysance, and brought into this realme, and bought by any person or persons within the same to sell agayne contrary to thys acte, sixe shilling eyght pence'.[29]

This put an end to any dealing in foreign-bound books. Native printing was protected by the decree that 'no person or persons inhabitant or resiant within this realm . . . shall buy . . . of any stranger born out of the King's obedience, other than of denizens, any manner of printed books brought from any the parts beyond the sea, except only by engross and not by retail . . .'.[30] This clause prevented an undenizened alien from retailing foreign-printed books. The English stationers were still not satisfied and further attempts were made to stop the importation of foreign books.

With the printing of Tyndale's New Testament in Cologne in 1525 and the government's attempts at stopping its sale, clandestine printing and religious censorship had begun in earnest and religious motives had got mixed up with economic ones in the attempt to ban the importation of foreign books. It would lead too far to go into these motives and their manifestations.

It may suffice to say that by 1557 the incorporation of the Stationers' Company virtually closed the booktrade to any foreign competition, ordaining that 'no person within this our kingdom of England . . . either by himself, or by his journeymen, servants or by any other person, shall practice or exercise the art or mystery of printing or stamping any book, or anything to be sold, or to be bargained for within this our Kingdom of England . . . unless the same person is, or shall be, one of the society of the foresaid mystery or art of a stationer of the city aforesaid, at the time of his foresaid printing or stamping, or has for that purpose obtained our licence . . .'.[31]

Thus was created what we would now call 'a closed shop' in an attempt to ban from the booktrade those who had been its most significant stimulus.

1. G. Pollard, *The English market for printed books* (Sandars Lectures, Cambridge, 1959), *Publishing History*, IV (1978). See also G. Pollard, 'The Com-

pany of Stationers before 1557', *The Library*, 4th series, xviii (1937–8), pp. 1–38.

2. E. Armstrong, 'English purchases of printed books from the Continent', *The English Historical Review*, xciv, no. 371 (April 1979) and for information below.

3. G. D. Painter, *William Caxton: a quincentenary biography*, London, 1976, pp. 62–3. L. Hellinga, *Caxton in Focus*, London, 1982, pp. 48, 83.

4. H. R. Plomer, 'The importation of books into England in the fifteenth and sixteenth centuries', *The Library*, 4th series, iv (1923–4), pp. 146–50. H. R. Plomer, 'The importation of Low Country and French books into England, 1480 and 1502–3', *The Library*, 4th series, ix (1928–9), pp. 164–8. N. J. M. Kerling, 'Caxton and the trade in printed books', *The Book Collector*, iv (1955), pp. 190–99. E. Armstrong, *art. cit.*

5. E. G. Duff, *A Century of the English Booktrade*, London, 1905, pp. xi–xii.

6. R. Juchhoff, 'Johannes de Westfalia als Buchhändler', *Gutenberg-Jahrbuch* (1954), pp. 133–6.

7. E. G. Duff, *op. cit.* p. xiii.

8. E. G. Duff, *op. cit.* G. Pollard, Sandars Lectures, 1959. W. Page (ed.), *Letters of Denization and Acts of Naturalization for aliens in England, 1509–1603* (Huguenot Society Publications vol. viii), London, 1893.

9. *op. cit.*

10. G. D. Hobson, *Blind-stamped panels in the English booktrade, c. 1485–1555*, London, 1944.

11. J. B. Oldham, *English blind-stamped bindings*, Cambridge, 1952. Idem, *Blind panels of English binders*, Cambridge, 1958.

12. H. M. Nixon, 'William Caxton and bookbinding', *Journal of the Printing Historical Society*, xi (1976–7), pp. 92–113.

13. G. Pollard, 'The names of some English fifteenth-century binders', *The Library*, 5th series, xxv (1970), pp. 193–218.

14. References to books in Cambridge University Library are to numbers in J. C. T. Oates, *A Catalogue of the fifteenth-century printed books in the University Library Cambridge*, Cambridge, 1954.

15. *Boekbanden uit vijf eeuwen*, Ghent, 1961, no. 20, pl. vii.

16. E.g. on J. Balbus, *Catholicon*, Lyons, 1503 (Corpus Christi College, Oxford).

17. A. Hulshof and M. J. Schretlen, *De kunst der oude boekbinders*, Utrecht, 1921, p. 15, pl. IX, nos. 13 and 15.

18. E.g. on B. Sacchi de Platina, *Liber de vita Christi*, Nuremberg, 1481 [and] W. Rolewinck, *Fasciculus temporum*, n.p.,n.d. (Pembroke College, Cambridge).

19. D. E. Rhodes, 'Account of cataloguing incunables in Oxford College Libraries', *Renaissance Quarterly*, xxix (1976).

20. G. Pollard, *art. cit.* (*The Library*, 1970). But see also pp. 111–12 above.

21. On W. Rolewinck, *Fasciculus temporum*, Louvain, 1476 (ill. in J. W. Holtrop, *Monumens typographiques*, The Hague, 1857, pl. 130).

22. G. D. Hobson, *Bindings in Cambridge Libraries*, Cambridge, 1929, pl. xv, no. 13.

23. This tool occurs on a ms. Diurnal (BL, Add. MS 40153) that belonged to the Canons Regular of St Augustine at Utrecht and also on books that came from the Hieronymushuis illustrated by Hulshof and Schretlen, *op. cit.*, pl. III, no. 3.

24. 1484/5 to before 1509. See G. Pollard, *art. cit.*

25. M. M. Foot, 'English and foreign bookbindings 11', *The Book Collector*, xxviii (1979), p. 554; see also article 11 above.
26. Magninus Mediolanensis, *Regimen sanitatis*, Louvain, [1484–85] (Bodley, Auct. Q. supra I. 14).
27. E. G. Duff, *op. cit.*, p. xx.
28. Ibid.
29. W. H. J. Weale, *Bookbindings and rubbings of bindings in the National Art Library*, vol. I, London, 1898, pp. xxix–xxx.
30. E. G. Duff, *op. cit.*, p. xxii.
31. Ibid., p. xxvii.

The rubbings used for the illustrations have been taken from a variety of previously identified bindings. The choice of these bindings was largely accidental and mainly based on their condition. It is irrelevant to the argument to describe the individual books covered by these bindings.

14 A Franconian Binding, c. 1475
(1982)*

It is the fate of almost every bibliographical census that as soon as it is published more items of the same nature as those listed appear or more information about them is found. Professor Schmidt-Künsemüller's monumental *Corpus der gotischen Lederschnitteinbände* (Stuttgart, 1980) is no exception. Item 376 mentioned under the heading 'lost or hidden bindings' has now been found. Recently a search through the Paul Hirsch music collection in the British Library brought to light a cut-leather binding elaborately decorated with floral and leaf shapes and an armorial shield on a dotted ground. Hirsch bought this book in November 1921 from Joseph Baer who had acquired it at the Wassermann sale in Brussels.[1] Earlier the book belonged to the Franciscan monastery of St Anna at Bamberg. In 1803 Heinrich Joachim Jaeck described that library as containing over 3000 books, including many incunabula. The majority of these went to the Königliche Bibliothek in Bamberg, but over a third was left behind. What happened to these books either then or at the dissolution of the monastery in 1806 is not known.[2] The first owner of this binding remains unknown. Dr Adolph Schmidt suggested[3] that the arms belonged to a German family that had distinguished itself at the siege of Acre. It proved impossible to establish which of the many German families whose arms are charged with one or more keys were in fact present at that time. A member of the Falkenberg family took part in this third crusade,[4] but Baron Froberg-Montjoye, for instance, did not go to Palestine until the late thirteenth century.[5] The cut-leather work is very similar to that on a number of bindings illustrated by Schmidt-Künsemüller and has been attributed to Geldner's 'Lederschneider I' who worked in Franconia, possibly in Bamberg.[6]

1. Galerie Georges Giroux, Oct./Nov. 1921, *998*.
2. *Bavaria franciscana antiqua*, I [Munich, 1955], pp. 450–72.
3. Letter to Mrs Hirsch, 6 Nov. 1921.
4. J. Siebmacher, *Erneuert und vermehrtes Wappen-Buch*, Nuremburg, 1696, I,

* English and Foreign Bookbindings 20, *The Book Collector*, XXXI, pp. 76–7.

Fig. 14.1   Isidore, Saint, Archbishop of Sevile, *Etymologiae*, Strasburg,
[*c.* 1473] (BMC I, 57).
Brown calf decorated with cut-leather work, lower cover.
424 × 295 × 52 mm.
British Library, Hirsch, I, 256.

134, 182. R. Röhricht, *Beiträge zur Geschichte der Kreuzzüge*, II, Berlin, 1878, p. 332.
5. Siebmacher, II, 35. *Versailles. Salle des Croisades*, Paris [1842], p. 50.
6. F. Geldner, 'Bamberger und Nürnberger Lederschnittbände', *Festgabe . . . für Karl Schottenloher*, Munich, 1953.

15 A Binding Made at Coesfeld, c. 1478

(1979)*

In February 1979 the British Library acquired two collections of sermons by Petrus de Palude, printed at Strasburg in 1493 and 1494, bound together in blind-tooled brown calf over wooden boards.[1] The book once belonged to the Charterhouse 'Castrum S. Mariae' at Wedderen near Duelmen, but the binding has none of the characteristic Duelmen tools. Further investigation brought to light nine other bindings,[2] all made of brown calf over wood and all decorated with the same tools, including two strips with 'ihesus' and 'maria', one wide, the other narrower and curved, a lamb-and-flag tool, a dragon, three different lion tools, eagles, various fleurs-de-lis, a tool depicting the Resurrection, a pot with thistles, various roses and a very characteristic tool showing a bear and a lion clutching a tree. Three of the bindings have a tool showing a small crown flanked by the initials I and O, possibly those of the binder. Three bindings have a contemporary ownership inscription of the Augustinian convent Marien-brink ('collis Mariae') at Coesfeld. The 'large Sisterhouse' at Coesfeld near Münster in Westphalia was founded in 1425. In 1427 the sisters were given a house on the Klinkenberge by Johann Vischer, their first rector. Papal sanction followed and the Bishop of Münster granted them permission to build a church.[3] When the convent was visited in September 1571 the nuns owned a small library.[4] The convent was suppressed in 1803.

1. IB. 2176 and IB. 2177.
2. Gregorius, *Liber dyalogorum*, MS (Bodley, Broxbourne 1531); *Liber Festivalis*, MS (BL, Add. MS 15457); Lactantius, *Opera*, MS (Wolfenbüttel, Herzog August Bibliothek, Cod. Guelf 56); *Pontifical*, MS (J. Brassinne, *La Reliure Mosane*, Liège, 1932, II, pl. CXIV); Albertus Magnus, *Compendium theologicae veritatis*, [Deventer], n.d. [and] Bernoldus, *Distinctiones de tempore et de sanctis* [Deventer], n.d. (Cambridge University Library, Inc. 3.E.4.1. (2913–14, Oates 3445–6); Cyprianus, *Epistolae*, [Deventer, 1477] (E. Hannover, *Kunstfaerdige Gamle Bogbind*, Copenhagen, 1907, pl. 3); J. Nider, *Formicarius*, [Cologne], n.d. (BL, IB. 3006, BMC I, 194); Cassiodorus, *Ecclesiastica et tripartita historia*, [Cologne, before 6 May 1478] (BL, IB. 4030, BMC I, 245).

* English and Foreign Bookbindings 10, *The Book Collector*, XXVIII, pp. 412–13.

Fig. 15.1   M. A. Cassiodorus, *Ecclesiastica et tripartita historia* [Cologne
before 6 May 1478].
Brown calf, blind tooled. 305 × 205 × 54 mm.
British Library, IB. 4030.

N. Falcutius, *Sermones medicinales*, Pavia, 1484 (Glasgow University Library, Hunt. Bx 1.13).

3. F. Darpe, *Codex Traditionum Westfalicarum*, VI, Münster, 1907, pp. 41–5; B. Sökeland, *Geschichte der Stadt Coesfeld*, Coesfeld, 1839, p. 41.

4. W. E. Schwarz, *Die Geschichtsquellen des Bistums Münster*, VII, Münster, 1913, p. 95.

16 A German Binding, *c*. 1485
(1981)*

On 14 and 15 March 1572, *c*. 85 manuscripts and an unspecified number of printed books from the convent Sancta Maria Virginis at Wöltingerode near Goslar arrived in the library of Duke Julius of Braunschweig-Lüneburg at Wolfenbüttel.[1] Four hundred and nine years later the manuscripts—having spent almost two centuries, from 1618 until the early nineteenth century, in the University library at Helmstedt—are again in Wolfenbüttel. One of the printed books, Gerard of Zutphen, *Tractatus de spiritualibus ascensionibus* [with other tracts], Lübeck, 1490, with the inscription 'auff wolfenbüttel aus waltingenroda ankhomen den 14 Martij aō [15]72', is now in the British Library.[2] Though 'Sancta Maria Virginis' was founded in 1174 as a Benedictine monastery, it soon became a convent for Cistercian nuns, and one of the Abbesses, Elizabeth von Burgtorff, who was elected in 1430 and who re-enforced the discipline in the convent, donated several manuscripts to the library.[3] Five of these have been bound in brown calf over wooden boards, tooled in blind with diamond-shaped tools depicting flowers, fleurons, fleurs-de-lis, acorns and eagles; round tools showing roses, a lamb-and-flag and the head of Christ; rectangular tools, one with a climbing plant and one with a dragon; and a large square tool showing a pierced heart. The same bindery bound several other manuscripts for the convent as well as a number of books without Wöltingerode provenance, one of which, a Nuremberg *Psalterium* (Creussner, n.d.)[4] belonged to Henry Davis and is now at the New University of Ulster at Coleraine.

1. W. Milde, 'Die Wolfenbütteler "Liberey-Ordnung" des Herzogs Julius von 1572', *Wolfenbütteler Beiträge*, I, Frankfurt, 1972, pp. 135–6.
2. IA. 9898: BMC II, 558.
3. J. B. Lauenstein, *Historia Diplomatica Episcopatus Hildesiensis*, Hildesheim, 1740, II, pp. 259–64. H. A. Lüntzel, *Geschichte der Diöcese und Stadt Hildesheim*, Hildesheim, 1858, II, pp. 227–31.
4. BMC II, 452–3.

* English and Foreign Bookbindings 19, *The Book Collector*, xxx, pp. 522–3.

Fig. 16.1   *Psalterium*, Nuremberg: F. Creussner, n.d.
Rebound with the original covers onlaid. 215 × 145 × 42
mm.
New University of Ulster, Coleraine: Henry Davis Gift
(P.1168).
Photograph by kind permission of the Librarian.

17 A Binding from Hamersleben, *c.* 1510

(1981)*

In 1107–08 Reinhard von Blankenburg, Bishop of Halberstadt, founded the monastery 'Domus Sancti Pancratii' of the Canons Regular of St Augustine at Osterwieck an der Ilse.[1] In 1109 the monastery, too much disturbed by the noise of the local market, was moved to Hamersleben, north-east of Osterwieck, where it remained until its dissolution on 19 September 1804.[2]

Among the manuscripts and printed books belonging to the 'Helmstedt' collection in the Herzog August Bibliothek at Wolfenbüttel is a group of at least fifteen late fifteenth- and early sixteenth-century books bound in brown calf or hide over wooden boards and decorated in blind with the same set of tools, the most characteristic of which are a large round stamp with the Sacred Monogram surrounded by rays, a large square stamp showing a pelican with her brood, and a diamond-shaped stamp depicting the Christ child. A small diamond-shaped eagle tool and various fleurons occur frequently as well. Seven of these have the provenance 'Liber monasterij beati pancracij martiris In hamersleue Ordinis canonicorum regularium Halberstadensis diocesis', often with the word 'completus' or 'comparatus' and the date, ranging from 1510 to 1521. Sometimes the prior Bernardus Fabri (1502–1540) is mentioned, and the provenance inscription and the chapter headings are frequently rubricated. Two more volumes have an unspecified 'hamersleue' provenance with the dates 1504 and 1524, and two others have the characteristic rubrication. They were all bound during the first quarter of the sixteenth century, probably in the monastery itself, or at least by one binder who worked for the house. The binding illustrated found its way from Hamersleben via the monastery of St Ludger near Helmstedt into the University Library there, and thence to the Herzog August Bibliothek.[3]

1. K. Bogumil, *Das Bistum Halberstadt im 12. Jahrhundert*, Cologne, 1972.
2. S. Kunze, *Geschichte des Augustiner-Klosters Hamersleben*, Quedlinburg, 1835.
3. O. von Heinemann, *Die Handschriften der Herzoglichen Bibliothek zu Wolfenbüttel, Abteilung* I: *Die Helmstedter Handschriften*, Wolfenbüttel, 1884–88.

* English and Foreign Bookbindings 18, *The Book Collector*, xxx, pp. 380–81.

Fig. 17.1   Johannes Gerson, Minor Works [Latin], MS, 15th century.
Brown calf over wood, tooled in blind. 219 × 155 × 48 mm.
Lower cover.
Herzog August Bibliothek, Wolfenbüttel, Cod. Guelf.
Helmst. 657.

18 A Binding Made at Klus, 1526
(1983)*

The Herzog August Bibliothek at Wolfenbüttel possesses a large number of books and manuscripts from the Benedictine monastery of St Mary and St George at Klus, near Gandersheim. Many of these are bound in blind-tooled brown calf or hide, some are in sheep and a few are in white, stained leather, and several have on the upper cover a title label with a library shelfmark in red. A number of identical tools occur on all these bindings and there is little doubt that they were made at the monastery, which had a library as well as a scriptorium and a bindery.[1] Three groups can be distinguished. The first consists of thirteen bindings covering manuscripts and books produced during the 1460s and 1470s or earlier, and one book has on the end-leaf a manuscript note dated 1483. Eleven tools connect this group with another, of at least 22 bindings. Three of these have an inscription to the effect that they were bound at Klus by the monk Johannes de Braclis who also wrote (at least part of) two of the manuscripts. One binding inscription is dated 1490. Johann von Brakel worked from c. 1485 and died in 1525.[2] He is likely to have been responsible for all bindings in this group. The third group, which has five tools in common with von Brakel's work and four tools with group 1, consists of six books printed between 1481 and 1517. The binding illustrated belongs to this group and has an inscription that it was bound in 1526. Another book in a binding decorated with the same tools was not presented to Klus until 1531 and it seems probable that this group was bound after von Brakel's death.

1. H. Herbst, 'Das Benediktiner Kloster Klus bei Gandersheim . . .', W. Goetz (ed.), *Beiträge zur Kulturgeschichte des Mittelalters und der Renaissance*, 50, Leipzig/Berlin, 1932.
2. H. Herbst, 'Johannes von Brakel', *Archiv für Schreib- und Buchwesen*, IV (1930). Johann von Brakel wrote and bound Cod. Guelf. Helmst. 547 and 533 (no inscription but same hand); he bound Cod. Guelf. Helmst. 596 and Helmst. Qu.H.62 (the latter has the date 1490).

---

* English and Foreign Bookbindings 27, *The Book Collector*, xxxii, pp. 450–51.

Fig. 18.1   Bartholomaeus Anglicus, *De proprietatibus rerum*, Strasburg, 1485.
Brown calf tooled in blind. 313 × 209 × 67 mm.
Herzog August Bibliothek, Helmst. Qu.H.22.1.

Part IV
GOLD-TOOLED BINDINGS

The technique of decorating bindings by impressing heated tools through gold leaf into the leather is of Islamic origin. Gold-tooled bindings were made in Morocco from the thirteenth century and the practice was well established in the second half of the fourteenth century in the Mamluk empire and Iran.[1] It took at least half a century more before this technique reached the West. The earliest European gold-tooled binding may well have been made in Florence early in the fifteenth century;[2] several Italian examples are known that may date from the 1450s. By the third quarter of the century gold-tooling was widely known in Italy and by the end of the century it had reached Spain. The first atelier regularly to practise gold tooling in Paris was that which worked for Louis XII early in the sixteenth century. During the 1520s and 1530s it became a practised habit and the Parisian binders never looked back. Their German colleagues continued to tool in blind, very successfully, especially on the much-used white pigskin, although panels and rolls were also used with gold leaf. The first English gold-tooled binding probably dates from 1519 but for the next ten years the technique remained largely experimental.

This Part discusses examples of gold-tooled bindings, dating from the late fifteenth century to the 1860s. The majority were made by named binders. This may give the false impression that from the sixteenth century onwards craftsmen either signed their bindings or are otherwise known by name. Nothing is further from the truth. The vast majority of decorated bindings made all over Europe during the sixteenth and seventeenth centuries were produced by anonymous craftsmen, and it is rare to find a signed binding of this period or to be able to link a name, known from archival sources, with an actual product. Historians have been compelled to distinguish groups of bindings by the tools that were used to decorate them and by combinations of tools, in order to establish workshops which could then be given a nickname. It is not until the eighteenth century that we can begin to attribute bindings on any scale and with any confidence to real, identifiable people.

1. A. R. A. Hobson, *Humanists and Bookbinders*, Cambridge, 1989, p. 21 (with literature).
2. Ibid, pp. 24–5, fig. 17.

19 A Spanish Mudéjar Binding of the end of the Fifteenth Century

(1987)*

Gold-tooled leather bindings were produced in the Islamic world as early as the middle of the thirteenth century.[1] From there the technique of impressing a heated tool through gold leaf came to Europe, first to Florence early in the fifteenth century, then to Venice and Bologna in the second half of the century and, in the 1480s and 1490s, to Naples and to Rome.[2] Neapolitan examples probably inspired the gold-tooled bindings produced for Matthias Corvinus at Buda.[3] Neapolitan and/or direct Moorish influence caused the emergence of gold tooling in Spain at the end of the fifteenth century. The frequently-quoted Aragonese royal inventories of 1410 and 1458, in which the Catalan word 'oripell' is used to indicate gold decoration on some of the bookbindings in the royal library, are not sufficiently clear as to which technique was used. They may refer to the use of punched dots on gesso, found both on Spanish and on Italian bindings of the period, but no examples of Spanish gold-tooled bindings of the first half of the fifteenth century have survived.

Only three[4] examples of gold-tooled mudéjar bindings have been published and to these a fourth may now be added. Of the previously-known specimens, two cover Books of Hours. One is a manuscript c.1440, now in the Pierpont Morgan Library[5] and said to have been bound c.1500; the other probably dates from the end of the fifteenth century. It belonged to Sir Sydney Cockerell and Major Abbey and is now in a private collection.[6] A third, in the Musée Condé at Chantilly, covers a *Devocionario* for Joanna the mad, begun c.1482 and presented to her c.1498–99. The text has some additions that can be dated c.1500–1502,[7] but one presumes that the manuscript was bound before it was presented. The example illustrated here, also in a private collection, covers an Ordinary of the brotherhood of Saint Narcissus and has been tentatively dated c.1490.[8] The binding is undoubtedly contemporary with the manuscript. It is of brown goatskin over wooden boards, tooled in blind and gold to a strapwork design. The twisted rope tool appears to be identical to that used on the Book of Hours in the Pierpont Morgan Library.

---

* English and Foreign Bookbindings 40, *The Book Collector* XXXVI, pp. 100–102.

Fig. 19.1 Ordinary c. 1490.
Brown goatskin, tooled in blind and gold. 246 × 182 × 16 mm.
Private Collection.

1. A Moroccan example of 1256 is illustrated in D. Miner, *The History of Bookbinding 525–1950*, Baltimore, 1957, no. 52, pl. XV. Another part of the same Qur'ān in an identical binding is British Library, Or. 13192. An Egyptian or Syrian binding with gold tooling from the 13th–14th century is illustrated in G. Bosch and others, *Islamic Bindings and Bookmaking*, Chicago, 1981, p. 88, no. 3.

2. A. R. A. Hobson, 'Two Renaissance Bindings', *The Book Collector*, vii (1958), p. 265. H. M. Nixon, *Sixteenth-Century Gold-Tooled Bindings in the Pierpont Morgan Library*, New York, 1971, no. 1. P. Needham, *Twelve Centuries of Bookbindings*, New York/London, 1979, nos. 28, 32 (with literature). The late twelfth-century French binding in the Pierpont Morgan Library has probably been decorated with gold paint (Needham, no. 15). See also A. R. A. Hobson, *Humanists and Bookbinders*, Cambridge, 1989, pp. 24–30.

3. See P. Needham, *op. cit.*, no. 31 (with literature).

4. The example in the Henry Davis Gift to the British Library (see *The Book Collector* xviii (1969), p. 37, pl. Xb and Fig. 60.10b below is decorated with gold paint.

5. H. M. Nixon, *op. cit.*, no.1; P. Needham, *op. cit.*, no. 34.

6. H. Thomas, *Early Spanish Bookbindings xi–xv Centuries*, London, 1939, p. LXXXVIII (pl. L may possibly be a fifth example). Sotheby's, i.XII. 1970, 2890.

7. J. Meurgey, *Les principaux manuscrits à peintures du Musée Condé à Chantilly*, Paris, 1930, pp. 172–5.

8. I am most grateful to Monsieur François Avril of the Bibliothèque Nationale for his dating of this manuscript and for his notes on the manuscripts from the Cockerell/Abbey collections and at Chantilly.

20 A Binding by Maestro Luigi, c. 1547

(1976)*

In his fascinating book *Apollo and Pegasus*[1] A. R. A. Hobson identified both the original owner of the well-known bindings with the Apollo and Pegasus plaquette and the three binders who worked for him. Two of these binders worked for the Vatican library and are mentioned in the accounts of the library's expenses: Maestro Luigi and Niccolò Franzese. Maestro Luigi first appears in the accounts on 12 December 1542 and occurs regularly until 1565 when there is a gap in the records. Niccolò Franzese, who came from Rheims, was probably a little older; he is first mentioned in the privy purse accounts of 1537 and worked for the Vatican until his death in 1570–71. Both binders used closely similar, mainly solid tools, though Niccolò owned some hatched tools as well. The 'Julius III' tool[2] and several other solid, floral and decorative tools which belonged to Luigi's stock occur on a 1547 Venice Breviary in the British Library and on Girolamo Muzio's *Discorso*, Milan, 1548, in the Broxbourne Library.

Niccolò was not only the more experimental binder of the two but also the more prolific, and six more bindings from his shop can be added to Mr Hobson's list:[3]

Quintus Horatius Flaccus, *Carmina*, Venice, 1501 (John Rylands, R. 52151)
Missale Romanum, Venice, 1505 (Broxbourne Library, R.912, H. M. Nixon, *Broxbourne Library*, 34)
Juan Boscan Almogaver, *Las Obras*, Salamanca, 1547 (BL, G.10955)
Francesco Petrarca, *Opere*, Venice, 1547 [and] Lodovico Dolce,
Espositione de tutti i vocaboli, Venice, 1548 (Fitzwilliam Museum, Cambridge)
Primaleon, *Historia*, Venice, 1548 (Trinity College Cambridge, Grylls 6.76)
Francesco Sansovino, *Diverse Orationi volgarmente scritte da molti huomini illustri*, Venice, 1561 (BL, C.66.c.22).

1. A. R. A. Hobson, *Apollo and Pegasus*, Amsterdam, 1975.
2. Ibid, p. 65, Fig. 30.
3. Since the publication of this article, several more bindings from this shop have come to light.

* Foreign Bookbindings XIX, *The Book Collector*, xxv, p. 529.

Fig. 20.1   *Breviarium Romanum*. Venice, 1547.
Brown morocco, tooled in gold and blind. Lower cover.
243 × 170 × 67 mm.
British Library, C.47.g.8.

21 A Binding by Thomas Krüger, 1573

(1981)*

Thomas Krüger, possibly the son of the binder Nikolaus Krüger of Wittenberg and himself a binder, started work not later than 1560. A number of his panels were signed, either with his full name or with his initials, and some were dated.[1] The earliest date on his panels is 1562 but Haebler describes two Krüger bindings with the date 1560 tooled on the cover. Krüger married three times and died on 17 May 1591.[2]

The large Melanchthon panel on this binding, dated 1563[3] and with Cranach's device at the bottom, was copied from a woodcut by Cranach dated 1561,[4] showing Melanchthon wearing the same fur-trimmed robe, neckcloth and shoes as on the panel, but with a closed instead of an open book in his right hand and a cap in his left. The face and hair are remarkably alike. The same woodcut served as example for the panels of other Wittenberg binders, such as those signed by Severin Rötter and Nikolaus Müller.

The lower cover of the binding illustrated has a purely decorative panel, unsigned and unrecorded, of a type quite common in Germany in the late sixteenth century.[5] The large corner fleurons, composed of solid tools and gouges, the elaborately tooled spine and the gilt, gauffered and painted edges make this binding stand out among Krüger's usually simpler and often blind-tooled bindings. The book was dedicated to Anne of Denmark, Electress of Saxony, and the painted arms of Denmark and Saxony on the fore-edge suggest that this was the dedication copy.

1. H. Herbst, 'Der Wittenberger Buchbinder Thomas Krüger', *Zeitschrift für Bücherfreunde*, N.F.XIX (1927), pp. 45–60. U. Thieme and F. Becker, *Allgemeines Lexicon der Bildenden Künstler*, Leipzig, 1907–50, vol. 21, p. 603. K. Haebler, *Rollen- und Plattenstempel*, Leipzig, 1928, vol. I, pp. 249–54. E. Schmidt-Herrling, 'Einbände von Thomas Krüger', *Festschrift E. Stollreither*, Erlangen, 1950, pp. 285–93.
2. M. Senf, 'Die Wittenberger Buchbinder', *Zentralblatt für Bibliothekswesen*, XXVIII (1911), pp. 208–14 (n.34).

* English and Foreign Bookbindings 17, *The Book Collector*, xxx, pp. 232–3.

Fig. 21.1   Johann Carion, *Chronica Carionis ... Auffs newe in
Lateinischer Sprach beschrieben, und ... vermehret ...
durch Herrn Philippum Melanchthonem, und Doctorem
Casparum Peucerum*, Wittenberg, 1573.
Brown calf, gold tooled. 320 × 202 × 80 mm.
British Library, Henry Davis Gift.

3. Weale, R.740; Herbst, n.4 (the scroll reads 'PHILIP. MELAN' not 'MELACTH'), Haebler, n.VIII. None of these mentions the date.
4. This woodcut occurs on fol. a vi verso of the book illustrated. A Bartsch, *Le peintre graveur*, Vienna, 1803–21, vol. VII, p. 300, n.153. G. Hirth, *Kulturgeschichtliches Bilderbuch*, Leipzig and München, [1881–90], vol. II, n.1026. See also H. Zimmermann, 'Holzschnitte und Plattenstempel mit dem Bilde Luthers', *Jahrbuch der Einbandkunst*, I (1927), pp. 112–21.
5. A similar panel is illustrated by O. Mazal, *Europäische Einbandkunst*, Graz, 1970, *Abb.* 155.

22 A Binding by Jean de Planche, c. 1570

(1978)*

In his 'Elizabethan gold-tooled bindings', *Essays in Honour of Victor Scholderer*, Mainz 1970, H. M. Nixon identified the Huguenot immigrant binder Jean de Planche as the son of Jehan Desplanches of Dijon; he outlined Jean's first five years in London and listed nineteen bindings made by him there. New evidence has come to light which suggests that 'Rouen' in Landsdowne MS 202 ('John de Planche and John Piccard of Rouen Stacion's') refers to de Planche as well as to Piccard, and though de Planche may have been born in Dijon, he certainly came to London from Rouen. Jean de Planche's stay in London can be extended by at least another four years, and four more bindings produced before 1575 can be added, as well as fifteen others which are decorated with some of de Planche's tools and cover books printed between 1577 and 1624.

The years from 1572 to 1575 brought Jean into conflict with the authorities of the French Church.[1] Late in May 1572 he married at the Barbican Helaine Couppe, the daughter of a shoemaker at Temple Bar. Three weeks later he was accused of bigamy. Jean acknowledged the existence of a previous wife in Rouen, but denied any obligations to her, having proved 'par suffisans tesmoins telle quelle est' and having told his new wife and parents-in-law that she was 'une paillarde a Rouen'. The case was referred to the Bishop's chancellor and Jean was excluded from the Eucharist. Enquiries among the people from Rouen found Madame de Planche innocent of her husband's charges, and the affair dragged on inconclusively for another three years.

Meanwhile Jean seems to have continued in his trade. A 1573 Geneva Beza, now at Emmanuel College, Cambridge, was bound by him and decorated with the same corner-pieces as are found on the binding illustrated, on another copy of Foxe's *Book of Martyrs*, London, 1570 with Archbishop Matthew Parker's arms, now at Trinity College, Cambridge, and on a 1570 London Euclid bound for Robert Dudley.[2]

---

* English and Foreign Bookbindings 5, *The Book Collector*, XXVII, pp. 230–31.

Fig. 22.1 J. Foxe, *Book of Martyrs*. London, 1570, vol. I.
Brown calf, gold tooled. 382 × 252 × 65 mm.
Cambridge University Library, K*.7.15(A).

1. A. M. Oakley, *Actes du Consistoire de l'église française de Threadneedle Street, Londres vol.II, 1571–1577*, London, 1969.
2. Quaritch, catalogue 937, 1974.

23 A London Binding, c. 1638
(1982)*

In the preceding article I listed four bindings made by Jean de Planche during his last years in London. One of these, covering a 1573 Geneva Beza, is decorated with a centre piece made up of four large corner blocks. These same corner blocks turn up later, probably after Jean de Planche had left London, on seven bindings, one of which, a 1616 Leiden *Common Prayer* [and] *Bible*, also has a large centre block which belonged to Bateman.[1] The other six cover J. Guillemeau, *The Frenche Chirurgerye*, Dort, 1597 (Hatfield, 11825 P 3); J. de Serres, *A General Inventorie of the History of France*, London, 1607 (BL, C.82.f.10); *Common Prayer*, London, 1616 (Queen's College, Oxford, 80.D.8); *Common Prayer, Bible* [and] *Psalter*, London, 1616 [and] 1624 (John Rylands University Library, Manchester, 21121); J. Smith, *The Generall Historie of Virginia*, London, 1624 (Queen's College, Oxford, Sel. c. 106); and L. Guicciardini, *Description de touts les Pays-Bas*, Amsterdam, 1625 (Quaritch, Catalogue 1921, 35). The bindings of both the 1616 Leiden *Common Prayer* [and] *Bible* and the 1616 London *Common Prayer* are also decorated with small tools that were used on the *Common Prayer, Bible* [and] *Psalter* at the John Rylands. This binding has in the centre the Stuart Royal Arms[2] used for James I, as well as a number of small curving and fleuron tools that are found on another binding for this King, on A. Thevet's *Pourtraits et Vies des Hommes illustres*, [Paris, 1584].[3] Three more bindings from this shop cover W. Shakespeare, *Comedies, histories and tragedies . . .* London, 1632 (University Library, University of Michigan, Shakespeare Collection, PR2751. A2), *Annotations upon all the Books of the Old and New Testament*, London, 1645 (BL, C.36.l.2) and the binding illustrated here.[4]

1. M. M. Foot, *The Henry Davis Gift*, vol.I, London, 1978, p. 48, no. 54.
2. One of sixteen variants. This same block is used for Charles I on the Guicciardini and on the binding illustrated.
3. W. Y. Fletcher, *English Bookbindings*, London, 1895, pl. XXXIV. H. M. Nixon, *Royal English Bookbindings*, London, 1957, pl. 7.
4. For five more bindings by Jean de Planche's successor, see M. M. Foot, *The Henry Davis Gift*, vol.II, London, 1983, p. 77, no. 46.

* English and Foreign Bookbindings 23, *The Book Collector*, XXXI, pp. 482–3.

Fig. 23.1 G. Sandys, *A Paraphrase upon the Divine Poems*, London,
1638.
Gold-tooled brown morocco, lower cover. 346 × 227 × 27 mm.
British Library, C. 83.i.7.

24 A Binding, probably made in Amsterdam, *c.* 1670

In the summer of 1970, I published as 'Foreign Bookbindings VI'[1] a binding which I misattributed to Bruno Spanceerder, having walked straight into the trap set at the end of the nineteenth century by Horlois, a Leiden dealer, for Mr N. de Roever. This well-respected scholar had bought a fine gold-tooled binding which had on one of its fly-leaves a trade card depicting a man holding a walking-stick and accompanied by a dog, amidst heraldic foliage, topped by a ship in full sail, and below it: 'Bruno Spanseerder/Boeck Binder in Opreght/Schoon Zijgreijn Leer/tot Amsterdam'.[2] De Roever described and illustrated this binding in *Oud Holland* IX (1891). However, it transpired that Horlois had pasted the trade card into the book in the hope of a better sale. The binding was subsequently attributed to Albert Magnus, the best-known Dutch binder of the period,[3] and later described as ?French.[4]

It is time to set the record straight. The binder who bound Mr de Roever's *Nouveau Testament* (1664) was also responsible for three other bindings. The finest of these is a large Bible, printed by the widow and heirs of Johan Elzevier in Leiden in 1663.[5] The same roll, showing alternating sitting and flying birds amongst vine branches and several of the same fleurons and curl-tools that decorate this Bible, also turn up on the binding of a manuscript [William III, Stadtholder of the United Provinces *etc.*], *Discours sur la Nouriture de son Alt. Monseig.[r] le Prince D'Orange*, written in 1654, which was lot 609 in the Mensing sale,[6] while identical curl and fleuron tools can be seen on the binding illustrated here.

Alas, Spanceerder, about whose life a certain amount is known,[7] will have to rejoin the many Dutch seventeenth-century binders whose names cannot be confidently linked with the multitude of fine and trade bindings produced in Amsterdam at that time.

1. *The Book Collector*, XIX (1970), pp. 214–5.
2. The binding covers *Le Nouveau Testament*, The Hague, J. & D. Steucker, 1664. The trade card, with the Spanceerder family crest and making a punning reference to Bruno's name (spanceeren = to walk), appears to be authentic.

Fig. 24.1 *Apologie pour la Maison de Nassau*. Madrid, 1664.
Mottled brown calf, gold tooled, with the arms of William III.
183 × 107 × 30 mm.
British Library, C.46.c.13.

3. Philopegus (pseud. for J. A. Loeber), *De geschiedenis van de boekband*, 1935, who exploded the Spanceerder attribution and accused Horlois.
4. *Albert Magnus en zijn tijd, zestiende en zeventiende eeuwse Amsterdamse boekbanden*, Catalogus van de Tentoonstelling in Museum Willet Holthuysen, 21 juli–21 sept. 1961, Amsterdam, 1961 (introduction and no. 60).
5. Royal Library, The Hague, 41.A.13. I am grateful to Dr J. Storm van Leeuwen for sending me a rubbing of this binding. It was no. 60 in the exhibition catalogue by J. Storm van Leeuwen, *De meest opmerkelijke boekbanden uit eigen bezit*, The Hague, 1983.
6. Sotheby's, 17 Dec. 1936.
7. *Book Collector*, XIX (1970), p. 215.

25 A Binding by the Charity School Binder, *c.* 1670–73

William Blake of Covent Garden, woollen draper, son of Francis Blake of Highgate, Esq., was founder and house-keeper of the Ladies Charity School on Highgate Hill, where 'near forty Poor, or Fatherless Children' were 'taught to Read, Write, and Cast Accompts'.[1] In a *Merlinus Anonymus* for 1655 the 'new Hospital at *Highgate*' is mentioned[2] and in 1680 a bequest was made to the 'Ladyes Hospital founded by Master Blake at Highgate'.[3] Blake intended his own 'Sumers Recess from London', once the Banqueting House of the Earls of Arundel, as 'Lodgings of Retyrement' for the Hospital's governors.[4] In 1682 he acquired Dorchester House, across the green, as a boarding house for girls, and during the next six years six houses were built on the estate. Apart from their rent and occasional contributions from a few London parishes, a number of pious and wealthy ladies were the main source of income for the school.[5] Blake's attempts to encourage their donations, preceding his *Silver Drops*, cannot have been totally successful. Having mortgaged his property and alienated his family, he was imprisoned for debt in the Fleet, and in 1687 the parish of St Giles-in-the-Fields offered £10 towards his release. His will was proved in 1695.[6]

Of the thirteen presentation bindings I have seen, twelve have the name of the recipient tooled on the upper cover. At first glance they seem to fall into four separate groups. The first group consists of bindings for Lady Delamere (BL, C.183.a.34), Madam Smyth (Fig. 25.1), Madam Thomas (Bodleian Library, Broxbourne Collection, 565/74.20), Madam Haymes (BL, C.67.b.26) and Madam Sewsby (V & A, Drawer 35, L 1646–1882).

The second group consists of bindings for Mrs Gregory (P. Grinke), Mad^m Semens (Christie's 18–19.7.1988, *12*), Mad^m Newland (Providence Public Library, Rhode Island)[7], and Dr Cox (Bryn Mawr College, PA).[8] One binding in a private collection, which does not have a name tooled on the cover, is equally elaborately decorated and has the same tools as the other bindings of this second group. Two bindings, one for Lady Alitia Devoo (York University, XVI.L.26), the other for Madam Dixon (formerly in the collection of Mr Henry Davis) have a number of tools in common. Furthermore, they form the link between the first and second

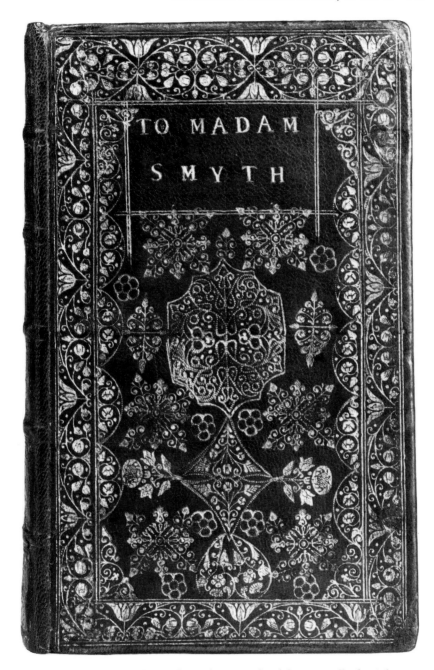

Fig. 25.1   W. Blake, *The Ladies Charity School-house Roll of Highgate*,
etc. *Silver Drops, or Serious Things* [London, *c.* 1670].
Red morocco tooled in gold. 157 × 97 × 27 mm.
British Library, 291.a.28.

group. One tool that occurs on two bindings of group I also decorates the binding for Madam Dixon, while both bindings have a large drawer-handle tool that is also found on the bindings for Mad^m Newland and Dr Cox. It is therefore likely that all twelve bindings were made in the same shop.

The odd one out is a binding for Madam Millar (Maggs Catalogue 1705, no. 75). Although it was made about the same time as the other presentation bindings and although it has a few tools that are similar to those used on the other twelve, it does not seem to have come from the same bindery.

1. W. Blake, *The Ladies Charity School-house Roll of Highgate*, etc. *Silver Drops, or Serious Things* [London, c.1670], pp. 1–2.
2. Fol. A8ᵛ (BL, E.1488(4)).
3. P.C.C., 1680, 124 (quoted in *LCC*, p. 53).
4. Sir George Gater and W. H. Godfrey (eds.), *London County Council Survey of London*, vol. XVII *The Village of Highgate*, London, 1936, pl. 39: Blake's drawing of *c.* 1688, showing the school, Dorchester House and his own house. See also pl. 40, 51 and pp. 52–4, 60–61, 90 and 148.
5. In the copy of *Silver Drops* at BL, 4400.n.16, 25 names have been added in manuscript.
6. P.C.C., 1695, 228.
7. I am grateful to Mr L. J. Bauer for this information.
8. I am grateful to Mr J. Tanis for this information.

26 A Binding by Alexander Ogstoun, c. 1680

(1980)*

In his *History of the Art of Printing*, Edinburgh, 1713, James Watson relates how 'in 1688, Mrs. *Anderson* [the King's Printer] . . . fell Tooth and Nail upon the Booksellers: And . . . seiz'd a good Quantity of Bibles brought from *London*'. One of these Edinburgh booksellers was Alexander Ogstoun[1] who not only had the temerity to import London-printed Bibles, but who bound them, together with the *Psalms in meeter*, printed by Mrs Anderson's late husband, in the most delightful onlaid and gold-tooled bindings known to have been produced at Edinburgh during the last quarter of the seventeenth century, and signed them on the fore-edge 'A. Ogsto[u]n fecit'. As well as his signature and rather crudely painted flowers, all but one of the fore-edges show a wreath containing the text 'A vertuous woman is a crown to her husband' (Prov. 12:4), and three are dated 1675, 1678 and 1680 respectively.[2] On 13 February 1680 Ogstoun became a Burgess of Edinburgh and a Guildbrother 'being well commended by H. M. Advocate and many of the College of Justice, and likely also to be useful to the good toun'[3] and on 16 April he married Martha Stevenson who bore him four children, at least two of whom, Alexander and James, adopted their father's trade.[4] It is likely that the 1676 Edinburgh *Bible* [and] *Psalms* (1675) with the fore-edge dated 1680 was a wedding gift from Ogstoun to his bride. Ogsto[u]ne's name occurs in several deeds dated 1685 and 1687;[5] in 1686 the binder John Reid worked for him as a journeyman,[6] and in 1690 he died and was buried on 29 March at the North side of the Greyfriars Burying-Ground.[7] His widow succeeded to the bookseller's business and survived him by almost 48 years.[8]

The binding illustrated belonged in 1723 to Agnes Keith, whose daughter Margaret Orme used it to record her marriage to James Keir in 1750, and the subsequent births of her ten children. Her youngest son John left his bookplate in the Bible as well as some additional notes about the family's history, some of which he transcribed from another 'old Bible the property of Elizabeth Forster', his paternal great-grandmother. The

---

* English and Foreign Bookbindings 13, *The Book Collector*, XXIX (1980), pp. 255–7.

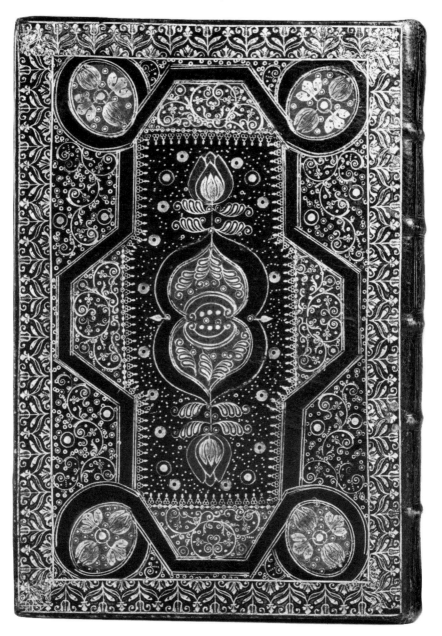

Fig. 26.1   *The Holy Bible*, London, 1680 [and] *The Psalms in meeter*,
Edinburgh, 1676.
Lower cover. Black morocco onlaid in citron and red and
tooled in gold. 174 × 120 × 35 mm.
Private collection.

granddaughter of John's eldest brother William married the great-grand-father of the current owner.[9]

Several of Alexander Ogstoun's tools also turn up on the binding of Boethius, *De Consolatione Philosophiae*, Leiden, 1671, in the Broxbourne Library.[10]

1. Sir John Lauder, Bart, Lord Fountainhall, *Historical Notices of Scotish Affairs*, Edinburgh, 1848, vol. II, p. 866.
2. *Bible*, London, 1603 [and] *Psalms in meeter*, Edinburgh, 1676: National Library of Scotland, Bdg. s. 108 (dated 1675); *Bible*, Edinburgh, 1678 [and] *Psalms in meeter*, Edinburgh, 1676: NLS, F.5.f.13 (no wreath, dated 1678. I am grateful to Mr John Morris for descriptions and xeroxes of these two bindings); *Bible*, Edinburgh, 1676 [and] *Psalms in meeter*, Edinburgh, 1675: Sotheby's, 27 June 1887, 252 (dated 1680); [*Bible*, London, 1675]: Sotheby's, 26 May 1930, 82; *Bible*, London, 1680 [and] *Psalms in meeter*, Edinburgh, 1676: private collection, see Fig. 26.1 (I am grateful to the present owner for permission to publish this binding).
3. C. B. B. Watson (ed.), *Roll of Edinburgh Burgesses and Guild-Brethren 1406–1700*, Edinburgh, 1926.
4. H. Paton (ed.), *The Register of Marriages for the Parish of Edinburgh 1595–1700*, Edinburgh, 1905. M. Wood (ed.), *Edinburgh Poll Tax Returns for 1694*, Edinburgh, 1951. F. J. Grant (ed.), *The Commissariot Record of Edinburgh. Register of Testaments, pt. III, 1701–1800*, Edinburgh, 1899 (James Ogstoun's will was registered on 31 Aug. 1714).
5. Scotland, General Register House, *Index to the Register of Deeds*, vols. XXV, XXVII: 1685, 1687, Edinburgh, 1959, 1961.
6. H. Paton (ed.), *The Register of the Privy Council of Scotland . . . A.D. 1686*, Edinburgh, 1930, p. 159.
7. H. Paton (ed.), *Register of Internments in Greyfriars Burying-Ground, Edinburgh, 1658–1700*, Edinburgh, 1902.
8. F. J. Grant (ed.), *op. cit.* (Martha Stevenson's will was registered on 20 Jan. 1738.)
9. Sir J. B. Burke, *Burke's . . . Landed Gentry*, London, 1939 (Campbell of Auchendarroch).
10. H. M. Nixon, *Broxbourne Library*, London, 1956, no. 81.

27 A Binding by William Cox, 1684

(1977)*

A 1679 Oxford Bible in the British Library has a fore-edge painting of flowers and insects underneath the gold, with the admonition to 'search the Scriptures', a quotation from St John 5:39, also used on fore-edges of books bound by Lewis and the Naval binder. This edge is signed 'Wm Cox Fecit 1684'.

Two stationers called William Cox occur in the registers of the Stationers' Company. The elder was made free in 1597 and had several apprentices during the first two decades of the seventeenth century.[1] The younger had two apprentices during the 1630s and 1640s,[2] and either could have been assessed at one shilling in 1632.[3] Neither William would probably have been young enough in 1684 to produce a delicately tooled binding. A reference from Professor M. Treadwell led me to find a third William Cox, who is described as 'Bookbinder' in the parish registers of St George, Southwark. On 28 April 1698 he married Abigail Simpson of that parish, who died in November of the same year. Nineteen months later William married Anne Greenfielde, who bore him two children, Robert, who was christened on 21 November 1703 while the Coxes lived 'at Widow Cattersons in the Mynt', and Anne, who was christened in June 1705. The address is given as 'King Street in the Mynt', from where they moved to Duke Street, also 'in the Mynt', where William died in April 1709.

1. E. Arber, *A Transcript of the Registers of the Company of Stationers of London 1554–1640*, London, 1875.
2. D. F. McKenzie, *Stationers' Company Apprentices 1641–1700*, Oxford, 1974.
3. W. A. Jackson, *Records of the Court of the Stationers' Company 1602 to 1640*, London, 1957.

* English and Foreign Bookbindings 3, *The Book Collector*, XXVI, pp. 566–7.

Fig. 27.1 The Holy Bible. Oxford, 1679.
Black morocco, gold tooled. 200 × 155 × 52 mm.
British Library, C.109.r.2.

28 A Binding, possibly made by Thomas Norris, 1685

(1984)*

In 1670 Isaac Vossius, son of the great Dutch classical scholar Gerard Vossius, one-time tutor to Queen Christina of Sweden, settled in England. He was created a D.C.L. at Oxford in the same year and three years later Charles II presented him to a vacant prebend in the royal chapel of Windsor. He was frequently seen at the court and his erudition and scepticism gave rise to a variety of anecdotes. In his *Variarum obser-vationum liber*, printed by Robert Scott in 1685, he expressed himself in flattering terms about his adopted country and his adopted monarch. A number of copies of this book have a dedication to Charles II,[1] printed on a separate leaf and inserted in a variety of places in the first gathering. Most copies are in blind-tooled brown or mottled calf but four copies,[2] with the dedication leaf inserted between the title-page and A3 (signed A2), are bound in red morocco and tooled in gold to a panel design with an elaborate centre piece built up of floral curls.

The same curl tools were used by Christopher Norris senior on the bindings he made for Maurice Johnson in the 1750s.[3] As Christopher Norris probably inherited his father Thomas's business and as he was not made free until 1703, it is possible that Thomas Norris was responsible for these presentation bindings. Thomas was apprenticed to Benjamin Harris, turned over to Mary Harris and made free in 1687. He lived in Aldersgate Without and later in St Giles without Cripplegate and on London Bridge. He retired to Highgate where he died in 1732.[4]

1. Of the 21 copies I have seen or seen descriptions of, twelve have the dedication leaf. I am especially grateful to Paul Morgan for his help.
2. British Library, 88.g.7; Cambridge University Library, Rel.c.68.2; Marlborough Rare Books; Maggs Bros. The latter three are almost identical. The BL binding is slightly simpler.
3. M.M. Foot, *The Henry Davis Gift*, vol. I, London, 1978, pp. 87–94.
4. E. Howe, *A List of London Bookbinders 1648–1815*, London, 1950; D. F. McKenzie, *Stationers' Company Apprentices 1641–1700*, Oxford, 1974; M. M. Foot, *op. cit*, p. 91.

---

* English and Foreign Bookbindings 29, *The Book Collector*, xxxiii, pp. 206–7.

Fig. 28.1   I. Vossius, *Variarum observationum liber*, London, 1685.
Red morocco tooled in gold. 235 × 180 × 35 mm.
Cambridge University Library, Rel. c. 68.2.

29 An Amsterdam Binding, *c.* 1700
(1977)*

The Vanandetzi family were active as Armenian printers and publishers in Amsterdam from 1685 to 1717. Mattheos Vanandetzi worked with Wuskan of Erivan, the publisher in 1666 of the first Bible printed in Armenian, from whom he learnt the art of typography. Mattheos established his own business, and *c.* 1685 ordered a new fount of Armenian type from Nicolaas Kis and bought a printing press from the widow of Christoffel Conradus.[1] Nine years later he was joined by his cousin Thomas, who became the financier and publisher of the firm and by Thomas's nephews Loukas, who was its author and editor, and Michael. A number of copies of several books from their press survive in their original, rather crudely-tooled, brown calf bindings, decorated with the same curls, fleurons, two bird-in-vine rolls and four Crucifixion stamps: all clearly the work of one bindery. Moses Khorenac'i's Genealogy of 1695[2] was bound there and so were two copies of the 1696 Imitation of Christ,[3] three copies, one in two parts, of a 1698–1700 New Testament,[4] six copies of a 1702 Hymnal,[5] and a 1704 Service book.[6] Wuskan of Erivan also used this shop, which bound his 1664 Hymnal[7] and three copies of his 1668 New Testament.[8] The British Library copy of the 1666 Bible[9] has the same Crucifixion stamp as occurs on one of the Hymnals,[10] but all the other tools are different. Four of the bindings belonged to John Sharp, Archbishop of York, who received the Vanandetzis during their visit to England and introduced them to the Queen on 26 March 1707.[11]

1. M. M. Kleerkooper and W. P. van Stockum, *De Boekhandel te Amsterdam*, The Hague, 1914–16, p. 774.
2. Durham University Library, Bamburgh, Z.IV.45.
3. Ibid, Z.IV.18; John Rylands Library, 3778.
4. Amsterdam, Universiteits Bibliotheek, 974.G.45; BL, 218.b.24–25. D. Parikian (June 1980).
5. BL, Or.70.aa.4, 17021.a.22; Durham University Library, Bamburgh, Select 30,31; Fitzwilliam Museum, Cambridge; John Rylands Library, 14603.
6. Amsterdam, Universiteits Bibliotheek, 974.G.47.

* English and Foreign Bookbindings 2, *The Book Collector*, xxvi, pp. 386–7.

Fig. 29.1   New Testament (Armenian), part 2, Amsterdam, 1700 (lower
cover).
Brown calf, gold tooled with the cypher of George III added;
rebacked. 150 × 90 × 48 mm.
British Library, 218.b.25.

7. Christ Church College, Oxford, e.8.28.
8. BL, Or.70.aa.3; John Rylands Library, 21534; A. Schmidt, *Bucheinbände* . . . *in der Landesbibliothek zu Darmstadt*, Leipzig, 1921, pl. LXXII.
9. BL, Or.70.bb.2.
10. John Rylands Library, 14603.
11. Thomas Vanandetzi, *Peregrinationis suae in Europeam* . . . *narratio*, Oxford, 1707.

30 A Binding by the Geometrical Compartment Binder, *c.* 1703
(1986)*

In *English Bookbindings* xc H.M. Nixon discussed the work of the Geometrical Compartment Binder. The same shop bound at least five copies of Joseph Gander, *The Glory of Her Sacred Majesty Queen Anne, in the Royal Navy* (London, 1703). The book was printed for the author and these are most probably the author's presentation copies. Four of these (British Library, C.183.c.18; University Library, Cambridge, SSS. 36.9; Bodley, Broxbourne, 38.8, and a copy seen at Maggs Bros. in 1986, which was lot 2234 in the Heber Sale, pt 2) are in very similar bindings, two in black morocco, one in red, and the British Library copy in olive-brown morocco, tooled to identical designs for which the same tools have been used. The covers have been clearly marked up with blind lines prior to tooling in gold. All four have identical metallic varnish end-papers, printed in gold on a dark pink ground. The same paper has also been found on a pair of empty wrappers in the Olga Hirsch collection which, according to a manuscript note, once contained a sonata by G. de Zotti (Venice, 1707).

The fifth copy, now in the King's Library of the British Library, is bound in red morocco with black onlays to which the cypher of King George III has been added. The tooling of the spine is identical with that on the other four copies. All five have gilt and gauffered edges. The end-leaves of the King's Library copy consist again of metallic varnish papers, not very common in English bindings of the early eighteenth century, but this time a different floral block has been used in gold on purple paper. It resembles papers produced in Augsburg at the end of the seventeenth and the beginning of the eighteenth century.

* English and Foreign Bookbindings 36, *The Book Collector*, xxxv, pp. 76–7.

Fig. 30.1 J. Gander, *The Glory of Her Sacred Majesty Queen Anne, in the Royal Navy* (London, 1703).
Olive-brown morocco, tooled in gold. 215 × 167 × 20mm.
British Library, C.183.c.18.

31 A Middelburg Binding, c. 1750–58

(1973)*

This mosaic binding is unusual in being 'backless', the effect being produced by stabbing, instead of sewing, and cutting the back of the leaves to form the fourth gilt edge.

In design it closely resembles a mosaic binding illustrated in Marlborough Rare Books catalogue 40, no. 30, covering two volumes of A. Seba, *Locupletissimi Rerum Naturalium Thesauri*, Amsterdam, 1734–5, in red morocco, with inlays of black morocco and green paper. This binding also has an eight-pointed star in the centre, heart-shaped compartments in the corners and is tooled in gold with a great variety of leaves and flowers and with small cupids shooting at winged hearts with the motto, 'in hoop' (hoping). On the upper cover is tooled, 'S. Mandelgreen fecit MDCCLVI'. Some of the floral tools, such as the pair of small, drooping flowers, a pair of carnations, a pair of curving flowers and a sunflower tool also occur on the binding illustrated.

Suenonius or Swenonius Mandelgreen was a printer[1] and stationer in Middelburg, who worked between 1736 and 1758. He lived at the sign of the 'Augburgschen Bijbel' at the Groote Markt. He is known to have been an auctioneer as well and must have had his own bindery. He died on 10 September 1758.[2]

A small group of related bindings, also possibly of Middelburg origin and similar in style, cover A. C. Mattheus, *Verzameling van Inleidingen*, a MS on paper, written in Middelburg between 1729 and 1735,[3] B. van Akerlaecken, *Genealogien*, n.p. [Sevenberghe], 1627,[4] dedicated to Frederik Hendrik, and three volumes of a 1663 Leiden Bible.[5] The endpapers of the Mattheus MS are of the same pink, yellow and green flowered paper as was used for lining the contemporary pull-off case of gold-tooled brown sprinkled calf, which contains the binding illustrated.

1. He is mentioned as printer in the city accounts for 1756–7.
2. A. M. Ledeboer, *De Boekdrukkers, Boekverkoopers en Uitgevers in Noord-Nederland*, Delft, 1872.

* Foreign Bookbindings XVII, *The Book Collector*, xxii, p. 209.

Fig. 31.1   L. Smids, *Schatkamer der Nederlandsche Oudheden*.
            Amsterdam, 1711.
            Dark red morocco, gold tooled, with inlays of painted vellum
            and heart-shaped onlays of green silk. 191 × 138 × 41 mm.
            British Library, Henry Davis Gift.

3. M. M. Foot, *The Henry Davis Gift*, vol. II, London, 1983, no. 315.
4. BL, C.38.l.10.
5. Chester-Beatty Library, 114B.

32 A Binding by Christiaan Micke, c. 1755

(1980)*

With the publication of Jan Storm van Leeuwen's meticulous study of bookbinding in The Hague in the eighteenth century,[1] it has become possible to attribute a number of bindings hitherto classed as '18th-century Dutch' to specific ateliers. My own group IX, mentioned in *The Henry Davis Gift*, Vol. I, London, 1978, pp. 252–3, can now be attributed to the First Stadtholder's bindery, a highly productive shop that worked from c. 1722 until 1793 and that may have been run by the Stofvoet family. Recently the British Library acquired a copy of Jan van Hout, *Der stadt Leyden dienst-bouc* [Leiden], 1602 (C.115.s.24), bound by this bindery for the owner of the 'lion collection'.[2] After 1749 the work from this shop deteriorated, and from c. 1750–70 the highest quality binding work made in The Hague was produced by Christiaan Micke. One of ten children, he was baptized on 12 August 1714, registered as apprentice with the Hague Booksellers' Guild in 1727 and worked independently from before 1743. He worked for the Stadtholders William IV and V. The gold-tooled red morocco binding with a central onlay of green morocco, illustrated here, was made by him and covers three lavishly illustrated descriptions of Stadtholder William IV's funeral. One of Micke's decorative leaf tools[3] seems identical with one used on the binding of a 1499 Venice Firmicus Maternus which belongs to my group V;[4] this could have been acquired by Micke after 1724 when the binder of Group V had ceased work.

1. J. Storm van Leeuwen, *De achttiende-eeuwse Haagse boekband in de koninklijke Bibliotheek*, 's-Gravenhage, 1976.
2. For this unidentified collection, see ibid., p. 58.
3. Ibid., p. 401, tool 67.
4. M. M. Foot, *The Henry Davis Gift*, vol. I, London, 1978, p. 258, no. 28.

* English and Foreign Bookbindings 12, *The Book Collector*, XXIX, pp. 82–3.

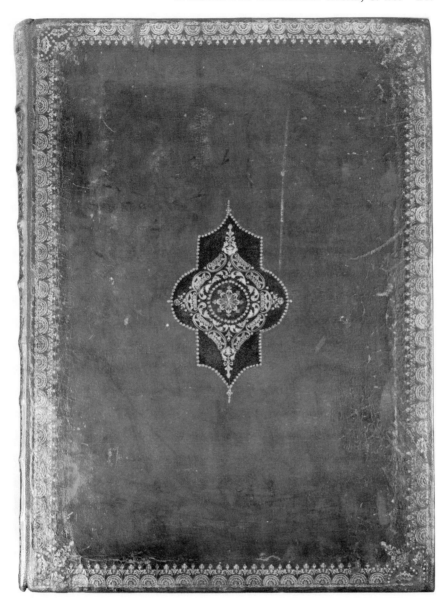

Fig. 32.1   *Laatste Eere ofte Historische Beschrijving en nauwkeurige*
afbeeldinge der plechtige begraaf-ceremonie . . . van wijlen
zijne doorluchtige Hoogheid Willem Carel Hendrik Frizo,
's-Gravenhage, 1752 [and two other works 1752–5].
Red morocco, onlaid in green, gold tooled. 520 × 380 × 44 mm.
British Library, C.128.k.8.

33 An Eton Binding of the 1760s by Roger Payne

(1983)*

In *The Book Collector*, 1963, Howard M. Nixon illustrated an early binding made in Eton by Roger Payne. As Mr Nixon pointed out, bindings from this period of Payne's life are rare and the tools used to decorate them do not occur on his numerous and well-known London bindings of the 1790s. I would like to add five more bindings to Payne's early Eton œuvre. Four are tooled with the same rather stiff fleurons that grace the turn-ins of Nixon's discovery: two cover a two-volume set of Horace Walpole's *Catalogue of Royal and Noble Authors* (1759), now in the Arts of the Book collection at Yale University Library; one is on a 1762 Baskerville *Common Prayer* and *Psalms* in the British Library (C.129.b.14) with elaborate doublures, and the fourth is illustrated here. The roll along its outer edge also occurs on a copy of Plinius Caecilius Secundus, *Vite de' Rè di Roma, et altri Rè*, Venice and Bologna, 1669 (British Library, C.46.a.21). Like the binding illustrated, the latter belonged to William Petty, Earl of Shelburne (later Marquess of Lansdowne), and has his bookplate, as well as his cypher on a label on the spine. The Xenophon formerly belonged to Henrietta Louisa Fermor, Countess of Pomfret, Lady of the bedchamber to Queen Caroline. After the Queen's death she left the Court and travelled with her husband in France and Italy where she acquired a three-volume set of Trissino, now in the Henry Davis Gift to the British Library, and where she may have bought the Xenophon. She died on her way to Bath in December 1761. Her granddaughter Sophia, only child of her eldest daughter Lady Sophia Carteret, married the Earl of Shelburne in 1765. It is possible that Payne bound the Xenophon for Lady Pomfret in 1760–61; alternatively, Shelburne had the book rebound, though the label with his cypher was added at a later date, possibly after the death of his first wife in 1771.

---

* English and Foreign Bookbindings 25, *The Book Collector*, xxxii, pp. 202–3.

Fig. 33.1   Xenophon. *Le Guerre de Greci*, Venice, 1550.
Gold-tooled blue morocco. 200 × 132 × 24 mm.
British Library, C.47.d.14.

34 A Binding by Roger Payne, 1796

(1978)*

In 1797 Thomas Payne, bookseller in Castle Street, offered for sale a copy of 'Fuller's History of the Worthies of England, *portrait and index, elegantly bound in russia by R. Payne, gilt leaves*, £4 14s 1662'.[1] This was cheap at the price considering that two years before Payne had offered the same work 'bound in russia' for £3 3s and that Roger Payne at that time charged between £2 11s and £4 14s 6d for binding a folio in russia leather. Moreover, it was 'the finest Large Copy without any Stains or spots [Roger Payne had] ever . . . seen'.[2] The reason for this bargain was that Roger, when finishing the binding, had forgotten 'to refer to the order & Finished Fuller according to yᵉ. Taste for English History with oak Leaves [and] Acorns'; consequently he 'sett a smaller price on yᵉ. Bookbinding than I can well afford to do. The Book being Bound so remarkable Well'.[3] The excuse for his mistake was 'my being before Finishing Dugdale'.[4] This is almost certainly the set of Dugdale's works which Roger bound in 1796 for Sir Richard Colt Hoare. The bindings were ordered through Thomas Payne. In a letter of 15 June 1796 Roger wrote to Thomas, 'I propose to Finish all the Dugdale uniform. But to make a difference in the English History by using Acorns & Oak Leaves'.[5] This suggests that the Fuller was bound later that summer.

Thomas Payne sold the book to William Beckford and, in 1822, it went with the contents of Fonthill Abbey to John Farquhar. In October 1823 the library was sold by Phillips; Fuller's *Worthies* fetched £7 5s.[6] Beckford may have recaptured it, as it was in the Beckford sale[7] where Quaritch bought if for £32 10s. Five years later Quaritch sold it for £48.[8] It belonged to Mrs Caroline Poole of Pasadena, California, and was acquired by the British Library in 1978.

1. *A New Catalogue for the Year 1797 . . . to be sold . . . by Thomas Payne*, no. 699.
2. Letter from Roger to 'Mr. Payne' with Fuller's *Worthies* 1662.
3. Ibid.

* English and Foreign Bookbindings 7, *The Book Collector*, XXVII, pp. 534–5.

Fig. 34.1 T. Fuller, *The History of the Worthies of England*. London,
1662.
Brown russia, gold tooled. 358 × 229 × 56 mm.
British Library, C.144.k.8.

4. Ibid.
5. Houghton Library, Dept of Printing and Graphic Arts, Harvard University.
6. *The valuable Library of Books in Fonthill Abbey*, Sept.–Oct. 1823, 2461.
7. Sotheby's, 13 July 1882, 3191.
8. *General Cat.*, Vol. iv, 1887, 22766.

35 A Binding by Devers, c. 1770–83

(1972)*

To the two bindings attributed on dubious grounds by L. Gruel[1] to *Claude* Devers, and the six bindings hesitantly attributed by L. M. Michon[2] to his son, a further twelve can be added; four of these are in the John Rylands Library in Manchester, two in the British Library, one in Keble College, Oxford, one in the Fitzwilliam Museum, Cambridge, one in 'La Grange', Cologny, Geneva, and three in private collections. They form a group of similar mosaic bindings in red or green morocco, onlaid in yellow, green or red with border compartments and often with heart and flower shapes. Small solid tools are used, mainly stars, crosses, various flowers, curls and fleurons. Frequently the spine is decorated with onlaid strips to a lozenge design; the end-leaves are of pale blue silk and the edges are gilt. The 1748 Gresset from the Schiff collection[3] and possibly the two examples mentioned by Gruel have no onlays but are decorated with the same tools. Eight bindings are signed (either at the top or at the bottom of the spine): DEVERS or RELIE PAR DEVERS. Gruel's doubtful example is the only one containing a ticket. There are a number of differently signed Devers bindings mentioned by C. Ramsden[4] and attributed to various members of the Devers family in Lyons. These all have quite different tools and are of later date. The Devers who was responsible for the group of bindings considered here must have worked before 1783 when two or possibly four of his bindings were sold in Paris. They belonged to Louis César de la Baume le Blanc, duc de la Vallière, governor of the Bourbonnais. I have found no bindings by him on books printed after 1783. Eleven or possibly fourteen of the bindings mentioned belonged to Count MacCarthy-Reagh and were sold in 1817.

1. L. Gruel, *Manuel historique et bibliographique de l'amateur de reliure*, Vol. II, Paris, 1905, p. 61.
2. L. M. Michon, *Les Reliures Mosaïqueés du XVIIIᵉ Siècle*, Paris, 1956, p. 46.
3. S. de Ricci, *French signed bindings in the M. L. Schiff collection*, New York, 1935, I, 99.
4. C. Ramsden, *French Bookbinders 1789–1848*, London, 1950, pp. 70–71.

* Foreign Bookbindings, XIII, *The Book Collector*, XXI, p. 107.

Fig. 35.1   *Dialogi Decem*, n.p. [Cologne], 1473.
Red morocco, onlaid in yellow and green and tooled in gold.
Arms of T. Grenville added. 290 × 210 × 30 mm.
British Library, G.8988.

36 A Binding by James Scott, c. 1779

(1982)*

Having read, indeed more than once, Mr Loudon's full account of the binders James and William Scott (London, 1980), having used it on several occasions, but not until very recently having got round to expressing my appreciation of this excellent book (review *Book Collector*, XXXI, 1982, p. 378), I would like to make an act of contrition for this delay by publishing five bindings by James Scott which have come to my attention since Mr Loudon's book appeared. The most elaborate undoubtedly belongs to Scott's rococo period and dates from about 1775. It covers yet another copy of the 1770 Foulis edition of Milton's *Paradise Lost* (Loudon lists six) and is decorated with the Corinthian column (Ar1.4), a crowned grotesque face (An. 1), a fountain (Ar3.5), two pairs of birds (Zo. 2–5), a thistle (Bo. 22) and a number of floral swags and rococo flourishes. It belongs to the Grolier Club in New York. From about three years later dates the red morocco binding on Kincaid's *Bible* [and] *Psalms* (1773) which has the Moses [John-the-Baptist] tool (An.6) on the spine and a heavy roll (Ro1.7) surrounding a panel with a fan-shaped tool (Bo. 21), a finial (Ar3.6), swags, flourishes and leaf tools. This binding and the next one, a much plainer tree calf affair decorated with a single roll (Ro1.6), belong to Patrick King. The latter, covering three volumes of Rousseau's *Emilius or a Treatise of Education* (Edinburgh, 1768), shows the tall trophy-column (Ar1.5) on the spine. Another very simple binding decorated with a single roll only (Ro1.10) to which the arms of George III have been added later (re-backed) covers the presentation copy to the King of J. Anderson's *Observations on . . . Industry* (Edinburgh, 1777); it has Scott's oval ticket on the title-page (BL, 34.d.18). Mr Loudon has given sufficient proof that the trophy-column was in fact a roll. On the binding illustrated here it was partially used along the short sides, and two little naked feet are just perceptible on top of the wreath containing the profile head.

---

* English and Foreign Bookbindings 22, *The Book Collector*, XXXI, pp. 340–41.

Fig. 36.1   R. Colvill, *The Caledonians*, Edinburgh, 1779 (presentation
copy to Walter Hamilton, Lord Provost).
Brown tree calf tooled in gold. 269 × 199 × 16 mm.
British Library, C.108.f.5.

37 A Binding by James Campbell, 1781

(1985)*

The *Royal Kalendar* for 1767 to 1770 lists James Campbell as bookbinder to King George III.[1] Charles Ramsden has found in the Royal Archives at Windsor bills for considerable sums for binding work done by Campbell, the first of which is dated Christmas 1766.[2] According to the various London trade lists and directories,[3] James Campbell, stationer and bookbinder, lived in the Strand from 1773 until his death on 2 April 1784,[4] in 1775 at no. 110 and from 1778 at 103.

When George III established his private bindery at Buckingham House, Campbell recommended John Polwarth who had been working for him as a journeyman, and who was engaged as head finisher. According to the Jaffray papers, 'In 1780 Mr. Pratt Senr. worked at Buckingham House . . . under Mr. Armstrong'.[5] If this is true, the bindery at Buckingham House was probably established by that date, but one should bear in mind that John Jaffray's memoranda, based on conversations with elderly binders, were written at least 60 years after the event.[6]

In 1781 Sir Horace Mann's nephew (later the second Baronet) took four sets of Galuzzi's *Istoria del Granducato di Toscana* (Florence, 1781) printed on 'carta cerulea' (thick, blue-ish Italian paper) 'to Mr. Campbell the bookbinder in the Strand' to have them bound: one set for presentation to George III and three sets for Horace Walpole.[7] The set for the King is in the King's Library at the British Library. The tools used on these bindings also occur on several other bindings in the King's Library and they ended up among the finishing tools used in George III's private bindery.[8]

1. The *Court and City Register* names W. Shropshire as royal binder from 1762 to 1788 (notwithstanding the fact that he died on 17 October 1785: see *Gentleman's Magazine*, LV, 1785, p. 837). The same source gives Campbell as royal binder for 1770 only. No royal binders are mentioned in 1760 and 1761. According to the *Royal Kalendar*, W. Shropshire held the position from

---

* English and Foreign Bookbindings 33, *The Book Collector*, xxxiv, pp. 214–16.

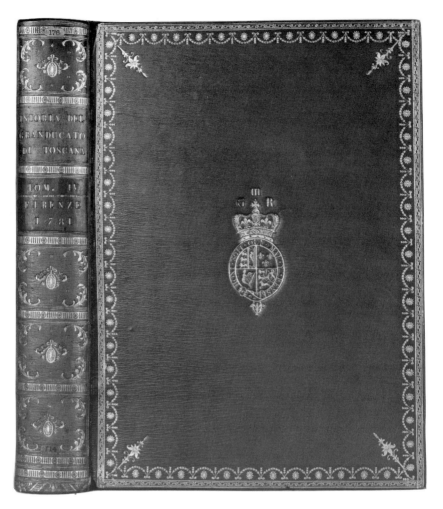

Fig. 37.1   R. Galluzzi, *Istoria del Granducato di Toscana*, 5 vols.,
Florence, 1781, vol. IV.
Gold-tooled straight-grain morocco. 297 × 222 × 50 mm.
British Library, 176.f.14.

1770 to 1788; the position was vacant from 1789 to 1792; Th. Lowndes was royal binder from 1793 to 1799, and Wm. Armstrong from 1800 to 1820.

2. C. Ramsden, 'Bookbinders to George III and his immediate Descendants and Collaterals', *The Library*, 5th series, XIII (1958), pp. 186–93.

3. *Lowndes London Directory*, 1773–1784; *The London Register of Merchants and Traders*, 1775; *A Complete Guide to . . . London* (J. Osborn), 1783; J. Pendred, *The Earliest Directory of the Book Trade . . . 1785* (ed. G. Pollard, London, 1955).

4. *Gentleman's Magazine*, LIV (1784), p. 316.

5. J. Jaffray, *A Collection of Manuscripts related to the Art and Trade of Book-binding*, vol. IV, p. 224 (typescript in the British Library); see also E. Howe, *The London Bookbinders 1780–1806*, London, 1950, pp. 59–62. On Armstrong, see note 1 above.

6. The date of the establishment of the bindery at Buckingham House is still not certain. The Jaffray papers suggest in or before 1780; E. Howe, *op. cit* gives 1780, but in *A List of London Bookbinders 1648–1815*, London, 1950, Howe says Polwarth was the first binder to be engaged and he was working for the King in 1786; C. Ramsden, *art. cit.*, gives between 1786 and 1788 as the starting date; H. M. Nixon, *English Royal Bookbindings in the British Museum*, London, 1957 gives *c.* 1786, but in *Five Centuries of English Book-binding*, London, 1978, he says that the bindery was established by 1780. More work in the Royal Archives is obviously necessary.

7. A. T. Hazen, *A Catalogue of Horace Walpole's Library*, London/New Haven, 1969, vol. 2, pp. 543–4.

8. Ink impressions of the tools used in the bindery at Buckingham House (now in the royal bindery at Windsor Castle) are in the British Library.

38 A London Rococo Binding, 1782

(1979)*

Edward King presented to George III his *Observations on Ancient Castles*, London, 1782, bound in red morocco, decorated in gold with floral and ornamental rococo tools which occur on five other bindings, all covering books printed between 1763 and 1778.[1] Very similar variants of a number of these tools are found on eight bindings attributed to John Ernst Baumgarten.[2] Three of the tools used on these 'Baumgarten' bindings each occur in two closely similar variants. On the 1763 *New Testament* which belongs to the same group as King's presentation, two parrots eye each other from behind tall rococo shells. Both parrots and shells are found on Santi Bartoli's *Receuil de peintures antiques*, 1757,[3] attributed to Baumgarten. A smaller rococo shell also turns up on bindings of both groups. To complicate matters further, the palmette tools which form the border of the 1778 *Evangeliae* look suspiciously similar to those on a 'Baumgarten' binding and the vase tool on the spine of King's *Observations* seems the same as that used by Kalthoeber, Baumgarten's successor.

It seems unlikely that Baumgarten would have owned more than one close variant of the same size of at least six tools. He, or Kalthoeber, might have bought them as part of a deceased binder's stock, but both groups of bindings seem to have been made during the same three decades. It may be that Huttner's observation of the borrowing habits of the next generation of German binders in London already applied in Baumgarten's day.[4]

1. *New Testament* [Greek], Oxford, 1763 (Sotheby's, 30 October 1962, 390); [A collection of engravings, Paris, *c.* 1765] (British Library, Henry Davis Gift); *The Regulations . . . of the Household of . . . Northumberland*, London, 1768 (Broxbourne Library, R.1568); Ariosto, *Orlando Furioso*, Birmingham, 1773 (Sotheby's, 1 November 1976, 29); *Evangeliae*, Oxford, 1778 (BL, 2.b.14).
2. H. M. Nixon, 'Baumgarten's Will', *Festschrift Ernst Kyriss*, Stuttgart, 1961, mentions seven, and an eighth covers J. Abravanel, *Dialogi di amore*, Venice, 1541 (National Library of Scotland, Af. ⅜.10).
3. Sotheby's, 27 April 1948, 658.

* English and Foreign Bookbindings 8, *The Book Collector*, xxviii, pp. 110–11.

4. J. C. Huttner, 'Ueber einige Vortheile und bequeme Handgriffe der Buchbinder in England', *Englische Miscellen*, VI, Tübingen, 1802, p. 28, 'Sie kommen oft zu einem der dortigen grossen Buchbinder, und sagen: leiht mir doch eure Stempel! dort sind sie, antwortet er, nehmet!'

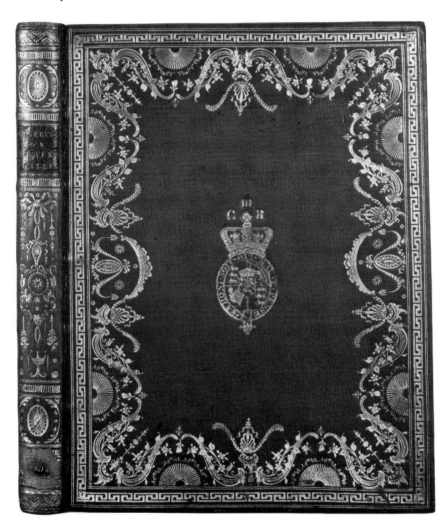

Fig. 38.1   E. King, *Observations on Ancient Castles*, London, 1782.
Red straight-grain morocco, gold tooled. 288 × 228 × 30 mm.
British Library, 141.e.13.

39 A Binding by Gabriel de Sancha, c. 1790

(1979)*

In article 38, I illustrated a rococo binding made in London in 1782 decorated with tools closely similar to those used by Baumgarten and to those used on the binding illustrated here, which is signed on the spine SANCHA F.

Gabriel de Sancha[1] was born on 18 March 1746, the son of the printer, publisher and bookbinder Antonio de Sancha. At the age of fourteen he was sent to Paris on a government grant to learn the art of bookbinding. In 1766 he was appointed binder to the Cámara and from 1773 he worked in Madrid in his father's publishing house and ran the bindery. In 1782 he compromised one of his father's servants and promised to marry her. Incensed, his father despatched him abroad, this time on a journey to England, France and the Netherlands. Six years later he married Manuela Moreno Tejada, the daughter of a family friend. When Antonio died in 1790 Gabriel inherited the printing business and 'that concerning the binding of books, such as presses of all kind, gilding and cutting tools . . .'. Gabriel's younger brother Antonio worked with him until 1797. The influence of Sancha's foreign travel is clearly discernible in his work. He bound à la Derome, imitated Padeloup, Dubuisson and other Parisian binders, and brought rococo and neoclassical designs back from England. His tool catalogue reproduced by P. Vindel,[2] shows how closely he had various French and English examples copied.

One of the other binders to receive grants to study abroad was Pascual Carsí y Vidal, who went to London where he married Maria Clark—he may be the 'Carsee' who 'learned the art at Baumgarten's',[3] although Baumgarten died in 1782 and Carsí y Vidal is first mentioned back in Madrid in 1797.

---

1. M. López Serrano in: *Archivo Español de Arte*, 1945, pp. 1–16; 1950, pp. 115–31. (pl. 1 shows two Sancha bindings similar to the one illustrated here).
   ——in: *Revista de Bibliografía Nacional*, 1946, pp. 391–9.

* English and Foreign Bookbindings 9, *The Book Collector*, xxviii, pp. 256–7.

2. P. Vindel, *D. Antonio de Sancha, encuadernador*, Madrid, 1935. M. López Serrano says Gabriel, his brother and son (rather than his father) used the tools.

3. Jaffray MS. E. Howe, *A List of London Bookbinders 1648–1815*, London, 1950, pp. xxxiv, 9.

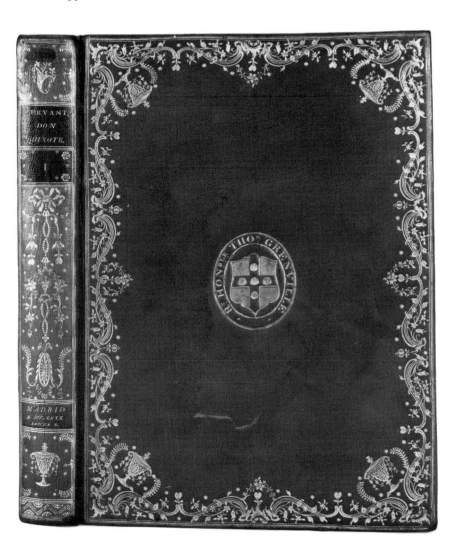

Fig. 39.1   M. de Cervántes, *El ingenioso hidalgo Don Quixote de la Mancha*. Madrid, 1780.
Red morocco, gold tooled. 307 × 234 × 45 mm.
British Library, G.18295.

40 An Irish Binding by William McKenzie, 1784

(1989)*

William McKenzie was apprenticed to William Gilbert, a bookbinder turned bookseller, and was freed as a Stationer on 4 July 1780.[1] In 1783 he married Sarah, widow of William Hallhead, formerly bookseller to Trinity College Dublin. On his marriage McKenzie took over Hallhead's appointment as Bookseller and Stationer to the University, as well as his (and formerly Leathley's) premises at 63 Dame Street. For the next twelve years he provided books and bindings for the library; he also supplied stationery and he printed the 1791 edition of the College *Statutes*. His relations with Trinity College Dublin were not without difficulties. He appears to have supplied defective sets, made mistakes in numbering series, sent unwanted materials and, on occasion, overcharged. By 1795 he had exasperated the College Librarian to such an extent that he was dismissed.[2] The year before he had moved to 33 College Street and in 1811 he is mentioned as printer and stationer at 7 Merrion Row.[3] He died in the spring of 1817.

His work, which he sometimes signed with an engraved ticket, is easily recognizable. As a rule he used green goatskin or tree calf and tooled the covers with a border roll, occasionally adding a central arms-block. The books are usually sewn on three sawn-in cords, producing a flat spine, frequently decorated with coloured labels and onlays and elaborate gold tooling. He was fond of a distinctive green, yellow, pink and black spot-marbled paper which he used for end-leaves; he sewed his headbands with red and white silk, and often marbled or stained the edges of the leaves.

1. J. McDonnell and P. Healy, *Gold-tooled Bookbindings commissioned by Trinity College Dublin in the Eighteenth Century*, Leixlip, 1987, pp. 58–67. C. Ramsden, *Bookbinders of the United Kingdom (outside London) 1780–1840*, London, 1954, pp. 241–2, M. Craig, *Irish Bookbindings 1600–1800*, London, 1954, p. 21.
2. For details see J. McDonnell and P. Healy, *op cit.*
3. *Wilson's Dublin Directory*, 1794 and 1811.

---

* English and Foreign Bookbindings 47, *The Book Collector*, xxxviii, pp. 66–7.

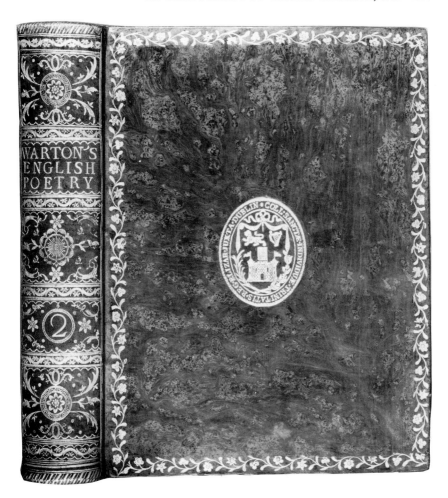

Fig. 40.1   T. Warton, *The History of English Poetry*, 3 vols. London,
1774–81 (vol. 2).
T.C.D. Prize binding of gold-tooled tree calf. 272 × 210 × 49 mm.
British Library, C.155.a.10.

41 A Binding by Bartholomew Frye, *c.* 1820

(1988)*

There is still some uncertainty about the origin and activity of Bartholomew Frye. According to T. W. Hanson he was a German immigrant who may have worked for Edwards of Halifax.[1] We know for a fact that by 1816 he worked as a bookbinder in the Causeway in Halifax where he was still active in 1820; that he worked at some unspecified date in Manchester, and that by 1824 he is mentioned at 34 Clare Street in Liverpool. His namesake, perhaps his relative, Gerard B. Frye, also a bookbinder, worked from 1818 till 1821 in Manchester, first at 2 Park Street, Redbank and then in Riding's Court, St Mary's Gate. Subsequently he is found at Bartholomew's address in Liverpool in 1825. Apart from scraps of information that may be gleaned from local directories,[2] fourteen bindings are known that can be attributed to Bartholomew.[3] Eleven of these are signed, nine at Halifax and two at Manchester. They have certain decorative features as well as certain tools in common. All but two (one in russia and one in vellum) are in straight-grained morocco; eight volumes have either drawings or engravings, below transparent vellum inlaid in the covers, and eleven have fore-edges painted with water-colour scenes beneath the gold. The latter two characteristics, as well as the place of work, may have made Hanson connect Frye with Edwards.

Several questions remain. The books inside Bartholomew's bindings range in date from 1793 to [*c.* 1820]. There seems to be some doubt as to where and when a *Book of Common Prayer*, printed for John Reeves, was published.[4] Could Frye have worked in Manchester before he came to Halifax? The relation between Bartholomew and Gerard is unclear. Both were binding at the same time in different places before arriving with a year between them at the same address in Liverpool. It is possible that Bartholomew died in 1824 and left his shop to Gerard. No bindings have emerged that can confidently be assigned to Gerard Frye.

1. Whether he came from Hanover or Osnaburgh seems in doubt. See T. W. Hanson, 'Edwards of Halifax', *Paper, Reports, etc. read before the Halifax*

---

* English and Foreign Bookbindings 44, *The Book Collector*, xxxvii, pp. 92–4.

Fig. 41.1   *An Essay on the Origin of Coats of Arms* (ms. unfinished), [c. 1820].
Green straight-grained morocco, tooled in blind and gold.
321 × 255 × 36 mm.
British Library, C.154.k.5.

    Antiquarian Society (1912) p. 193. C. Ramsden, *Bookbinders of the United Kingdom 1780–1840*, London, 1954, p. 76. H. M. Nixon, *Twelve Books in Fine Bindings*, London, 1953, p. 73, note 4. Sotheby's, 19 June 1967, *1597*.

2. *Commercial Directory . . . Ashton, etc.*, 1816, 1818–19–20. *Manchester Directory*, 1821. *Gore's & Kelly's Directory of Liverpool*, 1825. Baines, *History of the County of Lancaster*, Liverpool, 1824–25, vol I (Liverpool Directory). See also C. Ramsden, *op. cit.*

3. Eight volumes are mentioned in G. D. Hobson, *English Bindings 1490–1940 in the Library of J. R. Abbey*, London, 1940, no. 101. Three are in the Ramsden collection in the British Library (C.151.d.3, C.154.k.4, C.154.k.5). One was sold at Sotheby's, 24.vii.1951, *75* (and was lot 619 in the Doheny Sale III, Christie's, New York, 1–2 February 1988; lot 620 in this sale was Hobson, Abbey, *101*, and Sotheby's, 19.vi.1967, *1597*). One was sold by Maggs, Catalogue 1075, II (1987), *254* (now in the British Library, C.188.a.9) and one belongs to the National Trust and is at Speke Hall, near Liverpool (I owe this reference to Dr N. Pickwood).

4. Sotheby's, 24.vii.1951, *75* ascribes it to 'Oxford 1817', while the Doheny Catalogue, III, *619* states 'London [1801]'. I am convinced that both catalogues describe the same book. It has the Manchester ticket. The other Manchester ticket is found in C.154.k.4 (London, 1809).

42 A Binding by Thomas Mullen of Dublin, c. 1827–30

(1986)*

George Mullen, bookbinder at Dublin (1803–48) has been mentioned in the literature more than once,[1] but his relative, George junior and his namesakes (and possible relatives), John and Thomas, have not received much attention.

George junior is described in Wilson's *Dublin Directory* for 1822 as a bookseller and stationer at 38 Nassau Street, also George senior's address. His appearance explains the wording on a ticket in a copy of S. Collet, *Relics of Literature* (London, 1823) once in Ramsden's own collection, bound in plain boards, which states 'George Mullen Bookseller, Stationer, and Bookbinder, 38 Nassau Street, Dublin, late with R. Triphook, Bond Street, London'. Triphook was a Bond Street bookseller in the early 1820s and George the younger obviously worked for him before setting up in Dublin.

John Mullen, who is described in the Dublin directories as bookbinder and account-book manufacturer, occurs in 1839 and 1840 at 81 (Upper) Abbey Street and in 1841 at 22 Bachelor's Walk.

Thomas Mullen, whose alleged appearance in 1816 at 27 Anglesea Street is probably due to a misprint in Ramsden, occurs for the first time in the *Dublin Directory* for 1827 at 20 Anglesea Street. He is still there the following year, but by 1829 he had moved to 21 Anglesea Street where he is mentioned for the last time in 1830. During this seemingly very short career he produced several signed gold- and blind-tooled morocco bindings, only four of which I have seen, though there are presumably more examples in Irish collections. Two belonged to Ramsden and are now in the British Library. One of these covers Fénelon's *Livre de prières* (Paris, 1826); the other is illustrated here. Two more are in a private collection. One, a copy of Byron, *Sardanapalus* (London, 1821) is decorated with the same rolls that are found on the binding illustrated. The other, on J. E. Anderson's *Dissertatio medica* (Edinburgh, 1824) shows a very striking roll with large animals, birds and insects. It formerly belonged to Major J. R. Abbey. All four have Thomas Mullen's ticket.

---

* English and Foreign Bookbindings 39, *The Book Collector*, xxxv, pp. 494–5.

1. Seymour de Ricci, *British and Miscellaneous Signed Bindings in the Mortimer L. Schiff Collection*, New York, 1935, nos. 41–3. G. D. Hobson, *English Bindings in the Library of J. R. Abbey*, London, 1940, no. 112. C. Ramsden, *Bookbinders of the United Kingdom, 1780–1840*, London, 1954, p. 244. M. Craig, *Irish Bookbindings*, Dublin, 1976. H. M. Nixon, *British Bookbindings presented by K. H. Oldaker to . . . Westminster Abbey*, London, 1982, no. 69.

Fig. 42.1   Bartolomeo Pinelli, *Nuova raccolta di cinquanta costumi pittoreschi*, Rome, 1817.
Blue straight-grain morocco, tooled in gold and blind. 132 × 180 × 17 mm.
British Library, C.150.c.4.

43 A Binding by Archibald MacLiesh, 1837
(1986)*

Archibald MacLiesh, bookbinder, lived in Bishop Wearmouth, Sunderland. The Directories for 1827, 1828 and 1829 mention him at Cumberland Street.[1] He appears in the Durham Poll-Book for 1832 as living in Pratt's Buildings,[2] and by 1834 he had moved to Bedford Street.[3] I have not been able to find any directories that include Co. Durham for the years between 1835 and 1848 and by that date MacLiesh is no longer listed. W. Mitchell has illustrated MacLiesh's binder's ticket which gives his address as Cumberland Street.[4] The binding illustrated is signed on the doublure of the upper cover 'MACLIESH BINDER.' and has a tooled leather label on the first end-leaf stating that this copy was 'Presented to Miss Mary Lowe by Archibald MacLiesh. Bishopwearmouth, 1837.' The binding covers Thomas Paine, *Rights of Man* and the fore-edge has a painting beneath the gold showing the bridge over the Wear near Sunderland, which was built in 1793–5, mainly from a design by Thomas Paine.

In 1785 Paine had started to design a single-arched iron bridge to span the Schuylkill river. A model was exhibited at the Pennsylvania State House on New Year's Day 1787. Franklin advised Paine to present his model to the Academy of Sciences in Paris, which he did on 21 July. Paine then went to England where he submitted his model to the Royal Society, registered a patent, and reached an agreement with the Walker brothers of Rotherham to build an experimental arch. In May 1790 the 110-foot long bridge was brought to London where it was exhibited at Lisson or Leasing (later Paddington) Green. It was taken down after a year and not used again. However, the materials and most of the principles were used to build the bridge over the Wear.[5]

---

1. W. Parson and W. White, *History, Directory and Gazetteer of the Counties of Durham and Northumberland*, Newcastle, 1827–28. J. Pigot & Co., *National Commercial Directory for 1828–9*, London [1828].
2. I owe this reference to Mr R. J. Roberts, who also tells me that MacLiesh is not mentioned in the 1837 Poll-Book.

---

* English and Foreign Bookbindings 37, *The Book Collector*, xxxv, pp. 214–15.

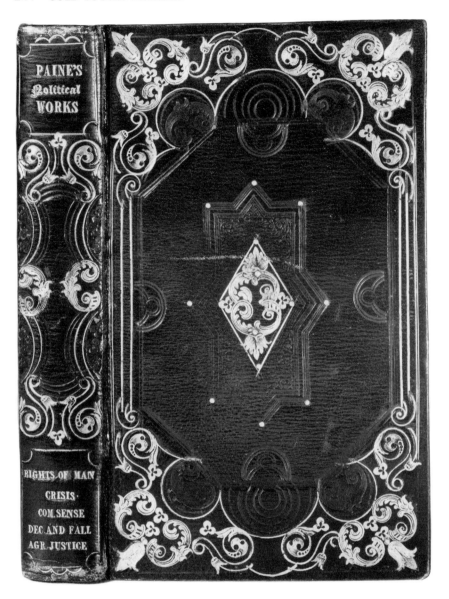

Fig. 43.1 Thomas Paine, *Rights of Man, etc.*, London, n.d.
Dark red straight-grain morocco, tooled in gold and blind.
168 × 108 × 27 mm.
British Library, C.183.aa.12.

3. J. Pigot & Co., *National Commercial Directory*, London, 1834. I. Slater, *Royal National Commercial Directory*, Manchester and London, 1848.
4. W. S. Mitchell, 'Bookbinders' Tickets', *Durham University Journal*, Dec. 1953, no. 15.
5. F. Oldys, *The Life of Thomas Paine*, London, 1791; A. Williamson, *Thomas Paine*, London, 1973; D. Powell, *Tom Paine The Greatest Exile*, London, 1985.

44 A Binding by M. M. Holloway, *c.* 1862

(1980)*

Marseille Middleton Holloway is first mentioned in the London directories in 1836 as an engraver, printseller and publisher, living in the house of Thomas Bristoll, an engraver and copperplate printer, at 22 King William Street. On 9 September 1837 he married Anna Smith,[1] and by Michaelmas he was paying rates for a house at 14 Henrietta Street, where three years later his son Marseille was born. In 1844 the family moved to 25 Bedford Street, and two years later he added printing to his activities. From 1853 he donated annually to the Bookbinders' Pension Society and employed Andrew Shaw, a journeyman binder.[2] Several Holloway bindings, 'admirably executed' and 'very elegant', were on show at the Great Exhibition of 1862;[3] the binding for Dudley Coutts Marjoribanks illustrated here dates from this time. Marjoribanks, who was a Berwickshire magnate and Liberal M.P., later first Baron Tweedmouth, owned a number of bindings signed M. M. Holloway.[4] In 1864 Marseille jr joined his father, and by 1873 they had widened the firm's scope and owned a gallery where they sold pictures, drawings, objects of art and vertu. From 1874 they no longer employed a bookbinder and the next year both father and son retired to their country houses: Marseille to Woodhurst at Oxted, where he died in 1878,[5] and Marseille Middleton to Hillbrow, Streatham, which he already owned in 1870, and where he died at the age of 88 late in 1897.

1. On his marriage certificate he is called 'Gentleman', like his – by then deceased – father Charles.
2. Shaw collected subscriptions to the pension fund at Mr Holloway's from 1854 to 1860, when this was done by A. Colvill. By 1863 Shaw was 67 years old and infirm, and in 1875 he qualified for a trade pension.
3. *The Bookbinders' Trade Circular*, August 1862, p. 135.
4. Hodgson & Co., 11–12 November 1948. Another one is in the British Library, at C.68.h.15.
5. His widow is still mentioned at Woodhurst in 1895.

* English and Foreign Bookbindings 14, *The Book Collector*, XXIX, pp. 406–7.

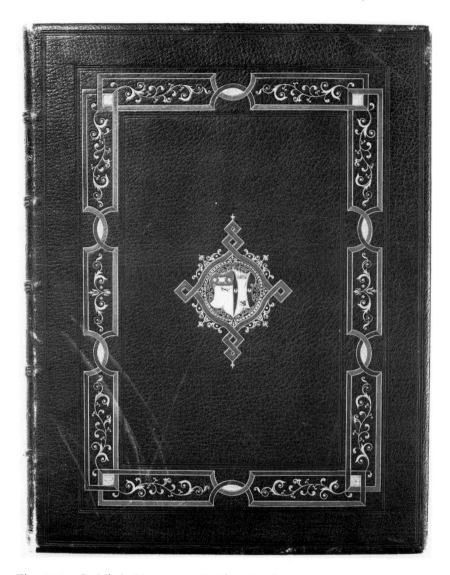

Fig. 44.1   G. Libri, *Monuments Inédits*, London, 1862.
            Blue morocco with coloured onlays, gold tooled. Arms and
            monogram of D.C. Marjoribanks and his wife Isabella Hogg.
            505 × 395 × 35 mm.
            British Library, Henry Davis Gift.

45 A Binding by Westleys & Co., 1864

(1982)*

Francis Westley became a Freeman of the Stationers' Company on 7 October 1800, after having been bound to George Westley, bookbinder, for seven years.[1] From 1805 until 1820 he worked as bookbinder, and from 1817 also as stationer, at 11 Friar Street, Blackfriars.[2] In 1819–20 he established a booksellers' business at 10 Ave Maria Lane, Stationers' Court, where he was joined by A. H. Davies in 1827. The firm Westley & Davies, booksellers and publishers, stayed at Stationers' Court until 1837, while Francis Westley kept his bindery in Friar Street where he is listed among the inhabitants of St Ann's, Blackfriars as a rate collector and under-churchwarden.[3] In 1837 the bindery in Blackfriars became known as Westley, Son and Jarvis. The son, Josiah, had been apprenticed to his father in 1827. The firm had become one of the largest in London; they employed over 40 men and were involved in various trade disputes.[4] From 1838 they called themselves bookbinders and embossers, and from 1842 to 1848 the firm's name was Westleys & Clark. The next year Josiah Westley's & Co. is listed, still in Friar Street, and the business continued as Westleys & Co. from 1850 until 1900 when the name changed to Trickett, Westleys & Co. It seems that Francis retired in 1841; Josiah left the firm in 1859–60 and was succeeded by Frederick William Westley.

They mainly produced blocked cloth bindings; Josiah took part in the Great Exhibition of 1851 with gold-blocked bindings, 'all in bad taste',[5] and Westleys & Co. won a prize medal for many specimens of blocking at the Great Exhibition of 1862. One of their exhibits was a green cloth binding virtually identical to the one illustrated here.[6]

1. D. F. McKenzie, *Stationers' Company Apprentices, 1701–1800*, Oxford, 1978. E. Howe, *A List of London Bookbinders, 1648–1815*, London, 1950.
2. *Holden's Triennial Directory*, 1805–24; *Kent's [London] Directory*, 1810–27; *Robson's Improved London Directory*, 1820–42; *Pigot & Co.'s London . . . Commercial Directory*, 1822–40; *The Post Office Annual [London] Directory*,

---

* English and Foreign Bookbindings 21, *The Book Collector*, XXXI, pp. 214–15.

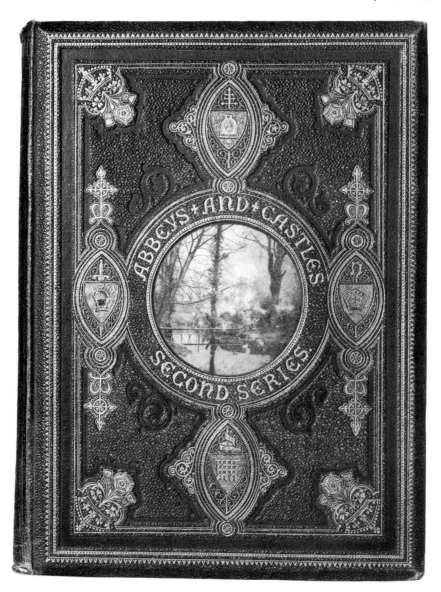

Fig. 45.1   W. Howitt, *Ruined Abbeys and Castles of Great Britain and Ireland. Second Series.* London, 1864.
Blue cloth blocked in blind and gold with a photograph onlaid in the centre. 228 × 167 × 30 mm.
British Library, C.44.d.7.

1800–1900; *The Business Directory [London]*, 1864–1900 (also for information below).

3. St Ann Blackfriars, 'Inhabitants List, 1702–1855', Guildhall Library, MS 1071.
4. E. Howe and J. Child, *The Society of London Bookbinders*, 1780–1951, London, 1952, pp. 109–35.
5. *The Bookbinders' Trade Circular*, 1850, p. 44.
6. Ibid., 1862, p. 143.

Part V
UNUSUAL MATERIALS

In the previous Parts only bindings made of leather have been discussed. Although until the second half of the nineteenth century leather was the most common material for binding books and although it has remained so for fine binding, other materials have been—and are being—used as well. Metal and ivory were deployed for treasure bindings; tortoiseshell, wood, straw, plaster of Paris, paper, and fabrics of various kinds were all used,[1] and nowadays one also finds bindings made of plastics.

Plain coloured paper was frequently used for covering pamphlets or acted as a temporary cover for a sewn book. Decorated paper was used by binders as end-papers and also served as wrappers, especially for sheet music. This Part starts with the description of a collection of decorated papers, now in the British Library, followed by a few examples of paper bindings. Two decorated wooden covers, produced more than 400 years apart, are also described.

1. For examples see M. M. Foot, *Pictorial Bookbindings*, London, 1986.

251

46 The Olga Hirsch Collection of Decorated Papers

(1981)*

In 1968 Mrs Olga Hirsch, the widow of Paul Hirsch the celebrated music collector, bequeathed to the British Library her collection of decorated papers, consisting of over 3,500 sheets of paper and about 130 books in paper wrappers or with decorated end-papers, as well as her eminently useful small reference library on paper making and paper decorating.

After her marriage in 1911, Olga Hirsch, née Ladenburg, started to learn bookbinding in order to be able to give the necessary professional attention to the repair of her husband's music library. She was trained at the Buchbinderei Ludwig in Frankfurt am Main, and started her truly remarkable collection from the need to match the paper for the end-leaves and wrappers of many of the music books.

She also collected bookbindings and owned several Italian, French and German Renaissance bindings, such as one with Grimaldi's Apollo and Pegasus device,[1] a nice binding attributed to Claude de Picques,[2] the 1544 Lyons New Testament bound by Wotton's binder C for presentation by Theoderic von Thüngen to Richard von der Kher,[3] and the unusual and lavishly tooled round binding by Caspar Meuser which was lot 336 in the Abbey sale of 22 June 1965.[4] Her seventeenth- and eighteenth-century examples included bindings with the arms and cyphers of Louis XIII, XIV and XV, an English Restoration binding on a 1641 Prayer-book, and bindings with tickets of Padeloup and Derome le jeune.[5] This collection was dispersed after the Hirschs's arrival in England in 1936.

The papers, collected originally for practical reasons, but soon for their own beauty and interest, increased significantly with the purchase in January 1916 from the Munich dealer Jacques Rosenthal of a collection of 2,000 pieces of eighteenth- and nineteenth-century marbled, block-printed and embossed paper. This was the start of almost 50 years of acquisition and exchange, study and arrangement, that made Mrs Hirsch one of the foremost authorities on decorated papers and her collection one of the most comprehensive of its kind.

The papers are arranged in boxes and folders according to the techniques

* *The British Library Journal*, VII, pp. 12–38.

used to decorate them, each type in chronological order so far as it could be established. This is extremely difficult to do with any certainty as papers were imported and exported widely, were used long after they had been manufactured, and were imitated as fashion and profit dictated.

Though several articles about the collection have been published,[6] and though Albert Haemmerle in his outstanding work *Buntpapier*[7] used it extensively, no comprehensive catalogue has yet been completed. I will not attempt here to list the papers individually, but I will try to deal with the main categories established by Mrs Hirsch and to describe and illustrate a few examples with emphasis on the hand-made papers.[8] A list of the signed and identified eighteenth- and nineteenth-century papers is appended. The earliest known decorated papers are the monochrome brush-coated papers that are found on the backs of playing cards and in *alba amicorum*. In the Württembergisches Landesmuseum at Stuttgart is a pack of playing cards the backs of which have been lined with red-painted paper; one of these shows a watermark that can be dated between 1428 and 1433.[9] A recipe book from the convent of St Katharine at Nuremberg of *c.* 1470 describes the methods of making the dyes for these monochrome papers, as well as how to make flock paper.[10]

Another early technique for decorating paper already used in the second half of the sixteenth century is sprinkling. The Olga Hirsch collection contains both brush-coated and sprinkled papers from the late seventeenth to the twentieth century; matt, semi-matt and glossy brush-coated papers; monochrome and polychrome sprinkled and sprayed papers. Some of these were obviously used as wrappers.

Flock paper is made by covering either the whole surface of the paper, or that part of the paper which is to show the design, with adhesive and then with coloured wool dust. It was already known in Italy in the mid-fifteenth century. This technique was used to make wall hangings, both of textile and of paper, and became popular, especially in England, in the sixteenth, seventeenth and eighteenth centuries. In 1634 Jerome Lanyer applied for the exclusive right to manufacture flock wall hangings 'which hee calleth Londrindiana',[11] fourteen years after Le François, an artisan from Rouen, had 'invented' his *tontisses*. In the mid-eighteenth century English flock papers were shipped to France to become the height of fashion in Paris where they were soon copied. Didier Aubert, a former apprentice of J.-M. Papillon, made it his speciality and produced 'toiles veloutées . . . fort supérieures aux papiers d'Angleterre'.[12] Examples are now quite rare and the two sets of Italian flock end-papers in Ospizio degli Armeni in Roma, *Ode tratta dall'Armeno* (Venice, 1834) (Hirsch B27) date from the 1830s. The paste-downs and first free leaves show a dark-green flock pattern stencilled on to a roller-printed pale-green paper;[13] the second pair of end-leaves is a roll-patterned ombré paper showing blue, white and pink stripes, with a curving design stencilled in red flock.

The earliest dated European wood-block print, now in the John Rylands University Library at Manchester, depicting St Christopher bearing the Christ Child, dates from 1423.[14] Wood-blocks were cut in relief, leaving the design standing; this was then coated either with water-based ink or with printing ink or water-colour, and the paper was either rubbed down on to the block or the block was used in a press. A yellow paper with a red floral design, printed probably c. 1490 in the south of France with a wood-block meant for textile printing, was found in the binding of three tracts printed in Paris in 1508 and 1514[15] and was acquired by Mrs Hirsch in 1937 (Hirsch J1). A Venetian wood-block-printed paper of c. 1535 was used to cover the boards of six tracts by Savonarola (Venice, 1512–17). The block is printed in black ink and shows on the upper cover Christ expelling the money-changers from the Temple, surrounded by four medallions containing Church fathers, and on the lower cover the expulsion of Adam and Eve from Paradise and four medallions containing Patriarchs (Hirsch BJ3).[16] Another sixteenth-century block-printed paper with a design of small triangles in black on yellow probably comes from southern France and dates from c.1550 (Hirsch J2).[17] It was once used as a wrapper for *La Magnificence de la superbe et triumphante entree de la noble et antique cité de Lyon faicte au treschrestien Roy de France Henri deuxiesme* (Lyons, 1549), and was lined with a piece of binder's waste in the form of a printed *Pronostication nouvelle pour l'an 1549*.

Block-printed papers were also used to line the backs of playing cards; two fragments of white paper printed in black with a design of diamonds containing stylized flowers were probably used in this way and may have been made in Germany c. 1600 (Hirsch J3, J4).[18] Another fragment (Hirsch J5) with a design of fleurs-de-lis in diamonds, also printed in black, seems too large to have served the same purpose.

In sixteenth-century France the 'cartiers-feuilletiers-maîtres-dominotiers-imprimeurs d'histoires', who were gathered into one corporation with statutes dating back to 1540,[19] manufactured and sold not only religious images and playing cards but also variously decorated paper destined for a variety of uses: to line boxes, cupboards and chests, as wrapping-paper, for book-papers and even already for hanging on the wall. The decree of Louis XIV of 1686 forbidding the importation and manufacture of 'indiennes', cheap decorated and painted cotton material used as wall hangings, gave a boost to the manufacture of a substitute: 'tapisserie de papier'. In his *Dictionnaire universel de Commerce* (1723–30), Savary des Brulons declared that by the end of the seventeenth century these papers had reached such perfection that there was no house in Paris, however magnificent, without a room hung and agreeably decorated with wallpaper.[20]

Fig. 46.1   A Paris Dominotier paper by Les Associées, style no. 229
(Hirsch B73).

A major innovation was the invention by Jean Papillon (1661–1723) of wallpaper with a continuous design. Either he or his son, Jean-Michel, or possibly Didier Aubert, was the engraver of a wood-block with a design of flowers and butterflies signed PAPILLON, printed in black and coloured by hand in red, blue, brown, yellow, pink and green, four pieces of which were used to cover the boards of J. Necker, *Compte rendu au Roy . . . au mois de Janvier 1781* (Paris, 1781) (Hirsch B106).[21] Another Paris firm, established like the Papillons in the rue St Jacques and engaged in the printing and selling of religious images as well as of decorated paper, that of Les Associées (1750–62), made a wallpaper with a bold floral design printed in black and hand-coloured in blue, signed in the border A PARIS CHEZ LES ASSOCIE NO 44 (Hirsch J1388). They also produced, as their style no. 229, a paper with a design of diamonds, formed by bands covered with little hearts and with flowers on the intersections, each diamond containing a flower on a background of vertical lines, printed in black and coloured by hand in yellow and red. This was used for the wrapper of [C. J. Dorat], *Le Célibataire, comédie en cinq actes* (Paris, 1776) (Hirsch B73, Fig. 46.1).

The 'dominotiers', who derive their name originally from the popular religious pictures they made and sold, and who during the eighteenth century mainly concentrated on the manufacture of, and trade in, decorated papers and specifically block-printed papers, were not only active in Paris. A great many firms are known to have existed in the provinces, in places like Orléans, Rouen, Besançon and Tournay. Orléans seems to have been an important centre and firms like Sevestre Le Blond, its successor Perdoux, Letourmy, and Rabier-Boulard are represented in the Hirsch collection. Jean-Baptiste Sevestre (1728–1805) married in 1751 the daughter of Jean Le Blond (1688–1771) and was taken into his father-in-law's firm. A paper signed LEBLOND ET SEVESTRE is illustrated by H. Clouzot.[22] After Le Blond's death Sevestre signed his papers SEVESTRE LEBLOND and two papers with this signature are Hirsch J1391–2. Sevestre Le Blond's no. 323 (J1391) shows a design of intersecting lines with flowers on the intersections dividing the sheet into diamonds, each containing a circle. It is printed in pink on white paper and coloured by hand in yellow and blue. A manuscript label on what was the upper cover shows that it was once used for the wrapper of '6 Sonates de Mr Giovanni de Cröner 1780. mon maitre de violon' (Fig. 46.2). No. 188 (J1392) has a pattern of diamonds and dots printed in blue. A lithographic reprint of this paper was used by Bärenreiter Verlag at Kassel for the covers of its [1936] edition of Kaspar Ferdinand Fischer, *Spielstücke, Erste Folge* (Hirsch J2713). In 1780 Sevestre sold his business to Pierre-Fiacre Perdoux who worked in Orléans until 1805. A floral and dotted-diamond pattern printed in blue and hand-coloured in pink is signed PERDOUX NO 416 (Hirsch J1397). Another

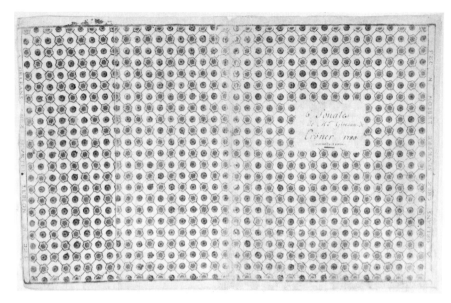

Fig. 46.2   An Orléans Dominotier paper by Sevestre Le Blond, style no.
323 (Hirsch J1391)

Orléans firm, the house of Letourmy, was founded *c.*1774 by Jean-Baptiste
Letourmy. He was succeeded by his son Jean-Baptiste (1781–1843)
'Letourmy, libraire, place du Martroi 39, du côté du Barillet, chez lequel
on trouve un assortiment divers de papiers-peints, papier tontisse et tout
ce qui concerne la Dominoterie'. The latter occurs in the *Calendrier
historique d'Orléans* for 1785 under 'Manufactures de papiers peints'.[23]
Two nice papers printed in blue on white signed LETOURMI are in the
Hirsch collection: one (style no. 14) with a diamond-and-dot pattern
(Hirsch J1404), the other (no. 190) with a design of leaves and flowers,
coloured by hand in pink and green (Hirsch J1405).

In 1812 Jean-Baptiste Letourmy sold his business to Mademoiselle Anne
Boulard who married Michel Rabier. Their firm Rabier-Boulard was active
from 1813 to 1843. A simple patterned paper of blue stars and dots on
white was their style no. 31 (Hirsch J1390).

Perhaps the first large-scale French publishers' bindings were made in
Orléans for the 36-volume 'Bibliothèque des meilleurs Poëtes Italiens'
issued by L. P. Couret de Villeneuve. The wrappers are printed in red
showing within a frame of foliage on the upper cover a cartouche with
'Des Livres de la Bibliotheque de M' followed by a blank space for the
owner to complete, above two putti and a dog climbing a rock. The lower
cover has two scenes with putti among trees and baroque ornaments
and is signed and dated 'michelin. 1785'. The spine is divided in eight

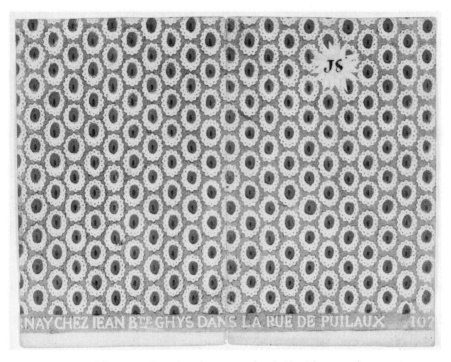

Fig. 46.3   A Tournay Dominotier paper by J.-B. Ghys, style no. 107
(Hirsch J1402)

compartments with conventional fleurons, title and volume number. The
Hirsch example (Hirsch BJ4) covers two volumes of Niccoló Carteromaco,
Ricciardetto (Orléans, 1785).[24]

At Tournay Jean-Baptiste Ghys worked first in the rue de Pont and
later in the rue de Puilaux. Four sheets, two with style numbers (no. 9
and no. 66)[25] have his name and the earlier address (Hirsch J1398, 1401),
and two (Hirsch J1402–3) were made in the rue de Puilaux. One of these,
showing an all-over design of objects strongly resembling lace doilies,
printed in pink on white paper, was his style no. 107 (Fig. 46.3). All these
six sheets, as well as a number of unsigned Dominotier papers in the
collection, were used as wrappers and have white paper stars with a
manuscript number or a letter and number pasted on the upper cover.

The most colourful and decorative of the eighteenth-century wood-
block-printed papers are the cotton papers. The blocks, often made of
pear wood and sometimes furnished with metal pins or strips, were used
to print textiles as well as papers. They were first produced from c.1735–40
and reached their artistic summit in the 1760s, 1770s and 1780s. They
were the most common type of decorated paper in Italy, France, Germany

and Holland, where a charming example printed in pink, purple and yellow paste colours on white paper may have been made c. 1760. The design shows flowers, fruit, part of a town and a huntsman leading a leopard on a chain, all against a background of dots made by metal pins driven into the wood-block (Hirsch J335).[26] A German cotton paper of about the same date, printed in red, green and yellow paste colours, with a design of leaves and flowers on a background of stripes, was once used for the cover of a music book, as is clear from the white paper label on the upper cover which reads 'Oboe, vel Flauto Primo' (Hirsch J351). A sheet of paper with an identical design, now in the Kupferstichkabinett of the Staatliches Museum at Berlin, is reproduced by Haemmerle.[27] The Italian cotton papers include two sheets signed by Carlo Bertinazzi of Bologna; one, his style no. 111 (Hirsch J1093), shows broad horizontal bands containing floral and decorative festoons printed in black on yellow; the other (Hirsch J1092), a design of leaves dividing the paper into compartments containing a flower or a sprig of berries, is printed in pale mauve and is extremely similar to the paper used as a wrapper for D. F. Leonardi's *Educazione* (Lucca, 1783) (Hirsch B62) which is signed ANTONIO BENUCCI FIREN[ZE].[28] A late eighteenth-century Venetian printed wrapper on Caterino Mazzola, *Orazione* (Venice, 1776) shows a rococo design with the arms of Monsignor Federico Maria Giovanelli, Patriarch of Venice, to whom the *Orazione* is addressed, on a semis of stars, printed in green on cream-coloured paper (Hirsch BJ 15, Fig. 46.4). Two early nineteenth-century Viennese wood-block-printed wrappers cover plays by A. F. Iffland published by J. B. Wallishausser. *Selbstbeherrschung. Ein Schauspiel in fünf Aufzügen* (1801) is stabbed in wrappers with a floral design within a frame, printed in blue and red paste colours, and once belonged to the Fürstlich-Starhemberg'sche Familien Bibliothek at Schloss Eferding (Hirsch BJ2a). *Die Brautwahl. Ein Schauspiel in einem Aufzuge. Für die k.k. Hoftheater* (1808) has pale-green wrappers, printed in black with a frame of palm leaves and ribbons surrounding the Austrian Imperial Eagle on the upper cover, and a floral ornament on the lower (Hirsch BJ2).

Paste colours as used in the manufacture of many cotton papers were already known at the end of the sixteenth century and were employed in various ways to make paste papers. The simplest technique is that of covering two sheets of paper with coloured paste, putting them together pasted sides inwards, and rubbing the upper surface gently, before pulling them apart to reveal a veined design. Rings, strips of felt or pieces of string could be sandwiched between the paste-covered sheets and would leave their marks on the paper. Simple designs were created by drawing patterns in the wet paste with combs, sticks, rolls or with one's fingers. This type of paper, with a design drawn into the usually bright or dark

Fig. 46.4   Venetian printed paper wrapper with the arms of F. M. Giovanelli (Hirsch BJ15).

pink, strong royal blue or drab olive paste, flourished in eastern and central Germany during the last third of the eighteenth century as 'Herrnhuter Papier'. The name derived from the religious community at Herrnhut in Saxony where papers of this type were made.[29] There are several specimens in the Hirsch collection, such as a dark-pink paper with a combed and finger-printed design (Hirsch J2338, Fig. 46.5); a strong blue paper decorated with a comb and a bookbinder's decorative roll (Hirsch J2363); another blue example with a design drawn into the wet paste with a two-pronged comb and with the fingers, which serves as the end-leaves of *Tagzeiten von dem Hochwürdigsten Geheimnisse des Altars* (St Blasien, 1771) (Hirsch B24); and olive paste-paper wrappers on *Raths- und Stadt-Calender . . . 1775* (Frankfort, n.d.) where the design has been drawn with a comb and a stick and stamped with a small simple wood-block (Hirsch B79).

A quite different kind of paste paper was made by using wood-blocks, which could either be covered with coloured paste and used to print the design, or used blind by impressing them into the wet paste. The raised design of the block would push the paste aside, thus effecting a higher concentration of colour along the outline of the design, while the block itself would pick up some of the coloured paste and leave a paler impression behind. This can be seen on a sheet made *c.* 1760 where an elaborately carved block was pressed into a multi-coloured paste ground (Hirsch J2386).[30] A wood-block similar to that used for this paper, also dating from the second half of the eighteenth century, now belongs to the Buntpapierfabrik A.G. at Aschaffenburg and is illustrated by Haemmerle.[31] Simple brushed, daubed and spattered papers were also often made with paste colours. Modern artists and craftsmen have taken to the manufacture of paste papers; among many very attractive examples is an early twenti-eth-century paper made by the Frankfort bookbinder Eduard Ludwig with a design of thistles drawn and dabbed into the purple paste (Hirsch J2684).

Until C. W. Woolnough's *The Art of Marbling* appeared in 1853, the technique of marbling paper had been shrouded in much deliberate mystery. Like other techniques for decorating paper, marbling was intro-duced into Europe from the East. The art was flourishing in Turkey and Persia during the second half of the sixteenth century. Marbled papers make their earliest appearance in Europe *c.* 1575 in the *alba amicorum* of German travellers, where they are found in combination with Turkish silhouette papers. Two pale-green silhouette papers occur in an *album amicorum* that belonged to Kaspar Koch,[32] and has entries dating from 1583 to 1649, some written in Rome and many in Basel (Hirsch B1). The book also contains eighteen pictorial water-colours and four painted coats of arms. Silhouette papers were made by cutting a pattern out of thin leather, soaking it in colour, and pressing it in between a folded sheet of

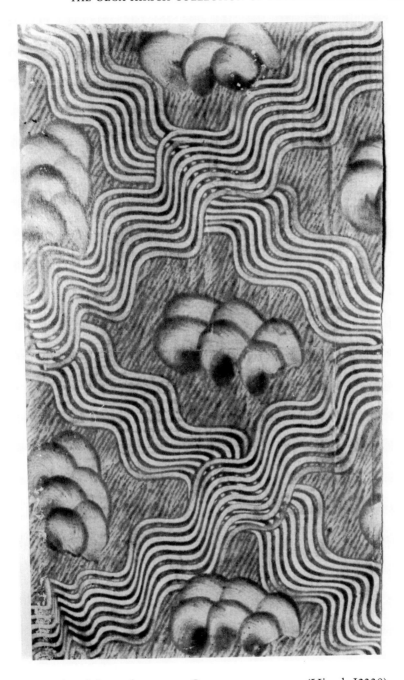

Fig. 46.5 An eighteenth-century German paste paper (Hirsch J2338).

paper previously dampened with alum water, after which the paper was brushed with glair and polished. Nine different Turkish silhouette papers, one of which is almost identical with a paper in the Stadtbibliothek at Nuremberg,[33] are found in the *album amicorum* of I. Pfinzing von Henfenfeld of Nuremberg. This consists of the title-page, text and engravings of a copy of [Jacob van der Heyden], *Speculum Cornelianum* (Strasburg, 1618) mounted on blank paper and interleaved with these silhouette papers as well as with a fair number of German marbled papers with stencilled patterns (Hirsch B3, Fig. 46.6).[34] Another *album amicorum*, with early seventeenth-century German papers marbled on both sides of the sheet, consists of pages 15–57 of Dirk de Bry, *Emblemata Saecularia* (Frankfort, 1596), 50 allegorical engravings and 50 engraved empty armorial shields, all mounted, as well as eight painted coats of arms, the 69 sheets of marbled paper, and several blanks. It belonged to a son of Johann Georg, Elector of Brandenburg, and the entries are dated 1604–7 (Hirsch B2).[35] The pale colours of the marbling make it a suitable background for the written entries and remind one of the Persian 'Ebru' papers which were often marbled in faint or pale colours and used either for grand manuscripts or as writing-paper for high dignitaries. Sir Thomas Herbert in *Some Yeares Travels into Africa & Asia* (London, 1677) relates how the King of Persia's name is 'usually writ with gold upon paper of a curious gloss and fineness varied into several fancies, effected by taking oyl'd colours and dropping them severally upon water, whereby the paper becomes sleek and chamletted or vein'd . . .'.[36] Sir Thomas visited Persia in 1627, and the account of his travels first came out in 1634. No mention of the Persian paper is made in this edition, but the 1677 edition has many additions, including the quoted passage. Before that date, however, Pierre de l'Estoile recorded in his *Memoires journaux* for December 1608 the gift of a small Chinese book bound in marbled paper to his friend Pierre Dupuy, and in May 1609 he gave to the same recipient 'Six Feuilles de mon Papier Marbré beau par Excellence, que ie lui avois promis'.[37] George Sandys in his *Relation of a Journey begun An: Dom: 1610* (London, 1615, p. 72) describes how the Turks 'curiously sleeke their paper, which is thicke; much of it being coloured and dapled like chamolets; done by a tricke they haue in dipping it in the water'. Francis Bacon in his *Sylva Sylvarum* (London, 1627, p. 192) talks about the Turkish 'Art of Chamoletting of Paper', and John Evelyn in his address to the Royal Society in January 1662 gives 'An Exact Account of the Making of Marbled Paper'.[38] Athanasius Kircher, who wrote about almost every subject under the sun, also discoursed on marbling,[39] his work forming the basis for much that was written on the subject for the next 50 years. La Caile in his *Histoire de l'imprimerie et de la librairie* (Paris, 1689, p. 213) attributes the inven-

Fig. 46.6   A seventeenth-century German marbled paper with a stencilled pattern (Hirsch B3).

tion of marbled paper to Macé Ruette, while Diderot and d'Alembert (tom. x, 1765) call it of German origin.

There are many examples in the Hirsch collection of the fine combed marbled papers so frequently found as end-papers in French seventeenth- and eighteenth-century bindings (e.g. Hirsch J1461–4), as well as of the larger combed marbles made in France and Holland (e.g. Hirsch J1466–86), and of drawn combed marbled papers (Hirsch J1640). Another well-known and frequently used type of marble is the French curl, called in French 'à la tournique' and in German 'Schneckenmarmor' (eg. Hirsch J1721–66), the 'invention' of which has been attributed to Nicolas Denis Derome. The nomenclature of the various kinds of marbles in different languages is confusing to say the least. Spanish marbles (or 'Griechische Marmor') have a ripple effect which is obtained by agitating the size bath;[40] a modern specimen was made by E. Seymour of the Fancy Paper Company, London, in 1956 (Hirsch J2011). The German bookbinder, teacher and writer on decorated paper, Paul Kersten, who worked for the Buntpapierfabrik A.G. of Aschaffenburg from 1898 to 1901, made in 1899 a series of marbled papers in various colours showing a feathery Christmas tree on a stone marbled ground which he called 'Jugend Marmor' and which he presented to Mrs Hirsch in 1902 (Hirsch J1802–10).

Among the different kinds of marbled papers made in Turkey are the 'Hâtip-Ebru' papers where coloured flowers are formed with a feather on a marbled ground. Haemmerle illustrates an example in the Musuem für Buch und Schrift in Leipzig made c. 1650.[41] This technique is still practised in Istanbul as shown by a red hyacinth on a brown stone marbled ground made by Professor Necmeddin Okyoy, now Hirsch J3526a(5) (Fig. 46.7). The best-known contemporary English firm of marblers was no doubt that of Douglas Cockerell & Son, directed by Sydney Cockerell at Grantchester near Cambridge until his death in November 1987. Mrs Hirsch knew and obviously liked both father and son and owned a large number of whole sheets and samples of their work. The variety of patterns is astonishing and ranges from the traditional combed marbles in blues, reds, greens and browns (e.g. Hirsch J2151)[42] and the less usual intricately drawn marbles in fiery colours (e.g. Hirsch J2154a) to a set of charming 'doodles' made in 1957, among which is a haughty-looking swimming duck in grey, brown, beige and pink (Hirsch J2160h). Sydney Cockerell's pamphlet *Marbling Paper* (Letchworth, [1966]) is a model of clarity.

German eighteenth-century metallic varnish papers ('Bronzefirnispapie-re') and embossed papers ('geprägten Brokatpapiere') form a large and important section of the Hirsch collection. Two of the nicest metallic varnish papers are illustrated in colour by Haemmerle,[43] one signed by Jakob Enderlin, the first maker of this type of paper (Hirsch J11–11a), the other probably made by Georg Christoph Stoy (Hirsch J7). Another

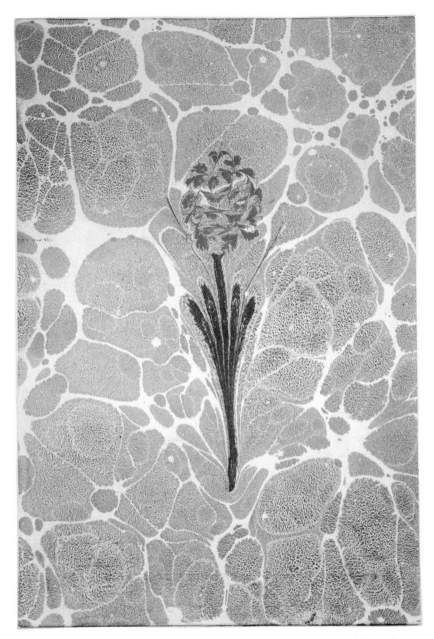

Fig. 46.7   A 'Hâtip-Ebru' paper made in Istanbul by Necmeddin Okyoy (Hirsch J3526a(5)).

metallic varnish paper with part of Stoy's signature has a design of fruitbaskets and acanthus leaves in gold on a red ground (Hirsch J34), while a sheet with a pattern of flowers and fruit printed in gold on green is signed with the initials of Simon (or Salome) Haichele (Hirsch J14).

Unlike the metallic varnish papers where the design is printed with a wood-block on previously coloured paper using a varnish-based metallic ink, the embossed papers were made with thick engraved copper plates and leaf metal. Both techniques owe much to the experiments of Jeremias Neuhofer of Augsburg who in the 1690s, with the cooperation of the designer Jakob Enderlin, tried to improve the quality of cotton printing.

The significant improvement in the manufacture of embossed papers was the use of a copperplate printer's rolling press. The design could be either cut in relief or in intaglio and was printed on paper, previously coloured with or without the use of stencils. A proof sheet which shows the design in blind on a stencilled multi-coloured ground is Hirsch J78.[44] The majority of these papers were made in Augsburg, Nuremberg and Fürth, the best examples dating from the first three decades of the eighteenth century.[45]

Among the Augsburg makers of embossed papers represented in the Hirsch collection is Mathias Merktl (Merkel, Merkli, Maerktl, Maerckli). He came from Günzburg and married in 1724 in Augsburg Maria Magdalena Segmüller. In 1731–2 he fell out with Abraham Mieser over the production of metallic papers but later obtained, for a consideration, Mieser's right to make gold and silver paper. A bold floral design embossed in gold on white paper is signed in the border MAERCKLI (Hirsch J141).[46] A famous name among the Augsburg embossed-paper makers is that of Georg Christoph Stoy. He was born in Nuremberg in 1670 and became a decorated-paper merchant and paper-embosser in Augsburg where he married in 1703 Anna Barbara Enderlin, the sister of Jakob Enderlin and the widow of the painter and paper-marbler Mathias Fröhlich. Stoy took over Fröhlich's decorated-paper business as well as his imperial 'Privilegium impressorum' for leather and metallic papers, which was renewed for him in 1709 and published.

Stoy's range of work can be judged from his two sample cards now in the Staatliche Kunstbibliothek in Berlin and illustrated by Haemmerle.[47] As well as his metallic varnish paper mentioned above, the Hirsch collection contains part of a sheet signed by him and embossed with a floral design in gold on a multi-coloured paper (Hirsch J47). Another, unsigned, fragment in gold on pink paper was embossed with the same plate (Hirsch J219), and a whole sheet of this paper, now at the Germanisches National Museum in Nuremberg, is illustrated by Haemmerle.[48] The wrapper for Benjamin de Barckhaus's inaugural dissertation (Erfurt, 1721), decorated with animals, birds, a monkey and a boy (the latter two only partly

Fig. 46.8   An embossed paper by J. M. Schwibecher (Hirsch J218).

visible) among large acanthus leaves, embossed in gold on orange paper,
was made by him (Hirsch small box 4), and another fragment of a sheet
was embossed with the same plate, this time in gold on red (Hirsch J199).
Among the paper-decorators with whom Stoy quarrelled in 1739 about
his privilege was Johann Michael Schwibecher, who worked in Augsburg
from 1715 to 1748. In 1715 he married Anna Veronika Roth, the widow
of Johann Michael Munck the elder. He made and signed a sheet decorated
with an intricate hunting scene figuring a variety of wild animals, exotic
birds and finely attired huntsmen among dense foliage which is illustrated
by Haemmerle;[49] a fragment of a sheet embossed with the same plate in
gold on turquoise paper is Hirsch J218 (Fig. 46.8).[50] After Schwibecher's
death in 1748 this plate was bought by Marx Leonhard Kauffmann who
replaced Schwibecher's signature with his own: AUGSPURG BEY MARX LEON-
HARD KAUFMAN N34, on a sheet which is now in the Prentenkabinet of
the Rijksmuseum in Amsterdam.[51] An impression of this same plate was
copied by Johann Michael Reimund, the first Nuremberg paper-embosser
who worked from c. 1727 and who died in 1768, showing all hunters as
left-handed. Schwibecher's stepson Johann Michael Munck the younger
comes from another well-known Augsburg family of paper-decorators.

His father was a paper-marbler and his son, Johann Carl, made embossed papers in Augsburg from *c.* 1749 to 1794. Johann Michael the younger worked as an embossed-paper maker from *c.* 1739; he died before January 1762 when his widow married Johann Georg Eder who may have taken over part of Munck's business.

A fine collection of Saints is embossed in gold on mauve paper showing in the top row from left to right: 'Christus ies. Mater dei. S. Petrus. S. Paulus.' and in the bottom row: 'S. Moyses. S. David. S. Ioannes. S. Elias.' It is signed I.M.M.A.V.Nr 40 (Hirsch J251). Another sheet signed (though on the Hirsch paper almost invisibly) by Johann Michael Munck, style no. 66[52] (Hirsch J316), shows two rows of four rectangles embossed in gold on pink, each containing the alphabet in Gothic and Roman letters as well as the Arabic numerals 1 to 10. The capital A encloses the Christ Child, an orb in his left hand, his right hand raised in blessing, standing with his legs slightly spread. This sheet may have been copied or imitated by various Augsburg, Nuremberg and Fürth paper-embossers, one of whom was Munck's son Johann Carl whose signature appears on a sheet illustrated by R. Loring.[53] The Hirsch collection contains several of these alphabets, the poor child's horn book. Two sheets, one in gold on pink, the other in gold on purple, were made in the 1820s or 1830s by Johann Lechner of Fürth (Hirsch J317/18). On this paper only the capital As of the fourth and eighth rectangle contain the Christ Child, here sitting down. The other As have a fir-cone-type ornament (rectangles 1 and 5), the Aesculapian symbol (rectangles 2 and 6) or a mandorla (rectangles 3 and 7). The design of a sheet embossed in gold on dark pink with two rows of four alphabets, where all As enclose the Christ Child half leaning to the right with his legs together (Hirsch J319), is identical with that on yellow paper in the Staatliche Kunstbibliothek in Berlin which bears a trace of the signature of the Nuremberg merchant and decorated-paper maker Johann Georg Eckart.[54] A fourth variant, embossed in gold on dark pink, was also made at Nuremberg by Paul Reimund, who signed it as his style no. 60, and shows a reclining Christ Child in every capital A (Hirsch J320). Paul Reimund, son of Andreas Reimund, was baptized on 7 January 1764. He married first (1783) Helena Sabina Hoffmann, secondly (1789) Petronella Mendelein, and thirdly (1802) Anna Regina Vogelsang. He lived in the Weissgerbergasse where he employed, *c.* 1800, six workmen. In 1803 he is mentioned as master in the Nuremberg book of pattern makers ('Formschneiderbuch'); he died in 1815, but his widow was still in business in 1820. A fair number of sheets signed by him are in the Hirsch collection, such as a purple-grey paper embossed in gold with a design of flowers and fruit including simple four- and five-petalled flowers, tulips, daffodils and carnations, as well as berries, pomegranates, cherries and grapes. This was his style no. 17 (Hirsch J123).[55] A lovely pictorial

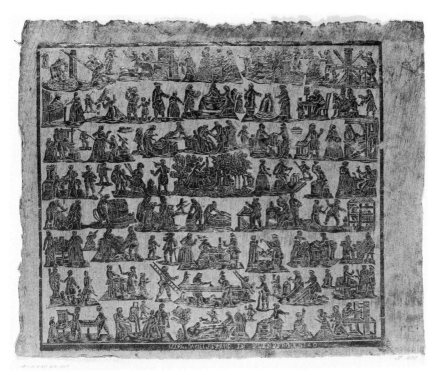

Fig. 46.9   An embossed paper by G. D. Reimund (Hirsch J303).

sheet signed by him showing five rows, each of five scenes with human figures, birds, animals, houses, a ship and a fountain embossed in silver on dark pink is Hirsch J281. His younger brother Georg Daniel was baptized on 28 February 1770. In the Nuremberg book of pattern makers he is mentioned as journeyman in 1795 and as master in 1801. He died in 1815. One of his sheets, style no. 40, embossed in gold on blue-green paper (Hirsch J303, Fig. 46.9) has eight horizontal rows of scenes depicting various crafts and professions, such as a baker and a copperplate printer (top row), a couple at a fountain (centre), a cooper and a paper maker (fifth row), a sculptor (seventh row), a painter and a printer (bottom row). It is a reversed copy of a sheet by Johann Carl Munck, style no. 141,[56] which was also copied in reverse, with differences in detail, by Paul Reimund (style no. 40);[57] a straight copy of the Munck sheet was made by Johann Georg Eckart.[58] Another sheet embossed in gold on clear-blue paper with seven rows of crafts and professions signed by Paul Reimund is described by Karl Theodor Weiss.[59] It dates from Goethe's childhood and is still in the Goethehaus in Frankfurt am Main. It has several scenes in common with Hirsch J303, such as the baker pursuing the dog that has stolen a bun, the girl escaping the printer's apprentice, the woman whose basket tumbles from her head, and the couple splashing each other at the fountain.

Georg Reimund, whose relation to the other Reimunds is not clear, also came from Nuremberg, but worked as a paper-marbler and paper-embosser in Augsburg where he married in 1746 the daughter of the paper maker Markus Lutz, and where he was still mentioned in 1755. His signature occurs on a white paper embossed with two sizes of gold stars used as end-papers for a copy of L. Senault, *Heures nouvelles tirées de la Sainte Ecreture* (engraved throughout, Paris, n.d.) (Hirsch B7), a type of paper often found in French books but not necessarily of French origin.

Simon Haichele, whose initials were found on one of Mrs Hirsch's metallic varnish papers (J14, see p. 268 above), made several of the embossed papers in the collection. A paper in a bold floral design embossed in gold on a multi-coloured ground, signed along the edge AUG. BEY. SIMON. HAEICHELE. CUM. PRI. S. C. [M.] forms the wrapper of *Affectus Humani. Argumentum quinque meditationum . . . Meditatio V. Tristitia* (Munich, 1758) (Hirsch small box 2). The same plate was used, also in gold on a multi-coloured ground, this time coloured with the aid of stencils, on a sheet a fragment of which is Hirsch J46. Two different embossed papers, one with a floral design in gold on dark red, the other with a design of bands, fruitbaskets and leaves in gold on yellow, the latter signed HAEICHEL C.P.S.C.M., are used as paste-downs and end-leaves in the gold-tooled red morocco binding on *Biblia, Das ist: Die gantze Heil. Schrift* (Basel, 1753) [and] *Neu-verbessertes Kirchen Gesang-Buch* (Basel, 1750) (Hirsch B8). The paste-down of the upper cover has a cut-out and hinged heart-shaped compartment over a piece of red morocco tooled with the initials H. SM. and the date 1758. In 1739 Simon Haichele asked the *Rat* of Augsburg permission to make 'Turkish papier', as his wife Salome had been doing since 1723. His request was refused but in 1740 Haichele held an imperial privilege for his metallic and coloured papers. The initials SH with which many of his papers are signed could equally well have been used by his wife.

As well as purely decorative designs, floral and leaf designs, designs with animals and birds, pictorial designs, saints and alphabets, a fashionable motif on embossed papers is one that gets its inspiration from Chinese landscapes, showing that the influence of the Far East on art during the eighteenth century had also reached the German paper-decorators. Stunningly beautiful Chinoiserie papers were made by Joseph Friedrich Leopold in Augsburg, and by Johann Köchel and Georg Popp in Fürth.[60] An unsigned paper with a scene of Chinese figures and animals among leaves and flowers embossed in gold on a multi-coloured ground serves as end-leaves for an eighteenth-century gold-tooled black morocco Scottish binding on *The Holy Bible* (Oxford, 1739) (Hirsch B11).

During the last third of the eighteenth century the artistic quality of these papers deteriorated; the designs became simplified and sometimes banal, while the engraving became less detailed and coarser. Papers such as those produced by the firm G. N. Renner & Abel during the second quarter of the nineteenth century show considerably less refinement than the earlier work of say Stoy and J. M. Munck. A plate with an engraved design of Adam and Eve in Paradise being tempted by the serpent and surrounded by animals and birds was used in gold on dark-blue, green, orange, and white paper (Hirsch J295–8). Of even less artistic merit are the embossed-paper publishers' bindings in which the 'Bibliothèque de la Jeunesse Chrétienne' was issued by A. Mame & Cie of Tours in the 1850s and 1860s. The nicest example in the Hirsch collection is a red flock-paper binding embossed in gold with a floral design on Baptistin Poujoulat, *Récits et souvenirs d'un voyage en Orient* (Tours, 1850) (Hirsch BJ22).

In the sections on paste paper and marbled paper I have already mentioned a few modern artists. The Hirsch collection contains a considerable number of modern papers made by various techniques, both by machine and by hand, for only two more of which is there room here. One is a roller-printed paper designed by Professor Otto Hupp at Munich in 1904. It has an intricate design with Art Nouveau elements and is embossed in gold on dark green (Hirsch J3107, Fig. 46.10). Mrs Hirsch possessed several of Professor Hupp's papers all printed with heated rollers (J3106–7c). The other is a work of art in grey and brown, with hints of yellow and a few spots of dark red, that rises far above the run-of-the-mill, often mechanically produced, decorated papers of the twentieth century; this was made by Eva Aschoff who worked in Freiburg in the Breisgau. She used oil paint for the background and water-colour mixed with paste for the drawing (Hirsch J3611). Mrs Hirsch acquired this and two more, equally beautiful, large sheets of her paper in 1958.

When E. A. Entwisle wrote his article on 'The Hirsch Collection of Decorated Papers' in *The Connoisseur Yearbook* (1961), he mentioned that Mrs Hirsch was compiling a bibliographical catalogue of her collection. This, alas, was never finished. Mrs Hirsch catalogued the reference books, as well as the books in paper wrappers and with decorated end-papers, but no catalogue of the papers themselves was ever compiled, though her arrangement of the papers according to their manufacturing process is very helpful for anyone consulting the collection.

As a start to classifying and grouping the papers a little more precisely, a list of the eighteenth- and nineteenth-century signed and identified papers follows, arranged in alphabetical order by maker's name. The Hirsch numbers of the signed papers are printed in roman; the attributions, based

Fig. 46.10   Roller-printed paper designed by Otto Hupp, 1904 (Hirsch J3107).

on comparison with the signed sheets or, in a few cases, on the description given by Haemmerle in his 'Verzeichnis' are given in italic. A few publications in paper wrappers have no identification number and are quoted by their short title and imprint.

Eighteenth- and Nineteenth-Century Signed and Identified Papers in the Olga Hirsch Collection

Associées, Les (Paris): B73 (style no. 229); J1385/6 (no. 43); J1387 (no. 68); J1388 (no. 44).

Benucci, Antonio (Florence): B62.

Bertinazzi, Carlo (Bologna): J1092; J1093 (no. 111).

Deyser, P.(?) (Augsburg): J302.

Eckart, Johann Georg (Nuremberg): *J319* (a copy of P. Reimund's J320).

Eder, Johann Georg (Augsburg): B96 (no. 3), same plate on J139 (no. 3).

Enderlin, Jacob (Augsburg): J11/*11a*.

Ghys, Jean-Baptiste (Tournay, rue de Pont): J1398 (no. 9); J1399; J1400; J1401 (no. 66); (Tournay, rue de Puilaux): J1402 (no. 107); J1403.

Haichele, Simon (Augsburg) (see also p. 277: Augsburg): B8; Poenitentia (Munich, 1753) (no.11); Die aus Liebe zusammen getrettene . . . Gesellschaft (Frankfort, 1754); Affectus Humani (Munich, 1758), same plate on J46; J14 [SH]; *J166; J176*.

[Imprenta de Guasp (Mallorca): J3590–7 are REPRINTS from blocks used by the Imprenta de Guasp.]

Kauffmann, Marx Leonhard (Augsburg); *J218* (see also Schwibecher).

Keck, Maria Barbara (Augsburg): J210; *J209* (this plate was later used by J. C. Munck).

Köchel, Johann (Fürth): *J51/51a; J53*; J214; J259, same plate on J260–2 (signature hardly visible).

Kost, Johann Friedrich (Fürth): J37 (no. 86), same plate on J140.

Lauti(?) Besançon: J1406.

Lechner, Johann (Fürth): J36 (no. 1); J294 (no. 9); *J317*, same plate on J318 (no. 26).

Leopold, Joseph Friedrich (Augsburg): J38; J39 (no. 39); J40, same plate on J97.

Letourmy, Jean-Baptiste (Orléans): J1404 (no. 14); J1405 (no. 190).

[Maisch, Johann (Nuremberg): J3599 is a REPRINT from a block used by Maisch *c.* 1850.]

Merer, David (Augsburg): J45 (no. 71).

Merktl, Mathias (Augsburg): J141.

Meyer, Johann Wilhelm (Augsburg): J41 (no. 14); J42 (no. 32); J117 (no. 29); J137 (no. 13).

Michelin (Orléans): BJ4.

Müller, Johann Friedrich (unknown): *J211*.

Munck (Augsburg): Religio (Munich, 1795) (signature incomplete); B77 (signature incomplete); J116 (signature incomplete, see also Munck, J. M.).

Munck, Johann Carl (Augsburg) (see also p. 277: Augsburg): Affectus Humani (Munich, 1758), different part of probably the same plate on Virtus Christianorum heroica (n.p., 1767) (no. 25); J43 (no. ?); J119 (no. 23); *J209* (see also Keck); J254 (no. 73?), same plate on J255–8; J279; J301 (dated 1782, no. 224, *J304* is a copy in reverse of J301).

Munck, Johann Michael (Augsburg): Affectus Humani (Munich, 1760); B107 (no 18); J44 (no. 16); *J49*, same plate on *J50*, *J52*, J113 (no. 13), and J118 (no. 13); *J104*, possibly different part of the same plate on *J109*; *J115*; J116(?) (signature incomplete); *J143* (J2714 is a modern copy of J143); *J144*; *J240*; J251 (no. 40); J316 (signature hardly visible).

'Papillon' (Paris): B106.

Perdoux, Pierre-Fiacre (Orléans): J1397 (no. 416).

Popp, Georg (Fürth): J187; *J217*.

Rabier-Boulard (Orléans): J1390 (no. 31).

Reimund, Andreas (Nuremberg): J247.

Reimund, Georg (Augsburg): B7; *J101*, same plate on *J233*; J142; *J213* (see also Stoy).

Reimund, Georg Daniel (Nuremberg): J246 (no. ?); J303 (no. 40).

Reimund, Johann Michael (Nuremberg): B. G. Geierus, Dissertatio Iuridica (Frankfort, 1754, a copy of a sheet by Schwibecher: *J218*, see also Kauffmann).

Reimund, Paul (Nuremberg): J120 (no. 19); J121 (no. 127); J122 (no. 212); J123 (no. 17), same plate on J125 (no. 17); J124 (no. 22); J126 (no. 11), same plate on J127 (no. 11); J128 (no. 36); J129; J243 (no. 36: though different from J128); J263 (no. 132); J281; J299 (no. 130); J307 (no. 61); J310 (a coarse copy of this sheet is *J311*); J320 (no. 60) (see also Eckart).

[Remondini (Bassano): REPRINTS signed 'Stampi Remondiniani PESP' of blocks used by the Remondini firm: J1313, J1321, J1322, J1323, J1324, J1326, J1327.]

Renner, G. N. & Abel (Nuremberg): J132, same plate on J133–5; J272, same plate on J273–8; J290, same plate on J291–3; J295, same plate on J296–8; J321.

Schindler, Johann Paul (Fürth): J130 (no.8), same plate on J131.

Schwibecher, Johann Michael (Augsburg): Affectus Humani (Munchen, 1758); *J57*; J136; *J218* (this plate was later used by Kauffmann).

Sevestre-Le Blond (Orléans): J1391 (no. 323); J1392 (no. 188) (J2713 is a modern copy of J1392).

Steber, Andreas (Nordlingen): *J160*.

Stoy, Georg Christoph (Augsburg): B. de Barckhaus, Dissertatio Inauguralis (Erfurt, 1721) same plate on *J199*; J34; J47, same plate on *J219; J56; J100*; J138; *J195; J197a-b; J213* (this plate was later used by G. Reimund).

Wolff, Jeremias (Augsburg): F. B. Eckher, Quaestio quid hominem homini prudenter faciat acceptum (Ingolstadt, 1764) (no. 103).

The following papers have incomplete signatures and could only be attributed to their place of origin:

Augsburg: Fundamenta Virtutum (n.p., 1768); J216 (possibly first used by Simon Haichele and consequently by Johann Carl Munck); J241/2.

Fürth: J286 (no. 109).

Paris(?): J1393 (no. 294).

Notes

1. P. Hirsch, *Eine Kleine Bücherschau*, Frankfort, 1920, no. 173.
2. Illustrated in : M. Lanckorówska, 'Die Bibliothek Paul und Olga Hirsch', *Philobiblon*, iii, 10 (1930), opposite p. 442.
3. Now in the British Library, Henry Davis Gift P. 1304; see M. M. Foot, *The Henry Davis Gift*, vol. I, London, 1978, p. 151.
4. P. Hirsch, *op. cit.*, n. 181. C. Schmidt, 'Aus der Sammlung Olga Hirsch', *Buch und Bucheinband, Festschrift H. Loubier*, Leipzig, 1923, pp. 194–8, pls. 23–4.
5. P. Hirsch, *op. cit.*, nos. 63, 194, 200, 206, 188, 204, 212.
6. H. P. R. Finberg, 'The Hirsch Collection of Decorated Papers', *Signature* (July 1939), pp. 47–53. O. Hirsch, 'Decorated Papers', *The Penrose Annual*, li (1957) pp. 48–53. E. A. Entwisle, 'The Hirsch Collection of Decorated Papers', *The Connoisseur Year Book* (1961), pp. 57–61. A. Haemmerle, 'Die Buntpapiersammlung Olga Hirsch', *Philobiblon*, x, 2 (1966), pp. 104–9. Printing Historical Society, *Newsletter* xii (Feb. 1969), item 9. See also O. Hirsch, 'Notes on Decorated Papers in the Collection of Mrs. Olga Hirsch displayed for members of the Double Crown Club, 23 June 1955' (typescript). O. Hirsch, 'Alte Buntpapieren', *Blätter für Buchgestaltung und Buchpflege* (1932), pp. 8–13, and O. Hirsch, *Holzschnitt-Umschläge und Buntpapiere*, Cologne, Bibliophilen-Gesellschaft, 1959 contain many references to her own collection. The latter article was also published as 'Alte Buntpapiere' in *Allgemeiner Anzeiger für Buchbindereien* (1959), pp. 186–94, and in French as 'Couvertures aux bois gravés et papiers multicolores', in *La Reliure* (Sept.-Nov. 1960 and Jan., May, Sept. 1961).
7. A. Haemmerle, *Buntpapier, Herkommen, Geschichte, Techniken, Beziehungen zur Kunst*, Munich, 1961. A number of copies of this book have at the end instead of '150 Jahre Buntpapierfabrik A.G. Aschaffenburg' (pp. 1–24) an appendix, printed on different paper (pp. 197–251) consisting of 'Verzeichnis von Brokat-Papieren', a descriptive catalogue, arranged alphabetically by maker's name, of signed metallic varnish papers and embossed papers, followed by a section on anonymous papers (a number of Hirsch papers are

included). References to this appendix are given as A. Haemmerle, 'Verzeichnis'.

I owe most of the information for the historical sections of this article to Dr Haemmerle's book. See also N. J. Barker's review in *The Book Collector*, x (1961), pp. 482–9.

8. Most of the papers described here were on exhibition in the British Library (King's Library) from 20 Feb.–14 June 1981.

9. A. Haemmerle, *op. cit.*, p. 26, pls. 13–14.

10. Ibid., pp. 28–30, 33–4, pls. 5–17, 19–22.

11. N. McClelland, *Historic Wall-papers*, Philadelphia, London, 1924, pp. 53–5.

12. H. Clouzot and C. Follot, *Histoire du papier peint en France*, Paris, 1935, pp. 23–36.

13. A Haemmerle, *op. cit.*, pl. 18.

14. C. Clair, *A Chronology of Printing*, London, 1969. For early techniques of printing wood-blocks see 'A Fifteenth-Century Horror Comic', *The Times Literary Supplement* (29.1.1971), p. 135 (I am grateful to Dr Lotte Hellinga for this reference).

15. St. Cyrillus, Patriarch of Alexandria, *Commentarius in Leviticum*, Paris, 1514; idem, *Thesaurus*, Paris, 1514; idem, *Opus in Evangelium Joannis*, Paris, 1508. The paper is illustrated by A. Haemmerle, *op. cit.*, pl. vi.

16. U. Hoepli, *Vendita . . . della . . . Libreria De Marinis*, Milan, 6–9 May 1925, no. 185, pl. xxxii; L. Baer, *Mit Holzschnitten Verzierte Buchumschläger*, Frankfort, 1923, no. xii; M. Sander, *Copertine Italiane illustrate del Rinascimento*, Milan, 1936, pl. viii; O. Hirsch, 'Couvertures aux bois gravés', *La Reliure* (Sept. 1960), fig. 2.

17. A. Haemmerle, *op. cit.*, pl. 51.

18. Ibid., pls. 52–3.

19. J.-P. Seguin, 'Des siècles de papiers peints', Musée de Rennes, *Trois siècles de papiers peints* (Nov.-Dec. 1967).

20. In England the first patent for making 'paper for hanginge' was granted to Richard and Edward Greenburg in 1636; see Commissioners of Patents, *Patents for Inventions. Abridgments . . . relating to . . . paper*, London, 1879.

21. M. M. Foot, 'A Parisian Paper Binding, c. 1781', *The Book Collector*, xxix (1980), p. 568. See below article 50.

22. H. Clouzot, *Le Papier peint en France du XVIIᵉ au XIXᵉ siècle*, Paris, 1931, pl. v. For these firms see H. Clouzot and C. Follot, *op. cit.*, p. 20; P. L. Duchartre and R. Saulnier, *L'imagerie populaire*, Paris, 1925, pp. 355–64; R. B. Loring, *Decorated Bookpapers*, Cambridge, Mass., 1952, pp. 40–41.

23. P. L. Duchartre and R. Saulnier, *op. cit.*, p. 363; H. Clouzot and C. Follot, *op. cit.*, p. 20.

24. G. Godron, 'Quelques travaux de dominotiers orléanais de la fin du XVIIIᵉ siècle', *L'art populaire en France* (1933), p. 83; De Cardenal, 'Evolution générale de la décoration de la couverture du livre', *Bulletin du bibliophile* (1938), p. 348; G. Barber, 'Continental Paper Wrappers and Publishers' Bindings in the 18th Century', *The Book Collector*, xxiv (1975), pp. 45–6; M. Breslauer, *Fine Books in Fine Bindings* (Catalogue 104), no. 100. See also M. M. Foot, *Pictorial Bookbindings*, London, 1986, p. 44, pl. 41.

25. O. Hirsch, *The Penrose Annual* (1957), fig. 12.

26. A Haemmerle, *op. cit.*, pl. 145.

27. Ibid., pl. 155. A very similar paper but without the stripes in the background and with purple instead of green leaves and flowers is Hirsch J451.

28. A. Haemmerle, *op. cit.*, pl. 137.
29. Ibid., pp. 139–44.
30. Ibid., pl. 121.
31. Ibid., pl. 122.
32. It probably belonged to both father and son. One of these silhouette papers is illustrated by A. Haemmerle, *op. cit.*, pl. 26.
33. Ibid., pl. 28; another one is illustrated by O. Hirsch in *The Penrose Annual* (1957), pl. 5 and in *La Reliure* (Sept. 1960), fig. 4.
34. There are 41 sheets, five of which are marbled on both sides; one is illustrated by A. Haemmerle, *op. cit.*, pl. 41; others by O. Hirsch in *The Penrose Annual* (1957), pl. 4 and in *La Reliure* (Sept. 1960), fig. 3.
35. A Haemmerle, *op. cit.*, pl. 40; O. Hirsch, *The Penrose Annual* (1957), pl. 3.
36. p. 294; on p. 298 he continues: 'their paper is very glossie, and by dropping oyl'd-colours chamletted and veined like marble'.
37. Now in the Bibliothèque Nationale. A. Haemmerle, *op. cit.*, pp. 48–9, pl. 37.
38. BL, Sloane MS. 243, fols. 96–8.
39. A. Kircher, *Ars magna lucis et umbrae*, Rome, 1646, liber X, Magia Pars II, 'Chartae Turcico more pingenda ratio', pp. 814–15.
40. A note on the back of Hirsch J2011 describes how the paper is agitated when being put down on the surface of the size bath. See also R. B. Loring, *op. cit.*, pp. 27–8.
41. A. Haemmerle, *op. cit.*, pl. 36.
42. See also A. Haemmerle, *op. cit.*, pl. iv.
43. Ibid., pls. viii, xiii.
44. Ibid., pl. 69.
45. For information about the makers of these papers see A. Haemmerle, 'Augsburger Buntpapier', *Vierteljahreshefte zur Kunst und Geschichte Augsburgs*, iii (1937–8), pp. 133–79; and idem, *Buntpapier*, pp. 120–29.
46. Illustrated in H. P. R. Finberg, *art. cit.*
47. A. Haemmerle, *Buntpapier*, pls. 11–12.
48. Ibid., pl. 9.
49. Ibid., pl. 100.
50. O. Hirsch, *The Penrose Annual* (1957), pl. 18.
51. A. Haemmerle, 'Verzeichnis', no. 64.
52. Ibid., no. 266.
53. R. B. Loring, *op. cit.*, pl. 3.
54. A. Haemmerle, 'Verzeichnis', no. 9.
55. The same plate was used on blue paper (Hirsch J125).
56. A. Haemmerle, 'Verzeichnis', no. 219.
57. Ibid., no. 358.
58. Ibid., no. 8.
59. K. T. Weiss, 'Das Bild des Papierers', *Zeitschrift für Bücherfreunde*, xxxvi (1932), pp. 145–6. This sheet may be A. Haemmerle, 'Verzeichnis', no. 374.
60. e.g. A. Haemmerle, *Buntpapier*, pls. 87–90.

47 Ferrarese Woodcut Bindings of the Late Fifteenth and Early Sixteenth Centuries

(1991)*

Because of their ephemeral character and their fragility, not many fifteenth- and early sixteenth-century bindings decorated with woodcuts have survived. The known examples have either a woodcut on one or both covers, leaving the spine undecorated, or one woodcut covering both covers and spine. They fall into two distinct categories. The earliest ones, made in Augsburg in the 1480s and 1490s, are publishers' wrappers adorned with woodcuts designed for a particular book and produced by the printer of that book. The same woodcuts are found on several copies of the same book or sometimes on books printed by the same printer.[1] Italian woodcut bindings of this period, which form the second category, have no connection with the book they cover. They were produced, possibly on commission from the bookseller, by bookbinders who used woodcuts over boards as a cheap and decorative way of protecting a text. The same or very similar woodcuts are found on unrelated books printed by different printers. Italian woodcut bindings were made in Ferrara, where the earliest known example dates from *c.* 1490; they were produced in Venice about fifteen years later. They may also have been used in Bologna and were still current at the end of the seventeenth century.[2]

The example illustrated here (Fig. 47.1) belongs to a group of nine woodcut bindings produced in Ferrara. The earliest one shows on the upper cover two angels festooned with ribbons tied to a bouquet of fruit and flowers, and on the lower cover three angels holding an open book; bunches of leaves are suspended above their heads. Both groups of angels are surrounded by a frame of leafy sprays with formal flowers at the corners. The binding covers Jacobus Riccius, *Annotata in Logicam Pauli Veneti*, Venice, Guilelmus Anima Mea, Tridinensis, 5 Oct. 1488 (Hain 13909), bound together with Ralph Strode, *Consequentiae*, Venice, Bernardinus Celerius, 30 April 1484 (Hain 15095). The book has a fifteenth-

* *Vision of a Collector: The Lessing J. Rosenwald Collection in the Library of Congress*, Washington, 1991.

Fig. 47.1 Baptista Fregoso, *Anteros, sive Tractatus contra amorem*.
Milan: Leonardus Pachel, 10 May 1496.
Library of Congress, Rosenwald Collection 313.

century Ferrara provenance and it belonged to E. P. Goldschmidt and Philip Hofer.[3]

There are two versions of a woodcut depicting the Sacred Monogram and St George. A medallion with the Sacred Monogram is surrounded by a circle of rays and by a second circle of formalized clouds. Above and below this central ornament are masks, and four medallions with the symbols of the Evangelists appear in the corners. The whole is surrounded by an ornamental frame with vases, scrolls or garlands, palmettes and cherubs' heads. A similar frame surrounds a scene showing St George killing the dragon, with the anxious princess wringing her hands at the very edge of the picture, contained in a medallion surrounded by a circle of formalized clouds. Above and below this medallion are large urns with fruit and leaves, and floral sprays decorate the corners. The two pictorial parts of the cut are connected by a spine strip showing zigzag lines and small formal flowers. The whole appears to have been cut on one block of wood and was obviously meant to cover the boards of a book of roughly the same size as, or a little larger than, the cut. Two copies of this cut, which was dated by Heitz c.1496,[4] are known. One, in the Kupferstichkabinett in Berlin, is imperfect and does not cover a binding. The other covers Baptista Fregoso (Fulgosus), *Anteros*, Milan, Leonardus Pachel, 10 May 1496 (Hain 7393; BMC VI, 781; Goff F–329) and is illustrated here. It belonged formerly to Ferdinand Cortesi, Michael Cavalieri, Cernuschi, C. Fairfax Murray and Dyson Perrins, at whose sale at Sotheby's on 17 June 1946 (lot 121) it was bought by the Rosenbach Company. It now belongs to the Lessing J. Rosenwald collection in the Library of Congress.

A contemporary copy of this woodcut was dated by Baer c.1500.[5] Here St George and the Sacred Monogram have been reversed, resulting in St George facing right, while the symbols of the Evangelists have been moved to the opposite corners. The Sacred Monogram is plainer, and there are a number of minor differences in the details of the ornamentation. A copy of this cut is in the Nationalbibliothek in Vienna.

There are three very closely similar versions of a woodblock depicting St George and St Maurelius. The figure of St George killing the dragon, while the princess looks on, is lettered 'szorzi' and appears again in a medallion set in an ornamental background of branches and fleurons, the whole surrounded by a frame with vases, garlands and winged horses' heads. The spine part shows a zigzag line with quatrefoils and half quatrefoils. St Maurelius, the patron Saint of Ferrara, stands holding a crozier in his left hand and a model of his city in his right hand in a medallion on a similar background and within a similar frame. Inscribed behind his head is '.ɛ. MAVRELIO'.

The three known versions of this cut show minor differences, for example, in the colour of the horse's harness, the folds of the princess's robes and the buildings of Ferrara. Two variants are reproduced by Max Sandar[6] and were found, together with four different woodcuts, in the boards of a binding. These cuts were never used for their original purpose and may have been rejected by a binder who used them as waste instead. The third version was used for binding and is found on two books: Phalaris, *Epistolae*, Cremona, Franciscus Ricardus de Luere, 23 Jan. 1505,[7] and Paulus Venetus [Nicolettus], *Tractatus summularum logice*, Venice, Lucantonio Giunta, 1517, bound with Menghus Blanchellus, *In Pauli Veneti logicam commentum*, Venice, Johannes Leoviler, 1488 (Hain 3229).[8]

Three more Ferrarese woodcuts for bindings are known, two of which depict the Annunciation. One example was among the six woodcuts found in a binding mentioned above and is illustrated by Sandar.[9] It shows two very similar pictures of Gabriel announcing to Mary the news of her pregnancy. The scenes are contained in medallions, surrounded by ornamental curving branches with leaves and flowers, within a frame with garlands, palmettes, sun-faces and cherubs' heads. The spine portion is decorated with serrated zigzag lines forming diamonds and triangles, each with a whole or half double oval with a nimbus. The other Annunciation cut covers Franciscus Rappus, *Doctrinale Sacro de Maria Vergine*, Bologna, Hieronymus de Benedictis, 1511,[10] and depicts the angel on the upper cover and Mary on the lower. Both figures are contained in a medallion surrounded by leafy sprays, garlands and flowers, within a frame of branches with palmettes, vases and cherubs' heads. The last Ferrara example is purely ornamental. It was illustrated in the Summer 1977 issue of *The Book Collector* and covers Jacopo Sannazaro, *Libro pastorale nominato Arcadio*, Venice, Bernardinus Vercellensis, 1502.[11] The frame that surrounds the large floral and leafy sprays that form the central ornament consists of garlands, palmettes and horses' heads, with cherubs' heads in the corners.

The ornamental frames of all but the oldest of these Ferrara woodcuts are similar in style and reminiscent of the frame round the woodcut on the verso of the title-page of *Corona beatae Mariae Virginis*, printed in Ferrara by Laurentius de Rubeis or Lorenzo de' Rossi (BMC VI, 613). A number of woodcuts in works printed by Lorenzo de' Rossi[12] have a similar decorative frieze with garlands, palmettes, cherubs' heads or vases, while the central ornament on the binding of Sannazaro is reminiscent of the set of large initials in de' Rossi's St Jerome, *Epistolae*, 1497.

The woodcut opposite the first page of text of *Leggendario e vita e miracolo di S. Maurelio*, Ferrara, Lorenzo de' Rossi, 30 Dec. 1489 (BMC VI, 611), shows St Maurelius, a crozier in his right hand and a building, representing Ferrara, in his left hand. In 'Les livres à gravures sur bois', Gustave Gruyer describes two copies of this book, one of which has at the end of the text an additional woodcut depicting St George.[13] It is possible that the St George scene on the woodcut bindings is a free reversed copy of this cut.

The angel of the Annunciation in a woodcut that occurs opposite the first page of text of Jacobus Philippus [Foresti] Bergomensis, *De claris selectisque mulieribus*, Ferrara, Lorenzo de' Rossi, 29 April 1497 (BMC VI, 613) looks very similar to that on the binding of Rappus, *Doctrinale*. The similarities in style are close enough to suggest that the woodblocks for the majority of these Ferrarese woodcut bindings were made by one of the artists who worked for Lorenzo de' Rossi.

1. L. Baer, *Mit Holzschnitten verzierte Buchumschläge des XV. und XVI. Jahrhunderts*, Frankfurt am Main, 1923. L. Baer, *Holzschnitte auf Buchumschlägen*, Strassburg, 1936. O. Leuze, 'Mit Holzschnitten verzierte Buchumschläge des 15. Jahrhunderts' in *Festschrift für Georg Leidinger*, München, 1930, pp. 165–70. M. Müller, 'Der älteste bisher bekannte Buchumschlag', ibid, pp. 195–8. H.M. Nixon, *Broxbourne Library. Styles and Designs of Bookbindings*, London, 1956, no.6. P. Needham, *Twelve Centuries of Bookbinding 400–1600*, New York/London, 1979, pp. 117–19.
2. The well-known Italian woodcut wrappers of the eighteenth century were largely publishers' wrappers.
3. E.P. Goldschmidt, *Gothic and Renaissance Bookbindings*, London, 1928, no.36. See also L. Baer, *Mit Holzschnitten verzierte Buchumschläge*, 1923, no IV; L. Baer, *Holzschnitte auf Buchumschlägen*, 1936, no.6; P. Heitz, *Italienische Einblattdrücke in den Sammlungen Ravenna, Rom, Salzburg, Venedig, Wien*, pt.IV, Strassburg, 1934, and P. Heitz, *Italienische Einblattdrücke in den Sammlungen Berlin, Braunschweig, etc*, pt.V, Strassburg, 1935 (in P.Heitz, *Einblattdrücke des fünfzehnten Jahrhunderts*, Band 82–83), no.78.
4. P. Heitz, *op.cit.*, no.76. See also L. Baer, *op.cit.* (1923), no.V; L. Baer, *op.cit.* (1936), no.7 (with literature); P. Kristeller, 'Woodcuts as Binding', *Bibliographica*, I, London, 1895, pp. 249–57.
5. L. Baer, *op.cit.* (1936), no.8. See also L. Baer, *op.cit.* (1923), no.VI; P. Heitz, *op.cit.*, no.74.
6. M. Sandar, 'Copertine illustrate del Rinascimento', *Maso Finiguerra*, I, 1936, pp. 26–37, figs 1, 2. See also P. Heitz, *op.cit.*, no.75; L. Baer, *op.cit.* (1923), no.VII; L. Baer, *op.cit.* (1936), no.10.
7. A.W. Pollard, *Italian Book-Illustrations and Early Printing. A Catalogue of early Italian books in the library of C.W. Dyson Perrins*, Oxford, 1914, no.170.
8. H.M. Nixon, *op.cit.*, no.16.
9. M. Sandar, *op.cit.*, fig.3.
10. L. Baer, *op.cit.* (1923), no. VIII; L. Baer, *op.cit.* (1936), no.11; P. Heitz, *op.cit.*, no.77.
11. See also L. Baer, *op.cit.* (1936), no.9.
12. E.g. on the verso of the title-page and on the first page of the text of Hieronymus, *Epistolae*, and on the title-page of *Vita de Sancto Hieronymo*, Ferrara, L. de' Rossi, 12 Oct. 1497 (BMC VI, 614); on the verso of the

title-page and opposite the first page of text of Jacobus Philippus [Foresti] Bergomensis, *De claris selectisque mulieribus*, Ferrara, L. de' Rossi, 29 April 1497 (BMC VI, 613).

13. G. Gruyer, 'Les livres à gravures sur bois publiés à Ferrare', *Gazette des Beaux-Arts*, xxxviii (1888), pp. 89–102. Gruyer (pp. 96–7) states that the library at Ferrara has two 'editions' of the 1489 *Leggendario*, but he must mean two copies. It is perfectly possible that the woodcut of St George was added later.

48 An English Woodcut Binding, 1647

(1988)*

Lambeth Palace Library owns a copy of a rare 8° pamphlet by I. D. [J. Day, Rector?], entitled *Certaine Godly Rules concerning Christian Practice*, London (printed by T. W. for Thomas Knight), 1647. The pamphlet originally belonged to Frances Wolfreston.[1] The work was entered to Master [Clement] Knight on 8 January 1615 and the copyright was transferred to Thomas Knight, who had succeeded Clement at the Holy Lamb, St Paul's Churchyard, on 12 October 1629.[2]

The woodblock-printed covers form part of the pamphlet. The cut on the upper cover (A1) depicts the raising of Lazarus with an inset showing the return from Egypt, while the cut on the lower cover, printed on the verso of the last page of the text, shows the adoration of the Magi. The printers' fleurons on the upper cover are found in other works printed by T. W., as well as in *The Fables of Aesop paraphrased*, printed by Thomas Warren for A. Crook in 1651. Thomas Warren was apprenticed to the bookseller Thomas Knight in 1630. He was freed on 2 April 1638 and started in the trade as a bookseller in partnership with Joshua Kirton.[3] He began to print in 1645 and printed, either as T. W. or as Thomas Warren, until he was succeeded by his widow Alice in 1660. In 1656 and 1658 a large number of woodcuts in sheets were entered to him, but those found on the covers of Day's pamphlet are not listed.[4]

1. See P. Morgan, 'Frances Wolfreston and "Hor Bouks", a seventeenth-century woman book-collector', lecture to the Bibliographical Society, 21 October 1986, printed in *The Library*, sixth series, XI (1989), pp. 197–219.
2. E. Arber, *A Transcript of the Registers of the Company of Stationers of London 1554–1640*, London, 1875-7, III, 560; IV, 220. See also STC 6168.5 (1634), 6168.7 (1636). The 1647 edition is not in Wing.
3. D. F. McKenzie, *Stationers' Company Apprentices, 1605–1640*, Charlottesville, 1961, p. 91. Arber, *op. cit.*, III, 688; IV, 31. H. R. Plomer, *A Dictionary of the Booksellers and Printers . . . 1641–1667*, London, 1968, p. 189.
4. [G. E. Briscoe Eyre], *A Transcript of the Registers of the . . . Company of Stationers from 1640–1708*, London, 1913-14, II, pp. 46, 47, 48, 50, 187.

* English and Foreign Bookbindings 46, *The Book Collector*, XXXVII, pp. 394–5.

Fig. 48.1   I.D., *Certaine Godly Rules concerning Christian Practice*,
London, 1647.
Woodblock-printed paper covers. 133 × 87 × 2 mm.
Lambeth Palace Library, **G 4500.D.2.

49 An English Paper Binding, c. 1698

(1981)*

'Mr Tollet's Calendar, Secundum Usum Monasticum. Not yet finished—1697', a manuscript, with drawings, that belonged to Samuel Pepys, is bound in boards covered with two different metallic varnish papers. The first and the fourth quarters are of purple paper with black stencilled compartments, printed in gold with a wood-block showing leaves and flowers; the second and third quarters are of dark green paper printed in gold with a different floral design. The same paper that was used for the first and fourth quarters also covers an exchange of letters between Pepys and John Flamsteed, written in 1697, and a collection of twelve miscellaneous manuscripts dated 1612–85. The block with which the green paper of the second and third quarters was printed was also used to decorate the black paper wrappers of a set of manuscripts on 'Magick & Exorcisms'. Pink papers printed with this same block were used to bind Pepys's *By the King. An Establishment touching Salutes by Guns . . . 1688* and a collection of ten maps [*c.* 1702]; a green paper also printed with this block covers 'Papers of M^r. Hally's & M^r. Greaves's touching . . . Navigation', dated 1695–6. This block is very similar to that used to print a paper now at Leipzig, said to have been made in Augsburg *c.* 1705.[1]

A number of other paper wrappers in the Pepys Library at Magdalene College, Cambridge, decorated with leaves, flowers and various stars, also forming distinct groups, cover both printed books and manuscripts mostly dating from the 1690s. Haemmerle describes these metallic varnish papers as first being made at Augsburg *c.* 1692–5; if the papers in the Pepys Library are indeed of German origin, at least one London stationer must have been quick off the mark to import them. The patents granted in 1691–2 to Nathaniel Gifford and William Bayly for printing papers 'with severall engines'[2] may apply to the manufacture of embossed paper, although that was even less frequently used in England at the time.

1. A. Haemmerle, *Buntpapier*, Munich, 1961, pl. 62.
2. *Patents for Inventions. Abridgments of specifications relating to . . . ornamenting paper*, London, 1879.

---

* English and Foreign Bookbindings 16, *The Book Collector*, xxx, pp. 74–5.

Fig. 49.1   Mr Tollet's Calendar, MS.1697.
            Metallic varnish paper over boards. 350 × 280 × 3 mm.
            Pepys Library 2525. By permission of the Master and Fellows,
            Magdalene College, Cambridge.

50 A Parisian Paper Binding, c. 1781

(1980)*

Among the books and pamphlets in decorated paper in the Olga Hirsch collection at the British Library is a copy of Necker's *Compte rendu au Roy . . . 1781*, roughly stabbed, in boards lined with blue-grey paper, and covered with four irregularly matched pieces of a woodblock-printed paper on which the word PAPILLON is just visible. Three possible engravers of this block, which is printed in black and coloured by hand, present themselves: Jean Papillon (1661–1723),[1] wood-engraver and inventor of wall-paper with a continuous design; his son Jean-Michel (1698–1776), who made his first engraving when eight years old and who wrote *Traité historique et pratique de la gravure en bois*, Paris, 1766,[2] both of whom worked in an atelier 'Au Papillon' in the rue St Jacques 'vis à vis la fontaine de St Severin'; and the latter's former apprentice Didier Aubert who established himself *c.* 1735 in the rue St Jacques near the Hôtel de Saumur, also 'Au Papillon', and who from *c.* 1755 specialized in flock paper.

After his father's death, Jean-Michel Papillon devoted himself more and more to delicate engraving and in 1733 was elected to the Société des Arts. The seven plates which he designed for the 1738 edition of the *Encyclopédie*, but never used, show the technique of printing and colouring wall-papers as practised in the atelier in the rue St Jacques, as well as of hanging them.[3] Jean-Michel sold the family business to the widow Langlois who in 1740 lost a lawsuit against Aubert concerning the right to use the sign 'Au Papillon'. In 1752 Jean-Michel presented a collection of his engravings to the Bibliothèque Royale. These *Oeuvres des Papillons* to which he continued to add specimens of his own and his family's work, now in the Bibliothèque Nationale (Cabinet des Estampes), contain only seven sheets of wall-paper.[4]

1. His father Jean (1639–1710), also a wood-engraver, founded *c.* 1662 the atelier in the rue St Jacques.
2. *Supplément du Traité de la gravure en bois*, Paris, 1766 [in fact 1768], contains his autobiography. Jean-Baptiste-Michel (1720–46) was his younger brother.

* English and Foreign Bookbindings 15, *The Book Collector*, XXIX, pp. 568–9.

3. Illustrated in H. Clouzot and C. Follot, *Histoire du papier peint en France*, Paris, 1935.
4. Clouzot and Follot, *op. cit.*, p. 16.

Fig. 50.1 J. Necker, *Compte rendu au Roy . . . au mois de Janvier 1781*, Paris, 1781.
Woodblock-printed paper over boards, hand-coloured in red, blue, brown, yellow, pink and green. 284 × 228 × 25 mm.
British Library, Olga Hirsch collection.

51 A Sienese Panel, 1488
(1984)*

Over 100 painted wooden covers, used to protect and decorate the accounts of the Sienese exchequer, survive; the earliest dates back to 1258.[1] Until about 1310 two sets of accounts, written on vellum, were kept and adorned with wooden covers. One set contained the accounts of the chief Treasury official, the Camarlingo, the other set those of the receivers of monies paid into the exchequer, the Provveditori. The covers of the Camarlingo's accounts were decorated with his portrait, often showing him at work in his office. The accounts of the Provveditori simply bore their names and coats of arms. From about 1314 only one set of accounts on vellum was kept, with the covers combining both elements of decoration. From 1334 a gradual change took place in the theme of the decorative scenes. Treasury officials were sometimes depicted with their patron saints; religious and contemporary historical scenes appeared and became the norm from the early fifteenth century onwards. In the late 1450s paper instead of vellum came to be used for the accounts and consequently the account books no longer needed the heavy wooden panels to keep them flat. All the same, the officials continued to have their period of office commemorated by painted wooden panels to be hung in the Treasury. The last surviving example dates from 1682.[2]

The panel illustrated here depicts the return of the Noveschi to Siena, showing the armed exiles on horseback with their leader, Pandolfo Petrucci, on a white steed before the Porta di Fontebranda. Above the town walls are the Virgin and St Mary Magdalen.[3]

1. E. Carli, *Le tavolette di Biccherna*, Florence, 1950. R. W. Lightbown, 'The *Tavolette di Biccherna* of Siena', *Journal of the Society of Archivists*, II, 7 (1963), pp. 292 ff. (with literature). After this article had been written an advance copy of a splendid new reference work on this subject reached me: L Borgia and others, *Le Biccherne*, Rome, 1984.
2. Other Sienese institutions kept their accounts in a similar way. See *Le Biccherne* for an eighteenth-century example.
3. According to Carli, *op. cit.*, St Ediltrude. However, the 'crown' in her hand

* English and Foreign Bookbindings 31, *The Book Collector*, XXXIII, pp. 486-7.

Fig. 51.1   Painted wooden panel for the accounts of the *Biccherna* of
Siena, 1488. 500 × 335 mm.
British Library, Henry Davis Gift.

is in fact a container for ointment. *Le Biccherne* bears out the suggested identification, and so does Erica S. Trippi in her dissertation 'Matteo di Giovanni: Documents and a critical catalogue of his panel paintings', University of Michigan, 1987. She attributes this panel to Matteo di Giovanni.

52 A Pair of Bookcovers of the Late Nineteenth Century by I. F. Joni

(1985)*

In the preceding article I illustrated a fifteenth-century Sienese painted wooden panel. A number of nineteenth-century panels of this type exist and are not unknown in the literature.

The perpetrator, Icilio Federico Joni, a Sienese painter, gilder and restorer, illustrated two of his 'late fifteenth-century' *Tavolette* in his autobiography[1] and H. M. Nixon gave an excellent account of Joni and his work in a paper read at the sixth International Congress of Bibliophiles.[2]

Joni was born in Siena in 1865 or 1866, the illegitimate son of a quarter-master-sergeant in the Italian army. He worked as a young man in the shop of a gilder and decorator and began as a sideline to produce imitations of the wooden covers used for the Sienese tax accounts, about which he had read a pamphlet. As he never went to the Archivio di Stato to see the *Tavolette*, it is perhaps not very surprising that his covers are a far cry from the originals. Joni's bindings which purport to date from the last 40 years of the fifteenth century consist, unlike the original *Tavolette* (which by that time had evolved to framed pictures), of two wooden covers joined by a leather spine. These covers are often decorated with punched roundels, made with knitting needles, and have metal bosses and clasps. He favoured full-length figures, which he surrounded with borders painted blue and embellished with characteristic floral scroll work. He was in no way ashamed of his activities and indeed made some of these painted covers to order. In 1904 he produced a binding in the *Biccherna* style on commission for Lady Wantage which he signed 'Ioni di Senis faciebat'.

As well as the ten examples mentioned by H. M. Nixon, I have seen eight others, several of which have come to light in the late 1980s.

1. I. F. Joni, *Le Memorie di un pittore di quadri antichi*, Florence [1932] (an English translation was published by Faber and Faber in 1936).
2. H. M. Nixon, 'Binding Forgeries', *Transactions, VIth International Congress of Bibliophiles ... 1969*, Vienna, 1971.

---

* English and Foreign Bookbindings 35, *The Book Collector*, XXXIV, pp. 488–9.

Fig. 52.1   Painted wooden cover by I.F. Joni, late 19th century. 387 ×
285 mm.
British Library, C.109.k.18.

Part VI
COLLECTORS AND COLLECTIONS

During the period when most bindings, and certainly most fine bindings, were made to order, the collector played an important part in the creative process that led to the finished book. Most books were written and produced for the reader, but the bibliophile—the lover of fine books and fine bindings—provided the circumstances in which the craft of bookbinding could develop into an art. Not all collectors were bibliophiles, however. The scholar and the student who bought a text and had it bound (perhaps—for the more pecunious among them—with a little blind- or gold-tooled decoration, a name, a coat of arms, a place or date of acquisition, some fillets, a roll, modest corner and centre-pieces or a few fleurons) kept the binders' shops as usefully, and probably more fully, employed as did the publishers.

Those whose bindings served to protect the texts they needed and cherished provided the bread-and-butter work for the binders. Those who loved their books for their appearance as much as—or possibly even more than—for their contents provided the jam. A third category of collectors were those who received books in fine bindings as gifts, ranging from the recipient of his or her Sunday-best prayer book, the bride's marriage Bible, the recipient of an author's presentation copy, to the rich and powerful who were able to bestow preferment in return.

This Part starts with a general article on patrons of bookbinding, followed by individual collectors of all three types, and finishes with descriptions of two large historical collections, one made privately, the other formed collectively, both of which now belong to institutions.

53 Bookbinding Patronage in England
(1986)*

Bookbindings well made and lavishly embellished, have for centuries appealed to those bibliophiles whose book-collecting urge may have been less governed by the delight of scholarly pursuit than by the satisfaction of their aesthetic sense. The attraction of fine materials—soft and luscious leathers, creamy vellum, rich fabrics and, largely in earlier days, precious metals and glittering stones—has been known to lure many a scholar away from the straight and narrow path of learning.

In 384 St Jerome wrote scornfully of the wealthy Christian women whose books were written in gold on purple vellum and clothed with gems.[1] However, treasure bindings, made of precious metals decked with jewels, were often commissioned not to emphasize the grandeur of the individual owner, but to accentuate what was contained between these luxurious covers: the word of God. The Emperor Constantine is recorded as having ordered a Gospel Book to be bound in gold covers furnished with pearls and precious stones for presentation to the Great Church.[2] Eusebius, in his life of Constantine, describes the 50 luxurious Bibles the Emperor commissioned to be made for the churches of Constantinople.[3]

Nearer home, Judith of Flanders, a great patron of the arts, owned several Gospel Books in metal and jewelled bindings. In 1051 she married Tostig, the brother of Harold. About four years after Tostig was killed in Harold's victorious battle at Stamford Bridge (September 1066), Judith married Welf IV, Duke of Bavaria, who had founded the Abbey of Weingarten in 1056. Among Judith's many valuable donations to this Abbey was an illuminated manuscript Gospel Book on vellum written in England in the mid-eleventh century. It is bound in wooden boards to which a gold and silver-gilt cover has been attached. It has an engraved silver frame, gold filigree, jewels and figures cast in silver, then gilt and attached to the background. The silver-gilt figures represent Christ in majesty

* This article, based on a slide lecture given at a conference on Booktrade History in 1985, was printed in R. Myers and M. Harris (eds.), *Bibliophily* (Publishing History, Occasional Series, 2, Cambridge, 1986 pp. 1–21), where it was illustrated with 77 plates issued on two microfiches. As most of the bindings mentioned have been reproduced, I have made reference here to where they can be found.

sitting within a mandorla between two angels; below him is the Crucifixion with St Mary and St John.[4] The binding as well as the manuscript is said to be English work of the mid-eleventh century. Another of Judith's bindings, which she also gave to Weingarten, covers an illuminated manuscript Gospel Book in Latin, perhaps written in Canterbury, possibly in the second quarter of the eleventh century.[5] It is bound in wooden boards with a gold repoussé cover attached to the upper board. The cover has a gold filigree border encrusted with jewels and shows, in a central mandorla surrounded by symbols of the four Evangelists, the full-length figure of Christ in majesty. The cover has been attributed both to England and to Flanders, but no conclusive case has been made for either attribution.

Another material that attracted lovers of fine bindings was fabric. As early as the fourteenth century, the Felbrigge Psalter was clothed in canvas and embroidered with silver-gilt thread and coloured silks, showing the Annunciation on the upper cover (Fig. 53.1) and the Crucifixion on the lower. The earliest known English embroidered binding, it belonged to Anne, a nun in the convent of Minoresses at Bruisyard in Suffolk and daughter of Sir Simon Felbrigge, standard-bearer to Richard II.

Leather and vellum, however, have for long been the most frequently used materials for fine bindings and were employed for the majority of the examples to be discussed here.

The great patrons of bookbinding over the centuries lived and collected on the Continent rather than in Britain, with names like Grimaldi, Filareto, Grolier, Mahieu, Duodo and de Thou, to mention but a very few, coming immediately to mind. Of course, England had its own collectors of bookbinding but hardly anyone collected and commissioned on the same scale as, say, Grolier or Mahieu. The English royal house did not do too badly but compared with the French kings, especially of the sixteenth, seventeenth and eighteenth centuries, their collecting was of a different order of magnitude.

In the twelfth century it was Prince Henry of France, the son of Louis VI, who presented to the Abbey of Clairvaux the most celebrated group of glossed manuscripts of his own time which had been bound in Paris in blind-stamped brown calf. He patronized two ateliers, one of which bound a glossed manuscript of the Gospels according to Saint John, now in the Bodleian Library.[6]

These Romanesque bindings were also produced in England, though on a smaller scale (fewer have survived and probably fewer were made). Two ecclesiastical dignitaries encouraged their production: Henry of Blois, Bishop of Winchester, an active patron of the arts who may well have commissioned the writing and the binding of the Winton Domesday, and Hugh de Puiset, Bishop of Durham, whose four-volume manuscript Bible in Romanesque bindings was probably local work.[7]

Fig. 53.1 *Psalterium*, MS, early fourteenth century.
Embroidered canvas inlaid in eighteenth-century sprinkled calf.
British Library, Sloane MS 2400.

Dr Christopher de Hamel has argued[8] that the French Romanesque bindings were made in monasteries; they did in fact cease to be made in Paris about 1200 when the professional stationers made their entrance and lay craftsmen settled there to work for the university. Indeed, monasteries have continued to exercise a kind of institutional patronage: bookbinders (and other artists and craftsmen) could practise their craft without having to worry about where their next meal would come from. Not many examples of English monastic binding survive, owing to their destruction at the dissolution of the monasteries, but the wealth of stamped binding emanating from the German and Italian monasteries in particular is well known.

It is not always easy to know whether a binding was made for a particular patron and if so, who he was and whether he played an active part in keeping the binding trade going. Until early in the nineteenth century a large number of books were sold unbound, in sheets or stitched in wrappers, and it was the task of the owner to have them bound. Especially during the late sixteenth and seventeenth centuries the more elaborately decorated bindings were commissioned work. In a way, most owners of bound books in the past were patrons of bookbinding. There were bound books for sale, but these were usually prayer-books, Bibles, popular religious books, textbooks, schoolbooks or popular editions of the classics—in short, books likely to sell well. Some large stationers would have a limited number of copies ready bound for sale, but most other books were still in need of a binding when they were bought. The buyer could ask the bookseller to have a newly acquired book bound or he could take it to a craftsman he favoured. As most of the bindings thus obtained were fairly simple, I do not want to include them here, but one should not forget that this type of modest patronage by the not-so-rich gentleman of learning did exist and no doubt helped to keep the craft alive.

Though a great many English late fifteenth- and early sixteenth-century blind-tooled bindings survive, we do not as a rule know to whom they belonged nor by whom they were commissioned. There are a few exceptions: the only English binder to use cuir ciselé, a cut-leather technique, to decorate his bindings (a habit more common in Germany and Austria) was the Scales binder. He worked in London in the mid-fifteenth century and he carved the initials, or in one case the complete name, of the prospective owner into the leather of the cover.[9] Mottoes tooled or painted on the cover are another indication of private ownership and hence of private patronage. 'Mon bien mondain', a motto said to have been used by Humphrey, Duke of Gloucester, and adopted by his physician, Gilbert Kymer, Dean of Salisbury and twice Chancellor of the University of

Oxford, occurs on the bindings of two manuscripts written at Salisbury for Kymer and probably bound either there or in Oxford.[10]

Printers and publishers could (and can) be patrons too. During the late fifteenth and early sixteenth centuries important stationers appear to have been instrumental in having the books they sold bound. A well-known example is William Caxton who constantly employed one particular binder to bind books he had printed and wanted for presentation or for sale in his shop (Fig. 53.2). The same binder continued to work for Caxton's successor, Wynkyn de Worde. The Oxford stationers, Theodoric Rood and Thomas Hunt, may also have favoured one particular binder; a number of books printed by one and (possibly) sold by the other were bound in the same shop.[11] The London printer, Richard Pynson, seems to have patronized one particular binder at the end of the fifteenth century (Fig. 11.1 above).

Not all names and initials on bindings are those of the owners. Sometimes they are those of the binders themselves and sometimes, especially in the case of certain signed rolls or panels, they can be those of the engraver or, perhaps more frequently in England, of the publisher/bookseller who may even have owned a panel or roll and given it to a binder to bind a small number of his books for sale. These stationers can certainly be classed as patrons, be it of a somewhat commercial kind. John Reynes, Martin Dature, Nicholas Spierinck and Garrett Godfrey are all cases in point: they were important stationers who may have owned a bindery but who certainly owned signed rolls and panels which they could and did farm out.

Fabric or embroidered bindings were frequently commissioned. A splendid example covers the indentures between Henry VII and Abbot John Islip concerning the foundation of Henry VII's chapel at Westminster: the King's copy is now in the Public Record Office; the Abbot's is in the British Library (Fig. 53.3).

The earliest known English gold-tooled binding was commissioned: it covers Robert Whittington's *Epigrams* (in manuscript) and was presented to Cardinal Wolsey.[12] Another early sixteenth-century gold-tooled binding was presented to Henry VIII by his physician, Thomas Linacre.[13] Linacre, who had already had gold-tooled bindings prepared for Henry VIII in Paris, must have felt that this could equally well be done in England. It was probably his idea to use the royal arms block, made for use in blind, with gold leaf on this occasion.

The fact that a binding has a royal arms block does not necessarily mean that it was made for the king or queen. Members of the royal household were entitled to use the royal arms on their belongings, and in the case of bookbindings, blocks showing the royal arms, or even royal portraits, were on occasion used on ordinary trade bindings. All the same,

Fig. 53.2   *Cronica de regibus Anglie*, MS, fifteenth century.
Blind-tooled brown calf by the Caxton Binder (type C).
British Library, Add. MS 10106.

Fig. 53.3   *Indenture made betwene . . . King Henry VII . . . and John Islippe Abbot of . . . Westminster*, MS, 1504.
Red velvet with silver-gilt and enamelled medallions and clasps. British Library, MS Harl. 1498.

several English monarchs were presented with books elaborately decorated with their arms and/or initials. Some bear additional presentation inscriptions and in those cases it would be more just to call the donor rather than the royal recipient the binder's patron. (In such a case, though, the presentation binding could have been used to obtain a benefit or office, and the right to bestow such a benefit or office is another meaning of the word patronage.)

However, in owning libraries filled with specially bound books and in finding lavishly bound books acceptable as gifts, the kings and queens of England did exercise an important form of patronage towards the bookbinders of their time. A few examples will suffice: King Henry's binder produced bindings for the royal library of Henry VIII, as did his successor, the Medallion binder. The Greenwich binder also bound for Henry VIII, and the King Edward and Queen Mary binder bound for the royal library during the reigns of both these monarchs.[14]

A different way in which the crown exercised patronage in the late fifteenth century was the active encouragement of the importation of books, as well as of the immigration of stationers, printers and bookbinders. When in January 1484 an Act was passed to regulate and restrict the conditions under which foreigners could carry on business in England, a proviso was added exempting those involved in all aspects of the booktrade. This freedom for foreign immigrant stationers and binders was later retracted, and during the early sixteenth century a number of Acts made it increasingly difficult for them to live and work here. After an Act issued in 1534, the native binders in particular were protected by the fact that from then on the importation of bound books was forbidden. These Acts were meant for the protection of the native stationers—patronage again, though exercised for a different group of people. The Stationers' Company was very active in this protectionism, and by 1557 had closed the booktrade to any foreign competition, having created practically a closed shop.

Wouter Deleen, a Dutch Protestant pastor who belonged to the household of Henry VIII, patronized the Flamboyant binder on several occasions to provide New Year's gifts for his king. A copy of Herman, Archbishop of Cologne, *Ein Christliche in dem Wort Gottes gegrünte Reformation*, Bonn, 1543 (preceded by a letter from Wouter Deleen to King Henry VIII offering this book and sending a Latin version of selected parts), bound in brown calf and decorated with an exuberance of gold tooling, has the royal arms as well as a long inscription and the date 1545.[15]

It was not only the king and queen who received elaborately tooled bindings. Sir Nicholas Bacon, Lord Keeper of the Great Seal and the father of Francis Bacon, presented a finely bound copy of the works of St Basil in Greek to his very learned wife, Anne.[16]

Two important Elizabethan collectors of books and bindings, who both patronized a variety of binders, were Thomas Wotton and Robert Dudley, Earl of Leicester. Wotton obtained all his best bindings in Paris where he used three different ateliers.[17] Leicester firmly stuck to English craftsmen. All Leicester's bindings have his crest, a bear and a ragged staff in the centre of the covers even though they come from a number of different shops (Fig. 53.4). People like Wotton and Leicester, or like Grolier and Mahieu in Paris, would set a fashion for particular types of decorated binding, thereby creating a demand and consequently causing more work for the binders.

Leicester's royal friend and benefactor, Queen Elizabeth, in turn acted as a patron to bookbinding, both directly through having books for the royal library bound, and indirectly by having finely bound books presented to her. Though it has been said that her personal preference was for embroidered velvet bindings, she was also presented with finely decorated leather-bound books made by the most distinguished craftsmen of her day. The Initial binder, who also worked for Leicester, bound the dedication copy of Laurence Humphrey's translation of St Cyril of Alexandria, *Commentarii in Hesaiam*, Basel, 1563, presented to her by the translator.[18] Jean de Planche, a Huguenot immigrant, also bound several books presented to her.[19]

Sometimes authors directed their patronage of bookbinders towards themselves as well as towards the recipients of their work. William Bullein had a copy of his own work *Bullein's Bulwarke of Defence against all Sicknes*, London, 1562, bound for himself by the Initial binder and decorated with two large initials W and B.[20] Sir Robert Heywarde, Lord Mayor of London in 1571, patronized the ill-named Morocco binder,[21] and Archbishop Matthew Parker stands out as a binding patron among his contemporaries. Not only did he employ on occasion almost all the binders mentioned as being active during the second half of the sixteenth century (though the majority of his fine bindings were done in the workshop where the ninth-century Gospels of Maelbright MacDurnan were bound for him),[22] but he also employed in his own palace at Lambeth 'drawers & cutters, paynters, lymmers, wryters, and boke bynders'.[23] These Lambeth 'boke bynders' made the standard bindings for Parker's library, as well as from time to time the more splendidly decorated presentation bindings.[24]

English monarchs continued to receive bookbindings as New Year's gifts or presents on other occasions, as witness a very fine copy of Thevet, *Pourtraits et vies des hommes illustres*, Paris, 1584, decorated in an English imitation of the French fanfare style and presented to King James I around 1615,[25] or John Speed's *Theatre of the Empire of Great Britain*, London, 1611, presented to James' wife, Anne of Denmark, probably not long

Fig. 53.4   Marcus Antonius Coccius, Sabellicus, *Le Historie Vinitiane*,
Venice, 1554.
Gold-tooled brown calf for Robert Dudley, Earl of Leicester.
British Library, C.183.a.25.

before her death in 1619, now in Trinity College, Cambridge. The most important royal library in England in the early seventeenth century was not that of this king and queen, however, but that amassed for their son, Henry, Prince of Wales. It was an important collection of books bought to educate a crown prince, bound in rather simple standard bindings of brown calf, showing the prince's arms in the centre and Tudor emblems in the corners (Fig. 53.5). The fact that there were three different arms blocks and six different corner blocks, all found in various combinations, suggests that the books were farmed out in batches to different binders who were at the same time lent the blocks. They all seem to date from around 1610. Charles I was more interested in collecting pictures than in collecting a library, but like all monarchs he acquired bindings as gifts. An elaborately tooled copy of Williams, *The Right Way to the best Religion*, London, 1636, was presented to him in 1636 (Fig. 58.2).

Turning to the nobility who either collected books or had books thrust upon them, we encounter one of the great English family libraries, that of the Egerton family, Earls of Bridgewater. The library was founded by Sir Thomas Egerton, Lord Chancellor; a Saxton atlas decorated with his crest and probably bound for him towards the end of his life is now in the Huntington Library, San Marino, California (110105). His son greatly expanded the library. Other collectors were George Villiers, Duke of Buckingham, who owned an elegant white vellum binding on James I's *Workes*, London, 1616,[26] and Captain John Smith who presented a finely bound copy of his own *Generall Historie of Virginia*, London, 1624 to 'his approved kynd frend' Frances, Duchess of Richmond and Lennox.[27] All these were the kinds of people who attracted fine bindings rather than commissioned them.

One of the truly great collectors of the century, Sir Robert Bruce Cotton, had his important collection of manuscripts bound in red turkey. Cotton used to instruct his binders with written exhortations such as:

> Bind this book as strong as you can and very fair in the read leather let it be shewed [sewed] withe 3 double threads waxed and when it is backed and shewed send it me and I will mark wher you shall cutt it gett it as euen at the head as you can.
>   [Cut it] as I have marcked and [round?] it not to muche in the back for fear you put som leaves so forward that the[y] may be in danger of Cutting sett flowers of gold one the back and corners and mak it very fayre and lett me have it ready this night when [I] send about 5' in the afternoone.[28]

This shows a very detailed personal interest by a great scholar/collector in the structure as well as the appearance of his bound books.

Of course, binding patrons did not commission their bindings only in London. The universities were most active in keeping the local binders going and even some public schools, such as Eton, provided enough work

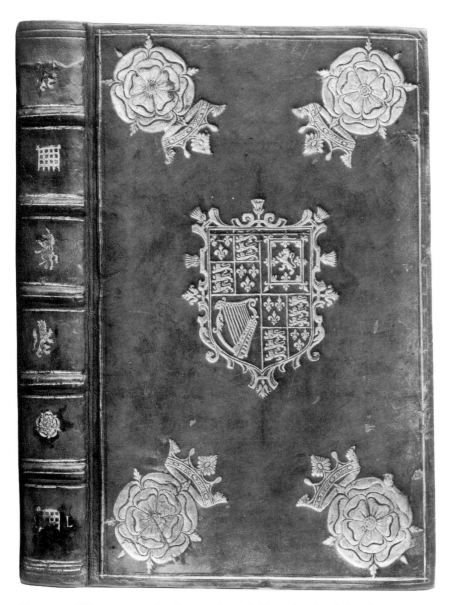

Fig. 53.5   Hieronymus Cardanus, *De subtilitate libri xxi*, Basel, 1554.
Gold-tooled brown calf for Henry, Prince of Wales.
British Library, C.78.e.4.

for the local craftsmen. The binder Williamson of Eton, who was described by Dudley Carleton in 1608 as having 'commonly his hands full of worke, and his head full of drinck',[29] bound several books for Sir Charles Somerset when he left Eton in 1604. It is not surprising that the universities furnished work for local binders. Scholars and students needed books and needed books bound, and from time to time the universities themselves issued publications which were then specially bound for presentation. We know a certain amount about the publications issued by Cambridge University and bound by several binders such as Boyse, Moody and a few unnamed others.[30]

From time to time the bookbinding trade has benefited from authors who believed that the dissemination of their ideas might be aided by the presentation of their work in handsome bindings. Lord Herbert of Cherbury is a case in point. Of his best known book, *De veritate*, six copies of the Latin edition (1633) and fourteen of the French edition (1639) are known in special bindings.[31] They all come from the same shop and are linked with bindings made by the man who worked for the printer and publisher John Bill.

When Charles II returned to England in 1660 to be restored to the throne, he received several presentation bindings: one, Foxe's *Book of Martyrs* bound by John Fletcher for £7 10s 0d, was presented to him by the Stationers' Company.[32]

The best-known binder of the Restoration period was Samuel Mearne. He was appointed royal binder to Charles II and made both the standard bindings for the royal library and lavishly decorated bindings for the King's own use.[33] Though royal patronage sounds an enviable thing, Mearne suffered much from royal non-payment of bills, to such an extent that on several occasions he refused to return the books until they were paid for. His widow was left to pursue the claim. The accounts show, however, that Mearne was paid for large numbers of books bound for the royal library and he does not seem to have done too badly, the more so as he also supplied bindings for members of the royal household and various other grand personages, and also bound the books supplied to the Dean of Windsor as Register of the Order of the Garter. Charles Mearne, Samuel's son, worked with his father and succeeded him as royal binder; several presentation bindings made by him are known.[34]

One of Mearne's contemporaries, William Nott—who may have been the binder who goes by the name of Queens' Binder A and who bound for Queen Catherine de Braganza—was patronized by Samuel Pepys who recorded in his diary for 12 March 1668/9:

> I took [W. Howe] in my coach with W. Hewer and myself towards Westminster, and there he carried me to Nott's, the famous bookbinder that bound for

my Lord Chancellor's library. And here I did take occasion for curiosity to bespeak a book to be bound, only that I might have one of his binding.[35]

Eight years earlier, on 15 May 1660, Pepys was sightseeing in The Hague. After recording his visit to the '*grand salle*, where we were showed the place where the States-generall sit in council', the diarist continues characteristically: 'After this to a bookseller's and bought, for the love of the binding, three books'.[36]

Samuel Pepys took a great interest in the binding of his books. He commissioned a number of binders to bind his library books in comparatively plain bindings with different styles of spine decoration, and he also owned more lavishly decorated bindings, such as a set of three manuscripts bound by the Queens' Binder B, probably commissioned by him in the second half of the 1670s.[37] In his capacity as secretary and later treasurer of the Navy Office, he received a number of gifts including some nicely bound books, witness a presentation copy of Barlow's *Aesop*, London, 1687.[38] All three presentation copies of this book that are known come from the same bindery.

I mentioned above binders patronized in Cambridge. In Oxford in the late seventeenth century Roger Bartlett, a London binder who had settled in Oxford after the great fire of 1666, worked for the university and is regularly mentioned in the university accounts; he also bound the Benefactors' Book of Magdalen College (1680) and that of St Edmund Hall (about 1685).[39] Another binder who apparently worked for the university towards the end of the century was Richard Sedgley. In 1699 he was paid £4 13s 0d by the Oxford University Press for binding the third volume of Wallis, *Opera mathematica*, 3 vols, Oxford, 1695–99, for presentation to the king.[40] He also bound the Benefactors' Book for three Oxford Colleges, and Dean Aldrich, whose books are now in the library of Christ Church, seems to have patronized him. Thomas Sedgley (possibly Richard's son) also worked for Oxford University during the first half of the eighteenth century and was employed to bind books for the Bodleian Library.[41]

An unusual, rather comical patron of bookbinding during the first quarter of the eighteenth century was Elkanah Settle, the City poet. He was considered a rising playwright in the 1670s, but by the beginning of the eighteenth century he had degenerated into a hack poet, scraping a living by retailing copies of topical political or personal verse. The personal poems celebrated the births, marriages and deaths of the noble and rich. The poems would be printed, often with a manuscript or decorated title-page and bound, usually in black turkey, embellished with large crude tools and the coat of arms of a possible recipient.[42] If the first recipient declined the honour, the leaf that contained the personal references would be cancelled, a new leaf substituted, the coat of arms on the binding would be covered with a piece of leather on which a different coat of arms was emblazoned, and Settle would call hopefully at the next great house. On at least one occasion he was lucky only at the third attempt.

Two more serious patrons of bookbinding as well as great collectors of books and manuscripts were Robert Harley, 1st Earl of Oxford, founder of the famous Harleian library, and his son, Edward, Lord Harley. In 1715 the son took over the management of the library which he enlarged considerably. He took a great deal of interest in the binding of the books and manuscripts and, thanks to the survival of the bills for binding (now deposited in the British Library), we know that Harley patronized first Richard Sedgley of Oxford, then John Graves and then Thomas Dawson of Cambridge. By 1715 books were sent for binding to Jane Steel[43] and by 1719 Thomas Elliott appears as one of Harley's main binders,[44] the other being Christopher Chapman. Harley's librarian, Humfrey Wanley,[45] kept a close eye on the bindings returned and is known on more than one occasion to have rebuked Elliott for careless lettering. Chapman started binding for the Harleian library in 1720.[46] At first his work seems to have satisfied Wanley, but gradually he took longer and longer to return the books and Wanley chided him for being too slow. John Brindley, who held the appointment of bookbinder to George II's queen, Caroline of Ansbach, also bound for the Harleian library.[47]

A binder who decorated his bindings in a style similar to that found on Harleian bindings, but whose finishing was more accomplished than either Elliott's or Chapman's, was Edwin Moore[48] who worked extensively for King's College, Cambridge. His predecessor Thomas Dawson bound for St John's College, Cambridge.

Both George, 3rd Earl of Cholmondeley and John Carteret, 2nd Earl Granville, patronized the same binder's shop in the 1740s. Carteret, the Whig politician, is not in the first instance known as a collector of books, but a binding on Plutarch, *Apophthegmata regum et imperatorum*, London, 1741,[49] and three other bindings from this same shop known to have been made for him, as all bear his coat of arms, suggest that he may have been a bibliophile as well as a scholar of repute.

Another large English country-house library is that of Lord Leicester at Holkham Hall. Several binders worked for the library, such as Jane Steel, John Brindley and Jean Robiquet, a French binder who lived in London. He spent long spells at Holkham in 1742 and 1748 and worked for the library until the death of the 1st Earl of Leicester (of the second creation) in 1759 (Fig. 53.6).

The antiquary Maurice Johnson patronized the London bookbinder Christopher Norris of St Paul's Chapterhouse Alley in the 1750s.[50]

One of the leading London binders of the 1750s and 1760s was Richard Montagu and his best patron was that staunchly patriotic republican,

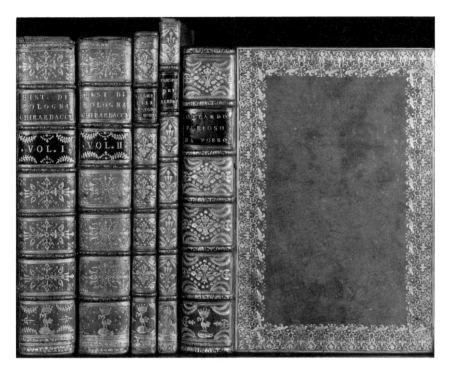

Fig. 53.6   A selection of books bound by Robiquet.
Holkham Hall.

Thomas Hollis. Hollis was a true patron of bookbinding, though it is for
the quantity rather than for the elaborate decoration of his bindings that
he should be awarded the palm. His standard bindings in red morocco
decorated with only a few emblematic tools on the covers are well enough
known. They were produced by Matthewman in the 1760s. Hollis was in
the habit of presenting whole libraries bound in this manner to deserving
institutions (such as Harvard and Berne). He also commissioned more
elaborate presentation bindings which were made by Montagu.[51]

A somewhat similar character to Thomas Hollis was Jonas Hanway
(1712–86), never mentioned without reference to an apparently quite
untrue record that he was the first person to carry an umbrella in London.
He was another eccentric philanthropist who sought to stimulate the good
causes he favoured by presenting elaborately bound books on the subject.
He used two binders, his later man used emblematic tools reminiscent of
those found on Hollis bindings.[52]

Apart from a little royal patronage, there seems not to have been much 'institutional' patronage in the eighteenth century. A fraternity which certainly stimulated the binding trade during the second half of the eighteenth century, though in limited quantity, was that of the Freemasons, who commissioned binders to bind Masonic works and to decorate them with specifically symbolic tools. One of these Masonic binders was John Lovejoy.[53]

Bindings specially produced and presented to mark a specific occasion remained in vogue. A binding by the firm of Edwards of Halifax was a wedding gift to Oliver Farrer and Anna Selina Fawcett whom he married in 1782;[54] it has their arms painted underneath the transparent vellum of the upper cover.

In volume I of my catalogue of the Henry Davis Gift,[55] I discussed Roger Payne and his patrons, the most faithful being his namesake, the bookseller Thomas Payne. Roger also worked for Walter Bowman, A. M. Storer, Michael Wodhull, the Reverend C. M. Cracherode, Thomas Grenville, Lord Spencer, Sir Richard Colt Hoare and many others. Payne's elaborate bills are frequently quoted and he seems to have been on personally friendly terms with a number of his patrons, especially with his doctor Benjamin Moseley.

An invasion of German binders, who played an important role in the binding trade in the West End of London, showed that during the second half of the eighteenth century London was a better place for a binder than Germany. Hüttner in *Englische Miscellen*, Vol. VI, 1802, gives a fascinating account of the state of the binding trade in England at that time and explains in detail the differences between the English and the German methods of binding. Prospects in England were much better than those in Germany. A German prince might have his whole library bound in calf, but even simple English gentlemen, like Cracherode or Colt Hoare, would have much of their library bound in the more expensive morocco. Andreas Linde, the first to arrive, was stationer and bookbinder by appointment to the future King George III; a binding on *Das neue Testament*, London, 1751, shows him at work for Prince George.[56] Others were Baumgarten, Kalthoeber (in whom George III took much interest), Walther, who bound a copy of *Novelle Otto*, London, 1790, for Colonel Thomas Stanley in 1791,[57] and Staggemeier and Welcher, who bound the copy of Horace, *Opera*, Paris, 1799, which Thomas Hope presented to the Royal Institution in London on 27 March 1805.[58] According to Thomas Dibdin, Hope 'gave the binder his plan . . . of book embellishment',[59] an example of a patron specifying the design.

Henry Bohn, the son of John Bohn who set up shop in Soho in 1795, wrote that 'at that time bookbinding in this country had fallen to a very low ebb, and the advent of the German workmen was generally welcomed'.[60] Another immigrant who established a successful firm in London

Fig. 53.7   R. Ackermann, *The History of Westminster Abbey*, London, 1812.
Red velvet with silver-gilt mounts designed by John Papworth, bound by Hering.
Westminster Abbey.

was Charles Hering who succeeded Roger Payne in the favour of Earl Spencer. Hering's bindery was also patronized by Thomas Grenville and Lord Byron. Hering's reputation earned him a commission from the curators of the Faculty of Advocates library in Edinburgh, and he bound Ackermann's own copy of his *History of Westminster Abbey*, London, 1812. (Fig. 53.7)

Two early- to mid-nineteenth-century witnesses of the English passion for collecting are Robert Southey, who in 1807 noted that 'there is, perhaps, no country in which the passion for collecting rarities is so prevalent as in England',[61] and R. P. Gillies who in 1851 derided his countrymen:

> There had sprung up a kind of *mania* for purchasing black letter volumes, although the purchasers themselves, from year's end to year's end, did not read, far less write, fifty pages consecutively. Among such people, it must be owned, the bibliographical propensity, though it had, indirectly, good results, was nearly as absurd as the *ci-devant* 'tulip-madness' in Holland.[62]

One of those 'good results', at least for the binders, was an increased demand to have those rarities suitably clothed.

An important patron of bookbinding during the end of the eighteenth and the beginning of the nineteenth century was King George III, as witness his magnificent library, now in the British Library, and this snide comment from a contemporary poet:

> Kings care not if we neither drink nor carve—,
> This is their speech in secret, 'Sing and starve.'
> And yet our Monarch has a world of books,
> And daily on their backs so gorgeous looks;
> So neatly bound, so richly gilt, so fine,
> He fears to open them to read a line!
> Since of our *books* a King can highly deem,
> The *Authors* surely might command esteem:
> But here's the dev'l—I fear too many know it—
> *Some* Kings prefer the *Binder* to the *Poet*.[63]

Not only did George III like and receive finely bound books as gifts, he had a private bindery at Buckingham House which operated from about 1780 [?1786] until a few years after his death in 1820. A number of elaborate bindings were executed by this bindery, such as George III's copy of Joannes Balbus, *Catholicon* (Mainz, 1460).[64]

Charles Lewis, the son of the German immigrant binder Johann Ludwig, having changed his name, became London's most fashionable and best-known binder, patronized by all the great collectors of the day. A binding made for Sir Mark Masterman Sykes with his arms on the covers and with Grenville's arms added later to the doublures covers Valerius Maximus, *Factorum et dictorum memorabilium libri*, Mainz, 1471, and shows Lewis at his best.[65]

In the 1830s a fashion for imitations of earlier binding styles took hold of the English collectors and the (not very successful) results do not speak well for the kind of interfering patronage about which I have hitherto said very little. I suspect that certain early collectors, such as Grolier and Wotton, took an active interest in the designs of their bindings, in the sense that they probably discussed the patterns and tools to be employed. There is virtually no factual evidence for a patron's dictating a design to a binder (though there is a certain amount of evidence for the colour of the leather being specified). Obviously, in the case where insignia, arms or mottoes were used, the owner must have stipulated the wish to have his mark of ownership on the spine or covers of his books, but how far the binder was left free, we can only guess. The nineteenth-century fashion for pastiche bindings shows that, at least in some instances, interference dictated by the taste of the collector was a bad thing.

About 1823, with the introduction of bookbinders' cloth, a big change was finally effected by which almost every book in a bookseller's shop was available ready bound in a publisher's binding. Though fine hand binding was carried on and is indeed still carried on, the easy availability of bound books profoundly changed the face of binding patronage. The rich and aesthetically fastidious continued to have their books bound specially, but the average book-buyer who bought his books for the contents and not for their appearance ceased to be even a modest patron of bookbinding in the sense I have been discussing. Of course, he willy-nilly patronized the machine and trade binders, but this is not under consideration here. The big firms of trade binders mostly turned out pastiches, and even hand binders aimed at a machine-like accuracy and perfection with pretty dead results.

A fresh wind into this stultifying atmosphere came with Thomas James Cobden-Sanderson (Fig. 53.8). When, at the age of 42, as a not very successful barrister, he decided to try his hand at bookbinding, he started the 'amateur' movement which has played such an important part in the subsequent history of the craft in England. He bound for his own family and friends and for the bookseller Bain, but in his own way he was a patron of bookbinding himself, not because he collected, but because he made his contemporaries aware of the joy of beautifully made and beautifully finished books.

The fact that I have talked entirely about England does not mean that binding patronage did not exist elsewhere in the British Isles. There is the very curious parliamentary patronage in eighteenth-century Ireland, where the most beautiful and lavishly decorated bindings were commissioned to cover the books of Parliamentary papers;[66] and Mr Loudon[67] has shown that in Edinburgh James Scott enjoyed the patronage not only of well-to-do collectors of books, but of booksellers and several institutions.

Patronage did not stop with the end of the nineteenth century. During the 1930s, 1940s and 1950s such private patrons as Major Abbey (whose collection was sold at Sotheby's during the mid-to-late-1960s) and Albert Ehrman (whose collection is now, through the generosity of his son, in the Bodleian Library) did a great deal to make bookbinding as an art better known and to encourage contemporary binders. Abbey's collection was used to mount several exhibitions of modern bindings in the late 1940s and 1950s, and Ehrman bought the products of his own time as well as those of the past. Henry Davis, whose taste was more conservative, nevertheless acquired a number of modern bindings, and his great generosity in donating his collection to the nation gives him a prominent place among patrons of bookbinding in this century. A book collector such as J. P. Getty Jr encourages public interest in the craft not least through his generosity in lending items of his collection to public exhibitions, and it is well known how much bookseller-collectors, such as Duval and Hamilton and Colin Franklin, have done and are still doing for the designer bookbinders of today. Even the periodical with the appropriate name of

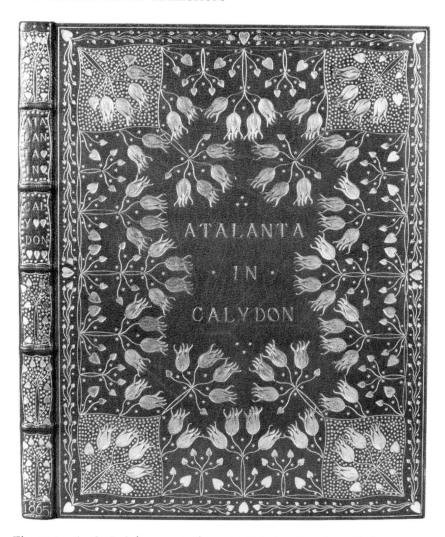

Fig. 53.8   A. C. Swinburne, *Atalanta in Calydon*, London, 1865.
Gold-tooled, green goatskin. Bound by T. J. Cobden-
Sanderson in 1888.
British Library, C.68.i.2.

The Book Collector excites interest in modern as well as ancient binding
through publication of articles on both subjects.

Patronage exercised by the crown has dwindled during the present
century. State patronage may not amount to much, but at least the Treasury provides funds for national institutions and pays out grants to

students. Institutional patronage continues, modestly; but if one realizes that the task of an institution is to build up an historical collection in which the current century has to take its place, while grappling with the problem of having to build a collection for the future with the knowledge, taste and means of the present, perhaps it is not negligible. Publishers such as the Folio Society occasionally commission fine binders to design an edition binding. A new kind of industrial patronage has emerged over the past few years. Banks and large firms have been known to provide financial support for binding conferences and exhibitions, and have sponsored individual binders. Private patronage, though again in this country not abundant, helps to keep the craft alive. In the matter of choice, private collectors who in the end have only themselves (or possibly their bank managers) to please, have a freedom no institution can afford.

The fashion in binding styles seems today to be set not by the collectors but by the binders themselves. Indeed, the Designer Binders are patrons as well as performers of their craft: Elizabeth Greenhill collects work by her contemporaries; all are active in organizing conferences and exhibitions; they institute competitions and award prizes; they travel round the world with suitcases full of their latest products; they strive to get bookbinding as an art more widely known and more widely appreciated. However, this is not entirely new (few things ever are): Elkanah Settle hawked his wares around and Roger Payne solicited his patrons for work. Perhaps the 1980s have not produced a Grolier or a Wotton, but all the same, in a few hundred years time, the late twentieth century will probably be considered as a period during which bookbinding patronage was alive and well.

1. J. P. Migne, *Patrologiae cursus completus . . . series Latina*, Paris, 1844–64, vol. xxii, col. 418.
2. J. P. Migne, *Patrologiae cursus completus . . . series Graeca*, Paris, 1857–1912, vol. cxxi, cols. 561–2.
3. Eusebius, Pamphili, Bishop of Caesarea, *Vita Constantini*, see Migne, *Patrologiae . . . series Latina*, vol. viii. Idem, *Life of Constantine*, London, 1649, Book iv, chapters 36–7.
4. P. Needham, *Twelve Centuries of Bookbindings: 400–1600*, New York/ London, 1979, no. 8.
5. Ibid, no. 9.
6. H. M. Nixon, *Broxbourne Library. Styles and Designs of Bookbinding*, London, 1956, no. 1.
7. M. M. Foot, 'Bindings' in *English Romanesque Art, 1066–1200*, Arts Council Exhibition, London, 1984, pp. 342–9.
8. C. de Hamel, *Glossed Books of the Bible and the Origins of the Paris Booktrade*, Woodbridge, 1984, chapter 6.
9. N. J. Barker, 'A Register of Writs and the Scales Binder', *The Book Collector*, xxi (1972), pp. 227–44, 356–79, pl. vii.

10. G. D. Hobson, *English Binding before 1500*, Cambridge, 1929, pl. 34.
11. Ibid, pl. 37.
12. *Fine Bindings 1500–1700 from Oxford Libraries. Catalogue of an Exhibition*, Oxford, 1968, no. 63.
13. H. M. Nixon, *Five Centuries of English Bookbinding*, London, 1978, no. 5.
14. For examples of all these see H. M. Nixon, 'Early English Gold-Tooled Bookbindings' in *Studi di Bibliografia e di Storia in onore di Tammaro de Marinis*, 4 vols, Verona, 1964, vol. III, pp. 283–308, pls, i, ii, iii, v.
15. I. G. Philip, *Gold-Tooled Bookbindings* (Bodleian picture books 2), Oxford, 1951, pl. 5.
16. H.M. Nixon, *Sixteenth-Century Gold-Tooled Bookbindings in the Pierpont Morgan Library*, New York, 1971, no. 28.
17. M. M. Foot, *The Henry Davis Gift*, vol. I, London, 1978, pp. 139–55.
18. H. M. Nixon, *Five Centuries of English Bookbinding*, London, 1978, no. 19.
19. H. M. Nixon, 'Elizabethan Gold-Tooled Bindings' in *Essays in Honour of Victor Scholderer*, Mainz, 1970, pp. 219–70, pls. 5, 6.
20. H. M. Nixon, *Five Centuries of English Bookbinding*, London, 1978, no. 20.
21. Ibid, p. 238, no. 18.
22. Ibid, no. 21.
23. BL, Lansdowne MS 17, fol. 63 (letter from Parker to Lord Burghley, 1572).
24. H. M. Nixon, *Five Centuries*, no. 23.
25. W. Y. Fletcher, *English Bookbindings in the British Museum*, London, 1895, pl. xxxiv.
26. *Fine Bindings 1500–1700 from Oxford Libraries*, Oxford, 1968, no. 137.
27. Ibid, no. 140.
28. BL, MS Cotton, Domitian A. VII, fols. 1, 84v [the original paste-downs].
29. Quoted in W. H. J. Weale, *Bookbindings . . . in the National Art Library*, vol. I, London, 1898, p. xlvii. See also R. Birley, 'The History of Eton College Library', *The Library*, 5th series, XI (1956), pp. 231–62, pls. vi, vii.
30. J. C. T. Oates, 'Cambridge Books of Congratulatory Verses 1603–1640 and their Binders', *Transactions of the Cambridge Bibliographical Society*, vol. I, part V, 1953, pp. 395–421; M. M. Foot, *The Henry Davis Gift*, vol. I, London, 1978, pp. 60–75.
31. H. M. Nixon, *Five Centuries*, no. 30. See also M. M. Foot, *The Henry Davis Gift*, vol. I, pp. 50–8.
32. H. M. Nixon, *Five Centuries*, no. 33.
33. H. M. Nixon, *English Restoration Bookbindings*, London, 1974, pls. 2–8; 13–21.
34. Ibid, pl. 34.
35. Ibid, p. 34; H. M. Nixon, *Catalogue of the Pepys Library at Magdalene College Cambridge, vol. VI: Bindings*, Woodbridge, 1984, no. 518, pl. 40.
36. H. M. Nixon, *Catalogue of the Pepys Library*, p. xiii.
37. Ibid, pl. 45.
38. Ibid, pl. 51.
39. H. M. Nixon, *English Restoration Bookbindings*, pls, 117, 118.
40. Ibid, pl. 122.
41. H. M. Nixon, *Five Centuries*, no. 59.
42. Ibid, no. 57.
43. Ibid, no. 58.
44. Ibid, no. 60.

45. C. E. and R. C. Wright (eds), *The Diary of Humfrey Wanley 1715–1726*, 2 vols, London, 1966.
46. H. M. Nixon, *Five Centuries*, no. 61.
47. Ibid, no. 64.
48. M. M. Foot, *The Henry Davis Gift*, vol. I, pl. opp. p. 80.
49. H. M. Nixon, *Five Centuries*, no. 63.
50. M. M. Foot, *The Henry Davis Gift*, vol. I, pp. 87–94.
51. H. M. Nixon, *Five Centuries*, no. 67 (see also no. 74 for a standard binding by Matthewman).
52. Ibid, no. 78.
53. Ibid, no. 75 (Loveday is a misprint for Lovejoy).
54. Ibid, no. 77.
55. M. M. Foot, *The Henry Davis Gift*, vol. I, pp. 95–114.
56. H. M. Nixon, *Five Centuries*, no. 66.
57. M. M. Foot, *The Henry Davis Gift*, vol. II, London, 1983, no. 195.
58. H. M. Nixon, *Five Centuries*, no. 81.
59. T. F. Dibdin, *Bibliographical Decameron*, London, 1817, vol. II, p. 520.
60. H. G. Bohn, 'Bookbinding', *Art Journal*, LXXV (1881), p. 196.
61. Manuel Alvarez Espriella (pseud.) [R. Southey], *Letters from England*, London, 1807, vol. I, p. 233.
62. R. P. Gillies, *Memoirs of a Literary Veteran*, London, 1851, vol. II, p. 2.
63. Peter Pindar (pseud.) [John Wolcot], *Works*, Dublin, 1796, vol. II, p. 393.
64. H. M. Nixon, *Five Centuries*, no. 84.
65. BL, G.9153. For another binding by Lewis, see H. M. Nixon, *Five Centuries*, no. 85.
66. M. J. Craig, *Irish Bookbinding 1600–1800*, London, 1954, frontispiece, pls. 1–17.
67. J. H. Loudon, *James Scott and William Scott, Bookbinders*, London, 1980.

54 Some Bindings for Foreign Students in Sixteenth-Century Paris

(1975)*

Ludovicus a Liliis or Ludwig Zur Gilgen[1] was born in 1547, the son of Aurelian Zur Gilgen, seigneur of Hilfikon,[2] a member of a patrician family from the canton of Lucerne. He studied at Freiburg in the Breisgau[3] and Dôle, continued his studies in Paris in 1565 and was at the university of Orléans two years later. Upon his return he became a member of the Grand Conseil, a year later in 1568 a member of the Petit Conseil and the following year saw him as Treasurer. He bought back the family mansion in 1571, founded the family library and died in 1577 at the age of 30.

Some of his books have strayed into this country. The Henry Davis Gift to the British Library contains a copy of Dioscorides, *Historia Plantarum*, Lyon, 1561, bound in brown calf, tooled in gold and silver with a cartouche[4] containing Zur Gilgen's arms—three fleurs-de-lis argent—in the centre, fleurs-de-lis in the corners, and lettered on the upper cover: LVDOVICVS|A LILIIS and on the lower cover: LVTETIAE 26. IVNI.|ANNO 1566 (Fig. 54.1).[5] Another calf binding, bearing the same inscription on the upper cover and lettered on the lower cover: LVTETIAE 19. IANVA.|ANNO 1566, covering five controversial religious works, printed in Paris between 1558 and 1562, is now in the Broxbourne Library.[6] This copy has a manuscript note on one of the endpapers: 'sum Ludovici à Lilijs Empt*us* . . . Lutetiae Parisio*rum* 19 Ianuarij, Anno 1566'. The fleurs-de-lis in the corners and the tools used for the lettering are the same as those used on the Dioscorides, but Zur Gilgen's arms are surrounded by a more formal hatched cartouche. This same cartouche occurs on several bindings, most of which cover books printed in Paris in the 1560s. Twenty-eight of these were bought in Paris between 1566 and 1569 on authority of Othmar II, abbot of the Benedictine monastery of Sanct Gallen, by one of his monks, Mauritius Enck who studied in Paris until 1571.[7] Among the books he brought back home were a Cologne Aristotle,[8] decorated with this cartouche and tooled on the upper cover: LIBER|SANCTI GALLI and on the lower cover: EMPTVS LVTETIAE|ANNO 1566, and three manu-

---

* *The Book Collector*, XXIV, pp. 106–10.

Fig. 54.1   Dioscorides, *Historia Plantarum* 1561.
British Library, Henry Davis Gift.

scripts, which are lettered on the upper cover: F.MAVRITIVS ENCK|MON. SG
GALLI COENOB.;[9] two have the title on the lower cover and all three are
tooled with their place and date of origin: LVTETIAE PARISIORVM|ANNO
DOMINI 1566.[10] Four more bindings with this cartouche, covering books
printed in Paris between 1543 and 1567, were acquired for the monastery
by an unknown buyer.

At least two other foreign students had their names tooled on bindings
decorated with this cartouche: 'Io.Ant.Salvius'[11] and 'Chilianus Berchtol-
dus'. Kilian Berchtold,[12] later Stadtschreiber of Munich, possessed a copy

of Paulus Aegineta, *Opus de re medica*, Paris, 1532,[13] bound in brown calf and tooled in gold with this cartouche, on the upper cover: CHILIANVS|BER-CHTOLDVS and on the lower cover: LVTETIAE|.7. APRILIS 1567. More than a dozen of the books he bought in Paris, which have his name tooled on the cover, are in the Bayerische Staatsbibliothek at Munich, such as a 1562 Cologne copy of *Annales Regum Francorum . . .*' which is dated on the lower cover: LVTETIAE 1566 AVGVSTI 14.[14] The oval centre-piece used on this binding also occurs on a 1554 Basel Appian,[15] which has hatched corner-pieces, the same as those used on two Paris Books of Hours,[16] where they are found combined with the cartouche which decorates the binding for Zur Gilgen in the Broxbourne Library, and on one[17] with several hatched tools. The cartouche on the Simon Vostre Book of Hours contains the initials MB, tentatively identified by Jean Porcher[18] as those of Marie Billart, née Fortia, the wife of Charles Billart, who was conseiller au Parlement de Paris and died between 1600 and 1610. This same cartouche occurs on four more bindings, two of which are at Trinity College, Cambridge. One covers a French translation of Aemilius Probus, *les Vies des plus grands, plus vertueux et excellents capitaines et personnages grecs et barbares*, Paris, 1568, which has a crowned ER added to the centre of the cartouche and an ownership inscription on one of the endpapers which reads: 'Henry Prñ de Gales'.[19] The other is H. Goltzius, *Fastos Magistratum*, Brugge, 1566,[20] in gold-tooled white calf, which has, besides the cartouche, the same hatched corner-pieces as occur on a 1565 Paris Breviary in the Broxbourne Library[21] and on a 1563 Paris Agapetus with the arms of Queen Catherine de Medici.[22] Another binding with this cartouche is illustrated by Dr Ilse Schunke,[23] and the fourth covers a 1556 Lyon Bible at the Bibliothèque Nationale.[24]

Some of the hatched tools which occur on the Book of Hours for M[arie] B[illart] and on the binding of J. Nestor's *Histoire des hommes illustres*, Paris, 1564, made for the future King Henri III in 1562,[25] and the corner-pieces used on both these bindings and on the 1554 Appian,[26] decorate a number of bindings previously[27] shown to have come from the atelier of Claude de Picques, such as that on a 1538 Paris Xenophon, with the arms of Queen Elizabeth made up of separate tools.[28] Many of the hatched tools are also found on the binding of *Annales et Croniques de France*, Paris, 1562,[29] where they occur in the company of Claude de Picques's well-known bat or butterfly tool.

Another German, Georg Emhard, had a 1568 Antwerp *Psalterium*[30] in five volumes bound for him by Claude de Picques in brown calf, tooled in gold with a cartouche, similar to but different from the hatched one used for Ludwig Zur Gilgen, Kilian Berchtold and others, containing on the upper cover: PARISI(IS) G.E. 1573 and on the lower cover: TV MEA XPE SALVS. This binding is decorated with the same large corner-pieces as were used on the presentation copy of S. Bouquet's *Recueil de l'Entrée de Charles IX*, Paris, 1572[31] for Catherine de Medici, for the binding of which Claude de Picques was paid in 1572.

1. L. Double, *Cabinet d'un curieux*, Paris, 1890, 57, supposes that 'Ludovicus a Liliis' stands for 'Louys de Lys', a descendant of a brother of Jeanne d'Arc, a suggestion that was repeated in Lardanchet, cat. 44 (1950), *100*. According to A. R. A. Hobson, *French and Italian Collectors*, Oxford, 1953, p. xvii, Tammaro De Marinis identified 'Ludovicus a Liliis' as a Swiss merchant from Zurich, called 'Ludwig Zugilden', J. H. Zedler, *Universal Lexicon*, x, Halle, 1735, refers under *Gilgen* to *Lilium* and registers *Gilgen, zur*, as a noble family from Lucerne. The *Dictionnaire Historique et Biographique de la Suisse*, Neuchatel, 1921–34, III, 414 gives *Zur Gilgen*, a patrician family from Lucerne, the name is a dialect form of Ilge = Lilie. See also H. J. Leu, *Allgemeines Helvetisches . . . Lexicon*, Zürich, 1747–65, tom. VIII. H. J. Holzhalb, *Supplement zu dem . . . Schweizerischen Lexicon*, Zürich, 1786–95.
2. 1521–48.
3. His name appears as 'Ludovicus a Lilijs Lucernensis' in the registers of the university of Freiburg on 23 June 1560; see H. Mayer, *Die Matrikel der Universität Freiburg i. Br. 1460–1656*, Freiburg im Breisgau, 1907–57.
4. This cartouche is similar to but not identical with those used on four bindings, all of which have the motto 'Patriae et Amicis', the date 1568, and identical hatched tools. They cover: Martialis, Antwerp, 1568 (Hotel Drouot, Paris, 15.XI.1971, *94*); Q. Horatius Flaccus, Antwerp, 1566, (John Rylands Library, R52174); Ovidius, Antwerp, 1566 (BL, C.47.a.7); Ovidius, Antwerp, 1567 (BL, C.47.a.8). The motto also occurs on Laertius Diogenes, Antwerp, 1566 (K. Westendorp, *Die Kunst der alten Buchbinder*, Halle, 1909, *37*) and on Livius, *Decades*, n.p. n.d. (K. Westendorp, *op. cit.*, *40*), combined with different tools.
5. From the collections of E. Waillet, Gemenitz, Yates Thompson and Miss Carol Graham.
6. Broxbourne Library, R.1395, from Double collection (*Cabinet d'un curieux*, *57*), Giraud Badin, cat. *Bibliothèque B* (1934), *49*, Lardanchet, cat. 44 (1950), *100*. See also H. M. Nixon, *Broxbourne Library. Styles and Designs of Bookbindings*, London, 1956, pp. 52–4. Since this article was published, a third binding has turned up with Ludovicus a Liliis' name on the upper cover and 'LVTETIAE II DECEMBRIS ANNO 1565' on the lower cover, but without the Zur Gilgen arms. It belonged to the librairie Paul Jammes in Paris.
7. E. Kyriss, 'Pariser Einbände der 2. Hälfte des 16. Jahrhunderts', *Börsenblatt für den Deutschen Buchhandel*, LI (June 1969), pp. 1515–28, Abb. 2, III, Abb. 3.
8. *Logica*, Cologne, 1565 [and] *Libri topicorum*, Cologne, 1561.
9. Or: S.GALLI, or: S.G. These are still in the St Gallen Abbey Library, MSS 1116–18.
10. In various forms: LVTET.PARIS.AN.DNI. 1566; LVTERIAE PARISIORV/ANNO DOMINI. 1566. See E. Kyriss, *op. cit.*
11. He owned a white vellum binding, tooled in gold with his name and this cartouche, covering M. A. Flaminius, *In librum psalmorum explanatio*,

Venice, 1564. See I. Schunke, 'Vademecum, um Einbände zu bestimmen', *Philobiblon*, x (1966), pp. 83–103, pl. 2 (quoted as '*Philobiblon*').

12. He must have been in Paris as early as 1542. See E. Ph. Goldschmidt. 'Die Einbände für Deutsche Studenten an Ausländischen Universitäten in 16. Jahrhundert', *Zeitschrift für Bücherfreunde*, N.F. xxi (1929), pp. 81–9.

13. Trinity College, Oxford, L.10.16. Another binding for him, decorated with this cartouche is described in Sotheby's catalogue, 11 May 1953, *35*.

14. F. Geldner, *Bucheinbände aus Elf Jahrhunderten*, Munich, 1958, pl. xlviii. Abb.62.

15. With the ex libris of Kevenhüller, see A. Nilsson, *Bokbandsdekorens stilutveckling*, Göteborg, 1922, pl. 34.

16. Paris, Hardouyn, illustrated by I. Schunke, *Philobiblon*, Abb. 4; Paris, S. Vostre, illustrated by J. Porcher, 'Documents sur la Reliure française au XVIᵉ siècle', *Humanisme et Renaissance*, i, Paris, 1934, pp. 165–6, fig. 11, and in *Catalogue de la Bibliothèque Henri Beraldi*, Paris, 1934, *15*.

17. J. Porcher, *op. cit.*, fig. 11.

18. J. Porcher, *op. cit.*, makes this identification on the grounds that another binding, illustrated by him on fig. 12, with the same cartouche, bears the name Marie Billart. However, the cartouche is not identical with the one on the binding illustrated in fig. 11. He also mentions a 1566 Basel Aristotle, bound for DOMINICVS MVRETANVS and decorated with 'the same placque', in a private collection in Paris.

19. Trinity College, Cambridge, II.6.36.

20. Trinity College, Cambridge, Y.17.18.

21. Broxbourne Library, R.1008.

22. H. Bouchot, *Les Reliures d'art à la Bibliothèque Nationale*, Paris, 1888, pl. XLI.

23. I. Schunke, *Die Einbände der Palatina*, Vatican City, 1962, pl. 138, Barb.K.XI.37.

24. Bibliothèque Nationale, Paris, Rés.A.5676.

25. Quaritch, catalogue, December 1921, pl. 38, *107*.

26. According to I. Schunke, *Philobiblon*, these corners also occur on a 1547 book from the library of Marcus Fugger, combined with a different cartouche and the name ANTOINE MARLANCHON.

27. 'Foreign Bookbindings IX; X', *The Book Collector*, xx (1971), p. 69, p. 227. See also article 57 below

28. BL, C.66.c.2.

29. L. Gruel, *Manuel de l'Amateur de Reliures*, II, Paris, 1905, opp. p. 107.

30. F. Geldner, *op. cit.*, pl. xlviii, Abb. 64. This book has a manuscript note reading: 'Sum Georgii Emhardi. Emptus Lutetiae Parisiorum'.

31. BL, C.33.m.1. Illustrated in 'Foreign Bookbindings X', *The Book Collector*, xx (1971), p. 227, and below on p. 338.

55 A Binding by the Du Saix Master for Jean Grolier, c. 1538

(1983)*

Among the bindings sold at Sotheby's on 27 May 1983 was, as lot 505, an unassuming-looking but extremely interesting binding for Jean Grolier. At first glance it looked similar to bindings that used to be attributed to Claude de Picques, and it was indeed described as such by Dr S. G. Lindberg when he first catalogued the Nordbäck collection.[1] A closer look at the tools shows them, though similar in design, to be different from those attributed to de Picques. Three more bindings for Grolier were made in this shop[2] which Dr Ilse Schunke christened the Du Saix master.[3] All four have Grolier's Portio mea device on the lower cover and his ownership inscription in the form of 'Grolierii et amicorum' at the foot of the upper cover. The Fleur-de-lis binder, who also possessed similar solid tools, used the same form of ownership inscription, but not the motto. Claude de Picques or, if we agree to Mr Hobson's suggested re-attribution, Jean Picard used the motto and the ownership inscription, often with the addition of 'Io'.

Of the lesser-known Paris shops that worked for Grolier before c. 1538, Dr Schunke distinguished as well as the Du Saix master, the Heustace master and the Bayeux master.[4] The latter two were further discussed by Jacques Guignard.[5] The Du Saix master, named after Antoine du Saix for whom he bound a translation of Plutarch,[6] has hardly received any further attention. According to Jacques Guignard, the practice of tooling the ownership inscription and the Portio mea device on the bindings started c. 1538-9,[7] though Howard Nixon suggested an earlier date for the Fleur-de-lis group.[8] It is likely that the Du Saix master was patronized, on a few occasions only, c. 1538.[9]

1. *Reliures royales et précieuses dans la collection du Dr Gunder Nordbäck*, Zurich, 1975, p. 24. For a recent re-attribution of bindings for Grolier, see A. R. A. Hobson, *Humanists and Bookbinders*, Cambridge, 1989, pp. 267-71.
2. G. Austin, *The Library of Jean Grolier*, New York, 1971, 96.1, 163, 213.1.
3. *Gutenberg-Jahrbuch*, (1953), p. 166.
4. *Gutenberg-Jahrbuch*, (1950), p. 382; (1963), pp. 290-91.

* English and Foreign Bookbindings 26, *The Book Collector*, XXXII, pp. 324-5

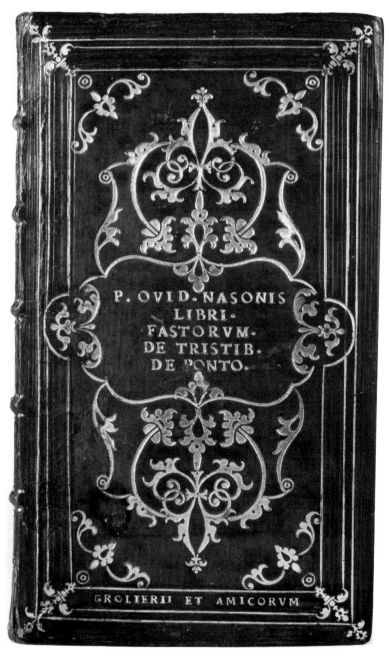

Fig. 55.1 Ovid, *Fastorum libri VI. De tristibus libri V. De Ponto libri IIII*, Venice (Aldus), 1502–3.
Brown calf tooled in gold. 174 × 103 × 28 mm.
British Library, C183.a.30.

5. *Mélanges oflerts à Julien Cain*, Paris, 1968, pp. 242–3 (Guignard identified a fourth, unnamed shop).
6. *Les Trésors des Bibliothèques de France*, IV (1933), pl. XIX.
7. *The Library*, 5th series, XXII (1967), p. 264 (the connection of the Du Saix master with Claude de Picques rests on misidentification of the fleur-de-lis tool).
8. *Bindings from the Library of Jean Grolier*, London, 1965, p. xiv.
9. Since this article was written, another binding by the Du Saix master for Grolier has emerged. It was sold in Paris (Hôtel Drouot, Ader Picard Tajan) on 19 May 1987, lot 73 and now belongs to a private collector.

56 A Binding by the King Edward and Queen Mary Binder, London, 1552

(1981)*

Alan Thomas's interest in bookbinding is apparent from his catalogues, most of which contain a section on bindings, and from chapter three of his *Great Books and Book Collectors* (London, 1975). The catalogues following the first Abbey sale of June 1965, where Alan Thomas bought lavishly, show a particularly fine display of collectors' pieces. The confrère, quoted in Catalogue 17, who remarked that Thomas's 'descriptions of bindings sounded like over-rich cake', meant no doubt that, as well as the best bookseller's butter, a basis of wholesome solid fact and a number of real plums made up the rich, appetizing and tempting whole.

The facts, the result of most meticulous and persevering investigation, speak for themselves and are clear to anyone who reads his catalogues. Of the plums I could mention several: the 1540 Basel Xenophon bound for Robert Dudley, Earl of Leicester, by the Dudley binder, now housed in the Broxbourne Library at the Bodleian;[1] a binding made by Marcantonio Guillery for Giovanni Battista Grimaldi, originally covering Bernardino Tomitano, *Ragionamenti della lingua Toscana* (Venice, 1545), now a remboîtage containing P. Giovio, *Gli Elogi. Vite . . . d'huomini illustri* (Venice, 1558) acquired by the University Library of Amsterdam;[2] a beautifully-tooled Claude de Picques binding on a Marlianus, *Urbis Romae Topographia* (Rome, 1544), from the Abbey collection;[3] and, from the same source, Plutarch's *Opera* (Frankfurt, 1599), in a pair of volumes bound by Williamson of Eton for Charles Somerset with his initials and the date 1604.[4] Similar bindings for him are now in the British Library (C. 128.k.3), the Bodleian Library, Broxbourne Collection,[5] and the Pierpont Morgan Library (PML 1113).

Another real plum, disguised as a rather tough and unassuming currant, found its way through Henry Davis to the British Library. Alan Thomas knew and liked Davis and described him as 'among the noble benefactors who have done so much for the great institution that we love'.[6] The book itself is imperfect and at first appeared somewhat puzzling. The text, a treatise on the Eucharist written in French, dedicated to Thomas Goodrich,

* C. de Hamel and R. A. Linenthal (eds.), *Fine Books and Book Collecting* [Festschrift for Alan G. Thomas], Leamington Spa, 1981, pp. 52–3.

Bishop of Ely, by François Philippe, and printed on vellum in the early 1550s, is bound in brown calf and tooled in gold to a design common in both France and England at that time. The binding provided the clue for the identification of the book. It was made by the King Edward and Queen Mary binder,[7] decorated with interlacing fillets painted black, fleurons, small flower tools, and a centre piece consisting of a monogram formed by the initials 'TGE' surrounded by the motto SI DEVS NOBISCVM QVIS CONTRA NOS. The initials 'AK' have been added later.

It was tempting to assume that 'TGE' stood for the dedicatee, Thomas Goodrich Eliensis, and F. B. Williams's *Index of Dedications and Commendatory Verses* (London, 1962) led to that work where most profound bibliographical secrets are already in print: the revised *STC*. No. 16430 is the translation into French by François Philippe of the new Prayer Book, at the revision of which Thomas Goodrich assisted, dedicated 'A tres reverend pere en Dieu Thomas Goodrik, Evesque d'Ely & Chancelier d'Angleterre'. A near miss, but *STC* 6003.5, a translation into French, also by François Philippe, of Thomas Cranmer's *Defence of the true and catholike doctrine of the sacrament of the body and bloud of . . . Christ*, sounded promising. The only known copy was described in great detail and illustrated in the Pforzheimer Catalogue (1, no. 237). This identified the Thomas-Davis book as *Defence de la vraye et catholique doctrine du sacrement du corps & sang de nostre sauveur Christ, . . . Translatée de la langue Angloyse en francoys, Par Francoys Philippe, serviteur de tres Révérend pére en Dieu, Thomas Evésque D'Ely, Chancellier d'Angletérre . . . Imprimeé a Londres par Pierre Angelin*, 1552. The Davis copy lacks the title-page, C3 and P6–8, and has, as well as the irregular pagination noted for the Pforzheimer copy, a pagination giving p. 62 instead of 64, 63 for 65, and so on. It consists, like the Pforzheimer copy, of 115 leaves—the faulty pagination accounts for that—but, unlike it, is printed on vellum.

W. Cole's *Extracts from the Registers of Ely*, IV (British Library, Add. MS 5827), has on fols 151[v] and 152[v] a drawing and description of Thomas Goodrich's arms with the initials 'TGE' and gives as his motto 'Si deus nobiscum quis contra nos'. It is more than probable that the Davis copy, printed on vellum and bound by a binder who worked for the Court, with the initials and motto of Thomas Goodrich tooled on the covers, is the dedication copy given to the Lord Chancellor by the translator who calls himself—not in the dedication but on the title-page—the bishop's 'serviteur'. According to Strype,[8] Goodrich 'procured a learned Frenchman, who was a doctor of divinity' to translate the new Prayer Book, and R. Masters'[9] calls Philippe 'a dependent' of Goodrich. The coincidence that on 10 March 1552 the Lord Chancellor, 'by virtue of the king's warrant. For nothing because all the fees are pardoned by the Lord

Fig. 56.1   T. Cranmer, *Defence de la vraye et catholique doctrine du sacrement du corps & sang de . . . Christ*, London, 1552. Gold-tooled brown calf. 145 × 90 × 30 mm. British Library, Henry Davis Gift. (Lower cover).

Chancellor's mandate', granted denization to 'Francis Phillipp',[10] opens the floodgates for further speculation.

1. A. G. Thomas, Cat. 1, 260; Cat. 3, 303; Cat. 5, 206; W. E. Moss, *Bindings from the Library of Robert Dudley, Earl of Leicester*, Manor House Press, 1934, no. 16; H. M. Nixon, 'Elizabethan Gold-tooled Bindings', *Essays in Honour of Victor Scholderer*, Mainz, 1970, p. 234, no. 3.
2. A. G. Thomas, Cat. 6, 283; Cat. 8, 226; Cat. 10, 208; Cat. 13, 225; A. R. A. Hobson, *Apollo and Pegasus*, Amsterdam, 1975, p. 182, no. 131.
3. A. G. Thomas, Cat. 17, 222.
4. A. G. Thomas, Cat. 19, 139; Cat. 21, 151.
5. H. M. Nixon, *Broxbourne Library*, London, 1956, no. 55.
6. A. G. Thomas, *Great Books and Book Collectors*, London, 1975, p. 82.
7. M. M. Foot, *The Henry Davis Gift*, London, 1978, vol. I, p. 25, no. 35.
8. J. Strype, *Memorials of ... Thomas Cranmer*, Oxford, 1812, I, p. 416; II, pp. 1035–6.
9. R. Masters, *The History of the College of Corpus Christi ... Cambridge*, Cambridge, 1753, p. 295.
10. Patent Rolls, 6 Edward VI, part IV [m.1]. His country of origin has been left blank.

57 A Binding for Jacques de Malenfant, c. 1560–66

(1971)*

Jacques de Malenfant was probably the son of Pierre de Malenfant, Sieur de Preyssac, later councillor of the *Parlement de Toulouse*, who married Cathérine de Minut on 12 September 1529.[1] Jacques was one of the almoners of Marguérite d'Angoulême, who sent him to Paris in November 1546 to continue his studies.[2] In 1565 his lament for Professor Adrien Turnèbe was published.[3] During the next year he acquired at least eleven books in which he wrote his name, place of origin and 'Paris 1566'. In 1570 he was back in Toulouse, living in his late father's house in the rue Fermat.[4] While in Paris he collected a number of books, 26 of which are known,[5] dated 1496–1566. He had probably all but one of them bound, usually in calf, adorned with open and hatched tools, hatched corner-pieces and a cartouche containing his name and arms (Fig. 57.1).

A very close copy of the cartouche used for Malenfant decorates a 1569 Paris Book of Hours (now British Library, Henry Davis Gift) with the name of Claude Berbis, as well as a 1562 Cologne Sacchi de Platina, which was bought in Paris by Mauritius Enck, a monk from St Gallen.[6] Although the cartouches are different, they were used in the same bindery, as the small open tools used on the binding for Claude Berbis occur on a number of bindings which in turn are decorated with tools that can also be found on the bindings for Malenfant.[7] Moreover, the pair of large corner-pieces that were used on the binding for Claude Berbis are identical with those on the white vellum presentation binding for Cathérine de Medici of the 1572 account of King Charles IX's entry into Paris (Fig. 57.2). It has the Queen's arms painted on both covers and a manuscript dedication 'A la Royne, Mere du Roy'. In the same year the royal binder, Claude de Picques, was paid 25 'livres tournois' for binding this copy and nineteen others in gold-tooled vellum.[8]

1. Fleury-Vindry, *Les Parlementaires français au XVIe siècle II, Parlement de Toulouse*, Paris, 1912, pp. 197–8.

---

* This article, Foreign Bookbindings IX, (*The Book Collector*, xx, p. 69) and Foreign Bookbindings X (Ibid, xx, p. 227) have been combined here and updated.

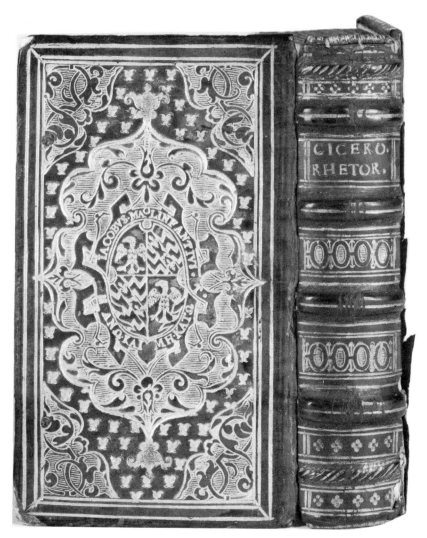

Fig. 57.1   M.T. Cicero, *Rhetorica*, Lyon, 1560.
           Gold-tooled brown calf, with the arms of Jacques de
           Malenfant. 126 × 72 × 31 mm.
           British Library, Henry Davis Gift. (Lower cover).

Fig. 57.2   S. Bouquet, *Bref et Sommaire Recueil de l'Entrée de Charles IX en sa bonne ville de Paris*, Paris, 1572.
White vellum, gold-tooled with the painted arms of Queen Cathérine de Medici. 273 × 195 × 23 mm.
British Library, C.33.m.1.

2. C. Artraud de la Ferrière-Percy, *Marguérite d'Angoulême, son livre de depenses*, Paris, 1862, p. 98.

3. In C. Roilet, *In tristissimum Adriani Turnebi morbum Academiae prosopopoeia*, Paris, 1565.

4. J. Chalande, 'Histoire des rues de Toulouse', *Mémoires de l'Académie des Sciences . . . de Toulouse*, 12, tom. IV, Toulouse, 1926, pp. 137–8.

5. Ten in A.R.A. Hobson, *French and Italian Collectors*, Oxford, 1953, p. 49 (n. 2 should be C.C. Rattey collection, Venice, 1528); a further thirteen were listed in M.M. Foot, *The Henry Davis Gift*, vol. I, London, 1978, p. 166, appendix II. Three more can be added: Bible [Hebrew], [Paris, *c.*1519–21]: Private collection; Valerius Maximus, Lyon, 1561: Private collection; Dionysius Halicarnassus, Lyon, 1561: Private collection. The last two have the 'Paris 1566' inscription.

6. E. Kyriss, 'Pariser Einbände,' *Börsenblatt für den deutschen Buchhandel*, LI (June, 1969).

7. M.M. Foot, *The Henry Davis Gift*, vol. I, London, 1978, pp. 157–8.

8. Ibid, p. 158.

58 Some Bindings for Charles I
(1984)*

The bindings from Charles I's library, now in the British Library, present a confused picture. Most, though, not all, came with the Old Royal Library in 1757 and can be identified by the presence of the Museum Britannicum stamps[1] and the successive press-marks showing their places in Montagu House and in the stacks of the British Museum Library before they were moved to the cases where they are kept today. Most can be traced in the Montagu House alphabetical author catalogue of the Old Royal Library[2] and a substantial number can be identified in the inventory of the Royal Library drawn up by Patrick Young in 1650 (C.120.h.6).[3] All have the royal arms stamped on both covers.[4]

Five different arms blocks and two different large blocks showing the Prince of Wales's feathers were used for Charles I when he was Prince of Wales, all of which had been in use previously for Prince Henry. A large number of arms blocks, varying both in size and shape, were used after Charles's accession. Several of these blocks had been employed on bindings for James I and a few were still in use after the restoration of King Charles II to the throne in 1660.

These arms blocks can be divided into five types: a large block without supporters but with decorative scroll work, frequently used for James I;[5] a large block with mask and claw handles of which at least sixteen variants are known, some also used for James I and Charles II; a large block with lion and unicorn supporters and garlanded with vine branches, used occasionally for James I and at least once for Charles II; and several kinds of round blocks without handles or supporters in roughly two sizes, the smaller of which is often found on small books in vellum bindings. The type with the mask and claw handles is the most common. In the British Library binding files it has been called the Stuart Royal Arms (SRA) and its sixteen variants have been numbered.

The first two variants, SRA I and II, were mainly used for James I. John Bill's binder used SRA I.[6] It is just possible that J. Norden's *England. An intended Guyde*, London, 1625 (C.77.d.16) was bound after James I's

* G. A. M. Janssens and F. G. A. M. Aarts (eds.), *Studies in Seventeenth-Century English Literature, History and Bibliography*, Amsterdam, 1984, pp. 95–106.

death but, though it has the SRA I arms block, it did not belong to the
Old Royal Library and may well have been made for a member of the
royal household. The one binding from Charles I's library decorated with
SRA II that I have found covers T. Harriot, *Artis analyticae praxis*,
London, 1631 (C.74.e.4).[7]

SRA III was used almost exclusively[8] for Charles I. It is found on
R. Crakanthorp, *Defensio Ecclesiae Anglicanae*, London, 1625 (C.82.d.3),
possibly bound before Charles's accession, as well as on L. Guicciardini,
Description de touts les Pays-Bas, Amsterdam, 1625,[9] H. Isaacson, *Saturni
Ephemerides*, London, 1633 (C.77.i.4),[10] and G. Sandys, *A Paraphrase
upon the Devine Poems*, London, 1638 (C.83.i.7).

Of SRA IV only one example is known, used for James I. SRA V (Fig.
58.1A) I have found on three bindings for Charles I. The *Speculum
Romanae magnificentiae*, [Rome, 1519–75] (C.77.i.11) tooled in gold with
this arms block and the initials CR may well have been the 'very great
book in fol. of prints being of several antiquities of Statutes and Roman
buildings . . . given to the King by the Earl of Exeter'.[11] The other two
bindings with this arms block cover Thomas Morton, *The Institution of
the Sacrament*, London, 1635 (C.47.k.4)[12] and J. Woodall, *The Surgeons
Mate; or, military and domestic surgery*, London, 1639 (C.77.h.18).

SRA VI is again known in only one example, on a binding probably
from James I's library.

SRA VII and VIII were used almost exclusively for Charles I. SRA VII
has been found on five or six bindings made during his reign, as well as
on a rather plain binding from the library of James I (C.83.k.1). Two
cover music books, the first of which, a 'Collection of English and Italian
Songs with Music' written in the eighteenth century in what was originally
a blank book ruled for music and bound in gold-tooled black goatskin
(Add. MS 27932), may have belonged to James I.[13] The second is the
'Music Book of William Lawes' written in the first half of the seventeenth
century and bound in gold-tooled brown calf (Add. MS 31432).[14] Four
bindings with the SRA VII block come from the Lord Herbert/Squirrel
bindery.[15] The presentation copy to Charles I of M. Raderus, *Bavaria Pia*,
Munich, 1628 (C.24.c.4), elaborately tooled with a border built up of
separate tools, large leafy corner blocks and the arms on a semis of
thistles and fleurs-de-lis, was illustrated by H. M. Nixon in *Royal English
Bookbindings in the British Museum*, London, 1957 (pl. 8). The other
three bindings cover copies of the same work: John Davies, *Antiquae
linguae Britannicae*, London, 1632. One copy (C.47.k.11) belongs to the
Old Royal Library and has the same leafy corner pieces that are found
on the Raderus. One was the author's presentation copy to the first Earl
of Bridgewater; it has an inscription dated 18 June 1632, is bound in olive-
brown goatskin decorated with the same corner pieces and is now in the

Fig. 58.1   Rubbings of Stuart Royal Arms blocks not illustrated
elsewhere: A. SRA V, B. SRA VIIID, C. SRA IX, D. SRA XII
(reduced).

H. E. Huntington Library in San Marino (60976). The third, in a light brown binding elaborately tooled with fleurons, the leafy corner blocks and a semis of thistles, is at Knole House.

SRA VIII occurs on two bindings, covering G. Williams, *The Right Way to the best Religion*, London, 1636 (C.21.e.14, Fig. 58.2), to which I will return later, and a *Book of Common Prayer*, (London, 1639 [and] *The Whole Booke of Psalmes*, London, 1640 (C.61.k.5).[16] Of the two examples of SRA VIIIA in the Old Royal Library, one occurs on a binding for James I (C.81.i.4), the other on one from Charles II's library (C.75.c.19). G. D. Hobson, in *English Bindings 1490–1940 in the Library of J. R. Abbey*, London, 1940 (pl. 19), illustrates a binding on G. Williams, *Seven Golden Candlestickes*, London, 1627, probably made for Charles I, which is decorated with this arms block.[17]

Of SRA VIIIB there is only one example in the Old Royal Library. This block was used by Daniel Boyse on the presentation copy for Charles I of Mercator's *Atlas*, Amsterdam, 1613 (C.18.e.15, now Maps C.3.d.8) bound in murray-coloured velvet and tooled in gold and silver.[18] The same block occurs on two elaborately gold-tooled copies of J. Selden, *Mare Clausum*, London, 1635, in black goatskin, one in the Henry Davis Gift to the British Library,[19] the other in an identical binding in the Sydney Jones Library in Liverpool (H.75.2). The book is dedicated to Charles I. Both copies look like presentation copies, but there is no evidence as to which was meant for the King. The copy of this book in the Old Royal Library (C.77.h.11) is also bound in black goatskin, but rather sparsely decorated with a narrow border and a different royal arms block.

This block, SRA VIIIC, was used during the reign of Charles I only and occurs on three more bindings, covering J. J. Boissard, *I-VI pars Romanae urbis topographiae et antiquitatum*, Frankfort, 1627, 28, 1597–1602 in six volumes (C.79.c.3), *Corpus Statutorum Universitatis Oxon*, Oxford, 1634 (C.24.d.6),[20] to which I will return later, and J. Puget de la Serre, *Histoire de l'Entree de la Reyne Mere . . . dans la Grande Bretaigne*, London, 1639 (C.37.l.9).[21]

Of SRA VIIID (Fig.58.1B) I have found only one example, on a binding covering the manuscript of T. Gardyner's 'Theological Tracts', 1627, dedicated to Charles I (Arundel MS.3).

SRA IX (Fig. 58.1C) was probably used for James I as well as during the reigns of both Kings Charles. The binding with Charles I's arms covers a *Book of Common Prayer*, London, 1629 together with the *Bible*, London, 1630 and *Psalmes in Meeter*, London, 1629 (C.47.f.13). It is made of brown calf tooled in gold with a semis of fleurons and large corner pieces.[22]

SRA X does not occur on any binding in the Old Royal Library in the British Library, but has been found on J. Smith, *The Generall Historie of*

Fig. 58.2   G. Williams, *The Right Way to the best Religion*, London,
1636: upper cover with SRA VIII.
British Library, C.21.e.14.

Virginia, London, 1624 in the Folger Shakespeare Library in Washington (22790).

Of SRA XI there is only one example in the British Library. It occurs on Vanderdoort's manuscript 'Catalogue of Pictures belonging to Charles I' (Add. MS 10112). It is bound in brown sprinkled calf and has the initials CR as well as the arms block and the date 1639. An identical binding on another copy of this manuscript is illustrated in R. R. Holmes, *Specimens of . . . Bookbinding, selected from . . . Windsor Castle*, London, 1893 (pl. 26).

The last variant, SRA XII (Fig 58.1D), has also only been found once. It decorates a 1636 London *Booke of Common Prayer* (C.36.l.1) in red goatskin, tooled in gold with a sun-roll border, fleurons and the initials CR. This book does not belong to the Old Royal Library; it reached the British Museum in 1857.

Frequently the same block was used by more than one binder and it is probable that the library bindings, as well as the bindings for the royal household, were ordered through the King's Printer or the King's Stationer who were issued with or had access to a variety of arms blocks owned by the Palace and who gave them with the books to be bound to the binder of their choice. In the Wardrobe accounts for the reign of Charles I there are several entries of payment to John Harrison, stationer, for binding books, mostly Bibles, Psalters and Service books, as well as for providing stationery.[23] The King's Printer is also paid on occasion for providing bound books, often unspecified, and again mainly Bibles and Service books.[24] Though John Bateman was still Royal Binder during Charles I's reign—he was last issued with a livery in 1639/40[25]—no bindings made by him for the King survive and only three bindings decorated with his tools carry the insignia of Charles as Prince of Wales. One of these is the presentation copy for Prince Charles of Sir Robert Dallington's *Aphorismes Civill and Militarie*, London, 1613 (C.46.i.11), bound in gold-tooled olive goatskin with Charles's arms and initials in the centre.[26] The other is a *Booke of Common Prayer* with *The Whole Booke of Psalmes*, London, 1615, recently acquired by the British Library (C.183.a.18), bound in gold-tooled brown calf, decorated with the Prince of Wales's feathers.[27] The third, now in a private collection, covers James I, *Workes*, London, 1616, and is bound in gold-tooled olive goatskin, also with the Prince of Wales's feathers. This feathers block was also used by Bateman on bindings for Prince Henry and it was still in use when the future King Charles II was Prince of Wales.[28] It occurs on one other binding for Charles I as Prince of Wales in combination with his initials, the date 1623, and a tiny rosette tool, covering Albrecht Dürer, *Hierinn sind begriffen vier Bücher von menschlicher Proportion durch Albrechten Dürer von Nürenberg erfunden und beschriben*, n.p. 1528 (C.82.g.9). This is almost certainly the book that was 'given to the King when he was prince by his Servant Vanderdort . . . a book in fol. of Wood Prince of Albardure [transcription error for "prints of Albrecht Durer"] being the inscription in high dutch of the proportions of men', mentioned in a list of books 'kept in his Maj:ᵗʸˢ Cabinet rome at Whitehall'.[29]

Very little is known of John Bateman's son Abraham, who shared the office of Royal Binder with his father. Except in the original grant of the office of Bookbinder to the King of 1604, Abraham is not separately mentioned. He presumably worked with his father, but only the elder Bateman appears to have been issued with a yearly livery and to have been paid regularly for binding or providing books.[30] Abraham was apprenticed to his father and freed by patrimony on 13 April 1607. He took his first apprentice on 27 June 1608 and two more apprentices have been recorded.[31] He may have been the 'Master Bateman' who went to the Lord Mayor's dinner on 29 October 1610 and who was mentioned as Renter Warden on 6 May 1618.[32] The last of his apprentices was freed in 1624, but by Thomas Johnson. It is useless to speculate whether Abraham died early or moved away, or whether he used a completely different set of tools so that his work cannot be connected with that of John. The last 'Bateman' binding covers a book printed in 1635[33] and the name Bateman is not found in the records after 1640.

The binder who worked for John Bill, the King's Printer, and who bound at least fifteen books for James I[34] made two bindings for Charles. One, on A. Gil's *Logonomia Anglica*, London, 1619 (C.21.b.8),[35] was made for Charles as Prince of Wales. The arms block that decorates this binding was previously used for Prince Henry and occurs on four more bindings for Charles.[36] The other binding covers William Lithgow's *Totall Discourse*, London, 1632.[37]

Two London shops seem to have been responsible for a fair number of presentation bindings for Charles I, both using a number of different blocks for the royal arms.

The smaller group comprises six bindings, mostly elaborately tooled with curls, fleurons, pointillé tools and four different arms blocks. Three of these are variants of the Stuart Royal Arms type: SRA VIII, SRA VIIIB and SRA VIIIC.

G. Williams, *The Right Way to the best Religion*, London, 1636, dedicated to Charles I, bound in brown goatskin elaborately tooled in gold to a panel design with tall fleurons in the outer border, small fleurons, curls of various kinds and flower vases, has the SRA VIII block in the centre (C.21.e.14). *A Book of Common Prayer*, London, 1639 [and] *The Whole Booke of Psalmes*, London, 1640, also with SRA VIII in the centre, has large leafy corner pieces of the type used by the Lord Herbert/Squirrel bindery and one fleuron tool found on other bindings of this group

(C.61.k.5).[38] The two lavishly tooled copies of Selden's *Mare Clausum*, London, 1635, with the arms block SRA VIIIB which I have mentioned already come from this same bindery, and so does the presentation copy of *Corpus Statutorum Universitatis Oxon.*, Oxford, 1634, printed on vellum with a manuscript dedication to Charles I from the Chancellor, Masters and Scholars of Oxford University (C.24.d.6). It is bound in black goatskin and tooled in gold to a panel design with various curls, tall fleurons and smaller fleurons around the arms block SRA VIIIC. The other binding from this group came to the British Library with the Henry Davis Gift. It covers *The Book of Common Prayer*, London, 1639 [and] *The Holy Bible*, London, 1639 [and] J. Downame, *A briefe Concordance*, London, n.d. [? 1633] [and] *The Way to true Happinesse leading to the Gate of Knowledge*, London, n.d. [? 1640] [and] *The Whole Book of Psalmes*, London, 1639, all bound together in gold-tooled brown goatskin decorated with curls and fleurons surrounding a round arms block.[39]

This same block was used by a shop responsible for nine or possibly ten bindings with Charles I's arms, the Lord Herbert/Squirrel bindery. It occurs on two bindings, both probably presentation copies to the King, one on A. Freitag, *L'Architecture militaire*, Leiden, 1635, in brown goatskin tooled in gold to a panel design with large corner and centre pieces built up of curls and fleurons,[40] the other on Charles Lodowick, Count Palatine's *Manifest . . . concerning the Right of his Succession*, London, 1637 (C.81.b.18) in dark olive goatskin, tooled in gold to a panel design with small rolls and fleurons at the corners. A different round arms block was used on a similar binding of brown goatskin also decorated with small rolls and a fleuron, covering W. Parks, *The Rose and Lily*, London, 1639, 38 (C.82.a.17).[41]

An entirely different arms block with large lion and unicorn supporters, frequently used by John Bateman on bindings for James I,[42] occurs on a semis of thistles and fleurs-de-lis and in combination with the triangle tools and the large leafy corner pieces that belong to the Lord Herbert/Squirrel bindery on a 1630 London *Book of Common Prayer* in brown goatskin in the H. E. Huntington Library (#45911).

Another arms block this bindery used has also got lion and unicorn supporters and is garlanded with vine branches. It decorates an elaborately gold-tooled brown goatskin binding on Julius Schillerus, *Coelum Stellatum Christianum*, Augsburg, 1627, at St John's College, Oxford (b.2.6).[43] The arms block which was on occasion used for James I and for Charles II occurs on two or possibly four more bindings for Charles I in the British Library.[44] A roll depicting curving vine branches which decorates the binding of the Schillerus at St John's is also used on a binding with the arms block SRA V covering T. Morton's *Institution of the Sacrament*,

London, 1635 (C.47.k.4). However, the other tools on this binding do not seem to have belonged to the Lord Herbert/Squirrel bindery.

Variant VII of the Stuart Royal Arms block was used by this shop and occurs on the presentation copy of Raderus, *Bavaria Pia*, Munich, 1628 (C.24.c.4), and on the three copies of Davies, *Antiquae linguae Britannicae*, London, 1632, all discussed above.

This leaves us with several bindings for Charles I unaccounted for. They are mostly presentation copies and four bindings, though not attributable to any specific bindery, are worth a brief description. Three were made for Charles as Prince of Wales and belong to the Old Royal Library. A 1622 London *New Testament* in Greek, dedicated to James I, is bound in brown goatskin and has the arms of Charles, Prince of Wales—on a block also used for Prince Henry—tooled in gold on a semis of small flowers (C.27.e.11). Aelfric, Abbot of Eynsham, *A Saxon Treatise concerning the Old and New Testament*, London, 1623, dedicated to Prince Charles, is bound in red velvet and tooled in blind with curved tools in the border, fleurs-de-lis in the corners and the Prince of Wales's feathers with the initials CP in the centre (C.65.l.1). A very splendid red silk binding embroidered with spangles, pearls, and gold and silver threads showing floral motives in the border, a large flower in each corner and the Prince of Wales's feathers within a wreath in the centre covers 'Cinquante emblemes chrestiens premierement inventez par la noble damoiselle Georgette de Montenay', the drawings and verses copied by Esther Inglis in Edinburgh, 1624, with a dedication 'To the thrice illustrious and most excellent Prince Charles' (Royal MS 17 D.XVI).[45]

The last binding was a New Year's gift to Charles I from Francis Stewart, Earl Bothwell, with a long presentation inscription dated 1 January 1636 (Eg. MS 1140). It covers a collection of treatises by Sir Nicholas Halse collected by Stewart under the title 'Great Britains Treasure', and bound in black goatskin, tooled in gold with several borders built up of small tools, the King's arms and initials on a semis of quaterfoils and the inscription 'TIBI SOLIO REX CHARISSIME', a suitable sentiment for a presentation and one that with a single alteration could well serve to grace this birthday gift.

1. S. Jayne and F. R. Johnson, *The Lumley Library*, London, 1956, p. 25, note 1.
2. Ibid., p. 23, p. 295, note 6.
3. Ibid., pp. 20–21. See also J. Kemke, *Patricius Junius*, K. Dziatzko (ed.), *Sammlung Bibliothekswissenschaftlicher Arbeiten* XII, Leipzig, 1898, pp. xxv–xxvi. The combinations of letters and figures quoted in brackets throughout this article are the current British Library press marks of the books discussed.

4. Royal arms do not necessarily denote royal ownership. However, most of the bindings discussed here are either elaborately decorated presentation copies or belong to the Old Royal Library, or both.

5. Used during Charles I's reign in two variants on: *The Book of Common Prayer* [and] *Psalmes*, London, 1630 (not from the Old Royal Library, possibly made for a member of the royal household; C.82.b.9) and on J. de Bie, *La France metallique*, Paris, 1634 (dedicated to Charles I, from the Old Royal Library; 603.k.3).

6. H. M. Nixon, *Five Centuries of English Bookbinding*, London, 1978, no. 28.

7. An example of this block used on a binding for James I is illustrated in H. B. Wheatly, *Remarkable Bindings in the British Museum*, London, 1889, pl. XLVIII.

8. A binding with this block, probably made for James I, covers a very elaborately tooled *Book of Common Prayer* [and] *Holy Bible*, London, 1616, at the John Rylands University Library, Manchester. The binding was made by the same shop that bound A. Thevet, *Pourtraits et vies des Hommes illustres*, Paris, 1584, for James I (C.22.f.4, illustrated in W. Y. Fletcher, *English Bookbindings in the British Museum*, London, 1895, pl. XXXIV).

9. B. Quaritch, Catalogue, 1921, *35*, pl. X. There is no copy of this book in the Old Royal Library.

10. The large corner pieces found on this binding are closely similar to but not identical with those used by the Lord Herbert/Squirrel bindery. Identical corner pieces occur on a *Book of Common Prayer*, London, 1639 [and] *The Whole Booke of Psalmes*, London, 1640 with SRA VIII (C.61.k.5).

11. Mentioned in a list of books 'kept in his Maj:^tys Cabinet rome at Whitehall' in Lansdowne MS. 1050, fol. 23^v. This MS is one of several copies of a 'Catalogue of Pictures, Books . . . belonging to King Charles I . . . drawn up by Vander Doort'.

12. This binding has a vine roll also used by the Lord Herbert/Squirrel bindery (see below).

13. This manuscript came to the British Museum with the Slade Bequest. Illustrated in H. B. Wheatley, *op. cit.*, pl. XXII. The corners that decorate this binding also occur on R. Brooke and A. Vincent, *A Discoverie of Errours*, London, 1622, with the arms of Charles, Prince of Wales (Maggs, Catalogue 665, *4*); H. Briggs, *Arithmetica Logarithmica*, London, 1624, for Charles, Prince of Wales (C.82.f.8); and Matthew Locke, 'Compositions for Consorts', autograph manuscript presented by Locke to Charles II in 1672 (Add. MS 17801). The sun tool also occurs on G. Coperario, 'Instrumental Fantasias', an early seventeenth-century manuscript with the same royal arms as occur on Locke's 'Compositions' (R.M. 24.k.3).

14. See J. P. Cutts, 'British Museum Additional MS 31432', *The Library*, 5th series, VII (1952), pp. 225–34.

15. M. M. Foot, *The Henry Davis Gift*, vol. I, London, 1978, section 4.

16. See note 10. This binding also shows a fleuron which links it with the group of bindings discussed below. The book belonged to Isaak Walton (see J. Bevan, 'Some Books from Isaak Walton's library', *The Library*, 6th series, II (1980), p. 260) and only reached the British Museum in 1897.

17. There is no copy of this edition in the Old Royal Library.

18. Illustrated in H. M. Nixon, *op. cit.*, n. 29.

19. M. M. Foot, *op. cit.*, vol. II, London, 1983, no. 86; illustrated in B. Quaritch, Catalogue, 1921, *36*, pl. XI.

20. Illustrated in W. Y. Fletcher, *op. cit.*, pl. XLVII.
21. This book came to the Old Royal Library with the library of John Morris and was probably issued in this binding. See T. A. Birrell, *The Library of John Morris*, London, 1976, no. 1277.
22. A third variant of the leafy corner pieces used by the Lord Herbert/Squirrel bindery; see also note 10. This book does not come from the Old Royal Library and may well have been bound for a member of the royal household.
23. PRO, LC 5/38, pp. 57, 106, 124, 157; see also pp. 65, 67, 116; LC 9/102, fols 13, 22ᵛ; LC 9/103, fols. 5, 17ᵛ, 20.
24. See Add. MS 5756, fols. 141 and 144. One more easily identifiable work, Foxe's *Book of Martyrs* 'in three Volumes bound in redd Leather & filletted', 'Received from the King's Printer this 24th of December 1641' (fol. 144) is not the copy in the Old Royal Library (C.78.i.3) which is bound in dark brown goatskin.
25. PRO, LC 9/103, fols. 41–41ᵛ; see also M. M. Foot, *op. cit.*, vol. I, pp. 40–43.
26. Illustrated in W. Y. Fletcher, *op. cit.*, pl. XXXVII. The same arms were also used by Bateman on bindings for Henry, Prince of Wales (see M. M. Foot, *op. cit.*, vol. I, p. 46, no. 18, p. 48, no. 42).
27. Illustrated in E. P. Goldschmidt, Catalogue 163, *211*.
28. R. R. Holmes, *Specimens of Royal Fine and Historical Bookbinding, selected from the Royal Library, Windsor Castle*, London, 1893, pl. 32.
29. Lansdowne, MS 1050, fols. 22ᵛ–24ʳ; for this entry see fol. 23ᵛ.
30. See M. M. Foot, *op. cit.*, vol. I, pp. 40–43.
31. D. F. McKenzie, *Stationers' Company Apprentices 1605–1640*, Charlottesville, 1961, pt. II (Bateman).
32. E. Arber, *A Transcript of the Registers of the Company of Stationers of London 1554–1640*, London/Birmingham, 1875–94, III, 692, 695.
33. M. M. Foot, *op. cit.*, vol. I, p. 49, no. 66.
34. H. M. Nixon, *op. cit.*, no. 28; also M. M. Foot, *op. cit.*, vol. I, p. 54 (the binding referred to in note 44 was made for Charles, not for Henry, Prince of Wales).
35. Illustrated in W. Y. Fletcher, *op. cit.*, pl. XL.
36. G. Primerose, 'Panegyrique a tres-grand et tres-puissant Prince Charles Prince de Galles', seventeenth-century manuscript in gold-tooled white vellum (Add. MS 27936). It has the same corner blocks, as well as the same arms blocks, as England [Laws and Statutes], *Anno regni Jacobi, Regis ... 21° ... At the Parliament begun ... the 19. day of February* (a fragment containing two acts), London, 1624, in gold-tooled vellum (C.77.h.17). M. Du Val, *Rosa Hispani-Anglica seu Malum punicum Angl'Hispanicum* [Paris, 1622?] in gold-tooled olive goatskin (C.46.f.1). Also probably on E. Grimstone, *The Imperiall Historie*, London, 1623, in gold-tooled olive goatskin (Quaritch Catalogue, 1921, *34*, pl. IX: the plate is not sufficiently clear to identify the arms block with certainty. The Old Royal Library copy of this book, 591.h.8, has been rebound).
37. Maggs, Catalogue 665, *5*. Neither of the two British Library copies of this edition belong to the Old Royal Library.
38. See notes 10 and 16.
39. M. M. Foot, *op. cit.*, vol. II, no. 93. There is no evidence that this book was bound for Charles I and it could have been bound for a member of his household. Other non-royal bindings from this shop are: *The Book of Common Prayer*, London, 1633/4 (C.130.i.2) and [Bible—Job], *Catena Grae-*

corum Patrum in Beatum Iob, London, 1637 (St John's College, Oxford, D.2.22).

40. M. M. Foot, *op. cit.*, vol. I, pp. 50 and 53 (illus.); vol. II, no. 71.

41. This book does not belong to the Old Royal Library. The same arms block that was used on Parks is found on P. Heylyn, *Ecclesia Vindicata*, London, 1657. According to a manuscript note, this is the author's presentation copy to Charles II (C.73.b.10).

42. M. M. Foot, *op. cit.*, vol. I, section 3, appendix.

43. Ibid., p. 58, no. 16.

44. G. Coperario, 'Instrumental Fantasias', early seventeenth-century manuscript in gold-tooled dark brown goatskin (R.M. 24.k.3, see also note 13) and F. Mason, *Vindiciae Ecclesiae Anglicanae*, London, 1625, in gold-tooled brown goatskin (C.18.b.15) could both have been bound for James I. The other two examples are: H. Hugo, *De Militia equestri antiqua et nova libri*, Antwerp, 1630, in gold-tooled brown calf (C.46.k.2) and J. Stow, *Annales*, London, 1631, 32° in gold-tooled brown calf (C.21.e.11) decorated with the same corners as are found on a *Bible* (1609) [and] *Prayer Book* (1636) illustrated by G. D. Hobson, *English Bindings 1490–1940 in the Library of J. R. Abbey*, London, 1940, no. 23. The binding for Charles II covers 'Compositions for Consorts . . . made by Matthew Locke', a seventeenth-century manuscript presented to Charles II in 1672 (Add. MS 17801).

45. Illustrated in W. Y. Fletcher, *op. cit.*, pl. XLVI. Could this be the 'Booke in french verse on sevrl Noble Ptr [Portraits] fol' mentioned in a list of manuscripts and English printed books at Whitehall, *c.* 1641 (Bodley, MS Smith 34, p. 107)?

59 A Binding for Caroline of Ansbach, 1722

(1988)*

Jean-Pierre de Crousaz, professor of philosophy and mathematics at Lausanne, dedicated his *Traité de l'education des enfans* to her Royal Highness, the Princess of Wales. This was Caroline of Ansbach, wife of the future George II. She herself had received part of her education from her guardian's wife, the Electress Sophia Charlotte. Liebniz was a frequent visitor during her youth and Caroline remained in contact with him after she followed her husband to England towards the end of 1714. Her own spelling left much to be desired and she never spoke English correctly. She was well-read in French history and conversed with her family in French. This French educational treatise was no doubt useful as Caroline had eight children.

The decorative curls and fleurons that cluster round the Prince of Wales's feathers in the centre of the binding of the presentation copy are also found on eight other bindings, five of which have metallic varnish paper end-leaves, not very common in England. They cover six books printed between 1582 and 1651, one (now empty) album and a manuscript that has been dated to the last quarter of the eighteenth century.[1] It seems that the bindery that produced them was active from before 1722 to c. 1780. The *Traité* came to the British Museum with the library of George III. It is probable that, when George II gave the Old Royal Library to the nation in 1757, he kept back some of his wife's personal books.

1. M. M. Foot, *The Henry Davis Gift*, vol. II, London, 1983, nos. 180, 181. In addition to the books mentioned there are the empty album (BM Prints & Drawings, 198*.b.2) and G. Lodi, *Amore prigioniero in Delo*, Bologna [1628?] (Marlborough Rare Books). The tools link with two more bindings: M. Maittaire, *Annales Typographici*, The Hague, Amsterdam, London, 1719–41, vols iv–v (B. Breslauer) and J. Bale, *Scriptorium illustrium maioris Brytanniae . . . Catalogus*, Basel, 1557 (BL, C.28.m.6).

---

* English and Foreign Bookbindings 45, *The Book Collector*, xxxvii pp. 240–41.

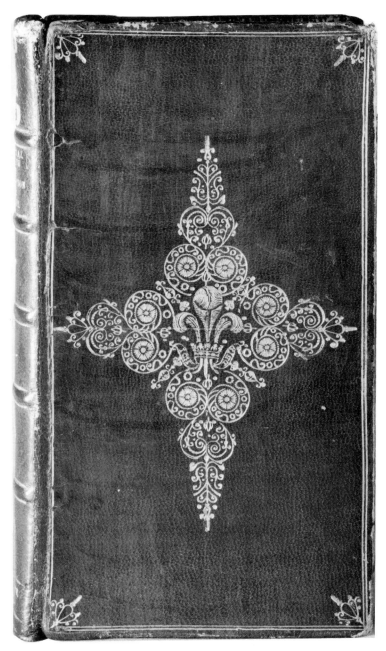

Fig. 59.1   J.P. de Crousaz, *Traité de l'education des enfans*, The Hague,
1722, 2 vols.
Red goatskin, tooled in gold. 174 × 100 × 30 mm.
British Library, 231.d.8,9.

60 The Henry Davis Collection: The British Museum Gift (1969)*

This article first appeared in the series 'Contemporary Collectors' (XLIV) in *The Book Collector* for 1969. At that time, Henry Davis, who had recently retired as managing director of a cable-making firm with factories in London and Belfast, was still adding to his outstanding collection of bookbindings.

He began collecting shortly before the Second World War and acquired early printed books, manuscripts and in particular decorated bookbindings which he presented to the British Museum Library in 1968. In the same year he gave his collection of rare and early printed books to the New University of Ulster at Coleraine, while the manuscripts were presented to the Fitzwilliam Museum in Cambridge in 1975. He was awarded a CBE in 1973. He died on 10 January 1977 in his eightieth year.

Henry Davis was a thoroughly knowledgeable collector who was prepared to back his own judgement. Yet he was always ready to take advice from experts both in the booktrade and in libraries. He was an extremely modest, kind and generous man who did a great deal of charitable work in an unobtrusive way, and who was much loved.

To make his bindings available to a wider public, he gave the British Library a showcase, in which a selection from his Gift is always on display. It is remarkable how his bindings filled many gaps in the British Library's collections, while duplicating very little. On looking at the bindings, one feature is immediately apparent: almost all the bindings are in a very good condition. There is no particular emphasis on any country or any period, though it is difficult to find many better and larger private collections of French eighteenth-century mosaic bindings. There are examples by Monnier—including a lovely white one *c.* 1750, with coloured floral onlays, signed *Monnier fecit* on both covers[1]—and from the workshops of the Padeloup and the Derome families (Fig. 60.1). Some are beautiful in design with large stylized flowers in different coloured leather; some very elaborate with shiny paper inlays and paintings, such as the one for the Comte de Langle of *c.* 1752 in dark blue goatskin with

---

* Contemporary Collectors XLIV, *The Book Collector*, XVIII, pp. 23–44.

a   b   c

Fig. 60.1   (from left to right). *L'Office de la Nuit*, Paris, 1745, 12mo.
Paris mosiac binding in red morocco with onlays of yellow,
bronze and white. Attributed to Derome. *c.* 1745. (Lower
cover).

L. Senault, *Heures Nouvelles*, Paris, 1680, 8vo.
Mosaic binding in brown morocco with yellow and red onlays
and pointillé tooling in the border. *c.* 1730.

Heures Nouvelles à l'usage de Rome, Paris 1749, 12mo.
Paris mosaic binding in white calf with multicoloured onlays
and gold tooling. *c.* 1750.
British Library, Henry Davis Gift.

elaborately tooled onlays of brown and red and his arms painted under
mica.[2] A 'rare bird' is one of the three copies of the *Office de la Semaine
Sainte*, Paris (N. Pepie), 1716, which has been attributed to Padeloup's
son-in-law Augustin Duseuil and was bound for the d'Orleans family[3] in
olive goatskin with red and orange onlays and tooled in gold. It has the
arms of Louise Adelaide, Mlle d'Orleans, in the centre of both covers.[4] In
addition to these there are some dentelle bindings of the eighteenth
century. The French seventeenth century is represented by finely tooled
pointillé bindings; an embroidered purple velvet binding for Marie de
Medici, the second wife of Henri IV of France (see Fig. 60.2a);[5] a most
unusual binding of black goatskin delicately tooled in gold to a design of
nine circular fans and four garlands, probably made for a collector named
le Riche (see Fig. 60.2b),[6] and a late fanfare binding with pointillé tools
and the arms of King James II and his second wife Mary of Modena,
bound for him after his abdication.[7] The collection contains fanfare and
imitation fanfare bindings of different kinds. A rather early and very

a   b

Fig. 60.2a   J. de Loyac, *L'Eupheme des François*, Bordeaux, 1615, 4ᵗᵒ.
Embroidered purple velvet binding for Marie de Medici.
c. 1615. (Lower cover).

Fig. 60.2b   C. Guichard, *Funerailles*, Lyons, 1581, 4ᵗᵒ.
Black morocco fan binding, probably made for le Riche.
c. 1600.
British Library, Henry Davis Gift.

beautiful example in golden brown goatskin, decorated with typical interlacing ribbons and hatched tools, is a two-volume Cicero (Paris, 1566).[8]
The highlights of France's greatest period of bookbinding, the sixteenth
century, are those bindings made in Paris on commission by the great
collectors of the time. Not only did French collectors patronize the best
artists and craftsmen available, but men like the Venetian Ambassador
Pietro Duodo, Thomas Wotton, the son of the treasurer of Calais, and
Marc Lauweryn, a widely travelled nobleman from Bruges, came to Paris
and had their books specially bound for them. Duodo had his books
decorated in a style particular to him, with an all-over pattern of small
ovals, formed by leafy sprays, with a small flower in each.[9] Among the
bindings for Wotton is an Aristotle[10] in brown calf with a black painted
interlacing ribbon and hatched and open tools. The most beautiful of these
bindings are the ones attributed to Claude de Picques, sometimes bound
in the so-called Greek style with raised headcaps and boards with grooved
edges, such as a dark brown goatskin example, gold-tooled with an interlacing ribbon and hatched tools, bound for the Augsburg banker Marx
Fugger, *c.* 1550 (see Fig. 60.3a).[11] Another binding in this style, on a non-

a   b

Fig. 60.3a   *Epistolae Graecae*, Venice, 1499, 4ᵗᵒ.
Claude de Picques binding in gold-tooled dark brown goatskin, bound for Marx Fugger. *c.* 1550

Fig. 60.3b   Ch. de Bouvelles, *Livre singulier et utile . . . de Geometrie* [and] D. de Sangredo, *Raison d'Architecture antique*, Paris, 1542, 4ᵗᵒ.
Binding for François I, in dark olive goatskin, tooled in gold with his arms and salamander. *c.* 1542.
British Library, Henry Davis Gift.

Greek book,[12] is a lovely small reddish-brown morocco one, inlaid in black in an arabesque design. Apart from a dark brown morocco binding for Grolier with an interlacing ribbon painted black and with solid tools,[13] and one for Lauweryn in brown calf with a painted interlacing ribbon and hatched tools,[14] there is a large Claude de Picques in crimson goatskin, onlaid in olive with a gold blocked cartouche, curving lines and hatched tools, decorated with black and silver paint.[15] Jean Grolier, the French patron of scholarship and book-collector, who was from 1532 treasurer of France, patronized other binders as well. There is one of the earliest bindings to bear his ownership inscription[16] on the cover, in brown goatskin, decorated in gold with arabesques and solid tools, of *c.* 1538.[17] Another Paris collector, the Secretary of Queen Cathérine de Medici, who mostly patronized the same binders, was Thomas Mahieu. A large Pausanias[18] was bound for him in *c.* 1560 in reddish-brown goatskin decorated entirely with gouges (small curves and straight lines) to a design which shows an early stage in the development of the fanfare style (see Fig. 60.4). Another Paris binding of a decade earlier is the one bound for François de Lorraine, Duc de Guise, in brown calf, gold-tooled, with an interlacing ribbon and open tools embellished with black, green and silver

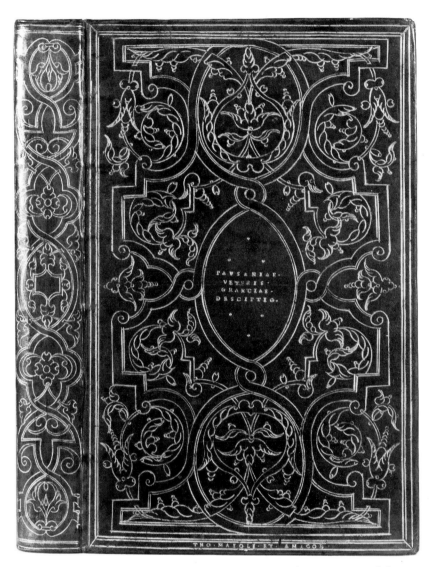

Fig. 60.4 Pausanias, *Veteris Graeciae descriptio*, Florence, 1551, fol.
Binding for Thomas Mahieu, in reddish-brown goatskin,
decorated in gold with gouges. *c.* 1560.
British Library, Henry Davis Gift.

paint, which has his painted arms in the centre.[19] Of roughly the same period is a fine brown goatskin binding, with a central oval onlay of dark brown, and compartments onlaid in black; its interlacing ribbon and the fleurons, tooled in gold, are decorated with black paint (see Fig. 60.5).[20]

Apart from bindings for these collectors, there are the ones made for Royal owners, French and foreign. There is a brown calf binding for Elizabeth I, Queen of England, tooled in gold with an interlacing ribbon and gouges on a dotted background with some black paint and the Queen's arms surrounded by small open tools in a centre oval.[21] For the French Royal Family there are books for Henry II and Diane de Poitiers; and for François I, one of c. 1542 in dark olive goatskin, tooled in gold with his arms and salamander (see Fig. 60.3b),[22] and one of c. 1531 with the same arms and badge in gold in the central rectangle of a brown calf binding.[23] Going back to the second decade of the sixteenth century, there is a binding from the first French bindery to use gold tooling, the *Atelier Louis XII*, in brown calf with gold and blind tooling in vertical strips.[24] The oldest French example is a Parisian Romanesque binding of c. 1200 in brown calf, decorated in blind with large stamps including a kneeling elder, a mounted knight and various monsters (see Fig. 60.6: lower cover).[25]

As the modern bindings form a group as such, the French twentieth-century examples will be left till later. Among the nineteenth-century examples, there are a few coloured paper bindings, stamped in gold with garlands and flowers, and a binding by Simier in blue straight-grain morocco with elaborate gold and jewelled mounts.[26]

The Swiss bindings are closely linked with the French ones, so closely sometimes that attribution can be difficult. This is the case with a group of bindings mostly in brown calf, tooled in gold with complicated interwoven ribbons and gouges, some with open or hatched tools, parts often closely covered with golden dots and, as their most distinctive feature, two masks of half-monster, half-human faces. These are to be found most frequently on sixteenth-century books, usually printed either in Geneva or in Paris. Two examples of this type in the Davis Collection have additional traces of black and silver paint, gilt and gauffered edges, and have a Geneva imprint.[27] The Diodorus Siculus (1559) was bound by the Geneva King's Binder, as was a sunk panel binding of c. 1565 in brown goatskin with an interlacing ribbon painted black and with lions' masks in sunk medallions in the corners. The central sunk panel is of gold-tooled white calf and shows traces of paint.[28] There is also a binding of 1563, probably of Genevan origin, in brown goatskin, tooled in gold with the arms of Frederic III, Elector Palatine (to whom the book is dedicated) in the centre of the upper cover and his motto on the lower cover.[29]

The English bindings form another comparatively large group. The oldest one is a twelfth-century Romanesque binding of undecorated white

Fig. 60.5   Herodianus, *Historiae de Imperio post Marium*, Venice, 1498,
fol.
Paris binding in gold-tooled brown goatskin with
compartments onlaid in dark brown and black. *c.* 1550
British Library, Henry Davis Gift.

Fig. 60.6 Gospels of St Matthew and St Mark. MS on vellum. [Paris, *c.*
1200], fol.
Paris romanesque binding in brown calf, decorated in blind. *c.*
1200. (Lower cover).
British Library, Henry Davis Gift.

leather over wooden boards with semi-circular flaps projecting from the head and the tail of the spine, and with its original brass clasp on a long leather thong, reaching from the centre of the outer edge of the upper cover almost to the middle of the lower cover.[30] The oldest decorated binding, which comes from a workshop which was one of the first to produce tooled bindings after the thirteenth century in England, is a Canterbury binding of *c*. 1470 of brown calf, blind-tooled to a different design on each cover with characteristic small squares and triangles and a number of different stamps, such as a row of trotting stags (see Fig. 60.7: lower cover).[31] A pattern of small squares again decorates a late fifteenth-century London binding by the 'Scales binder'.[32] Each cover is decorated in a different way with small blind stamps such as a four-leaf flower and a pelican in her piety. In the central rectangle of the lower cover the initials *RS*[33] are incised.[34] There are a few more late fifteenth-century blind-stamped bindings such as a Cambridge one signed *WG*,[35] and a number of blind-tooled bindings from London, Oxford and Cambridge, decorated with rolls and panels, signed and unsigned, dating from the sixteenth century.

An early sixteenth-century example comes from the Caxton Bindery.[36] Unfortunately only the lower cover has been preserved, decorated in blind with a border composed of separate stamps (two intertwining half crescents), enclosing a central panel divided by diagonal lines into compartments, within each of which there is either a small square stamp with a stylized flower and four fleurs-de-lis or a large square griffin stamp.[37] Other sixteenth-century bindings include a London binding for King Edward VI *c*. 1550 in brown calf with his arms made up of small tools in the centre, bound by the 'Medallion binder';[38] one bound for Queen Mary, *c*. 1554 in brown calf, tooled in gold with an interlacing ribbon, the Queen's arms and initials and the title of the book, by the binder who bound for her and for King Edward;[39] a brown calf binding by Jean de Planche on a Royal Charter of *c*. 1575,[40] gold-tooled with corner and centre blocks and hatched and solid tools with, in a centre cartouche, a profile portrait of Queen Elizabeth on the upper cover and her arms on the lower cover; and bindings for Elizabeth's favourite, Robert Dudley, Earl of Leicester, among which is a gold-blocked binding with L-shaped corner pieces, signed *E.D*, a sunk panel of punched velvet and a brown calf centre-piece with a sunk medallion with Dudley's badge.[41] This unusual combination of leather and velvet also occurs on a London *dos-à-dos* binding of *c*. 1567, containing two books,[42] bound back to back in gold-tooled and painted brown calf with a sunk panel of blue velvet (see Fig. 60.8). It comes from the same workshop as the 'Macdurnan Gospels'[43] at Lambeth Palace. There is another binding from this shop in brown calf, gold-tooled and decorated with white, red and black paint, with a border

Fig. 60.7 'Biblia Sacra'. MS on vellum [13th century], 4to.
Canturbury binding in brown calf, decorated in blind in a
different design on each cover. *c.* 1470. (Lower cover).
British Library, Henry Davis Gift.

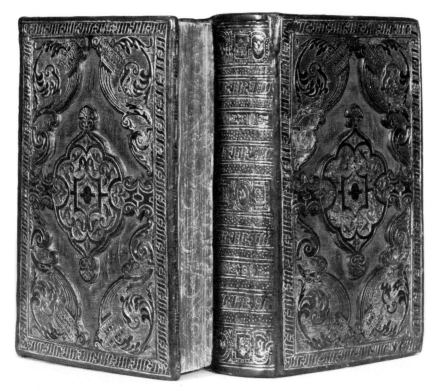

Fig. 60.8   *Le Nouveau Testament*, Lyons, 1564 [and] *Les Psaumes mis*
en rime, Geneva, 1565, 8ᵛᵒ.
London *dos-à-dos* binding in gold-tooled and painted brown
calf with a sunk panel of blue velvet. *c.* 1570.
British Library, Henry Davis Gift.

with knotwork tools and centre and corner blocks, a type of decoration
often found in this period.[44]

An embroidered binding for Queen Elizabeth, in red velvet worked
with silver thread in a floral pattern with her initials in the centre of both
covers, dates from the beginning of the seventeenth century.[45] Bindings
from the reign of James I include one for Henry, Prince of Wales, in
brown calf with his arms in the centre and a large fleur-de-lis in each
corner,[46] and a canvas binding embroidered with gold and silver thread
and coloured silks with the arms of James Montague, Bishop of Bath and
Wells, in the centre of each cover.[47] There is another embroidered binding
somewhat later of *c.* 1630, possibly made for John Davenant, Bishop of
Salisbury, in purple satin, embroidered with silver thread and coloured
silks in a floral design.[48] A couple of Cambridge bindings date from a few

years earlier. One is in greenish-blue velvet tooled in gold in a style practised by at least two Cambridge binders of the period,[49] and one in brown goatskin with red painted onlays and tooled in gold and silver in this same style; both are by Daniel Boyse (see Fig. 60.9).[50] A copy of Selden's *Mare Clausum*[51] of 1635, dedicated to Charles I, is bound in dark goatskin, elaborately tooled in gold with the King's arms in the centre. Another binding for Charles I comes from the workshop which bound for Lord Herbert of Cherbury and is in olive goatskin, tooled to a centre and corner design with small tools.[52] A Cambridge binding of *c.* 1660 is in black goatskin with red onlays and gold tooling.[53]

From the Restoration period date two bindings by the bearer of the best-known name in the history of English bookbinding: Samuel Mearne. Both are folios, one a Prayer Book of 1662[54] in black goatskin with traces of silver paint, tooled in blind and gold to a panel design with the crowned cypher of Charles II in the corners and the centre of both covers; and one a Cambridge Bible[55] in dark olive goatskin, onlaid to a cottage roof design and elaborately tooled in gold, also with Charles II's cypher. This Bible and its companion Prayer Book, now in the Broxbourne Library,[56] were possibly supplied for use in the Chapel Royal in 1666. Slightly later in date is a binding in black goatskin decorated with curls, fleurons and floral tools in gold, which has a fore-edge, painted underneath the gold, signed and dated: *Owen fecit, 1672.*[57] Another fore-edge painting, with the motto *Search the Scriptures*, is dated 1675 and comes on a book bound by the 'Naval binder'[58]—a man also employed by Samuel Pepys[59]—in brown goatskin, onlaid in red and citron and elaborately tooled in gold with large sprays of flowers and a mass of floral curls.[60] Less gay is a so-called sombre binding in black goatskin, decorated in blind with a number of distinctive tools, such as heads in profile, hands and moths,[61] and with *MM 1673* in the centre of both covers.[62] A third binding with the fore-edge painted underneath the gold comes from Oxford, from the workshop of Roger Bartlett, who settled there after the Great Fire of London. It is a typical cottage roof style binding of *c.* 1679 in orange-red goatskin with gold tooling and some black paint.[63] Two bindings of the last part of the century are a London needlework binding of 1688, with the date on the painted fore-edge, in white satin embroidered with silver thread and coloured silks, depicting on the upper cover Jacob wrestling with the angel and on the lower cover Jacob's dream;[64] and a signed binding by Alexander Cleeve[65] of *c.* 1690 in black goatskin, gold-tooled in a style reminiscent of the fanfare bindings.[66] Another late development of the fanfare style in gold-tooled red goatskin is the work of the 'Geometrical Compartment binder'[67] of *c.* 1700.[68] An imitation of this same style resulted in a mosaic binding of *c.* 1701 in red goatskin, with black and citron onlays and elaborate gold tooling.[69] The cottage roof style lives on into the eighteenth

Fig. 60.9   Edmund Spenser, *The Faerie Queene* [and other works],
London, 1609–11–12, fol.
Cambridge binding by Daniel Boyse in brown goatskin with
red painted onlays and tooled in gold and silver. *c.* 1630.
(Lower cover).
British Library, Henry Davis Gift.

century. There is an example of 1705, dated on the painted fore-edge, in black goatskin with brown, yellow and red onlays, traces of silver paint and much flowery tooling in gold.[70] From the beginning of the same century dates a copy of *Eusebia Triumphans* by the City Poet, Elkanah Settle,[71] dedicated to 'the Lords and Commons of England' in a typical Settle binding of black goatskin, decorated with rather coarse tooling in gold and the arms of Duncombe,[72] the recipient of this copy, in the centre of both covers.

The habit of painting the edges underneath the gold was carried on by (among others) the well-known family of binders from Halifax by the name of Edwards, who often decorated their fore-edges with landscapes in colour. They developed a process of making vellum transparent and adorned the covers of their bindings with paintings underneath the vellum, such as the monochrome Resurrection scene on the upper cover and the Crucifixion on the lower cover of a Baskerville Common Prayer and Psalter[73] of 1762, bound in the early 1780s. A large green goatskin folio bound after 1799, with a blue onlaid centre panel and onlaid borders in yellow and red, tooled in gold, comes from the workshop of Staggemeier and Welcher.[74] Another of the numerous German immigrant binders, H. Walther, made a mosaic binding *c.* 1791, of citron goatskin with blue and red onlays and gold tooling in a design copied from French work of the early part of the century.[75] There are also some books bound by Roger Payne, one of which, in gold-tooled brown Russia, still has the original bill that Payne presented to Dr Moseley on 19 August 1795, in which he describes at length the care he took to clean the pages and to bind the book 'in the very best Manner', for the sum of £0.17.6,'as per Agreement'.[76]

The English nineteenth century is widely represented. Among the bindings of the beginning of this period is one signed by T. Gosden in dark blue calf with a gold-tooled border and portraits of Izaak Walton and Charles Cotton, blocked in blind in the centre panels.[77] Throughout the century we find signed and unsigned bindings, mostly in leather, by binders such as Hering, Hayday, Bedford, Rivière, Zaehnsdorf, Sir Edward Sullivan and others.

The best examples from Ireland and Scotland are those from the eighteenth century. There was a complete series of Irish Statutes[78] in gold-tooled red goatskin, part of the Ulster Gift, and a number of odd volumes of the same work, one of which[79] is in a Dublin binding of *c.* 1782 of red goatskin with a central onlay of white paper, decorated with black paint and elaborately tooled in gold. Other Irish eighteenth-century bindings include a 1745 Virgil,[80] bound by the 'Parliamentary Binder A'[81] in red goatskin, tooled in gold with a roll with birds and a centre lozenge filled with small tools, such as flowers, feathers and more birds, and a concave lozenge onlaid in white in the centre; Charles Smith's *History of Cork*[82] in contemporary gold-tooled red goatskin; and a binding of crimson goat-skin with a central oval onlaid in green and decorated with tools from the workshop associated with the name of Abraham Bradley King.[83] There are a couple of nineteenth-century Dublin examples, bound by George Mullen with his ticket, in straight-grain morocco tooled in gold and blind and with a blind centre block.[84]

From Scotland come bindings with the familiar wheel and herringbone patterns, such as an Edinburgh binding of *c.* 1715 in dark goatskin, gold-tooled with a large central fan or wheel, with fish-scale decorations above and beneath it and large leafy sprays in the corners.[85] Also from Edinburgh comes a black goatskin binding of *c.* 1730, tooled in gold with leaf sprays in the corners, a central panel with outward-curving sides and a vertical middle line which has on both sides floral tools, parrots' heads and typical turnip-shaped tools,[86] a variant of which also occurs on a rather coarsely tooled Edinburgh binding of *c.* 1734, in red goatskin, tooled to a panel design with leaf sprays and fish-scale decorations in the wide outer border, and floral tools and leafy sprays emanating from a central spine.[87] Another red goatskin Edinburgh binding with a less distinctive herringbone pattern dates from *c.* 1760 and has tulips on both sides of a vertical row of circles, surrounded by characteristic large onion- or pear-shaped tools, and more floral decorations in the corners.[88] A late example of a special binding on a presentation copy of a thesis of 1792 is in red goatskin, tooled in gold with birds among branches, floral tools, a musical instruments tool, and typical rococo-style ornaments.[89]

Before embarking on a much smaller but no less interesting group formed by the German and Dutch bindings, an eighteenth-century Vien-nese binding of brown sheep, tooled in silver and gold, should be men-tioned. On the upper cover four border rolls surround a gold-tooled landscape with houses, trees, hunters and animals, above which in the centre is the coat of arms of Amandus Schickmayer, Abbot of Lambach,[90] with rococo-style floral decorations, and above that three chinoiserie fig-ures; the lower cover shows four frames, each with a landscape with animals in silver, and a fifth with the Abbot's arms in the centre of a landscape with houses.[91] The German bindings included a late fifteenth-century brown leather binding decorated on the upper cover with a broad frame filled with large rectangular tools depicting naked wild men and women hunting through branches of foliage, and a central panel, finely engraved with a Tree of Jesse, most probably designed by the illustrator of Schedel's Chronicle. The lower cover has a typical Nuremberg design.[92] This is now part of the Ulster Gift. Apart from a number of sixteenth-century blind-tooled bindings decorated with rolls and panels, among which is a binding from the Carthusian monastery of Duelmen (West-phalia) signed *HG*,[93] there is a very elaborately decorated binding of *c.*

1592 in brown calf, richly tooled in gold and painted with a portrait of the Emperor Charles V, bound by Lucas Weischner who, like the author of the book,[94] lived in Jena. From the first part of the seventeenth century dates a binding, decorated in a fashion which later seems to have become popular both in Germany and Holland and in Eastern Europe, of gold-tooled white vellum, pierced to show silks in different colours underneath. This example shows the gilt, gauffered and colour-painted edges, characteristic for both seventeenth-century Germany and Holland, depicting either a wealth of birds and flowers or, as here, different scenes or figures from the Old Testament.[95] From the first decade of the eighteenth century are two brown calf bindings, both tooled in gold with long sprays and rather large flowers, one from the monastery of Ettal with the coat of arms of the monastery on the upper cover and that of Abbot Placidus Seitz on the lower cover and with circular fans in the corners,[96] and one tooled with an interlacing ribbon decorated with black paint.[97] Later in the eighteenth century we get the so-called Peasant bindings, usually found on books printed in Germany, Holland, Switzerland, and Eastern Europe, of which a gay example is a binding in white vellum, of either German or Swiss origin, tooled in gold with a brown-painted ribbon dividing the covers into compartments, painted green and pink and decorated in gold, and a white centre compartment with a gold-tooled vase with large, richly coloured flowers.[98]

There is a slightly less gaudy Dutch specimen in white vellum with pink and mauve painted compartments, outlined by an interlacing ribbon and tooled in gold with floral curls, large flowers and drawer-handles of different sizes, with traces of silver paint.[99] Among the other Dutch eighteenth-century books is a Middelburg MS, written between 1729 and 1735[100] and bound in three volumes in red goatskin with black and citron onlays and tooled in gold, mostly with floral tools (see Fig. 60.10a), and a work by Ludolph Smids[101] in a so-called 'backless' binding[102] of red goatskin, gold-tooled and embellished with black paint, with four heart-shaped onlays of greenish-blue silk and a centre inlay of painted and tooled vellum, in its original case of gold-tooled sprinkled calf. The pride of the Dutch section of the collection is a large two-volume Elzevier Bible of 1669,[103] bound by Albertus Magnus in red goatskin, beautifully tooled in gold. A number of the tools are to be found on the Bible Magnus gave to his wife on the occasion of their marriage.[104] The sixteenth century in the Netherlands is represented by a number of blind-stamped bindings, such as an early one by Victor van Crombrugghe of Ghent;[105] examples of another Ghent binder Jan Ryckaert, who worked from 1511–46;[106] and a well-known *Spes*-panel from Louvain, signed *IB*, of about 1550.[107]

From Spain there is a late fifteenth-century Mudéjar binding in brown goatskin, decorated in gilt and blind to a different design on each cover[108]

a   b

Fig. 60.10a   A. C. Mattheeus, 'Verzameling van Inleidingen'. MS on
paper. [Middelburg] 1729–35, 4ᵗᵒ.
Dutch binding in gold-tooled red goatskin with black and
citron onlays. c. 1735.

Fig. 60.10b   Breviary for the use of Toledo. MS on vellum. [Toledo, late
fifteenth century], 4ᵗᵒ.
Mudéjar binding in gold-painted and blind-tooled brown
goatskin, late fifteenth century.
British Library, Henry Davis Gift.

(see Fig. 60.10b); a sixteenth-century binding with distinctive animal tools
in gold—a monkey playing bagpipes, a roaring lion, a duck, a stag and
a unicorn—placed between blind rolls;[109] and some seventeenth-century
manuscripts in contemporary bindings, elaborately decorated with rather
coarse tools, such as a brown calf binding of c. 1600, tooled in gold with
the Sacred Monogram and with rolls engraved with heads in medallions.[110]
A small mosaic binding of the eighteenth century is signed on the upper
cover: SANCHA F.[111] It is in gold-tooled white calf, onlaid in red and black
goatskin, with inlays of shiny paper in the corners and a chubby cherub
painted under mica in the centre.[112]
   There are a few Eastern European examples, such as a Polish binding
of c. 1527, bound for John Laski[113] in white leather, decorated in gold on
the upper cover, with the title of the book,[114] a border composed of
separate stamps showing two interlacing circles, corner fleurons and
Laski's badge in the centre. The lower cover has his badge in black.
Another Polish binding, of the first half of the eighteenth century, is
in brown goatskin, elaborately tooled with feathers and flowers, small
Crucifixion stamps and stamps of the Virgin with her Child, stamps

depicting the four Evangelists with their symbols, one in each corner, and in the centre an oval stamp with the Crucifixion on the upper cover, and King David praying on the lower.[115] From Russia comes a binding of c. 1800 in red goatskin with coloured onlays. The border is tooled in the neoclassical style fashionable all over Europe at this period.[116]

From farther East originate a number of Oriental bindings, the oldest of which is a very fine late fourteenth-century Egyptian one in brown goatskin, tooled in gold and blind to a centre and corner design (Fig. 60.11).[117] This is an early example of gold tooling which can be dated before AD 1400, since the Amir Aytmish al-Bajasi, for whom the book was written and bound, was executed in that year. Other Oriental bindings include a fifteenth-century Persian leather binding with a large central panel and a border, blocked in gold in a regular floral pattern, and doublures of red goatskin, with cut-out compartments, over gold-decorated coloured paper;[118] a number of seventeenth-century Persian bindings in blind- or gold-tooled leather or in lacquer, painted with flowers and nightingales among roses; and some Persian nineteenth-century lacquered bindings, such as a pair of empty covers, painted with a floral border and houses among trees round a central oval with nightingales and roses, and red doublures, elaborately decorated with birds in vine branches and, in a central oval, a hand holding a branch of flowers and bearing the inscription: 'The humble Lotfali of Shiraz in the year 1278' (AD 1861).[119]

The earlier Oriental designs were of considerable influence on the Italian binders of the fifteenth and sixteenth centuries, with bindings decorated with gold-blocked sunk compartments in the Oriental style persisting throughout the sixteenth century. They are to be found on a 1552 Petrarch[120] in brown goatskin with sunk panels, blocked with a floral pattern in dark red and gold, and finely decorated doublures, one of which has cut-out compartments with gold decorations over blue paper; and on a couple of Ducali: one of 1563 in red goatskin with a border and a centre panel, containing a number of sunk compartments, all finely blocked in gold, leaving a raised pattern of small flowers, painted brown;[121] and one of c. 1590, also in red goatskin and decorated in the same way, with the floral pattern painted in red and white, additional gold painted flowers on the leather, and the centre compartments decorated with the lion of St Mark on the upper cover and the arms of Benetto Amoro on the lower cover.[122] The collection also contains much earlier Italian bindings, the oldest of which is a Neapolitan binding of c. 1480 in reddish-brown goatskin with knotwork tooling in gold, bound for presentation to Cardinal Oliverius Carafa (see Fig. 60.12a).[123] A cuir ciselé binding of c. 1482 is probably of North Italian origin; it is in brown goatskin, both tooled in blind with small knotwork in the corners and worked by hand to fill the centre octagon with an interlaced and floriated ornament on a dotted

Fig. 60.11   Koran (pt 25). Arabic MS on paper in Naskh script. [Egypt,
late fourteenth century], fol.
Egyptian binding in gold- and blind-tooled brown goatskin.
Late fourteenth century.
British Library, Henry Davis Gift.

a   b

Fig. 60.12a   P. Balbi, The dedication of the *Epistola ad Theodosium* to the Cardinal of Naples. MS on vellum. [Italy, before Sept. 1479], 8[vo].
Neapolitan binding for Cardinal Oliverius Carafa in gold-tooled, reddish-brown goatskin. *c.* 1480.

Fig. 60.12b   M. Sabellicus, *Exemplorum libri decem*, Venice, 1507, 4[to].
N. Italian binding in gold- and blind-tooled brown goatskin. *c.* 1510. (Lower cover).
British Library, Henry Davis Gift.

background.[124] This binding, which resembles the Hispano-Mauresque bindings produced in Spain in this period, may be the work of a Jewish craftsman.[125] From the end of the century comes a binding of gold-tooled red goatskin with a cameo portrait of Alexander the Great, possibly made from an antique intaglio, in the centre.[126] A later cameo stamp depicting the head of Julius Caesar is to be found in the centre of a Philostratus[127] in brown goatskin, tooled in blind.

Before the French collector Jean Grolier started to employ his Parisian binders, he acquired, when treasurer of the French army in Italy, a number of books in Italian bindings, such as a Milanese plaquette binding of *c.* 1510, tooled in gold with a knotwork frame and small solid tools round a circular plaquette in blind in the centre of each cover, depicting on the upper cover the Judgement of Paris[128] and on the lower cover Orpheus playing to the animals.[129] Another one from Milan from the same period is in brown goatskin, tooled in gold to a panel design with a frame of linked circles and with solid tools on the corners of the frame, in the outer border and in the centre. On the first page of the text (A ii recto) are painted two circular medallions, one with a hand drawing a nail from the top of a hill with the motto *Aeque difficulter* and the other with Grolier's arms.[130] A North Italian binding in brown goatskin, tooled in gold and blind with three central ornaments, made up of floral and leaf tools round knotwork (see Fig. 60.12b) also dates from *c.* 1510.[131] A rare example, the design of which shows some Oriental influence, is probably a Venetian painted vellum binding,[132] very attractively decorated with arabesques, flowers and leaf shapes, outlined in black and painted in blue, red, green, yellow and gold, round a centre piece with the Sacred Monogram, surrounded by flowers on a deep blue-green background.[133].

The 1540s include a few Roman bindings: one of *c.* 1542 for Apollonio Filareto, chaplain to Pier Luigi Farnese, in olive-brown goatskin, gold-tooled with his device of an eagle soaring over a rocky coast in the centre;[134] one of *c.* 1545 by Niccolò Franzese, in red goatskin, tooled in gold with an interlacing ribbon painted black and with solid gold tools;[135] and another one of *c.* 1548 by Maestro Luigi, a binder who worked for Giovanni Battista Grimaldi to whom the ownership of these bindings has been attributed, in brown goatskin with a sunk medallion, depicting Apollo driving his chariot towards Mount Helicon, on which stands Pegasus.[136] A few come from Bologna, such as two volumes of a set of Cicero, one bound for Damianus Pflug and one for Nicolaus von Ebeleben, two German students in Italy at the time.[127] The one for Pflug is in reddish-brown goatskin, gold tooled with an interlacing ribbon, small tools, his name and the title of the book on the upper cover. It is dated on the lower cover, Bologna, 20 February 1543;[138] the one for von Ebeleben is in dark brown goatskin, similarly decorated and dated, Bologna, 20 July 1543.[139] From the same workshop comes a binding in olive goatskin, decorated in gold with the same tools and dated on the lower cover, Bologna, 27 June 1544.[140]

Less glamorous, but certainly not less interesting, is a Bojardo[141] in grey-brown paper over pasteboard covers, the upper cover decorated with a large woodcut of two angels holding a vase of lilies and a sheet. Few bindings of this very fragile type have survived. From the last quarter of the sixteenth century date a brown goatskin binding of *c.* 1572, tooled in gold, with a border with palm leaves and a circular centre, in a manner similar to bindings found on a number of other manuscripts connected with the Ferrero family of Sicily,[142] and an elaborately decorated red goatskin binding, tooled in gold with curved lines and solid and hatched tools, with floral decorations painted in silver in the border and the silver seal of Ludovicus Manin, Doge of Venice, attached to it by a red and silver plaited cord.[143] Throughout the sixteenth and seventeenth centuries we find bindings decorated with the tooled or painted arms of successive popes and cardinals. There is also a large embroidered example, worked with coloured silks and silver thread with the arms of Pope Benedict XIII in the centre.[144] Fan-pattern designs were common at this time all over Europe. An attractive, possibly Milanese, brown goatskin binding is tooled in gold with quarter fans in the corners and a large circular fan in the centre with semi-circular fans above and beneath it.[145]

The modern bindings form a category apart. In France, after a long period of imitations, the Marius-Michels, father and son, introduced new styles of decoration into bookbinding. An example is a signed binding by Marius Michel, of c. 1885, in black morocco with a bold inlaid floral design in light brown.[146] From twentieth-century France comes an onlaid binding by Mercier c. 1905 in citron morocco with blue and red onlays and pointillé tooling, in appearance strongly reminiscent of the earlier mosaic bindings. It has the monogram of Henry Walters of Baltimore in the centre.[147] A binding of c. 1950, signed *J. Antoine Legrain*, in black morocco with a small green onlaid circle and the title tooled in blind, gold and pink,[148] has a more contemporary look. So have two large bindings of the early 1960s, a Virgil,[149] beautifully bound in brown box calf with the Latin and English titles intertwined and onlaid in cream and fawn, signed and dated *P. L. Martin, 1961*, and a startling signed and dated Paul Bonet of 1962, in dark-green morocco, gold-tooled to a sun-burst design with coloured onlays.[150]

T. J. Cobden-Sanderson inaugurated a new style of bookbinding in England. There is a binding, signed by him and dated 1890, in maroon morocco, tooled in gold with a pattern of stylized roses.[151] He also designed a white pigskin binding, with a rose border round a panel with a gold-tooled inscription, executed in 1899 at the Doves Bindery which he established.[152] Also from the Doves Bindery comes a binding dated 1901, in red morocco, tooled in gold to a panel design with a wide border filled with leafy branches. The title of the book[153] surrounds a panel with three roses. A gay, onlaid binding of 1902, designed and finished by P. A. Savoldelli, comes from the Hampstead bindery. It is in brown morocco with coloured onlays and tooled with stylized oak leaves, grouped in a pattern of four circles round a central lozenge.[154] From the end of the nineteenth century is a binding by Charles Ricketts in red morocco, gold-tooled to a panel design with vertical lines, small crowns, feathers, round tools and small *Rs*.[155] His style influenced the earlier work of Miss Sybil Pye. Later she developed a distinctive style of her own based on coloured inlays, an example of which is a green morocco binding, inlaid in white vellum and tooled in gold to a cubist design, dated 1916.[156] Another binding of the beginning of the century is by Katharine Adams, in white vellum, gold tooled and painted with roses. On the spine is the inscription:

A. T. from K. A. It is a gift to Ann Thompson, a neighbour of the binder at Broadway, Worcestershire.[157] Miss Adams's tools are now in the possession of the British Library. The collection of modern English bindings is brought up-to-date with work by Elizabeth Greenhill, Edgar Mansfield, C. Philip Smith, Trevor Jones, Bernard Middleton and other living bookbinders.

References in Notes

BFAC: Burlington Fine Arts Club, *Exhibition of Bookbindings*, London, 1891.

GOLDSCHMIDT: Goldschmidt, E. Ph., *Gothic and Renaissance Bookbindings*, London, 1928, 2 vols.

HOBSON: *English*: Hobson, G. D., *English Bindings 1490–1940 in the Library of J. R. Abbey*, London, 1940.

HOBSON, *Thirty*: Hobson, G.D., *Thirty Bindings*, London, 1926.

NIXON, *Grolier*: [Nixon, H. M.], *Bookbindings from the Library of Jean Grolier*, London, 1965.

NIXON, *Twelve*: Nixon, H. M., *Twelve Books in Fine Bindings from the Library of J. W. Hely-Hutchinson*, Oxford, 1953.

S. cat.: Sotheby's catalogue. (Reference to item or lot is by italic numeral.)

1. On: M.T. Cicero, *De Amicitia Dialogus*, Paris, 1749.
2. On: *L'Office de la Semaine Sainte*, Paris, 1752.
3. A. Duseuil may have bound two more copies of the same book, one for Philippe II, Duc d'Orleans, and one for his wife, Françoise Marie.
4. L. M. Michon, *Les Reliures Mosaïquées du XVIIIᵉ Siècle*, Paris, 1956, p. 71, 149. *Ill.*: *Catalogue Bibliothèque R. Descamps-Scrive* (1925) I, *198*.
5. On: J. de Loyac, *L'Eupheme des François*, Bordeaux, 1615. Another copy of the same book was similarly bound for her son Louis XIII.
6. On: C. Guichard, *Funerailles*, Lyons, 1581. Le Riche's signature is on one of the fly-leaves. His signature occurs also in Platine, *Les Généalogies... des SS. Pères*, Paris, [1519], which has a very similar binding; *ill.*: Giraud-Badin, *Catalogue of the Gougy Sale I* (1934), *213*, pl. XVIII.
7. On: *Office de la Semaine Sainte*, Paris, 1691. *Ill.*: Fairfax Murray, *Catalogue of Early French Books*, London, 1910, *400*.
8. M. T. Cicero, *Opera Omnia*, Paris, 1566, 2 vols. This book, once in the collection of C. M. Cracherode, will after a separation of almost two centuries rejoin its fellows in Cracherode's library, bequeathed to the British Museum in 1799. *Ill.*: BFAC, pl. LVIII.
9. In red goatskin on: St Ambrosius, *Officiorum libri*, Paris, 1583 [and other works].
10. Aristoteles [and others], *Politicorum libri octi*, Paris, 1543; [and] I. le Fevre, *In Politica Aristotelis introductio*, Paris, 1535.
11. On: *Epistolae Graecae*, Venice, 1499.

12. On: St Augustin, *Las Confessiones*, Antwerp, 1555. *Ill.*: S. cat., 21 June 1965, *104*.
13. On: Z. Ferreri, *Hymni novi ecclesiastici*, Rome, 1525. *Ill.*: NIXON, *Grolier*, *35*.
14. On: M. T. Cicero, *Orationes*, Paris, 1543. *Ill.*: GOLDSCHMIDT, *206*, pl. LXXIX.
15. On: *Breviarum Romanum*, Lyons, 1556.
16. *Grolierii et Amicorum*.
17. On: I. Pontanus, *Opera*, Venice, 1513. *Ill.*: NIXON, *Grolier*, *17*.
18. Pausanias, *Veteris Graeciae descriptio*, Florence, 1551.
19. On: Appian, *Des guerres des Rommains*, Lyons, 1544. *Ill.*: Wilmerding sale cat. (Parke-Bernet), 5 Mar. 1951, *40*.
20. On: Herodianus, *Historiae de Imperio post Marium*, Venice, 1498.
21. On: N.Gilles, *Annales et Croniques de France*, Paris, 1562. *Ill.*: GOLDSCHMIDT, *231*, pl. XCI.
22. On: Ch. de Bouvelles, *Livre singulier et utile . . . de Geometrie;* [and] D. de Sangredo, *Raison d'architecture antique*, Paris, 1542.
23. On: A. Pio, *Opera*, Paris, 1531. *Ill.*: E. Ader, *Bibliothèque d'un Humaniste* (Dec, 1966), *83*, pl. V.
24. On: J. de Pins, *Divae Catherinae Senensis . . . et . . . Philippi Beroaldi . . . vita*, Bologna, 1505. *Ill.*: S. cat., 23 June 1965, *549*.
25. On: Gospels of St Matthew and St Mark. MS on vellum (MS Lat.), [Paris, *c.* 1200].
26. On: *Office de la Quinzaine de Pâques*, Paris, 1825. *Ill.*: Catalogue Bibliothèque R. Descamps-Scrive, (1925) II, *292*.
27. I. Sleidan, *Histoire de l'Estat de la Religion* [Geneva], 1557. *Ill.*: A. M. Boinet, *Bibliothèque de Madame Whitney-Hoff*, Paris, 1933, *666*, pl. CXXIX. Diodorus Siculus, *Bibliothecae historicae libri* [Geneva], 1559. *Ill.*: C. Sonntag, Jr., *Kostbare Bucheinbände*, Leipzig, Boerner I, [1930?] *38*, pl. XVII.
28. On: *Novum Testamentum* [Greek and Latin], [Geneva], 1565. *Ill.*: S. cat., 23 June 1965, *502*.
29. On: I. Tremellius, *In Hoseam Prophetam interpretatio*, [Geneva], 1563. *Ill.*: S. cat., 23 June 1965, *662*.
30. On: 'Liber Ezechialis'. MS on vellum (Lat.), written at Fountains Abbey, Yorkshire, in the latter part of the twelfth century.
31. On: 'Biblia Sacra'. MS on vellum (Lat.), [thirteenth century].
32. J. B. Oldham, *English Blind Stamped Bindings*, Cambridge, 1952, p. 25. G. D. Hobson, *Bindings in Cambridge Libraries*, Cambridge, 1929, pp. 14–24.
33. Those of the original owner?
34. On: [J. Charlier de Gerson, *De passionibus animae* (and other tracts)], [Cologne, 1470–3].
35. On: *Vocabularius utriusque iuris*, Basel, 1488.
36. J. B. Oldham, *op. cit.*, p. 27, pl. XXI.
37. On: Eusebius and the Ven. Bede, *Historica Ecclesiastica*, Hagenau, 1506. (2 pts, 30 last leaves of pt. 1 only, pt. 2 complete.)
38. G. D. Hobson, *op. cit.*, p. 79. On: *Bible* [Greek], Basel, 1545. *Ill.*: NIXON, *Twelve*, pl. I.
39. The 'King Edward and Queen Mary binder': H. M. Nixon, *The Book Collector* I (1952), p. 244. On: *Actes made in Parliament*, London, 1554. *Ill.*: S. cat., 19 June 1967, *1592*.

40. [Elizabeth I], 'Royal Charter of Confirmation in favour of the town of Dunwich'. MS on vellum (Eng.), [*c.* 1575] *Ill.*: S. cat., 2 Feb. 1960, *301*.
41. On: J. Asser, *Aelfredi Regis Res Gestae* [and other books], London, 1574. *Ill.*: S. cat., 1 Dec. 1942, *94*.
42. *Le Nouveau Testament*, Lyons, 1564; [and] *Les Psaumes mis en rime*, Geneva, 1565.
43. H. M. Nixon, *Five Centuries of English Bookbinding*, London, 1978, no. 21.
44. On: Matthew of Westminster, *Flores historiarum*, London, 1570.
45. On: *The New Testament*, Dort, 1603. *Ill.*: S. cat., 21 June 1967, *2048*.
46. On: T. Brahe, *Astronomiae instauratae mechanica*, Nuremberg, 1602. *Ill.*: S. cat., 20 June 1960, *213*.
47. On: *The Book of Common Prayer*; [and] *The Bible*, London, 1611; [and] *Psalmes of David in metre*, London, 1612. *Ill.*: S. cat., 24 Mar. 1942, *402*.
48. On: *Biblia Sacra*, London, 1585; [and] *The Whole Book of Psalmes . . . into . . . meetre*, London, 1587. *Ill.*: BFAC, pl. CXIII.
49. On: [*The Book of Common Prayer*]; [and] *The Holy Bible*; [and] *The Whole Book of Psalmes . . . into . . . meeter*, Cambridge, 1629. *Ill.*: S.cat., 15 Oct. 1945, *1927*.
50. On: E. Spenser, *The Faerie Queene* [and other works], London, 1609–11–12.
51. J. Selden, *Mare Clausum*, London, 1635. *Ill.*: Quaritch, *Cat. of English and Foreign Bindings* (1921), *36*, pl. XI.
52. On: A. Fritach, *L'Architecture Militaire*, Leiden, 1635. *Ill.*: HOBSON, *Thirty*, pl. XXI.
53. On: F. Quarles, *Devine Poems*, London, 1643; [and] Ib., *Emblemes*, Cambridge, 1643. *Ill.*: Lardanchet catalogue 46 (1952), *1568*.
54. *The Book of Common Prayer*, London, 1662.
55. *Holy Bible*, Cambridge, 1659.
56. H. M. Nixon, *Broxbourne Library. Styles and Designs of Bookbindings*, London, 1956, p. 148.
57. On: *The Holy Bible*, London, 1671; [and] *The Whole Book of Psalms*, London, 1669.
58. H. M. Nixon, *The Book Collector*, IV, 1955, pp. 45–6.
59. In the Davis Collection is a MS '*The Dementions and Burthen of his Ma^{ts} Ships*', bound by him for Pepys in gold-tooled red goatskin: *Ill.*: HOBSON, *Thirty*, pl. XXIV.
60. On: *The Holy Bible*; [and] *The Whole Book of Psalms*, Cambridge, 1673.
61. *Ill.* (tools): HOBSON, *Thirty*, pl. LVIIB.
62. On: *The Holy Bible*, London, 1660; [and] *Psalmes . . . in . . . Meeter*, London, 1661. *Ill.*: E. Almack, *Fine Old Bindings*, London, 1913, pl. facing p. 113.
63. On: T. Comber, *A Companion to the Altar*, London, 1678. *Ill.*: S. cat., 17 July 1944, *37*.
64. On: *The Book of Common Prayer*, London, 1680; [and] *The Holy Bible*, London, 1682; [and] *Psalmes*, London, 1680.
65. On the turn-in of the lower cover: *Cleeve fecit*.
66. On: *The Book of Common Prayer*, Cambridge, 1666; [and] *The Holy Bible*, Cambridge, 1663. *Ill.*: S. cat., 17 Oct. 1960, *778*.
67. H. M. Nixon, *Broxbourne Library*, London, 1956, p. 165.
68. On: J. Taylor, *A Dissuasive from Popery* [and other works], London, 1686. *Ill.*: S. cat., 17 July 1944, *215*.

69. On: Le Sieur de Royaumont, *The History of the Old and the New Testament*, London, 1701. *Ill.*: Parke-Bernet cat., 15 Dec. 1953, *43*.
70. On: *The Christian Religion*, London, 1705.
71. E. Settle, *Eusebia Triumphans*, London, 1702.
72. Sir Charles Duncombe, the banker and politician. He was expelled from the House of Commons in 1702 and died in 1711.
73. *The Book of Common Prayer*; [and] *The Whole Book of Psalms ... in ...' Metre*, Cambridge, 1762. (The book is in its original green goatskin slip-case.) *Ill.*: S. cat., 17 Oct. 1960, *759*.
74. On: T. Birch, *The Heads of Illustrious Persons of Great-Britain*, London, 1756. *Ill.*: S. cat., 22 June 1965, *393*.
75. On: *Novelle Otto*, London, 1790. *Ill.*: NIXON, *Twelve*, pl. XIV.
76. On: R. Saunders, *Physiognomie and Chiromancie*, London, 1671; [and] idem, *A Treatise of the Moles*, London, 1670. Both the binding and the bill are *ill.*: S. De Ricci, *British ... Signed Bindings in the Mortimer L. Schiff Collection*, New York, 1935, no. 10.
77. On: T. Zouch, *The Life of Isaak Walton*, London, 1823.
78. *The Statutes at large, passed in the parliaments held in Ireland 1310–1776*, Dublin, 1765–82, 10 vols. *Ill.*: Breslauer, cat. 87, *101*.
79. Vol. X, Dublin, 1782. *Ill.*: HOBSON *English*, *87*.
80. P. Virgilius, *Opera*, Dublin, 1745.
81. M. Craig, *Irish Bookbindings 1600–1800*, London, 1954, pl. 22.
82. Ch. Smith, *The Ancient and Present State of the County and City of Cork*, Dublin, 1750, 2 vols. *Ill.*: M. Craig, *op. cit.*, pl. 27.
83. M. Craig, *op. cit.*, pl. 15–17. On: D. A. Beaufort, *Memoir of a Map of Ireland*, Dublin, 1792.
84. On: G. Miller, *Philosophy of Modern History*, Dublin, 1816, 2 vols. *Ill.*: Sawyer cat. 242, (1957) *100*. And on: *The Proceedings of the Dublin Society*, vol. LII, Dublin, 1816.
85. On: *The Holy Bible*; [and] *Psalms in Metre*, Edinburgh, 1715.
86. On: *The Holy Bible*; [and] *Psalms in Meeter*, Edinburgh, 1730, 2 vols.
87. On: C. Ayntoun-Douglas, *Dissertatio medica inauguralis*, Edinburgh, 1734. *Ill.*: HOBSON *English*, *81*.
88. On: *The Holy Bible*; [and] *Psalms in Metre*, Oxford, n.d.
89. On: R. Forsyth, *Disputatio juridica*, Edinburgh, 1792.
90. 1746–94.
91. On: 'An album with drawings with a ms. index', [Vienna, *c.* 1750]. *Partly ill.*: S. cat., 12 Apr. 1954, *152*.
92. H. Schedel, *Libri Chronicarum*, Nuremberg: A. Koberger, 1493. *Ill.*: GOLDSCHMIDT, *38*, pl. XVII.
93. On: U. Pinder, *Speculum Patientiae*, Nuremberg, 1509; [and] A. Alveld *Super apostolica sede*, Leipzig, 1520.
94. E. Reusner, *Basilicon. Opus genealogicum Catholicum*, Frankfurt, 1592. *Ill.*: *Book Collector*, III (1954), pl. VI (facing p. 185).
95. On: *Psalmi Davidis metrorythmici*, Frankfurt, 1612. *Ill.*: HOBSON, *Thirty*, pl. XVII.
96. On: J. B. Braun, *Historia Augusta*, Augsburg, 1698.
97. On: L. Berger, *Thesaurus Brandenburgicus selectus*, Berlin, 1696–[1701], 3 vols.
98. On: *La Sainte Bible*, Bern, 1731. This binding of *c.* 1740 has been attributed to Bern. *Ill.*: Maggs Bros, cat. 830, *118*.

99. On: G. B. Marini, *Herodes Kinder-moordt*, Amsterdam, 1740.

100. A. C. Mattheeus, 'Verzameling van inleidingen', MS on paper, [Middelburg], 1729–35, 3 vols.

101. L. Smids, *Schatkamer der Nederlandsche Oudheden*, Amsterdam, 1711. *Ill.*: S. cat., 25 June 1965, *623*.

102. A binding of which the spine looks like the fore-edge.

103. *La Sainte Bible*, Amsterdam, 1669, 2 vols. *Ill.*: Breslauer cat. 91, (1959), *6*.

104. (On 30 September 1670). *Biblia*, Amsterdam, 1664. *Ill.*: *Bookbindings by Albert Magnus*, Amsterdam: University Library, 1967. pl. I.

105. On: I. A. Agurellus, *Iambicus libri II, Sermonum libri II, Carminum libri II*, Venice, 1505.

106. On: F. M. Grapaldi, *De partibus aedium*, Parma, 1506. *Ill.*: GOLDSCHMIDT, *145*, pl. LIV.

107. On: Epictetus, *Enchiridion Epicteti Philosophi inter Stoicos*, Louvain, 1550; [and] H. Verlenius, *Epicteti . . . Enchiridion*, Antwerp, 1550.

108. On: Breviary for the use of Toledo. MS on vellum (Lat.), [Toledo, late fifteenth century].

109. On: 'Carta executoria'. Proceedings on behalf of Philip II of Spain, against Don Alonzo de Mohedas, mayor of Medellin. MS on vellum, Granada, 1570. *Ill.*: Breslauer, cat. 74 (7 June 1952), *43*.

110. On: A collection of orders and privileges issued by the Inquisition in favour of various individuals. MS on vellum (Sp.), last entry dated 1614. *Ill.*: HOBSON, *Thirty*, pl. XVI.

111. Antonio de Sancha, 1720–90.

112. On: *Estado militar de España*, Madrid, 1783. *Ill.*: S. cat., 22 June 1965, *317*.

113. G. D. Hobson, *Bindings in Cambridge Libraries*, Cambridge, 1929, pl. XXI.

114. D. Erasmus, *Hyperaspistes diatribae . . .* 2 pts, Basel, 1526–7. On the title-page of pt 2 is an ownership inscripton in Laski's hand and a note reading: *Ab Erasmo missus, redditus circiter cal [-] Anni MDXX [-]. Ill.*: S. cat., 22 June 1950, *65*.

115. On: *Liturgy of the Ruthenian Uniate Church*, Lemberg, 1721.

116. On: C. Tacitus, *Opera*, Parma, 1795, 3 vols. *Ill.*: Breslauer cat., 97 (1963) *114*.

117. On: Koran (pt. 25), Arabic MS on paper in Naskh script [Egypt, late fourteenth century].

118. On: Koran, Arabic MS in Naskh script. The date in the colophon is 1291, but it is described in S. cat., 24 June 1941, *86*, as of a later date.

119. Lotfali of Shiraz: a celebrated Persian painter who worked mainly for the court.

120. F. Petrarcha, [*Opera*] *Con l'Espositione d'Alessandro Velutello*, Venice, 1552. *Ill.*: GOLDSCHMIDT, *217*, pl. LXXXV, VI, VII.

121. On: Instructions from the Republic of Venice to an unknown officer. MS on vellum (Lat.), signed and dated *Aloysius Zambius Secretarius*, 21 April 1563, *Ill.*: N. Rauch cat. I (1948), *69*.

122. On: Instructions to Benetto Amoro on becoming a member of the Council. MS on vellum (It.), [Venice, *c.* 1590]. *Ill.*: S. cat., 18 June 1962, *127*.

123. On: The dedication of the 'Epistola ad Theodosium' to the Cardinal of Naples by Petrus Balbi, Bishop of Tropaea. MS on vellum (Lat.), [Italy, before Sept, 1479].

124. On: Gregorius IX, *Decretales*, Venice, 1482. *Ill.*: *Rilegature Veneziane del XV e XVI Secolo*, Venice, 1955, II, pl. IV.

125. S. cat. (Mensing Sale), 16 Dec. 1936, *246*.
126. (Unfortunately damaged on lower cover.) On: *Anthologia Graeca*, Florence, 1494. *Ill.*: S. cat., 12 July 1948, *7*.
127. Philostratus, *De Vita Apollonii Tyanei*, [Italy, 16th cent.]
128. E. Molinier, *Les Bronzes de la Renaissance: les plaquettes*, Paris, 1886, *134*.
129. E. Molinier, *op. cit.*, *498*. On: Procopius, *De bello Gothorum*, Rome, 1506. *Ill.*: NIXON, *Grolier*, *2*.
130. On: J. J. Pontanus *Opera*, Venice, 1505. *Ill.*: NIXON, *Grolier*, *6*.
131. On: M. Sabellicus, *Exemplorum libri decem*, Venice, 1507.
132. I doubt Goldschmidt's assumption that the design is printed from a woodblock because of small differences in the design on upper and lower cover. See GOLDSCHMIDT, *192*, p. 74.
133. On: *Horae dive Virginis Mariae sec. verum usum Romanum*, Paris, 1511. *Ill.*: GOLDSCHMIDT *192*, pl. LXVIII.
134. On: P. Victorius, *Explicationes . . . in Catonem*, Lyons, 1542. *Ill.*: Fairfax Murray, *Cat. of Early French Books* (1910), *567*
135. On: F. Petrarcha, *Sonetti et Canzoni con l'espositione d'Alessandro Vellutello*, Venice, 1545.
136. On: G. Capella, *Commentarii*, Venice, 1539. *Ill.*: Quaritch, *Cat. of Bookbindings* (1889), pl. VI.
137. They both came to Bologna in 1542, where von Ebeleben stayed till 1548, while Pflug left for Rome in 1546 (GOLDSCHMIDT, pp. 271–5).
138. M. T. Cicero, *Orationes*, Volumen secundum, Venice, 1541. *Ill.*: GOLDSCHMIDT, *198*, pl. LXXII, III.
139. M. T. Cicero, *De Philosophia*. Volumen secundum, Venice, 1541. *Ill.*: GOLDSCHMIDT *198*, pl. LXXII, III.
140. M. Cato [and others], *Libri de re rustica*, Venice, 1533. *Ill.*: S. cat., 3 May 1951, *685*.
141. A. Bojardo, *Libro d'arme e d'amore nomato Philogine*, Venice, 1547. *Ill.*: S. cat., 10 Dec. 1957, *460*.
142. On: B. Ferrero, 'Notarial documents'. MS on paper (Lat.), Palermo, 1572–3. *Ill.*: S. cat., 14 Mar. 1961, *441*.
143. On: 'Grant of the degree of Doctor of Philosophy and Medicine in the University of Padua to Sanctiflorus Mundella of Brescia by Nicolaus Galerius'. MS on vellum (Lat.), Padua, 1576.
144. On: Th. à Kempis, *De Imitatione Christi*, Paris, 1640. *Ill.*: G. Libri, *Monuments Inédits*, London, 1864, pl. XXXIV.
145. On: G. Ripamonti, *Historiarum urbis Mediolani*, n.p., n.d.
146. On: M. Michel, *La Reliure Française*, Paris, 1880. *Ill.: Bibliothèque de H. Béraldi*, (1935) pt. 4. *126*.
147. On: J. de la Fontaine, *Les Amours de Psiche et de Cupidon*, Paris, 1669. *Ill.*: Wilmerding sale cat. (Parke-Bernet), 6 Mar. 1951, *360*.
148. On: M. Proust, *Du Côté de chez Swann*, Paris, 1913. *Ill.*: N. Rauch, 13 May 1952, *581*.
149. P. Virgilius, *Eclogues*, Munich, 1927. *Ill.*: Breslauer, cat. 94 (1961), *159*, pl. XX. See also Fig. 7.1 above.
150. On: P. Valéry [and others], *Paul Bonet*, Paris, 1945.
151. On: J. and W. Grimm, *Household Stories*, London, 1882. *Ill.*: HOBSON, *English*, 117.
152. On: G. Cavendish, *The Life of Thomas Wolsey*, London, 1893. *Ill.*: S. cat., 11 May 1960, *534*, facing p. 75.

153. *The Tale of King Florus and the fair Jehane* [trans. William Morris], London, 1893.
154. On: [C. J. Dorat], *La Déclamation théâtrale*, Paris, 1766.
155. On: M. Field, *Fair Rosamund*, London, Ballantyne Press, 1897.
156. On: T. S. Moore, *The Little School*, London, 1905.
157. On: Dante Alighieri, *La Divina Commedia*, Florence, 1907.

61 Some Bookbindings in the Herzog August Bibliothek

(1984)*

Any visitor who spends but a few days in the ducal library at Wolfenbüttel soon realizes what a treasure house the dukes of Braunschweig-Lueneburg have left to posterity. Perhaps not as immediately striking as the splendid manuscripts or Duke August's own library, but nevertheless well worth exploring, is the relatively little-publicized collection of bookbindings. Though Hermann Herbst devoted a small booklet to the binding collection and wrote several extremely interesting articles based on the bindings at Wolfenbüttel,[1] and though Dag-Ernst Petersen compiled a fascinating and beautifully illustrated study of some medieval bindings in the Herzog August Bibliothek, neither has more than dipped into the vast and varied sources of historic interest and aesthetic pleasure this library possesses. This article, a slightly edited version of a talk given during the 12th International Congress of Bibliophiles held at Wolfenbüttel in late September and early October 1981, cannot do more than give a taste of the variety and scope of the historical bookbindings in the ducal library.

The monastic bindings, to which the greater part of the talk was devoted, form by far the most interesting portion of the collection. I hope one day to compile and publish a list of bindings from the various monasteries now present in the Herzog August Bibliothek, but a great deal more work needs to be done before this is anywhere near complete, and only a few of these monasteries and their bindings are mentioned here.

Some examples from the work of German fifteenth- and sixteenth-century binders come next, followed by a few German eighteenth-century bindings and their ducal owners.

The selection of other European bindings is a purely personal one, limited by lack of space, and includes a very few examples each from Holland, England, Italy and France. I would like to emphasize that this is by no means a survey, but a mere indication of an as yet insufficiently explored part of the collections.

In 1928 E. P. Goldschmidt, in the introduction to his *Gothic and Renais-*

* *Treasures of the Herzog August Library. Rare Books and Manuscripts*, Wolfenbüttel, 1984, pp. 87–130.

sance Bookbindings pointed out how the religious reform movements of the first half of the fifteenth century carried in their wake the revival of book production and bookbinding. The two major reform movements in Germany were those of the Benedictine monasteries, centralized in the Bursfeld Congregation, and of the Canons Regular of St Augustine. The monastic reform, with its return to the strict observance of the rules of the religious orders and its emphasis on study, on reading and on writing, stimulated the formation of monastic libraries. Luther's Reformation, followed by the secularization of the monasteries, resulted in the dispersion of these libraries or, in the case of the territory belonging to Duke Julius of Brunswick which included part of the diocese of Hildesheim, in their incorporation in the ducal library. Duke Julius, the third son of Heinrich the younger, had from his youth been interested in books. He studied in Cologne and Louvain, and during a journey to France in 1550 he acquired the first books for his library. Julius, who had become heir to the dukedom when his two elder brothers died in the battle of Sievershausen (1553) and who was a proponent of the Reformation (and consequently not on very good terms with his father) lived in Hessen where he built up his collection of books. In 1567 he acquired the library of the late Nuremberg syndic Michael von Kaden (d. 1561), and when in the following year Heinrich the younger died, Julius moved with his library to Wolfenbüttel. In March and April of 1572 Julius's library was considerably enriched with books and manuscripts from the convents of Wöltingerode, Steterburg, Dorstadt, Heiningen, and Marienberg; other monastic libraries, such as those from Amelunxborn, Georgenberg and Klus followed later.

The growth of the library brought with it the need of a librarian and of a set of library rules. The first librarian, the composer Leonhard Schröter, stayed barely a year; to his successor Lukas Weischner, I will return later. The set of rules, Julius's 'Libereyordnung' of 5 April 1572, a decree in which the tasks of the librarian and the administration of the library were set out in ten points dealing mainly with the cataloguing and the use of the books, was described and printed by Dr Milde in the *Wolfenbütteler Beiträge*, 1 (1972). In 1575 Julius founded the University at Helmstedt. His son and successor, Heinrich Julius (who succeeded in 1589; d. 1613), followed in his father's footsteps and also collected books, and in 1614 his son, Friedrich Ulrich, transferred the library collected by his father and grandfather to the University of Helmstedt. The books arrived there in 1618 and from then until Duke August the younger moved his books from Brunswick to Wolfenbüttel in 1644, there was no library there. In the early nineteenth century the University of Helmstedt closed; the books were gradually brought back and now form the 'Helmstedt' collection in the Herzog August Bibliothek.

Of the *c.* 85 manuscripts that came to Wolfenbüttel from the convent

Sancta Maria Virginis at Wöltingerode near Goslar, 69 have an inscription indicating their arrival there on 14 March 1572 (I have also found, more or less by accident while looking for bindings rather than provenance, three printed books that came from Wöltingerode to Wolfenbüttel on that date, one of which is now in the British Library);[2] one manuscript came on the following day and one had come a year earlier. Several of these manuscripts were presented to the convent by the abbess Elizabeth von Burgtorff (abbess from 1430); two were given by the abbess and reformer Mecheldis von Schwiecheld (who, according to one inscription, gave many more books), and among several other benefactors was also the convent's *prepositus*, Henricus, who gave 26 books.

'Sancta Maria Virginis' was founded at Wöltingerode in 1174 by the three local counts Ludolf, Hoger and Burchard as a Benedictine monastery. Soon it became a convent for Cistercian nuns. A number of the manuscripts with Wöltingerode provenance are clearly bound in the same shop and are decorated with tools that are found on other bindings (without this provenance) in the Helmstedt collection. This includes a binding on a manuscript Alanus de Rupe, *Tractatus responsorius de psalterio beate Maria Virginis* [and other works] (Cod. Guelf. Helmst. 1035). A binding on a Nuremberg Psalter of c. 1484/5, now in the Henry Davis Gift to the New University of Ulster at Coleraine, also came from the same bindery (see p. 171, Fig. 16.1).[3]

On 12 April 1572 about 20 to 30 manuscripts and a number of printed books came to the ducal library from the convent of St Peter at Heiningen. According to a thirteenth-century legend this convent was founded by the widow and daughter of a German King Alfried whose death during a crusade in 1012 drove his sorrowing widow and child to take leave of the world. Historically this is most improbable, but an eleventh-century source indicates two noble ladies, possibly of the Billinger family, who under the guidance of Bishop Bernward, c. 1000 founded a convent for canonesses dedicated to the Mother of God and to St Peter, which they endowed with land in and near Heiningen. During the first century of its existence the convent went down-hill and 'sorores tam miserabiliter dissolutae sunt, ut locus ille non diceretur claustrum ancillarum Christi'.[4] Bishop Berthold I in 1126 summoned Provost Gerhard of Riechenberg to reform the convent and to induce the nuns to live a communal life in obedience and discipline, according to the Rule of St Augustine. Three centuries later reform was necessary again, and the Provost of the Windesheim monastery at Sülte, Berthold Ziegenmeier, was sent to Heiningen to re-introduce the 'vita communis', to abolish private property and to help the nuns to manage their affairs. The nuns were encouraged to practise arts and crafts and became proficient in tapestry work (a large figurative tapestry made at Heiningen by 59 nuns whose names are visible in the border is now

Fig. 61.1   Alexander Grammaticus, *Doctrinale*, Basel, 1486.
Bound in blind-tooled brown calf.
(August. 32.1. Gram.) (Lower cover).

in the Victoria and Albert Museum). They also copied books and they may have bound them. A number of manuscripts from Heiningen, now at Wolfenbüttel, have very similar bindings decorated with the same tools, and it is probable that these were made at the convent. An example covers a fifteenth-century manuscript *Quadragesimale* ... (Cod. Guelf. Helmst. 162). During the Reformation the convent was plundered several times and almost destroyed by the troops of Heinrich the younger. In 1572 the convent's library was absorbed into Duke Julius's library. As well as the group of manuscripts just mentioned, there is an Innocentius III, *Liber super officium misse* (Cod. Guelf. Helmst. 719), with the provenance 'liber sancti Petri apostoli claustri in Heyninghe', bound, probably not at the convent, in brown calf and decorated with tools showing a lamb-and-flag, an acorn with spiky leaves, a small round eagle and large MARIA stamp. This binding links with a whole group of bindings at Wolfenbüttel, covering manuscripts and printed books, a fair number of which belonged to Duke August's library, such as the copy of Alexander Grammaticus, *Doctrinale* (Basel, 1486: August. 32.1 Gram: Fig. 61.1).

The most important reform movement of the Benedictine monasteries in Germany originated in Klus, spread from there to Bursfeld, Reinhausen, Huysburg and all over Germany, becoming known as the Bursfeld Union or Bursfeld Congregation. The monastery dedicated to St Mary of the Holy Cross and to St George at Klus was founded in 1124 by Adelheid, the daughter of the Emperor Heinrich IV, abbess of Gandersheim. From 1134 it was occupied by monks from Cluny. By the time Johann Dederoth, a monk first at Reinhausen and then in the monastery of St Blasius at Northeim, who had encountered monastic reform during his travels in Italy, was elected abbot of Klus in 1430, the monastery of St Mary and St George had, like so many Benedictine monasteries, moved rather far away from the original Rule of St Benedict. Dederoth brought back the concepts of communal property and communal life and, when three years later in 1433 he became abbot of Bursfeld, he put his reformation ideas into practice there. The reformer, Johannes Rode, abbot of St Matthew in Trier, sent him four monks, two for Klus and two for Bursfeld, who brought Rode's Statutes to these monasteries. Dederoth also started to reform Reinhausen; he remained abbot both of Klus and of Bursfeld until his death in 1439. After his death Johann von Hagen was elected abbot at Bursfeld and became the organizer of the Bursfeld Congregation. In 1444 Huysburg joined the movement; other monasteries followed suit and the congregation grew in size and gained strength.

Most of our knowledge of Klus we owe to the monk Heinrich Bode who wrote a chronicle of his monastery, relating the events from the beginning of Dederoth's reform movement until 1539. The manuscript, which also contains a chronicle of Gandersheim, came to the Herzog

August Bibliothek during the seventeenth century (Cod. 19. 13 Aug. 4°).
After Dederoth's death Hermann Bornemann became abbot at Klus. Klus
was a small and poor monastery, but it gradually increased in size and in
wealth; under abbot Wedego (1460–1505) there were 32 monks, among
whom was 'frater Joannes Doliatoris, patria Braklensis', or brother Johann
von Brakel, a scribe and bookbinder to whom I shall return in a moment.
One of the results of Dederoth's reform movement was an increased
interest in study and books. The *Ceremoniae* of the Bursfeld Congregation
stipulate that the monks should 'scribere libros aut rubricare vel ligare,'
and it contains a separate chapter dealing with the tasks and duties of the
Armarius, the librarian.[5] Klus also owned a library as well as a scriptorium
and a bindery. Abbot Wedego was particularly concerned with the development of the library which during his abbacy increased through purchase,
donation and book production in the monastery itself. The books from
Klus often have the inscription 'Iste liber pertinet ad Clusam' or 'liber
sancti georgii in Clusa', and many of the books which are still in their
original binding have on the upper cover a title label with a library
shelfmark in red. The majority of the manuscripts and a number of the
printed books with Klus provenance are bound in blind-tooled brown calf
or hide; several are in sheep and some are in white, stained leather. A few
identical tools occur on all these bindings and there is little doubt that
they were made at Klus. A careful study of the tools suggests a division
into three groups.

The first group contains several bindings decorated with characteristic
fleurs-de-lis, fleurons and leaf tools. One binding (Cod. Guelf. Helmst.
13) covers a manuscript Nicolaus de Lyra, *Postilla super epistolas Pauli*
[and other religious works] and was bought for the library at Klus in 1465
from the priest Heinrich Ghuler or Ghiler, together with nineteen other
manuscripts. A manuscript in a binding decorated with the same tools, a
collection of Saints' lives, was—at least partly—written by Andreas Sote-
flesch at Klus in 1471 (Cod. Guelf. Helmst. 322). The other bindings of
this group cover manuscripts and books written or printed in the 1460s
and 1470s or earlier, and one book containing a printed *Ceremoniale
monachorum ordinis S. Benedicti* [and] *Ordinarius Benedictinus Bursfelden-
sis* [Marienthal, 1474–5], as well as a manuscript *De electione novi abbatis*
has on the end-leaf a manuscript note dated 1483 (Helmst. Qu. H. 74).
It is probable that this whole group (of thirteen bindings) was bound
during the late 1460s, the 1470s and the early 1480s. Eleven tools that
were used to decorate these bindings also occur on a group of at least 22
bindings all of which have either a round or an oval seal tool, and in
many cases both. The binding of a manuscript *Pars estivalis breviarii
fratrum . . . ordinis scti Benedicti* (Cod. Guelf. Helmst. 587) has the round
seal only; a binding showing both seals covers a fifteenth-century manu-

script, *De mystica expositione . . . misse libri* (Cod. Guelf. Helmst. 596). The inscription round the round seal reads 'Guill. de Lut' (Guillielmus de Luttere);[6] the letters round the oval seal form the name: 's'THIDERICI DE BRAC PLEBAN IN SESEN', i.e. Dietrich von Brakel, priest at Seesen, whom Hermann Herbst believes to have been a relative of the monk, scribe and bookbinder Johann von Brakel. Of this group of bindings three (two manuscripts and one printed book) have an inscription to the effect that they were bound in Klus by the monk Johannis de Braclis, who also wrote—at least part of—two of the manuscripts; one of the binding inscriptions is dated 1490.[7] I mentioned already that 'Joannes Doliatoris, patria Braklensis' or Johann von Brakel, occurs in the list of monks who were at Klus during the abbacy of Wedego, and in Bodo's chronicle his death is recorded in 1525. There are good reasons to assume that von Brakel worked from *c.* 1485 (or at least from before 1488), and he is no doubt responsible for all bindings in this group.

The third group shows the most distinct change of tools. Five tools link it with Johann von Brakel's work and four occur also on the earlier group, but several highly decorative tools—including a barking dog, a vase or pot containing a plant, the symbols of the four Evangelists, and a round tool that looks like a binder's mark and has the initials mk (possibly standing for monasterium Klus?)—occur for the first time. This last group contains six books printed between 1481 and 1517. But as one, a Bartholomaeus Anglicus, *De proprietatibus rerum* (Strasburg, 1485: Helmst. Qu.H. 22.1; see Fig. 18.1 above) has an inscription that it was bound in 1526 (after von Brakel's death), and as another, a collection of Pope Gregory I's works (1481–1502: Helmst. D. 109.4) was only presented to Klus in 1531, it seems likely that this whole group was bound after von Brakel's death by his successor.

Before Johann Dederoth became abbot of Klus, he was a monk at the Benedictine monastery St Blasius at Northeim (north of Göttingen). This monastery was founded sometime between 1083 and 1101. The foundation was planned by Count Otto of Northeim, but only carried out after his death (1083) by his three sons: Heinrich (d.1101), Siegfried and Kuno. Monks and nuns lived together in the same monastery until Duke Otto II of Brunswick *c.* 1234 instructed the then abbot, Eckbrecht, to move the young and comely nuns to a separate women's convent. The older nuns were allowed to stay out their days but no new women recruits were permitted. In 1463/4 St Blasius joined the Bursfeld Congregation.

Count Otto of Northeim had left manuscripts for the library of the monastery he intended to found and these were given to the monks by his sons. Warmond, the first abbot (d. *c.* 1144) had bought books for the library, and manuscripts were copied in the monastery itself. Two early library inventories, one written *c.* 1150, the other probably *c.* 1160–65, have been published by Hermann Herbst.[8] The old library was entirely destroyed and a new library was accumulated in the mid-fifteenth century and catalogued in 1592 by Johann Letzner.[9] Several books were presented to the monastery by the Erfurt dean Johannes Weidemann. During the troubles of 1521 the population of Erfurt stormed the houses of the clergy. Weidemann's house was also attacked, his servant thrown into the river, his furniture battered, his library broken up and his supply of communion wine looted. Weidemann himself only just managed to flee the town. When later in the year peace had been restored, Weidemann gave what remained of his library to St Blasius at Northeim. At least two of the books he presented were bound by Johann Helmstatt, an Erfurt binder who had matriculated at Erfurt University in 1458 and who worked for Weidemann from *c.* 1471/2. Helmstatt used a letter stamp to sign his bindings; an example of his work covers Clement V, *Constitutiones*, n.p., n.d. (Einband Sammlung 22.2.4. Jur. 2°). Another Erfurt binder who also used a name stamp was Nikolaus von Havelberg. He bound the two volumes of Rainerus de Pisis, *Pantheologia*, n.p., n.d., which were at St Blasius in 1517 (Helmst. E. 146. 2°).

The date 1517 occurs again and again in the ownership inscriptions of the monastery and were it not for at least one manuscript that had been written at St Blasius by the monk Heinrich Holthusen in 1497, one would presume that a large collection of books and manuscripts had either been bought or given at that date. 1517 is in fact the date that the library building was finished, as a note on the verso of the library inventory of *c.* 1150 states: 'Anno 1517 ist das gebew der sacristei und librarei zu Northeim vollendet und erfertigt und da hat man aus allen stifften und clostern Bücher dahin gegeben.'[10] It seems likely that when the books were moved to the new building they were rearranged and registered as belonging to the monastery.

Hermann Herbst has identified a number of the manuscripts that occur in Letzner's inventory of 1592, and I have found several printed books with St Blasius provenance that are mentioned in this list. One is no. 38: Meffreth, *Sermones de tempore* (n.p., n.d.: Helmst. E. 260. 2°), bound in white calf and decorated with tools that occur on two other bindings from Northeim as well as on three bindings from the Helmstedt collection without this provenance. The bindings from St Blasius at Northeim come from a variety of shops and can be linked with other bindings in the collection to form small groups.

I want to discuss one more monastery whose books and manuscripts have found their way into the Herzog August Bibliothek. This is the 'Domus Sancti Pancratii' of the Canons Regular of St Augustine, founded in 1107–8 by Reinhard von Blankenburg, Bishop of Halberstadt at Oster-wieck an der Ilse. In 1109 the monastery, too much disturbed by the noise of the local market, was moved to Hamersleben, north-east of Osterwieck, where it remained until its dissolution in 1804. One fifteenth-century manuscript, Johannes Gerson's minor works in Latin (Cod. Guelf. Helmst. 657; see Fig. 17.1 above), and six books printed between 1500 and 1519 have the ownership inscription 'Liber monasterij beati pancracij martiris In hamersleue Ordinis canonicorum regularium Halberstadensis diocesis', often with the word 'completus' or 'comparatus' and the date ranging from 1510 to 1521. Sometimes the prior Bernardus Fabri (1502–40) is mentioned, and the provenance inscription and chapter headings are frequently rubricated. Two more volumes have an unspecified 'hamersleue' provenance with the dates 1504 and 1524, and two others have the characteristic rubrication. They are all bound in brown calf or hide and decorated with the same set of tools that were used on the binding of Athanasius Alexandrinus, *Opera*, Paris, 1519 (Helmst. D. 132. 2°). At least four other books belonging to the Helmstedt collection, printed between 1498 and 1516, without a written provenance, come from this same shop.

After these largely anonymous monastic binders I would like to turn to a few German fifteenth- and sixteenth-century craftsmen whose names are known. I have already mentioned the Erfurt binders Helmstatt and von Havelberg, some of whose signed bindings belonged to the monastery of St Blasius at Northeim. Another Erfurt binder, Caspar Strube, signed the binding of a 1483 Strasburg Bible (Bibel Sammlung 4° 129). No other town seems to have had so many binderies that signed their work as Erfurt: at least 21 Erfurt binders used name stamps. They have attracted a fair amount of literature, two of the best-known Erfurt binders both matriculating at Erfurt University in 1455: Johann Fogel and Ulrich Frenckel. In the matriculation book Fogel is registered as 'Johannes Voghel de Francfordia'. His first datable binding covers a matriculation book and was made in 1456. He worked until 1461. At least 30 bindings by him are known.

Ulrich Frenckel worked in Erfurt at the same time. According to the entry in the matriculation book he came from Hirschau (though it is not known from which of the ten places in Germany that bear that name he originated). He started binding in 1456 and, like Fogel, bound a volume of the University's matriculation book and worked for the students there. Like most of Frenckel's work I have seen, the binding on Clement V, *Constitutiones* (Mainz, 1471: August. 1.6 Jur. 2°: Fig. 61.2), is made of brown hide over wooden boards and is decorated with typical Erfurt tools, including a barking dog, a pierced heart, a deer and Frenckel's name stamp. Both covers are protected by metal bosses and metal bars which are no doubt partly responsible for the still excellent condition of the binding. Frenckel seems to have worked in Erfurt until *c.* 1480.

Fig. 61.2   Clement V, *Constitutiones*, Mainz, 1471.
Bound by Ulrich Frenckel in blind-tooled brown hide.
(August. 1.6. Jur. 2°).

Fig. 61.3   Nicolaus de Lyra, *Moralia super totam Bibliam*, Strasburg, *c.*
1479.
Bound by Johannes Grieme in blind-tooled brown hide.
(August 18. Th.).

A binder who may possibly have worked in Strasburg, though nothing seems to be known about him, was Johannes Grieme. He used his name tool as well as four remarkable bird tools and—on the lower cover—four less unusual tools depicting the symbols of the Evangelists to decorate Nicolaus de Lyra's *Moralia super totam Bibliam* (Strasburg, *c.* 1479: August. 18. Th.: Fig. 61.3).

Less cut and dried is the identity of the bookbinder who bound a copy of Gasparinus Barzizius, *Epistolae* (Basel, 1472: Einband Sammlung 158.3. Qu. 2°: Fig. 61.4) for Hans von Thill and who signed himself 'mair.b.b'. Much ink has flown in attempting to identify him with Meir Jaffe, and more in counter-attempts to distinguish him from this Jewish scribe, illuminator and cut-leather artist from Ulm. The literature on German cut-leather binding is weighty, culminating in the monumental *Corpus der Gotischen Lederschnitt-einbände* (Stuttgart, 1980) by Professor F. A. Schmidt-Künsemüller, but the argument surrounding Meir Jaffe and 'mair.b.b' (Mair, *buchbinder*) has remained unproven. If I may try to sum up the argument: Otto Mitius firmly located the bookbinder who made the cut-leather bindings decorated with—what turned out to be—'mair.b.b.'s' tools at Bamberg. Hermann Herbst, who published all seven Wolfenbüttel examples and who discovered the 'mair.b.b' stamp, attributed them to Nuremberg (basing his attribution on the fact that their original owners belonged to two Nuremberg patrician families). Husung went an important step further in discovering a decree of the Council of Nuremberg, dated 4 July 1468, giving permission to 'Meyerlein', a Jew from Ulm, to reside in their town from that date until 11 November of the same year, and instructing this 'Meyerlein' to bind several books for the Council's library. Husung also discovered a Pentateuch (now in the Bayerische Staatsbibliothek at Munich) bound and decorated with cut-leather work and signed in Hebrew: 'The Pentateuch for the Council of Nuremberg, long life to it, Meir Jaffe, the artist'.

The identification of 'Meir Jaffe' with 'Meyerlein' can hardly be disputed. Husung described Meir Jaffe as a wandering Jewish cut-leather artist who came from Ulm, worked in Nuremberg from 4 July to 11 November 1468, then probably went to Bamberg where he made the several cut-leather bindings which have an early Bamberg provenance, before returning to Nuremberg to make the cut-leather armorial bindings for the patrician family Von Thill. Both Herbst and Husung wrote about Hans Hack von Sul, called von Thill, who was a member of the Nuremberg Council and who in January 1481 married Klara Imhoff. There are eight armorial bindings which have been decorated in cut-leather work with Von Thill's arms only (e.g. Fig. 61.4), and were therefore made before that date, and two armorial bindings which have Von Thill's arms impaling Imhoff that can confidently be attributed to after the date of his

Fig. 61.4   Gasparinus Barzizius, *Epistolae*, Basel, 1472.
Bound by 'mair.b.b.' for Hans von Thill in blind-tooled brown
hide decorated with cut-leather work.
(Einband Sammlung 158.3.Qu.2°).

marriage. All these bindings are also decorated with a set of tools among which is the scroll tool signed 'mair.b.b' (an example covers G. Merula, *Enarrationes satyrarum Juvenalis*, Treviso, 1478: Einband Sammlung 156.5 Qu. 2°). Husung was quite convinced that Meir Jaffe and 'mair.b.b' were the same man, a conviction shared by E. P. Goldschmidt who pointed out a striking resemblance of technique and style of the cut-leather work on the Von Thill bindings with that on the Pentateuch for the Nuremberg Council. Geldner then upset the applecart by stating that he could discern at least three different leather cutters who worked for or with the binder who signed himself 'mair.b.b.'. He numbered them leather cutter IV (whom he equated with Meir Jaffe), V and VI (whom he held responsible for the Von Thill bindings). In a footnote he threw doubt on his own argument by suggesting the possibility that the leather cutters were not different people but that one man may have used different patterns or examples. He went further to argue a Bamberg origin for the 'mair.b.b' bindings, having discovered in the town accounts of Bamberg that in 1476 a certain Ulrich Meyer was paid to bind a town law book. This has alas not been preserved, but a later Bamberg law book (1481–97), for the binding and the paper of which an unnamed binder was paid in 1480, turns out to have been the work of 'mair.b.b'. Geldner concluded that 'mair.b.b' was Ulrich Meyer of Bamberg, a conclusion with which Professor Schmidt-Künsemüller agreed.

There are weak links in both arguments. The Pentateuch for the Nuremberg Council has not got any small tools to connect Meir Jaffe with 'mair.b.b', the identification of Jaffe with 'mair.b.b' resting entirely on a similarity of technique and style of the cut-leather work. How dangerous and subjective such a basis for argument is, is made clear by Geldner and Schmidt-Künsemüller who also founded their argument on the technique and style of the cut-leather work and came to a totally different conclusion. Geldner's weakness is that the law book mentioned in the 1476 Bamberg accounts has not been found and that the binder of the later law book has not been named. A travelling cut-leather artist who was also a bookbinder would solve the contradiction of the Nuremberg provenance of the Pentateuch and the von Thill bindings on the one hand, and the Bamberg provenance of the law book and of other Bamberg books on the other. However, until more archival evidence is found either to connect or to disconnect Meir Jaffe and 'mair.b.b', the question remains unsettled.

We tread firmer ground about a century later with the second ducal librarian and bookbinder Lukas Weischner from Jena who succeeded Leonhard Schröter at the end of 1572. Among Weischner's tasks was to bring the library into proper order and keep it so, to fill the gaps in the collection by buying books and binding them, weekly to clean the library, and not to let anyone in or lend books without the Duke's permission. He earned

30 *Thaler* per annum and got his winter and summer Court livery and his board and lodging free. He was allowed to keep a journeyman and was given an extra 20 *Thaler* to acquire bookbinders' tools which were to remain the property of the ducal library. He lived in Riddagshausen—which he found inconvenient—until 1575 when he asked permission to work for the newly founded Helmstedt University. He was duly appointed bookbinder to the University, but living now even further away from Wolfenbüttel, found that he could not fulfil his duties as ducal librarian, though he continued—at a reduced rate of payment—to bind for Duke Julius's library. As well as working for the University library (which acquired but few new books), Weischner bound for the professors and students at Helmstedt. It was apparently not a great financial success and Weischner had to press Duke Julius for payments due to him; he also complained about the price of vellum and leather. In 1579 his old father, Hans, asked for his son to be released from his duties in order to help him at Jena. This must have been agreed, for by 1588 Lukas is mentioned as librarian and bookbinder to the University there. He died in 1609.

Hermann Herbst published[11] a letter from Duke Julius requesting Weischner to bind three books, one of which, a *Corpus Doctrinae* of 1576 (64.8 Theol. 2°) is in the Herzog August Bibliothek. Through comparison of the tools used on this binding and of those used on a number of dated bindings made for Duke Julius it is possible to identify Weischner's work now at Wolfenbüttel. Among the rather gaudily decorated bindings, for which Weischner used rolls, large floral tools and smaller tools, is a Plantin Polyglot Bible (1568–73: Bibel Sammlung 2° 2b: 1–8) bound in eight volumes in brown calf, tooled in gold and decorated with coloured paint, volume III of which is illustrated here (Fig. 61.5). All volumes have on the upper cover a portrait of Duke Julius, the initials VGGIHZBVL (Von Gottes Gnaden Iulius Herzog Zu Braunschweig Vnd Lueneburg) and the date 1573, and on the lower cover Julius's arms. Julius's son, Heinrich Julius, married in 1585 Dorothea, the daughter of the Elector August of Saxony. She owned a set of Luther's works printed at Jena between 1572 and 1580, bound in brown calf in eight volumes (plus an index volume), every one of which has been decorated to a different design (Einband Sammlung Li. 4° 265, vol. III: Fig. 61.6). They are the work of Caspar Meuser, second court binder at the Court of the Elector of Saxony. Meuser probably came from Suhl or Suhla in Thüringen. He was employed by the court binder Jakob Krause as his 'guetenn tuchtigen gesellen' in 1574 and worked with Krause for the next four years until his appointment as second court binder with a workshop of his own in 1578. In volume I of my book on *The Henry Davis Gift* (London, 1978), I have devoted a whole chapter to Meuser which I will not repeat here. Krause died in 1585 and Meuser acquired his tools. He remained court binder first to

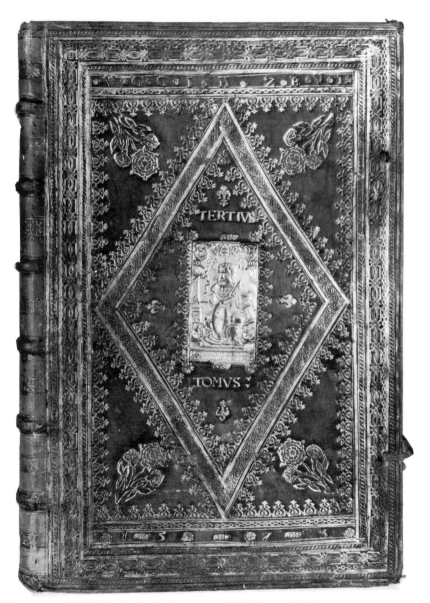

Fig. 61.5 *Biblia* [Polyglot], Antwerp, 1568–73, vol. III.
Bound by Lukas Weischner in gold-tooled brown calf
decorated with coloured paint.
(Bibel Sammlung 2° 2b: 1–8).

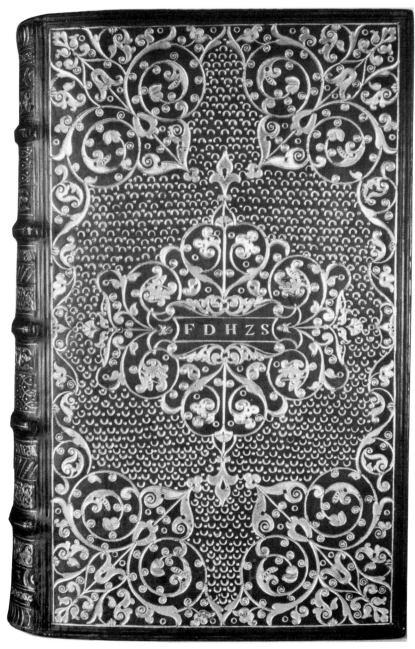

Fig. 61.6   M. Luther, *Alle Bücher und Schriften*, Jena, 1572–80, vol. III.
Bound by Caspar Meuser for Dorothea of Saxony in gold-
tooled brown calf.
(Einband Sammlung Li.4° 265).

August and then to Christian I and Christian II until his own death in 1593. The bindings for Dorothea have her initials (Frederricke Dorothea Herzogin Zu Sachsen) and the date 1583 on the spine, and all have gilt, gauffered and painted edges with her arms on the fore-edge.

The son of Dorothea and Heinrich Julius, Friedrich Ulrich, gave his father's and grandfather's library to the University at Helmstedt. He died childless (1634) and was succeeded by Duke August the younger. One of August's grandsons was Ludwig Rudolph who was born in 1671, the younger son of Anton Ulrich. During 1685–87 he travelled in Italy, France and the Netherlands, and after his return he served in the Emperor's army. When in 1714 Anton Ulrich died, Ludwig Rudolph inherited Blankenburg which he ruled as a separate state. His court was quite splendid and quite expensive, and when in 1731 his elder brother August Wilhelm died childless, Ludwig Rudolph succeeded him as Duke of Braunschweig-Lueneburg.

Among the bindings at the Herzog August Bibliothek are two sets of Johann Schilter's *Thesaurus Antiquitatum Teutonicarum* (Ulm, 1728–27) Einband Sammlung Ln. 2° 2) in three volumes. One set is bound in purple-stained vellum, the other in pink, and both are painted with a wide border showing animals, birds and cherubs among foliage (the purple set shows a stag and a horse, and has lions instead of cherubs) around, on the upper cover, the arms and, on the lower cover, the monogram of Ludwig Rudolph. Volume II of the pink set is illustrated here (Fig. 61.7). Ludwig Rudolph's monogram also occurs on the upper cover of one of two copies of J. F. Lampe's Dissertation (Helmstedt, 1720), bound in orange velvet and embroidered with gold and silver thread and coloured silks, which sports on the lower cover the prancing horse that forms the crest of the Dukes of Braunschweig-Lueneburg (Einband Sammlung Gn. 2° 2 Ex.). Another copy of this Dissertation, similarly bound and embroidered, has the monogram of Ludwig Rudolph's first cousin and son-in-law, Ferdinand Albrecht II (Einband Sammlung Gn. 2° 3 Ex.).

In 1690 Ludwig Rudolph had married Christine Louise, daughter of Albrecht Ernst von Oetingen. They had four daughters, the youngest of whom, Antoinette Amalia, married in 1712 another of Duke August's grandsons, Ferdinand Albrecht II, whose embroidered binding I have just mentioned. Their son, Karl I, was born in 1713 and married in 1733 Philippine Charlotte, daughter of King Friedrich Wilhelm I of Prussia. On the occasion of their marriage they were presented with a poem by B. H. Brockes, *Daphnis Hirten-Gedicht auf den Vermählungs Fest des Printzen Carls und . . . Printzessin Philippinen Charlotten (etc.)*, bound in pink silk and embroidered with gold and silver thread and coloured silks showing a rococo cartouche around two shields with their respective

Fig. 61.7   J. Schilter, *Thesaurus Antiquitatum Teutonicarum*, Ulm,
1728–27, vol. II.
Bound for Ludwig Rudolph in pink-stained vellum decorated
with paint.
(Einband Sammlung Ln.2° 2).

crests: the prancing horse of Braunschweig and the Prussian eagle (Einband Sammlung Gn. 2° 32: Fig. 61.8). A year later, J. G. Pertsch published in Leipzig (1734) his *Versuch einer Kirchen-Historie*, which he dedicated to Karl. The presentation copy to the heir to the Dukedom was bound in pale blue velvet and embroidered with silver thread depicting, on the upper cover, Karl's monogram (2 Cs addorsed) and on the lower cover his crest (Einband Sammlung Tm. 484: Fig. 61.9). The presenteation copy to Philippine Charlotte is similarly bound. In March 1735, Ludwig Rudolph died and when Ferdinand Albrecht II died six months later, Karl I became Duke of Braunschweig-Lueneburg. It was during his reign that Lessing was appointed ducal librarian in 1770.

During and after Karl's reign the court binder was Friedrich Bartholomaeus Widemann. He is called the 'Hofbuchbinder' in the introduction to Johann Jakob Heinrich Bücking's *Die Kunst des Buchbinders* (Stendal, 1785). Bücking was a medical man and a druggist at Wolfenbüttel who wrote several books on such subjects as the extracting of teeth and the treatment of broken knees. In the introduction to his bookbinder's manual Bücking explained how he had got to know the court binder Widemann through the many illnesses he and his family had suffered. He described Widemann as a man who seemed born for his craft and who combined his talents with 56 years of experience. Through watching Widemann at work and through discussing his metier with him, Bücking was able to write his remarkably useful handbook, at the end of which are two folding plates, drawn (or composed) by Widemann, illustrating, as well as several bookbinders' presses, instruments and various stages of sewing, a number of rolls and decorative tools which clearly belonged to Widemann. Several of these (e.g. a crested roll, a large flower tool and a small 3-leaved clover plant) are found on the binding of a 1730 Tübingen Bible (Bibel Sammlung 2° 96a) made of brown marbled calf and elaborately tooled in gold, largely to a floral design, with gilt, gauffered and painted edges, which has been signed in the bottom compartment of the spine 'Widemann fecit Wolfenbüttel MDCCLXIV' (Fig. 61.10). After 35 years of experience as a bookbinder, Widemann was certainly a master of his craft and one of whom the town of Wolfenbüttel can rightly be proud.

In order not to give the impression that all the bindings in the Herzog August Bibliothek are of German origin, I have selected a few other western European bindings, a selection that is far from representative and based on a purely personal choice.

A Dutch binding of brown-stained calf, tooled in gold with gilt, gauffered and painted edges, covers a New Testament and Psalter printed at 'sHertogenbosch in 1666. The tools used to decorate this binding are closely similar to those used by Holland's best-known seventeenth-century

Fig. 61.8   B.H. Brockes, *Daphnis Hirten-Gedicht*, Hamburg, [1733].
Bound in 1733 for Karl I and Philippine Charlotte in pink silk,
embroidered with gold and silver thread and coloured silks.
(Einband Sammlung Gn.2° 32).

Fig. 61.9   J.G. Pertsch, *Versuch einer Kirchen-Historie*, Leipzig, 1734.
Bound for Karl I in blue velvet embroidered with silver thread.
(Einband Sammlung Tm. 484). (Lower cover).

Fig. 61.10 *Biblia*, Tübingen, 1730.
Bound in 1764 by F.B. Widemann in gold-tooled brown
marbled calf, signed and dated.
(Bibel Sammlung 2° 96a).

binder, Albert Magnus, who worked in Amsterdam, where this book was
most probably bound (Bibel Sammlung 973: Fig. 61.11). A Hague binder
who figures prominently in Dr Storm van Leeuwen's *De achttiende-eeuwse
Haagse boekband* (The Hague, 1976) was Christiaan Micke. He was born
in 1714, one of a family of ten, was registered as an apprentice with the
Hague booksellers guild in 1727 and set up independently as a bookbinder

Fig. 61.11   *Het Nieuwe Testament* [and] *Psalmen*, 'sHertogenbosch,
1666.
Bound, probably in Amsterdam, in gold-tooled brown-
stained calf.
(Bibel Sammlung 973).

in 1743. He worked for Stadtholders William IV and V and bound a 1663 Leyden Bible (Bibel Sammlung 2° 147a).

Also in the 'Bibel Sammlung' is a two volume Oxford Bible (1717: Bibel Sammlung 2° 115: Fig. 61.12) bound in England in red goatskin tooled in gold in the so-called Harleian style, though not by any of the binders who worked for the Harleian Library. I have found the same tools on several bindings in the British Library and in Cambridge, all covering books printed between 1715 and 1725.

One of the works of which Thomas Hollis, 'citizen of the world' (as he called himself), lover of liberty and generous donor of books, had several copies bound to present to libraries in his own country and abroad, was the 6th edition of John Wallis's *Grammatica linguae Anglicanae* (London, 1765), printed at Hollis's own request and under his general direction. One copy, bound by Matthewman in gold-tooled red morocco, he presented with an inscription dated 1 January 1765 to the library at Wolfenbüttel (Kn 27). In June of the preceding year Matthewman's shop had burnt down and Hollis's emblematical tools had perished in the fire. A very similar set was engraved by Pingo, the medallist and seal engraver, and though the new set was not completed until 1767, some tools must have been ready earlier, for a numbr of copies of Wallis's *Grammatica*, all identically bound and decorated with tools from the new set, have either a presentation inscription or a provenance inscription dated 1765 or 1766.

There are several nice sixteenth-century Italian bindings in the library. One, in gold-tooled red-brown goatskin, covers a music manuscript in six parts (Cod. Guelf. 293 Vogel) and was made by the Venetian Apple bindery (named after one of its tools, not used on this binding). This atelier worked in the 1540s and 1550s for a number of well-known book lovers such as Johann Jakob Fugger, Thomas Mahieu (who owned one binding from this shop), Marc Laurin (who also owned one), Cardinal Granvelle and several distinguished Venetian families. Another Italian binding of about the same date or a little later covers Ariosto's *Orlando Furioso* (Venice, 1549: Einband Sammlung Lk 57: Fig. 61.13).

The Herzog August Bibliothek possesses a number of attractive sixteenth-century French bindings, such as a 1476 Venice Aristotle bound for Jean Grolier by the Cupid's Bow binder.[12] Two other binders who worked for Grolier are represented. One is the Mansfeld binder who owes his name to Peter Ernst, Count von Mansfeld who, while a captive of the French at Vincennes in the 1550s, acquired a number of books bound by this binder. A gold-tooled and painted brown calf binding covering four works printed in Rome and Venice between 1526 and 1535 was made by him (Einband Sammlung 108 Qu. 4°: Fig. 61.14). The other binder, until recently identified as Claude de Picques, bound a 1536 Venice Petrarch

Fig. 61.12   *Holy Bible*, Oxford, 1717.
Bound, probably in London, in gold-tooled red goatskin.
(Bibel Sammlung 2° 115).

Fig. 61.13 Ariosto, *Orlando Furioso*, Venice, 1549.
Bound in Venice, *c.* 1550 in gold-tooled red-brown goatskin.
(Einband Sammlung Lk 57).

(Einband Sammlung 30 Poet) in gold-tooled brown calf, embellished with coloured paint. Of later date is a fine architectural binding in brown calf, tooled in gold and decorated with silver and dark brown paint on Joannes Leo, *Description de l'Afrique* (Lyons, 1556: Einband Sammlung 6.11 Geogr. 2°: Fig. 61.15). The edges of this book are gilt and gauffered and the fore-edge is dated 1560.

Finally, I would like to mention two French blind-stamped bindings.

Fig. 61.14   Aesop, *Specchio di Esopo*, Rome, 1526 [and other works].
Bound in Paris by the Mansfeld binder in gold-tooled brown
calf decorated with coloured paint.
(Einband Sammlung 108 Qu.4°). (Lower cover).

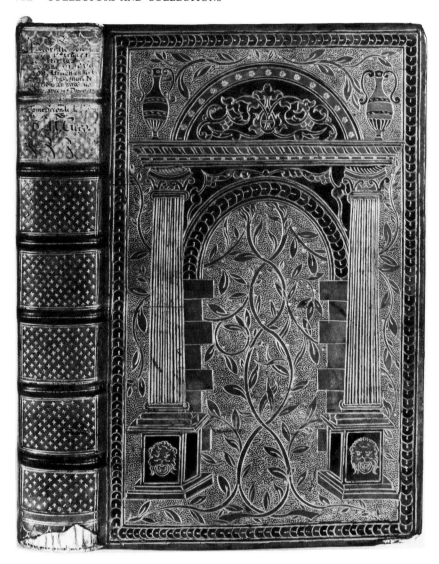

Fig. 61.15   Joannes Leo, *Description de l'Afrique*, Lyons, 1556.
Bound in 1560, probably in Paris, in gold-tooled brown calf
decorated with silver and dark brown paint.
(Einband Sammlung 6.11 Geogr. 2°).

Fig. 61.16   D. Erasmus, *Paraphrasis in Evangelium Matthei*, Paris, 1523.
Bound by Jean Norvis in blind-tooled brown calf.
(Einband Sammlung 1331.2 Th.).

One is decorated with two panels signed by the Paris binder Jean Norvis,
showing on the upper cover Bathsheba in her bath (signed 'Iehan Norvis')
and on the lower cover St Michael (signed 'I N'). Norvis' panels often
occur on duodecimos issued in Paris by Pierre Vidoue and this particular
pair has been found on several copies of Erasmus, *Paraphrasis in Evangelium Matthei*, printed in Paris by Vidoue in 1523. The library at Wolfenbüttel owns two copies of this edition so bound (Einband Sammlung 1331.2
Th.: Fig. 61.16, and C.21. 12° Helmst.). The other binding also has two
different panels; that on the lower cover consists of four vertical strips of
ornament, two of flies and two of four-petalled flowers, surrounded by a
floral border; the panel on the upper cover depicts St Yves holding an
open book and standing between two trees; it covers Ptolemy's Works in
Latin (Venice, 1493: Einband Sammlung 9.4 Astron. 2°: Fig. 61.17). This

St Yves panel also occurs on the binding of a manuscript at Corpus Christi College, Cambridge, in combination with a Saints' panel signed Julien des Jardins.

1. See 'List of works used,' nos. 19–30, also for literature mentioned below.
2. IA. 9898: *BMC* II, 558.
3. See article 16.
4. *Urkundenbuch des Hochstiftes Hildesheim*, I, no. 184, p. 165; see Taddey (List, no. 56), p. 28.
5. See Herbst (List, nos. 21, 25).
6. Königslutter, west of Helmstedt.
7. Johann von Brakel wrote and bound Cod. Guelf. Helmst. 547 and 533 (no inscription, but same hand); he bound Cod. Guelf. Helmst. 596 and Helmst. Qu. H. 62 (the latter has the date 1490).
8. List, no. 26.
9. Published by Herbst (List, no. 30), cols. 67–71.
10. Published by Herbst (List, no. 24), p. 359.
11. List, no. 22.
12. Illustrated in H. Lempertz, *Bilderhefte zur Geschichte des Buchhandels*, Cologne, 1853–65, X, pl. 6.

List of works used

1. J. G. R. Acquoy, *Het Klooster te Windesheim en zijn invloed*, Utrecht, 1875–80.
2. K. Bogumil, *Das Bistum Halberstadt im 12. Jahrhundert*, Cologne, 1972.
3. M. Buchberger (ed.), *Lexikon für Theologie und Kirche*, Freiburg, 1957–65.
4. J. J. H. Bücking, *Die Kunst des Buchbinders*, Stendal, 1785.
5. H. Bünting and J. Letzner, *Braunschweig-Lüneburgische Chronica*, Braunschweig, 1772.
6. H. Endres, 'Meister Ulrich Frenckel aus Hirschau' in *Festschrift H. Loubier*, Leipzig, 1923.
7. M. M. Foot, *The Henry Davis Gift: Studies in the History of Bookbinding*, vol. I, London, 1979, chapters 22 and 24 (and literature there).
8. F. Geldner, 'Bamberger und Nürnberger Lederschnittbände' in *Festschrift K. Schottenloher*, Munich, 1953.
9. E. P. Goldschmidt, *Gothic and Renaissance Bookbindings*, London, 1928.
10. E. P. Goldschmidt, 'Some Cuir-ciselé Bookbindings in English Libraries', *The Library*, 4th series, XIII (1933).
11. Y. A. Haase, 'Die Geschichte der Herzog August Bibliothek', *Wolfenbütteler Beiträge*, II (1973).
12. K. Haebler, *Rollen und Plattenstempel*, Leipzig, 1928–9.
13. M. Heimbucher, *Die Orden und Kongregationen der Katholischen Kirche*, Paderborn, 1933–34.
14. O. von Heinemann, *Die Handschriften der herzoglichen Bibliothek zu Wolfenbüttel. Abteilung I: Die Helmstedter Handschriften*, Wolfenbüttel, 1884–88.
15. O. von Heinemann, *Die herzogliche Bibliothek zu Wolfenbüttel*, Wolfenbüttel, 1894.
16. W. Heinemann, *Das Bistum Hildesheim im Kräftespiel der Reichs- und Terri-*

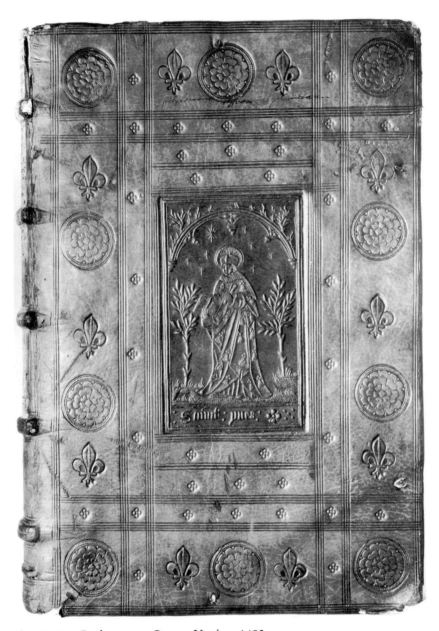

Fig. 61.17 Ptolemaeus, *Opera*, Venice, 1493.
Bound, possibly by Julien des Jardins, in blind-tooled brown
calf.
(Einband Sammlung 9.4 Astron. 2°).

torial-politik (Quellen und Darstellungen zur Geschichte Niedersachsens, 72), Hildesheim, 1968.

17. H. Helwig, *Handbuch der Einbandkunde*, Hamburg, 1953–55 (and relevant literature there).

18. H. Helwig, *Jenaer Buchbinder des 16. Jahrhunderts (Sammlung bibliothekswissenschaftlicher Arbeiten*, 46), Leipzig, 1937.

19. H. Herbst, *Alte deutsche Bucheinbände*, Braunschweig, 1926.

20. H. Herbst, *Braunschweigische Buchbinder des 16. Jahrhunderts (Sammlung bibliothekswissenschaftlicher Arbeiten*, 46), Leipzig, 1937.

21. H. Herbst, 'Das Benediktinerkloster Klus bei Gandersheim und die Bursfelder Reform' (*Beiträge zur Kulturgeschichte des Mittelalters und der Renaissance*, ed. W. Goetz, 50), Leipzig and Berlin, 1932.

22. H. Herbst, 'Der Braunschweigische Hofbuchbinder Lukas Weischner', *Jahrbuch der Einbandkunst*, I (1927).

23. H. Herbst, 'Erfurter Buchbinder des 15. Jahrhunderts', *Archiv für Buchbinderei*, XXVI (1926).

24. H. Herbst, 'Handschriften aus dem Benediktinerkloster Northeim' (*Studien und Mitteilungen zur Geschichte des Benediktiner-Ordens*, 50), Salzburg, 1932.

25. H. Herbst, 'Johannes von Brakel', *Archiv für Schreib- und Buchwesen*, IV (1930).

26. H. Herbst, 'Mittelalterliche Bücherverzeichnisse des Benediktinerklosters St. Blasius zu Northeim', *Archiv für Kunstgeschichte*, XIX (1928).

27. H. Herbst, 'Namenstempel und Namen von Buchbindern', *Zeitschrift für Bücherfreunde*, XXXIX (1935).

28. H. Herbst, 'Nürnberger Lederschnittbände' in *Die Bibliothek und ihre Kleinodien. Festschrift zum 250jähr Jubiläum der Leipziger Stadtbibliothek*, Leipzig, 1927.

29. H. Herbst, 'Wanderungen Erfurter Einbände', *Archiv für Buchbinderei*, XXVIII (1928).

30. H. Herbst, 'Zur Geschichte der Bibliothek des St. Blasiusklosters zu Northeim', *Braunschweigisches Magazin*, 1927, Nr. 5.

31. C. Hirsche, *Prolegomena zur einer neuen Ausgabe der Imitatio Christi*, Berlin, 1873.

32. M. J. Husung, 'Die Lederschnitt-Wappeneinbände des 15. Jahrhunderts', *Gutenberg Jahrbuch*, 1944–49.

33. M. J. Husung, 'Dreimal das gleiche mittelalterliche Lederschnittmotiv' in *Festschrift G. Leidinger*, Munich, 1930.

34. M. J. Husung, 'Geschichte des Bucheinbandes', Neu bearb. von F. A. Schmidt-Künsemüller, in *Handbuch der Bibliothekwissenschaft*, I, Wiesbaden, 1952.

35. M. J. Husung, 'Über den sogen. ''jüdischen Lederschnitt'' ' and 'Ein jüdischer Lederschnittkünstler' in *Soncino-Blätter*, I, Berlin, 1925–26.

36. K. Janicke, *Urkundenbuch des Hochstiftes Hildesheim*, Leipzig, 1896.

37. S. Kunze, *Geschichte des Augustiner-Klosters Hamersleben*, Quedlinburg, 1835.

38. E. Kyriss, *Die Einbände der Handschriften der Universitätsbibliothek Erlangen (Katalog der Handschriften der Universitätsbibliothek Erlangen, Band 6,2)*, Erlangen, 1936.

39. E. Kyriss, *Nürnberger Klostereinbände*, Bamberg, 1940.

40. E. Kyriss, *Verzierte gotische Einbände im alten deutschen Sprachgebiet*, Stuttgart, 1951–58.

41. J. B. Lauenstein, *Historia Diplomatica Episcopatus Hildesiensis*, Hildesheim, 1740.
42. G. W. von Leibniz, *Scriptores rerum Brunsvicensium*, Hanover, 1707–11, vol. III.
43. J. G. Leuckfeld, 'Antiquitates Northeimenses' in *Antiquitates Bursfeldenses*, Leipzig and Wolfenbüttel, 1713.
44. H. Loubier, *Der Bucheinband in alter und neuer Zeit*, Berlin and Leipzig, 1904.
45. H. A. Lüntzel, *Die ältere Diöcese Hildesheim*, Hildesheim, 1837.
46. H. A. Lüntzel, *Geschichte der Diöcese und Stadt Hildesheim*, Hildesheim, 1858.
47. W. Milde, 'Die Wolfenbütteler "Liberey-Ordnung" des Herzog Julius von 1572', *Wolfenbütteler Beiträge*, I (1972).
48. O. Mitius, *Fränkische Lederschnitteinbände des 15. Jahrhunderts (Sammlung bibliothekswissenschaftlicher Arbeiten, 28)*, Leipzig, 1909.
49. P. Needham, *Twelve Centuries of Bookbindings*, New York/London, 1979, chapter 21.
50. D.-E. Petersen, *Mittelalterliche Bucheinbände der Herzog August Bibliothek*, Wolfenbüttel, 1975.
51. A. Rhein, *Erfurter Buchbinder seit 500 Jahren (Festschrift zum 3. Reichsinnungstag des Buchbinder-Handwerks . . . in Erfurt)*, Erfurt, 1937.
52. F. A. Schmidt-Künsemüller, *Corpus der gotischen Lederschnitteinbände aus dem deutschen Sprachgebiet*, Stuttgart, 1980 (and literature there).
53. H. Schreiber-Dresden, 'Beiträge zur Erfurter Einbandforschung', *Archiv für Buchbinderei*, xxvii (1927).
54. P. Schwenke, 'Die Buchbinder mit dem Lautenspiel und mit dem Knoten' in *Festschrift K. Haebler*, Leipzig, 1919.
55. H. Sudendorf, *Urkundenbuch zur Geschichte der Herzöge von Braunschweig und Lüneburg und ihre Lande*, Göttingen, 1859–83.
56. G. Taddey, *Das Kloster Heiningen von der Gründung bis zur Aufhebung (Studien zur Germania Sacra, 47)*, Göttingen, 1966.
57. P. Volk, 'Die erste Fassung des Bursfelder *liber ordinarius*', *Ephemerides Liturgicae*, lvi (1942).
58. P. Volk, *Die Generalkapitel der Bursfelder Benediktiner-Kongregation*, Münster, 1928.
59. P. Volk, *Urkunden zur Geschichte der Bursfelder Kongregation*, Bonn, 1951.
60. W. Ziegler, *Die Bursfelder Kongregation in der Reformationszeit*, Münster, 1968.

All bindings illustrated in this article are in the Herzog August Bibliothek, Wolfenbüttel. I am grateful to the Herzog August Bibliothek for giving me permission to reproduce them here.

Part VII
PRESERVING THE PAST

The preceding Parts have been devoted almost exclusively to the history of decorated bookbinding. Decoration is not the only aspect of bookbinding that deserves consideration. But in order to be able to study the different components of a book—how it was made, what materials were used in its manufacture and how they were used—the book in all its original features needs to be available for scrutiny. The questions of what should be preserved, and why, are addressed in the articles that follow. In the first of these I have perhaps painted too bleak a picture. It was written ten years ago with the aim of provoking the audience of restorers and conservators at whom it was directed, and all adverse practices mentioned were based on observation; not all have been abandoned even now. It remains a sad truth that the binding historian of today still owes more to neglect than to enlightened conservation policy.

62 The Binding Historian and the Book Conservator
(1982)*

This title suggests that the binding historian and the book conservator are two separate people. This is, of course, not necessarily the case; ideally, every conservator would also be a binding historian and a bibliographer. That there is an antagonism between the bibliographer and textual critic on the one hand, and the conservator on the other was stated during a conference on the conservation of library materials in 1980 by David Foxon,[1] whose opening sentence, 'Bibliographical analysis depends on using evidence preserved in copies of a book to demonstrate how it was produced, but many sorts of vital evidence can be obliterated by conventional methods of repair or rebinding' was closely echoed by Christopher Clarkson who said, during the same conference, 'If left undisturbed, a text-block and its binding are of inestimable value to the development of bibliographical studies, while any encroachment by the restorer tends to lessen such value'.[2] If, as in this instance, both bibliographer and book conservator can agree on the vital importance of leaving the original evidence undisturbed, one has to ask why disasters of the kind I shall describe later do still happen, and why they happen so frequently. Why not leave well alone? The answer to this second question was intimated by Christopher Clarkson on the same occasion: 'Nonetheless certain conservation and restoration activities often have to be carried out to assure an object's stability and continued preservation'.[3] In other words, in a number of cases things cannot be left as they are if one wants them to continue to exist. Here the important distinction between public and private ownership should be made, as well as the possibly even more important distinction between public ownership as exercised by museums concerned with the preservation of objects for future generations, and that as exercised by libraries and archives where objects are preserved in order to be used. I will return to this matter of diverse and sometimes contradictory responsibilities later.

The first question, why do disasters happen, is perhaps most simply

* This paper is the edited and slightly expanded text of a talk given to the Institute of Paper Conservation on 29 January 1982. It was published in *The Paper Conservator*, VIII (1984), pp. 77–83.

Fig. 62.1 Finely rebound incunable

Fig. 62.2 Canvas binding

and most truthfully answered by identifying carelessness and a lack of knowledge as the chief culprits. I should add straightaway that this harsh judgement can be applied with equal justice to both bibliographers and conservators. Neither knows enough of the other discipline's requirements and techniques.

One could give many examples of the instances where carelessness and ignorance have resulted in the distortion or destruction of bibliographical evidence, but there is room here for only a few. They are not meant to rake up the mistakes of the distant and not so distant past, but rather to try to instill a sense of uneasiness, a feeling of alertness, an attitude of mistrust of the obvious solution, and, most important of all, a feeling for historical evidence and an awareness that the smallest detail can be of vital importance.

Nobody in his or her right mind is likely to rebind a seventeenth-century Bible in lavishly tooled and onlaid goatskin, bound by Samuel Mearne for one of Charles II's Royal Chapels. Even those with no knowledge at all of binding history can see that this is an artifact worth preserving. Today, with binders and conservators more aware of the value of original bindings, one need not have too much anxiety that a fifteenth- or early sixteenth-century blind-tooled binding would be destroyed. Whilst the great collectors in both England and France in the eighteenth and nineteenth centuries were eager to see the possibly rather tatty bindings on their incunabula replaced by the brightest and grandest of bindings that their own age could produce (Fig. 62.1), contemporary decorated bindings on most early printed books are now reasonably safe. On the other hand, a plain calf binding in a poor state of repair has fewer chances of survival, and a miserable-looking canvas binding (Fig. 62.2) has hardly

Fig. 62.3   Gold embossed paper
wrapper

Fig. 62.4   Blue-grey paper wrapper

any chance at all, notwithstanding the fact that eighteenth-century canvas bindings are now extremely rare, and, though they are nothing much to look at, show how tracts and school books were often issued. American canvas bindings of the eighteenth century are even scarcer, like the scruffy eighteenth-century American calf and sheepskin bindings, so many of which have been cheerfully rebound, while their importance as historical evidence was not even questioned. It is only recently that even binding historians have become interested in the cheaper end of the market, in the publishers' bindings or original paper wrappers in which so many books were first issued.

Only a very few binders nowadays (one hopes) would remove the colourful gold embossed paper wrappers from a pamphlet (Fig. 62.3), but one still has to ask what their reaction would be to a much more modest-looking, plain blue-grey specimen (Fig. 62.4). It is like this, however, that many pamphlets and tracts were issued in the eighteenth century, stabbed in plain or coloured paper wrappers; because they are not particularly flashy in appearance and are certainly fragile, they are now comparatively scarce. It does not take much imagination to see how our idea of the booktrade and the publishing trade would be distorted if none of these examples had survived. I want to go even a step further. Surely, one might say, a piece of brown paper used to wrap a bundle of papers found at Blickling Hall in Norfolk could be thrown away (Fig. 62.5). Perhaps, but it so happened that on this particular piece of brown wrapping paper, the bibliophile Thomas Rawlinson wrote the title (Fig. 62.6), and therefore this rather nasty brown paper provides the only evidence that its contents

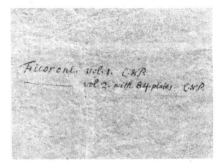

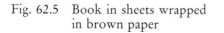

Fig. 62.5   Book in sheets wrapped   Fig. 62.6   MS inscription on
            in brown paper   brown paper

were once in his possession before they cast up at Blickling Hall. It tells us in this case even more: the brown paper hid a set of unbound sheets and most probably Rawlinson bought the work for Sir Richard Ellys, the theologian, whose library reached Blickling through his second wife's family. This may be an exceptional case, but it does show that one cannot be too careful before removing anything which may provide evidence for the history of a book and, in this case, the history of a collection.

Let us now consider some spines. Every sane person, having been asked to reback a set of *Philosophical Transactions* (1667–1704), once in the possession of Samuel Pepys and bound in brown calf with elaborately tooled spines (Fig. 62.7), will do his utmost to preserve these spines, but will a perfectly plain (though original) spine be preserved with equal care? Yet even a plain, undecorated and unlabelled spine can contribute to history: there can be traces of a label, perhaps a case of an early use of a label since lost; there may be traces of original lettering underneath a later label, providing evidence for early spine lettering.[4] Of course, not all spine labelling is original; on the contrary, late seventeenth- and eighteenth-century owners made a habit of having their older bindings lettered or provided with lettering pieces, and in some cases went so far as to have the whole spine of such a book re-tooled. It all contributes to the history of the book.

Other historical evidence may be removed with the spine. The modern shelfmark labels which most libraries are compelled to use to enable their staff to find books on the shelves are familiar to all. Most of them could be described as eyesores, but even eyesores can provide evidence for the history of a book, as is the case with an eighteenth-century German theological work which has the shelfmark label from a Jesuit College in Rotterdam (Fig. 62.8). Inside the book, the library stamp of the college and the shelfmark can be found on the fly-leaf, but without the fly-leaf,

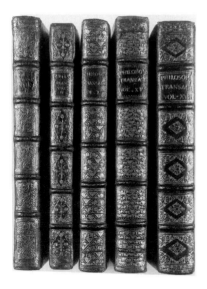

Fig. 62.7 Tooled calf spines on Pepys's *Philosophical Transactions*

Fig. 62.8 Shelfmark label on Jesuit owned book

the spine label would be the only indication of the provenance of this particular book. It can easily happen (usually through the over-enthusiastic application of leather dressing), that the shelfmarks on such spine labels become illegible; this is no reason for their removal. The shape of the labels may be characteristic enough to provide the clue as to which library the books once belonged.

A slightly more tricky problem arises when the label bearing a shelfmark obscures part of the tooling of a spine (Fig. 62.9). The temptation is to remove it, but it may identify the book as having come from a well-known collection (in this case that of the Duke of Portland). The 'obvious' solution, to lift the label and paste it inside the covers, is no solution at all: it would only lead the writer of the history of that particular library to believe that in some cases it was the habit of the librarian to have the shelfmark labels pasted inside the covers. Worse still, the book in question, because of the unorthodox position of its label, may never be recognized as having come from that library at all. Labels are an invaluable source of information, whether it is a binder's ticket or a library label. For example, tickets were used by Derôme le Jeune to sign the bindings made in his atelier, but a binder's ticket is by no means proof that the binding in which it occurs was in fact made by the man whose name is on the

Fig. 62.9   Shelfmark label over tooling

ticket. Apart from the complications of the kind which make the history of binding in eighteenth-century France such a maze and a quagmire (such as the habit of having a book forwarded by one man and finished by another, whilst the ticket is that of the head of the business who might have farmed the whole set of operations out to neighbouring workshops), there are good reasons to suspect that certain booksellers in the nineteenth century would paste a ticket from a dilapidated binding into a sound one in order to sell it as a signed piece of work. There are also cases where well-meaning but misguided librarians and conservators have wanted to preserve a ticket and, rather than lose it, have had it pasted into another book. Bookplates, whether of libraries or individuals, can supply equally valuable clues to the history of books and are equally liable to abuse and misuse.

When one comes to consider end-papers and paste-downs, one would hope that no-one would dream of disturbing a splendid gold-tooled leather doublure, nor would eighteenth-century paste-paper or embossed gilt end-papers be lightly discarded. Even plain vellum doublures and end-leaves are likely to be safe. But can the same be said of ordinary plain paper end-leaves? To disturb even the arrangement of the end-leaves can destroy an important indication of ownership as, in an extreme example, can happen with books once in the possession of Jean Grolier. In those cases where his name and motto were not tooled on the binding, as was the case with the books he owned before 1538, or where the original binding

Fig. 62.10   Norwich binder's inscription

Fig. 62.11   Mathewson binding inscription

has been replaced at a later date, the peculiar arrangement of the end-leaves (vellum paste-downs followed by a pair of white paper leaves, followed by a vellum leaf conjugate with the paste-down, followed by another pair of paper leaves) at the very least suggests the probability that Grolier once owned the book in question.

The paper of the end-leaves themselves can give an indication of the origin of a binding, though one has to be extremely careful with this; evidence provided by the paper can only be used to support an argument, hardly ever to clinch it. Manuscript notes on end-leaves can be of the greatest importance and almost always are of some interest. It need hardly be said that Coleridge's own annotations that cover the end-leaves and margins of copies of the first editions of his poems should be preserved come what may, nor should it be necessary to point out that a manuscript note on the paste-down of a seventeenth-century book stating that it was 'New bound' in Norwich in 1665 (Fig. 62.10) is of interest to the binding historian. However, a loose fly-leaf which carries an inscription recording that the book it came out of was bound by Mathewson in February 1725/6 for four shillings per volume (Fig. 62.11), is rendered virtually valueless as evidence because it can no longer be related to the book to which it belonged. This type of 'detached' evidence can, in fact, become positively dangerous when a binder, looking for eighteenth-century paper to use as end-leaves for a repaired book, decides to use it.

Manuscript notes denoting provenance are not limited to presentation inscriptions nor to names of individuals or country houses. A shelfmark, if it is distinctive enough or if it belongs to a known collection (and most shelfmarks are potentially distinctive), can indicate where the book came from. In the British Library, the early shelfmarks indicate whether a book belonged to Sir Hans Sloane, the old Royal Library, the King's Library or the Grenville Collection. Library stamps in the same Library's collections can indicate (by their colour and shape) whether a book was donated, purchased or came in by copyright, when it arrived in the library, whether it belonged to the foundation collections, or whether it came later from, for example, Sir Joseph Banks. There are numerous examples where the history of a library can be reconstructed from the number and sequence of the pressmarks in the books. Pepys's library at Magdalene College, Cambridge, is a good example. Yet all this information is lost when a binder discards an end-leaf, and it should not be forgotten that even the absence of a shelfmark may be significant. Transcribing the ownership notes or pressmarks is of course no solution, not only because there is the risk of wrong transcription, but mainly because the actual handwriting, the arrangement of the figures and letters, even the colour of the ink, can all provide evidence. Not only end-leaves with manuscript notes are of interest. From time to time one finds fragments of printing (binder's waste) used as paste-downs. It has happened that unknown incunable fragments have turned up in this way, but at the very least such fragments can provide a date postquam for the binding.

Not only can evidence be removed altogether, it can also be so disturbed that it is either lost or tells the wrong story. For example, the habit of many modern bookbinders of using old paper for the end-leaves of a book which they have rebound can lead to all sorts of confusion. Decorated (and sometimes signed) end-papers are often moved from book to book, thus upsetting all theories about their origin and use. Ownership notes from one book can turn up in another; manuscript pressmarks from a book in a particular library can suddenly occur on the fly-leaf of a totally different and unconnected book. Even the partial evidence provided by the paper itself can point in a totally wrong direction once the paper has been used in a different book. The lesson for the binding historian therefore is never to believe evidence provided by the end-papers of an obviously rebound book, or face the disillusion of finding that what look like and could have been the original end-leaves are in fact interlopers from another source.

Edges can cause problems as well. It is known that many fore-edge paintings are fakes. There are examples of genuine seventeenth- and eighteenth-century fore-edge paintings,[5] sometimes painted under gold, sometimes signed and dated, but many an elderly mother-in-law in the last century was made useful by being put in the back room of the bookshop and told to deploy her talent for sketching by producing washy watercolours on the edges of earlier books. But even then, one must not assume that such work is expendable and can therefore be lost through resewing without a thought. It is part of the history of the book, fake or original, and should therefore be preserved. There is the sad tale of a very faint example of what is probably a medieval fore-edge painting on a late

Fig. 62.12   Fore-edge title

Fig. 62.13   Over-cleaned title on
vellum spine

thirteenth-century manuscript. The manuscript needed re-sewing; the painting was so faint that its existence was not noticed; the edges of the leaves were shifted slightly in the course of rebinding, and now only traces of shapes and colours can be discerned. This is an extreme case, but one must be careful not to overlook the less conspicuous examples. Many medieval and a number of sixteenth-century books have their titles or pressmarks, or both, written on the fore-edge (Fig. 62.12). This was done because books used to be stored with their fore-edges towards the reader, either flat in piles in the medieval period, with the title written along the fore-edge or, later, when books were first stored upright in bookcases, again with their fore-edges outwards, with the title written across the fore-edge. Resewing inevitably disturbs the edges and can therefore obscure one of the sources of evidence of a book's provenance or even of its date. Of course, ploughing the edges removes the evidence altogether and can never be justified. The fact that an edge has been marbled or sprinkled can tell us something of the history of a book. Once again, Samuel Pepys's library can give us an example. At the start of his collecting career, Pepys had the edges of his books sprinkled; in the middle period he favoured marbled edges, and at the end of his life he reverted to sprinkling, often with red and brown colouring. Ploughing the edges of these books in the course of rebinding would remove these clues to the history of the collection. The practice of some trade binders to plough more and more off the edges of a book until whole portions of the text are unreadable is too deplorable to mention here.

A good case for taking special care in cleaning books can be made where there is a manuscript title, either on the spine, a normal habit, especially on vellum bindings of all ages and all too easily removed in cleaning (Fig. 62.13), or in the top compartment of the upper cover, often found on German calf or hide bindings of the fifteenth century.

The location of the title on a book is of significance, whether it occurs on one of the edges, the spine or the boards, for it indicates a habit of storing books—those on the boards indicate storage on lectern-like shelves. It is also potentially interesting to study the manuscript titles written across the spines of books because the handwriting itself may show up an early (or later) owner. In the Herzog August Bibliothek at Wolfenbüttel, a great many of the vellum and pigskin bindings have the titles written either directly on the covering material or on paper labels: all are in the same handwriting, which has now been proved to be that of their original owner, Duke August himself.

I mentioned earlier the possibility of distorting evidence. One very common example is that of repainted bindings. In France and in the Southern Netherlands in the mid-sixteenth century, owners were not satisfied with gold-tooled decoration only, but had the ribbon patterns formed by the tooling and the open tools themselves filled with silver and coloured paints. Unfortunately, in many cases this paint has flaked off and later owners often had these bindings repainted, sometimes so crudely as to obscure the original shape of the tools. There are also less obvious and sometimes hardly discernible cases of re-tooling and over-tooling, which again often spoil the evidence provided by the exact shape of the tool, and thus make the identification of the individually engraved tools of a binder or a bindery impossible. Distorting the exact shape of a tool by tooling over it ruins all chance of identification.

Having dealt with some of the trouble that restoring and rebinding can lead to insofar as immediately visible evidence is concerned, I would now like to turn to the destruction or distortion of the hidden 'invisible' evidence. For instance, the boards of a book are most usually hidden by the covering materials and paste-downs, but can have a story to tell. Wooden boards have very often been re-used over the ages (Fig. 62.14). Wood was comparatively expensive and, if not attacked by woodworm or rot, the wooden boards were virtually indestructible. It is clear from the pattern of lacing-in holes and tunnels made into the wood that the boards were often used more than once; that they were turned round or cut down to fit a smaller book. This, though it can be confusing for the unprepared, is well known and, with the help of X-rays, clearly discern-

Fig. 62.14   A re-used wooden board of a German binding.

ible. What is less common is that paste boards, millboards or straw boards
have been re-used. Being comparatively cheap and readily available, these
boards were as a rule discarded when a book was rebound. However, one
does come across misguided binders who, out of a wrong sense of history,
have kept old boards from disbound books, not to re-use them on the
same book, but to use them on other books. This can create havoc among
the theories as to when and where certain kinds of board were first used.

A different and equally disturbing point arises over the presence of
worm holes in the leaves of a book as well as the boards. The position
of the holes can be very helpful in establishing the original composition
of a book and the chronology of the different bindings it may once have
had. Tampering with them, specially in the way of invisible repairs, can
either obscure evidence or lead to the wrong conclusions being drawn.

Such sad tales could be continued for a long time, and the examples I
have given are far from exhaustive. However, I hope that by now the
point will have been taken, and I would now like to try to identify the
basic problem which is at the root of all these mishaps. Since the indis-
criminate rebinding of the nineteenth century, we have come a long way.
Binders and restorers are more alive to the claims of history, and librarians

and book owners in general know that there are other ways to make a book in bad condition re-usable than by rebinding it. One of the problematic questions is: where does the responsibility lie? Is it the owner of the book who, in the practical sense, has only himself to please, though it can be argued that morally his responsibility reaches much further? Is it the librarian or archivist who has to reconcile the irreconcilable in being compelled to preserve for the future the treasures of the past, whilst making them available for use in the present? Is it the binder or conservator who is given the contradictory tasks of restoring a book so that it is fit for use, while preserving all the historical evidence undisturbed?

In my opinion, everybody who has a hand in the preservation, conservation, keeping, repairing or any process affecting the physical existence of a book is responsible. The responsibility must be shared. Librarians' and owners' orders intelligently given should be intelligently queried and interpreted; if possible, carried out or, if need be, refused; certainly discussed. One hopes that this now happens more frequently than it used to. However, the lack of knowledge, the lack of care and the lack of communication on both sides is still staggering. I can count the book conservators who know enough about the history of binding not to fall into the obvious traps on the fingers of both hands, and the number of librarians and book owners who know about and understand binding and restoration techniques is not much, if at all, larger. This would not matter so much if each side were prepared to listen and to talk to the other. I have learned more in conversation and argument with binders than in reading most binders' manuals (always with the exception of Bernard Middleton's excellent book on the history of English binding technique).[6] Colleges of arts and crafts teach binding and restoration techniques, but no binding history to speak of, let alone bibliography. Universities and colleges of librarianship teach bibliography, too little binding history and practically no conservation techniques. One cannot blame people for not knowing enough, but one can blame them for not wanting to know. It is a sad state of affairs that lack of money and lack of understanding should make it so difficult for those who teach, as well as for those who want to learn, to impart and to acquire the knowledge necessary to preserve the book as an historical object and to recognize what is important to preserve.

1. David Foxon, 'Priorities in Book Conservation 3: A Bibliographer's View', *The Conservation of Library and Archive Materials and the Graphic Arts*, Cambridge, 1980, p. 146.
2. Christopher Clarkson, 'Priorities in Book Conservation 6: Priorities in Book Conservation', *The Conservation of Library and Archive Materials and the Graphic Arts*, Cambridge, 1980, p. 154.

3. Ibid., p. 154.
4. Although 1660 is commonly given as the date by which spine lettering was generally in use, there are Italian examples that date from the first half of the sixteenth century and Paris workshops practised lettering directly onto the spines only a little later. The earliest English example, by Williamson of Eton, dates from 1604.
5. For medieval painted edges see article 64 below.
6. Bernard C. Middleton, *A History of English Craft Binding Technique*, London, 1978.

Acknowledgements

The photographs for Figs. 62.1, 62.3, 62.5, 62.6, 62.12 and 62.13 in this article are reproduced by permission of the National Trust. That for Fig. 62.7 is reproduced by permission of the Master and Fellows of Magdalene College, Cambridge. All, with the exception of Figs. 62.7 and 62.14, were taken by Nicolette Hallet.

63 Preserving Books and their History

(1987)*

It is not unusual for librarians and historians of the book to blame the nineteenth and early twentieth centuries for the destruction of many early bookbindings. Institutions and private collectors alike are scolded for the wholesale rebinding of manuscripts and early printed books, and it is indeed striking that those libraries that were short of funds during the previous and present centuries still contain a wealth of medieval and renaissance bindings, often frail or dilapidated, but in their original state. Those institutions that managed to attract generous benefactions now display much polished calf or straight-grain morocco, finely decorated, often in suitably 'antique' styles, proudly featuring leather or silk doublures or colourful leather joints.

The tendency among well-off collectors and bibliophiles to have their prize possessions clothed and embellished by the best craftsmen of their day goes back much further. We do not know what state Grolier's copy of the 1476 Jenson edition of Pliny's *Historia naturale* was when he acquired it, but we do know that he took it to one of the best binders in Paris to have it put in brown goatskin, tooled in gold to a design of interlacing ribbons and solid tools, surrounded by an arabesque border, so fashionable in the late 1530s and early 1540s.[1] The original binding of Mahieu's copy of the *Hypnerotomachia Poliphili* (Venice, 1499) cannot have been totally ruined, nor can the book have been unbound since its pages are still in pristine condition, but nevertheless, he had it rebound by Claude (de) Picques in dark blue goatskin with an onlaid panel of pale brown and a border stained black and decorated in gold to an arabesque design with hatched and solid tools.[2] The results in both cases are wonderful, almost certainly much more aesthetically pleasing than the plain or blind-tooled leather that originally covered the then wooden boards, but the evidence of how these incunabula had originally been bound has disappeared.

During the second half of the eighteenth century a number of German bookbinders emigrated to England. It was known that the book lovers of

---

* *Bookbinder*, I, 1987, pp. 5–8.

London had their treasures bound in goatskin and appreciated the talents of a high-class finisher, while back home even the Princely libraries were seldom decked out in anything more luxurious than calf. Baumgarten, Kalthoeber, Walther, Staggemeier and Welcher all produced splendid work during the last quarter of the eighteenth century, though some of the books inside the lavishly-tooled red and blue morocco were printed one or more centuries earlier.

Thomas Grenville's collection of incunabula was famous already during his lifetime and Panizzi, then keeper of Printed Books and later Principal Librarian of the British Museum, secured them for the nation's library. Many were rebound by Roger Payne, Charles Hering and Charles Lewis: very fine bindings in their own right and a joy to handle, but one cannot help a slight feeling of historical loss. King George III was so much interested in bookbinding that he had his own bindery in Buckingham House which he is reputed to have visited at the most inconvenient moments.[3] There his 42-line Bible was dressed in blue morocco and decorated with finely-cut fleurons and dots.[4] Larger Gothic-style tools were held to be more suitable for the embellishment of the double boards of his Seneca, *Opera omnia* (Naples, 1475).[5] One wonders what was there before. In Paris in the nineteenth century, Bauzonnet, Capé, Niedrée, Petit, Thouvenin and many others rebound earlier books by order of their patrons.

But should we only blame the past? Some private collectors of today prefer a modern designed binding or even a glossy trade binding to the fading tree calf of their eighteenth-century first editions. Many libraries and institutions still rebind their deteriorating stock. Their argument that these books are read (and photocopied) to shreds and need more protection than can be provided by their original binding is a strong one, but is it not used too easily and too often?

The private collector, who has no obligations to the public and for whom excessive use cannot be a valid argument, still sends his early bindings to be touched up, sophisticated and in extreme cases re-tooled or re-painted. The result may look better, but is that sufficient reason for tampering with the structure or adding modern materials?

What is it that a book or binding historian values and that binders and restorers, almost always on command from librarians or owners, remove or distort? Virtually any action that changes the original condition of book or binding can be said to distort or destroy historical evidence. This is obviously not a practical attitude. A book consisting of paper with a pH of 4, with holes in the title-page, with torn and chipped edges, with badly broken sewing resulting in loose pages and sections, and bound in rotted sheep over crumbling boards, can obviously not be kept in its original state if one wants it to survive, and I would not advocate the maxim that all action is bad. Too much action, however, certainly is, and so is the wrong kind of action.

In the previous article[6] I set out a lengthy catalogue of incidents where the wrong action could lead or has led to the distortion or destruction of evidence concerning the book and its history. Accidents of this kind often happen with the best intentions and are largely due to lack of knowledge, lack of understanding or lack of care. What then to look out for?

In the scope of an article I cannot mention all elements I have found to be of importance for the study of the book, its binding and its history, let alone those that have not (yet) struck me as such, but I hope that a choice of aspects, which may not be totally obvious to all but which are nevertheless of historical or bibliographical interest, will convey the basic message that all evidence, however small and however hidden, is potentially valuable.

Conservators and binders who have studied medieval and post-medieval book structures and who have written and lectured in great detail on various aspects of the book and its constituent parts,[7] have made an invaluable contribution to the knowledge of librarians and binding historians. Their daily practical work increases their experience in a way that leaves 'theoretical' historians gasping with envy. Any binder, any restorer, any conservator has one tremendous advantage over any librarian or book historian.

When Graham Pollard studied the construction of early medieval bookbindings, he realized that neither the British Library nor the Bodleian Library would be prepared to disbind their manuscripts to help him in his research. He had to make do with X-ray photography and—though at first not easy to interpret—these X-rays taught him a great deal about the boards and the lacing-in patterns of the bindings he studied.[8] What X-rays do not show is what materials have been used and how. When taking a book down for repairing or rebinding, the binder or conservator is in a position to discover more about the original construction, about the materials and about the techniques used to apply these materials, than any historian who studies the book before it reaches the binder's bench, let alone those who see it after it has been restored.

Paper and vellum sometimes show blind impressions made by printers' furniture. Too much beating or pressing obliterates these impressions. Wormholes in paper and boards can help to establish the original composition of the book, as well as give some indication as to when the boards were attached. Sewing or stabbing holes can teach us much about methods of sewing. Fragments of sewing thread show what materials were being used and at what time. The presence of original cords or thongs can indicate when and where or under what circumstances certain materials were being used and how they were being used. They can show, for example, when and where and under what circumstances single leather thongs replaced alum-tawed split thongs; when and where raised cords were used, whether double or single or alternating; when the practice of sawing-in or recessing cords first started and for what kinds of books it became popular; which books were thought fit to be sewn on flat vellum thongs and where this habit flourished; or how many cords or thongs were thought necessary for various sizes of books at various times. One can also see what the sewing thread was made of and how it passed round, between or over the thongs or cords; whether there were thongs or cords in the first place or whether the thread itself linked the various sections together; how the kettle stitches were formed; whether and how often each cord or thong was circled at each sewing station; and when and where the custom of sewing several sections at a time started and how it developed.

Careful observation can teach us about the habits of rounding and backing, when these practices started and where; how the shape of the round changed with time; when square books were the norm and when the spine took on the shape of a mushroom or a quarter circle; how the amount of rounding and backing varied from place to place and even sometimes from binder to binder.

The variety and use of lining materials are equally fascinating. The vellum manuscript and printed waste that can be found giving strength to boards or spines can at best produce unknown texts or editions and at least provide a date *postquam* for the binding. How these lining materials were used, in what shape and in what quantity; when paper replaced vellum; when canvas or linen or mull was first introduced and where; when, where and with what the boards were lined; when the hollow back was first thought of and in what ways it was constructed, can all be explained by looking carefully and over a period of time at a sufficiently large number of deteriorated books. All these details can give us insight into workshop practices and into the social and economic circumstances that dictated these practices. It is well known that the increase in book production following the invention of printing had repercussions in the binding trade. The mechanisation of printing and binding techniques in the nineteenth century changed the whole attitude to book production and even to book purchasing. But equally, increases in book production in the second half of the eighteenth century necessitated the speeding-up of binding processes and a consequent change in techniques and habits. It has often been suggested that the emergence of false headbands, for example, was a direct result of this, which is no doubt the case. But it was not the first time that this particular economy had been thought of: false headbands were already used in Germany during the sixteenth century. Much of what has been said above about thongs, cords and sewing thread can equally be applied to headbands. Core material as well as sewing materials changed over the ages, and methods of sewing and tying down varied considerably from place to place. Patterns of lacing both cords and headbands in to the boards have been the subject of research and a wide variety has been recorded, ranging from triangularly-shaped tunnels in Anglo-Saxon (pre-Conquest) boards, via straight grooves of varying lengths in which the thongs could be pegged down in the middle ages, to parallel or staggered pairs of holes in limp vellum or pasteboard through which the thongs or cords were pulled that have been in use from the sixteenth century onwards.

The variety of the boards themselves must be obvious to every binder who has worked on early books, and it may have struck him how often wooden boards show signs of having been re-used over centuries. Fifteenth- or sixteenth-century leather can be found to cover a wooden board that has been turned round, while near the fore-edge traces can be seen of the kind of tunnels that were common several centuries earlier. It seems that pasteboard was not used in England before the first quarter of the sixteenth century, but an earlier form of it, consisting of layers of vellum glued together, may not have been as unusual as we now think. Leather boards are now very rare, but how many have perished in rebinding? When was millboard first introduced, and were pasteboard and millboard replaced by strawboard, or were all three used in parallel but for different kinds of binding? Every rotten board that is thrown unthinkingly into the bin can potentially lose us yet another clue to the practices of the past.

Every end-leaf that is being replaced can remove untold evidence of the book and its history. End-leaves are well-known hosts to binders' tickets or stamps, bookplates, ownership inscriptions, manuscript notes, library labels, library stamps, earlier shelfmarks and many other signs of provenance. Their material, be it vellum or paper, plain or decorated, their arrangement, and their watermarks can all contribute to our knowledge of when the book was bound, where and even by or for whom. Removing or altering any of this evidence leads to loss of knowledge.

Lettering pieces, labels or inscriptions on spines or covers can tell us something both of the provenance of the book and of earlier storage habits. Inscriptions on the fore-edge can do the same. Any treatment of the edges, be it decorative or informative, is invariably altered or distorted by re-sewing and destroyed by trimming. Covering materials, whether lavishly onlaid and tooled leather, plain vellum, canvas, or paper, can provide information about publishing and booktrade history, as well as about the time and place of binding. The way these materials have been treated and used, how they have been turned in, whether they have been lined and, of course, whether and how they have been decorated, can divulge workshop practices as well as indicate local fashions or the taste of individual collectors.

How to preserve all this evidence in its almost infinite variety? Books, when used, must be in a fit state for handling, and I do not have the answer to the perennial problem of how to preserve for the future the evidence of the past, while making it available for study in the present. This is a cleft stick in which all librarians and conservators are caught and from which I see no universally safe route of escape. All I can plead for is infinite care and patience in observing what evidence there is and equal care in attempting to keep as much as possible *in situ*, or to replace it after necessary treatment: to re-use the old sewing holes; to imitate the sewing structure, but only if the original has perished beyond redemption; to re-use—if at all possible—the original boards and lining materials; to re-use lacing-in grooves or holes; to preserve the spine or its fragments; to save and re-use lettering pieces, labels, tickets, bookplates, and always in the position where they were found; never to discard end-leaves if they can be saved nor to replace them with other 'old' paper from another source; to re-use the covers if not totally rotted away; in short, to keep as much as possible and in a way as faithful to the original as can be done. If saving proves impossible, photographic records or careful drawings are better than nothing.

Financial considerations will in many cases force librarians to take the cheapest option to preserve the text at the cost of the book as a physical object. The choice whether to spend a given sum on keeping a number of texts by microfilming them, or on preserving one object with all its historical and bibliographical evidence cannot be easy, nor should it be made lightly. Questions of importance of texts versus the value of (what may be considered) archaeological specimens will have to be balanced with great care: both contribute to knowledge.

Loss, alas, will be inevitable, but we should strive first of all to recognize what there is to lose and then do our utmost to keep it to an absolute minimum.

1. H. M. Nixon, *Bookbindings from the Library of Jean Grolier*, London, 1965, no. 70.
2. W. Y. Fletcher, *Foreign Bookbindings in the British Museum*, London, 1896, pl. xix. There is now some doubt as to whether Claude (de) Picques was indeed responsible for all bindings hitherto attributed to him. The tools used on these bindings link with those found on royal bindings for Henri II (when Gommar Estienne was royal binder) and on those for François II and Charles IX (when Claude (de) Picques held the office). It is possible that they all came from the atelier of an (anonymous) Paris finisher who was employed by both royal binders.

3. E. Howe, *The London Bookbinders 1780–1806*, London, 1950, p. 60.
4. H. M. Nixon, *Royal English Bookbinders in the British Museum*, London, 1957, pl. 16a.
5. *Ibid*, pl. 16b.
6. First published as 'The Binding Historian and the Book Conservator', *The Paper Conservator*, VIII, 1984 (published 1986), pp. 77–83. See article 62 above.
7. A few names immediately come to mind: Chris Clarkson, Michael Gullick, Bernard Middleton, Nicholas Pickwoad, Roger Powell and Janos Szirmai. Others, both in this country and abroad, have done equally valuable work and I beg their forgiveness for not mentioning them here.
8. G. Pollard, 'Some Anglo-Saxon Bookbindings', *The Book Collector*, XXIV (1975), pp. 130–59. Unfortunately, in some of the drawings of the X-rays the boards are reversed.

64 Medieval Painted Book Edges
(1989)*

Medieval painted book edges may be not as rare as would first appear. Paintings of the fourteenth and fifteenth centuries, especially those made in Italy and the Low Countries, often show apostles and saints holding books, either open, or closed with the upper cover uppermost and the fore-edge facing outwards. Several painters of the period went into enough detail to show that the covers of the books were frequently elaborately decorated—though it is of course impossible to see whether the gold that embellishes the covers was tooled or painted. They often show clasps and how these were fastened, and in many cases the edges of the leaves display decorative patterns. I have seen a number of paintings where the meticulous artist has made it quite clear that the decoration of the edges was the result of paint and not of gilding and gauffering.[1] Many Italian paintings show edges striped in red and gold or black and gold, similar to those that are still found in the sixteenth century,[2] some have elegant scroll work, while others display dots or zig-zag patterns of the kind that can be seen on several of the edges described below. It is not too fanciful to assume that these artists were painting what they saw, and the surviving evidence of the books themselves bears out that the habit of decorating the edges, certainly of the grander illuminated manuscripts, was not limited to Italy or the Low Countries, nor to the fourteenth and fifteenth centuries. I have seen painted edges on manuscripts dating from the tenth century onwards and produced in Greece, Italy, France, Germany, Switzerland, the Netherlands and England. It is not always easy to judge whether the edge decoration is contemporary with the manuscript itself; in some cases the manuscript was obviously bound or rebound at a later date, at which time the edges were decorated. In the discussion that follows I have tried to indicate, whenever possible, the relation between the manuscript, the binding and the edge painting.

Before embarking on a description of the edges themselves, I want to make the limitations of this study clear. First of all, it must be called 'work in progress'. I am convinced that many more examples of medieval

---

* *Studies in Book Making and Conservation in Honour of Roger Powell*, (forthcoming).

painted edges can and will be found so that the examples described here are just that: examples of different patterns. They do not pretend to be anything like a comprehensive listing. Secondly, I have limited myself to examples I have actually seen.[3] Thirdly, all examples described here are of European origin; I have not looked eastward. Fourthly, I have not gone beyond the fifteenth century. The main reason for this decision is that there is so much material from the sixteenth century onwards that it deserves separate treatment.

The painted edges that I have seen can be divided according to their designs into four categories: those with simple abstract patterns, those with more elaborate scrollwork (including a small group of flower patterns), those that display an indication of ownership in the form of a coat of arms, and those that show pictorial representation. All my examples occur on illuminated manuscripts; with four exceptions, these manuscripts are written on vellum. Originally, in most cases, the edges of the leaves would have been flush with the edges of the boards. Unhappily, the majority of the manuscripts described here have been rebound: only 21 out of 52 remain in an early binding. Rebinding, or rather resewing, has meant that the edges have shifted, to a greater or lesser degree, which makes the observation and identification of the pattern not an easy task. The late nineteenth- and early twentieth-century custom of heavy rounding and backing or, worse, the later twentieth-century habit of putting the sections on meeting guards have further obscured matters. In one case, a lavishly illuminated Flemish Psalter of the late thirteenth century (BL MS Royal 2.B.iii), the edges shifted to such an extent when the manuscript was rebound in the nineteenth century that the traces of paint are too faint to be distinguished as a pattern. It is probable that the edges were re-gilt when the manuscript was rebound, which further hides the painting. Nor is it possible to see whether whatever paint there was, was applied when the manuscript was first written and bound or whether the edge decoration was added later.[4]

The edges that show simple abstract patterns can be divided into three groups based on dots, circles and straight lines. The simplest pattern I have seen consists of black dots, irregularly spaced on the fore-edge and displayed in a zig-zag pattern on the bottom edge. The top edge shows faint traces of a linear zig-zag pattern in yellow. The decoration is difficult to see, not only because the manuscript, a Flemish fifteenth-century Book of Hours (BL Egerton MS 1147), has been rebound in the nineteenth century, but at some time in its history, probably at the time of rebinding, the edges were stained red, obscuring the original decoration. It is interesting to note that in a painting by a follower of Quentin Massys (1465/6–1530), showing St Luke portraying the Virgin and Child, there is a shelf of books lying and standing with the fore-edges towards the beholder, displaying an irregularly spaced zig-zag pattern of black dots.

A more sophisticated pattern shows circles with ornaments. The examples I have seen occur on Greek illuminated manuscripts. One is a tenth-century manuscript in Greek of the Four Gospels, Acts of the Apostles, Catholic Epistles, and Epistles of St Paul (BL Add. MS 28815). The binding consists of wooden boards covered in worn pink velvet. The lower cover shows traces of five bosses and four pairs of clasp attachments, while there are traces of pins for the clasps to fasten on, on the edges of the upper board. On the upper cover, silver-gilt plates have been nailed. Two strips, one along the top and one along the bottom of the cover, show repoussé half-length figures of the four Evangelists, St Peter and St Paul. Two strips running lengthwise along the edges of the board have scenes displaying the overthrow of the heretics Nestor and Noetus with inscriptions in Greek. The centre panel has repoussé figures of Christ in majesty enthroned between the Virgin and St John, surrounded by the symbols of the four Evangelists and two angels' heads.[5] The manuscript was re-sewn when it was re-backed. The edges are decorated in black and it is possible that the bottom edge once had an inscription which it is now impossible to see. The top and the fore-edges are painted with circles containing a St Andrew's cross, and between the circles are ornaments also shaped like a St Andrew's cross with triangular pinnacles in the top and bottom V formed by the cross. The edges of the second Greek manuscript, the Four Gospels written by Constantine, priest and notary, in the monastery of St Demetrius the Martyr in 1326 (BL Add. MS 11838), are painted in red and black and also show large circles, this time divided into segments by semi-circular bands. Between the circles are triangular leafy ornaments with serrated outlines connected by a twisted rope. The manuscript has a Greek binding of thick, not grooved, wooden boards covered in blind-tooled brown goatskin. The flat spine is lined with a canvas-like material. There are metal bosses at the corners and in the centre of the lower cover, and traces of two pairs of clasps, while holes for two pins can be seen in the edges of the upper board. Raised headcaps protect the four rows of silk headbands in a pink, green and white herringbone stitch. I am not sure about the age of the binding; it is possible that both it and the edge decoration date from the sixteenth century and should not be included here.[6]

Turning westward, we find linear patterns composed of St Andrew's crosses, diamonds or zig-zags. A simple drawing in black of small St Andrew's crosses can be found on the edges of a fifteenth-century collection of Hymns with the Litany, prayers and calendar in Latin (BL MS Harley 5765). Though the manuscript was rebound in the early eighteenth century, there is no reason to believe that the decoration is of later date than the manuscript. Another simple linear pattern of crossed and parallel lines with triangles, this time in red, occurs on the edges of a Psalter written *c.* 1210 at Worcester (Bodley, MS Magdalen College, Lat.100). It is bound in fourteenth-century pink-dyed sheepskin over wooden boards, with traces of two pairs of clasps on thongs with the catches very near the fore-edge of the lower board. It is possible that the crossed lines that decorate the edges of the leaves are in fact crossed arrows or spears. A northern English manuscript of religious poems and prose, written on paper in the first half of the fifteenth-century (BL Add. MS 37049), was rebound in 1969 and put on guards, with the usual sad consequences for the structure of the book. The edges have moved noticeably, but a criss-cross or diamond pattern in red and black, possibly formed by rows of zig-zag lines, can still be seen.

Diamond and zig-zag patterns are not uncommon. Second-hand evidence is supplied by Antonio Vivarini and Giovanni d'Alemagna who worked in Italy in the 1440s and who painted St Jerome holding a book, the edges of which are gilt and painted with a network of crossing lines in red, showing little red crosses in each diamond. A painting of 'Rhetoric' by Joos van Wassenhove, an immigrant from the Netherlands who worked for the Duke of Urbino during the second half of the fifteenth century, shows a book with edges painted to a bold design of two crossing zig-zag lines. The same pattern in black with possibly a trace of red adorns the edges of *Leges Angliae* (BL MS Harley 947). However, as this manuscript dates from the sixteenth century it falls outside the scope of this article. An earlier example is BL Stowe 941, Charters referring to the Sacristy of the Priory of St Neots, Co. Huntingdon, of 1286. It was rebound in red velvet, probably in the eighteenth century, and it belonged to Thomas Astle (1735–1803), Keeper of the Records in the Tower of London. The edges are painted in red and green in a single zig-zag pattern taking up the total width of the edge. One or two single zig-zags in red and black, forming diamonds and triangles, occur on the edges of *Tractatus de legibus et consuetudinibus regni Anglie tempore H. regis secundi* by Ranulfus de Glanville, written in England in the first half of the thirteenth century (MS Bodley 564). The manuscript has been rebound in blind-tooled calf, but the original fourteenth- or fifteenth-century wooden boards have been preserved. The edges of a manuscript *Dialogus Bartholomei Exoniensis episcopi contra Iudeos*, written in England early in the thirteenth century and bound in ?fourteenth-century alum tawed sheepskin over wooden boards (MS Bodley 482), have been decorated with two zig-zag ribbons outlined in black and painted green. There are black roundels in the diamonds and triangles formed by the zig-zags. The binding shows traces of one clasp, with the catch on the edge of the lower board, and of a chain attachment in the bottom right-hand corner of the upper cover.

Sometimes the zig-zag lines on the edges of the leaves are combined with ornamental leaves or floral shapes. The edges of an early thirteenth-century Psalter from Northern France (BL MS Harley 2895), rebound and put on guards in 1973, show a pattern closely similar to that seen on the edges of books in a painting by the Master of the Imagine Dominicane (1320–50), now in the Accademia in Florence, and on an English wooden painted Retable of *c.* 1335 where St Dominic and St Peter Martyr are depicted, both holding books, the edges of which show a large painted double zig-zag with ornaments in the triangles.[7] On the edges of the Psalter (BL MS Harley 2895) the design is outlined in black and shows also two parallel zig-zag lines over the total width of the edge, while the triangles formed by the zig-zag are filled with large acanthus-leaved flowers in red and green. There are also traces of gold. A similar large single zig-zag, outlined in parallel black lines with red fleurons or possibly fleurs-de-lis in the triangles, decorates the edges of a twelfth-century Durham manuscript of Miracles of the Virgin in Latin (Bodley, MS Laud. misc. 359). It was bound, probably in the second half of the thirteenth century, in alum tawed leather over wooden boards and has remnants of one clasp on a leather thong with a catch near the fore-edge of the lower board, as well as plaited leather headbands. The same basic edge painting design, but now formed by three crossing zig-zag bands or ribbons with acanthus-leaved flowers in the triangular compartments, also outlined in black, but painted in green, red and blue on a gold background, is found on a *Lectionarium ex Evangeliis per circulum anni*, written in an eleventh-century German hand (with nine later leaves inserted) (BL Add. MS 20692), rebound in modern red morocco. Of the leaves that have been inserted seven are in a twelfth-century hand and two in a sixteenth-century hand. The edges of the seven twelfth-century leaves have been painted, whereas I cannot discern a trace of paint on the edges of the sixteenth-century leaves. A manuscript of the first half of the fourteenth century of Henry of Bracton's *De legibus et consuetudinibus Angliae*, in an alum tawed leather binding over wooden boards, still has its alum tawed leather chemise (Bodley, MS Rawl. C. 159) and two pairs of clasps on long leather thongs, as well as traces of two more thongs at the head and tail of the upper cover, and four holes for pins in the lower cover. The protruding flaps of the chemise have protected the painted edges from fading and a zig-zag pattern outlined in black and painted red is clearly visible. The diamonds formed by the red zig-zag ribbon contain fleurons outlined in black, and the triangles between the diamonds have leaf shapes in black on a blue ground. Another example of a pattern of diamonds or lozenges, this time not formed by connected zig-zag lines, occurs on the edges of a Flemish Psalter written in the last quarter of the thirteenth century (Bodley, MS Liturg. 396). It is bound in red-dyed sheepskin over wooden boards, tooled in blind with an all-over pattern of various fleur-de-lis tools, round floral tools and rectangular tools, one containing a monster, the other a lamb-and-flag. Oddly enough, there are traces of two pairs of clasps hinging on the upper cover, while traces of catches can be found near the fore-edge of the lower cover, as well as two holes for pins much nearer the centre of the lower cover.[8] The binding could be Netherlandish and probably dates from the fifteenth century; the edge decoration seems to be of the same date. The edges are gilt and have a painted pattern of lozenges outlined in black. The two outer rows of lozenges are painted blue and contain a fleur-de-lis in gold, while the centre row of lozenges is painted red with a floral shape in a darker colour. It is just possible that these are heraldic charges that I have not been able to identify.

A Book of Hours, written in Paris c. 1412 with painted edges showing both straight and curved lines, was sold at Sotheby's on 2 December 1986 (lot 56). It is bound in fifteenth-century blind-tooled brown calf over wooden boards. The edges are gilt and have been painted in blue and red with traces of black and green, probably at the time the manuscript was bound. The top and tail edges show a design of two crossing zig-zag lines forming a row of large diamonds and two rows of triangles. The diamonds are filled with very small squares, while there is a flame or possibly an ivy leaf beneath an arch in each triangle. The manuscript has been rebacked and the edges have moved, but all the same it looks as if the fore-edge is decorated with two intertwining curved lines forming a similar pattern. The oval compartments are filled with dashes that may have made squares before the resewing, and we find again the flames or ivy leaves beneath arches.[9] Another case where the top and tail edges display a different pattern from that on the fore-edge is a thirteenth-century British manuscript Bible (part II) (Bodley, MS University College 116), still in its medieval wooden boards. The boards have lost their covering leather and the manuscript has been rebacked. There are traces in the wood of four pairs of clasps on thongs, probably hinging on the upper cover. The top and tail edges are painted in dark green with a single large zig-zag dividing the edges into triangles containing large fleurs-de-lis. The fore-edge has an elegant bold pattern, also in green, of curving lines forming inverted heart shapes, similar to patterns we will find in the next category of painted edges, those decorated with scrollwork.

Simple scrollwork with small roundels or leaves, largely in black, decorate the edges of an early fifteenth-century Book of Hours (BL Add. MS 18629), rebound in the nineteenth century. The edges have shifted and the pattern is difficult to see.

Three more examples of fairly simple scrollwork are in the Bodleian Library, Oxford. A copy of *Flores super regulam beati Augustini*, written in England c. 1400 is bound in contemporary alum tawed leather over wooden boards (Bodley, MS e. Mus. 139). The leather shows signs of having been dyed pink, there are four bosses or traces of bosses on each cover and there are traces of two pairs of clasps on thongs which hinge on the upper cover. The edges are painted with scrollwork in black. A late thirteenth-century English manuscript Psalter was bound, possibly in the fourteenth century, in reversed calf over wooden boards, showing traces of two pairs of clasps, while holes for pins to fasten the clasps on can be found near the centre of the lower board (Bodley, MS Lat. liturg. d. 41). The edges have been painted to a pattern of two pairs of curving lines in black forming an intertwining ribbon that shows traces of red paint. A more clearly visible intertwining ribbon, outlined in black and painted in red, forming a pattern of circles that are filled with black triangles on a red ground, occurs on the edges of Bede's Life of St Cuthbert, *etc.*, a Durham manuscript of the third quarter of the twelfth century (Bodley, MS Laud. misc. 491). It was rebound in seventeenth-century blind- and gold-tooled calf with the arms of Archbishop Laud, Chancellor of the University of Oxford.

More elaborate scrollwork with and without leaves and flowers can be found on a number of manuscripts. A late twelfth-century Peter Comestor, *Historia scholastica* at Durham Cathedral (B.I.33)[10] has been rebound, but the decoration, especially that of the fore-edge, is still visible. It also shows a row of circles, formed by intertwining curving lines, which contain leafy ornaments, flowers and what may be a bird, painted in green with traces of a lighter shade, while brown or possibly black paint was used for the outlines. The rubrics have been cropped, and so, in places, has the fore-edge pricking, but the edge painting may well date from the time the manuscript was finished and first bound. A Psalter and Hours of the Virgin, written in Oxford *c.* 1200–1210 (BL Arundel MS 157) may also have contemporary painted edges. When the manuscript was rebound in the late nineteenth century, the textblock was heavily rounded and backed and the pattern has been distorted. All three edges are gilt and painted with scrollwork on the top and tail edges, while the fore-edge displays intertwining curving lines with leafy ornamentation in red, green, black and blue. A mid-thirteenth-century English manuscript of Petrus Riga, *Aurora* (MS Bodley 822), still has its medieval binding of alum tawed leather over wooden boards, with remnants of two pairs of clasps hinging on the upper cover. The edges are painted to a vigorous design of scroll-work in green with green leaves and traces of red flowers. An elaborate scrollwork design, boldly painted in green, red and black, decorates the edges of Peter Comestor, *Historia scholastica*, written in England in the late thirteenth century (MS Bodley 748). The original, possibly fourteenth-century binding of alum tawed sheepskin over wooden boards has been tooled in blind, probably in the sixteenth century. The original fabric-covered headbands have been preserved and there are traces of two pairs of clasps. The edges of a late thirteenth-century Bible (Bodley, MS Lat. Bibl. d.8), bound in fourteenth-century alum tawed leather, once dyed pink with traces of two pairs of clasps hinging on the upper cover, show on a red painted ground a vigorous design, outlined in black, of a green curving ribbon with large green leaves.[11] A similar pattern of large green leaves in curving green lines, this time interspersed with smaller circles in red, embellishes the edges of a manuscript Cartulary of Glastonbury, 1342–48 (Bodley, MS Wood. empt.1). The manuscript has been rebound at least twice, once for Ralph Sheldon whose coat of arms has been preserved and onlaid on the present eighteenth-century binding of blind-tooled calf. Four more examples may date from the fourteenth century. The edges of the Statutes of England to 1320, a manuscript in Latin and French, written in England c. 1320 (Bodley, MS Rawl. C. 292), also have a scrollwork pattern with leaves in green and flowers in red. The fourteenth-century binding is of alum tawed sheepskin over wooden boards with traces of two pairs of clasps hinging on the upper cover, while holes for pins can be found near the centre of the lower board. An early fourteenth-century French Book of Hours with calendar, penitential psalms, the Litany and prayers (BL Add. MS 17444) is bound in contemporary French blind-tooled brown calf over wooden boards. All three edges are gilt and painted with scrollwork forming large curly inverted hearts adorned with leaves. The outline is in black, the leaves are green or orange and there are larger shapes in white. These, according to Weale-Taylor,[12] are busts of Kings and Queens, but they are no longer recognizable as such. A fourteenth-century English *Breviarium Romanum* (BL MS Sloane 2466) was rebound in 1984 and the manuscript was put on guards. Consequently, the edges have moved to such an extent that the painted scrollwork in black with unidentifiable shapes in red and white are difficult to see. In much better state of preservation is a fourteenth-century *Miscellanea Theologica* (BL Add. MS 11619) bound in alum tawed sheepskin over wooden boards with semi-circular tabs at head and tail, lined with pink silk and with traces of a whip stitch round the outer edge.[13] There are also traces of one clasp, but restoration has taken care to remove all evidence of the original location of the hinge or of the fastening. The edges have been painted in black, red and green with bold decorative scrollwork.

My last four examples of elaborate scrollwork date from the fifteenth century. A manuscript of *Statuta Anglicae*, written in Staffordshire c. 1400, now in Durham University Library (Mickleton & Spearman MS 27), has been rebound but the painted edges are still visible. The top edge shows curving lines that form large curly heart shapes of the kind we have seen before, while the tail and fore-edges have intertwining curving lines forming oval compartments with traces of further scrollwork. The outline is in black and the decoration is painted in green, pink and blue. A French Book of Hours of the use of Bourges, written c. 1410 (BL Yates Thompson MS 37), was put on guards and rebound in 1966. Though the edges have shifted slightly, the decoration is still clearly visible and seems to be contemporary with the manuscript. All three edges are gilt and have been painted in black with traces of green and red to a design of curving branches with leaves and flowers. A bolder scrollwork pattern in red and black is painted on the edges of Ludovicus de Cortosiis's alphabetical subject index to the canon and civil law (Bodley, MS Lat. misc. c. 58). The manuscript was written on paper in Germany in the early fifteenth century and shows black and red painted scrollwork in the top margin of fol. 1. It has been rebound in vellum, probably in the eighteenth century. A Flemish mid-fifteenth-century manuscript Book of Hours of Sarum use in the Fitzwilliam Museum, Cambridge (MS 1055–1975) has been rebound in nineteenth-century red velvet. The edges have shifted slightly, but the painting is still visible and is probably contemporary with the manuscript. The edges are gilt and show a pattern in green, red and blue paint of curving scrollwork with leaves and larger, possibly floral, shapes.

A small group of edges show floral patterns that cannot be classified as scrollwork. I have hitherto only found two examples. One occurs on a Swiss manuscript, the life and miracles of St Francis of Assisi, written in Latin by St Bonaventura and translated into German by Sibilla de Bondorff, a nun of the Order of St Clare in Lower Fribourg (BL Add. MS 15710). It was written on paper in the fifteenth century and is still in its original late fifteenth-century binding of brown calf over wooden boards, tooled in blind. The binding is signed 'fr.rolet.stosz', a Franciscan friar and bookbinder who worked in the second half of the fifteenth century in Fribourg.[14] The edges have been painted with a trellis work of green leafy branches with traces of red flowers. There is no reason to believe that the edges were not decorated at the same time as the manuscript was bound, probably in the 1470s. The other example embellishes the edges of a Paris Book of Hours written c. 1415–1420 (Getty Museum, Malibu, MS 22), rebound by Sangorski & Sutcliffe. The edges are gilt and have been divided into horizontal compartments. The top edge is divided into two by a large green branch, one part containing a pinkish-red flower, the other a blue periwinkle with foliage in green. The tail edge also has flowers but is difficult to see. The fore-edge is divided into three parts by broad green bands. Each compartment contains a flower with green foliage; the outer parts have blue flowers while the centre has an orange flower. One of the blue flowers may be a carnation, and very similar carnations can be found in the margins of the manuscript itself (e.g. fol. 242). Similarly, the other more stylized blue flower, the periwinkle, the pinkish-red flower and the orange flower that occur on the edges can all be found in the manuscript (e.g. on fols. 126ᵛ, 130ᵛ, 241, 246, 258).

The next category consists of edges that display the owner's coat of arms. All my examples date from the fourteenth and fifteenth centuries, and all but one are either English or French. The earliest manuscript in this group is Peraldus, *Summa de Vitiis*, Bestiary, and miscellaneous texts, written in England *c.* 1240–1255 (BL MS Harley 3244).[15] It has been rebound and the leaves have moved noticeably. The edges are gilt (gold painted?) and painted with what looks like a coat of arms with a crest or possibly mantling. There are traces of red in the sinister part of the shield. Four examples of English heraldic edges of the first half of the fourteenth century are better preserved and therefore easier to identify. A Psalter, written and illuminated in Northern France in the second half of the thirteenth century came to England where, in the fourteenth century, it belonged to Anne Felbrigge, a nun in the convent of Minoresses at Bruis-yard in Suffolk whose name occurs in the manuscript (BL MS Sloane 2400). She was the daughter of Sir Simon Felbrigge, standard-bearer to Richard II. The Psalter, rebound in the eighteenth century, still has its original embroidered covers inlaid in the later calf binding. The embroidery, in coloured silks and silver-gilt thread on a two-fold linen ground, shows on the upper cover the Annunciation and on the lower cover the Crucifixion. It can be dated *c.* 1300–1330.[16] The edges show traces of gilt (or gold paint?) and are painted to a bold pattern of two large zig-zag lines forming diamonds and triangles. The diamonds have the Felbrigge arms, *or* a lion rampant *gules*, while the triangles contain half or three-quarter fleurs-de-lis on a blue/green background. Another Psalter, written in the Diocese of Norwich in the beginning of the fourteenth century (Bodley, MS Douce 366) was presented to Norwich by Robert of Ormesby in the mid-1320s. At the time of presentation the manuscript was bound and the edges were decorated.[17] The binding is of pink-dyed leather over wooden boards and is covered with an alum tawed leather chemise which wraps round the volume. The edges are painted in gold, red, blue and green and show the arms of Norfolk Cathedral Priory and the See of Norwich. A Psalter written in Peterborough *c.* 1321–1341 (Bodley, MS Barlow 22) is also bound in alum tawed leather over wooden boards; the turn-ins show that the leather was once dyed pink. There are remnants of a chemise and the edges have been painted with the quarterings of the royal arms as borne by the English kings from Edward III till Henry V: *azure* a semis of fleurs-de-lis *or*, and *gules* three lions passant guardant *or*. The charges have been outlined in black and the tincture *or* was probably effected with yellow paint rather than with gold. A manuscript of Bede, William of Malmesbury, Martinus Polonius, *etc.*, written after 1330 for Robert de Wyville, bishop of Salisbury, with his arms on fol. 1

as well as on the fore-edge, has been rebound in eighteenth-century mottled calf (MS Bodley 712). Besides Wyville's arms, the edges show scrollwork with large fleurons painted in red and black. The curving ribbon is left uncoloured on a red or black ground while the fleurons are in the contrasting colour. An English manuscript of the first half of the fourteenth century, a *Bible historiale* in French, in two volumes (BL MS Royal 19.D.IV & V), rebound in eighteenth-century brown russia, has edges painted in blue, red and gold. On a blue ground two zig-zag ribbons, outlined in black and painted in gold, form a row of large diamonds with connecting knots. These diamonds are alternating red and blue and show, on a red ground, a coat of arms, paly of six *or* and *azure*, and, on a blue ground, a coat, *gules* a fess *or*. The paly coat is clear and may be that of Sir Matthew Gurney. The other coat is indistinct and may have other charges besides the fess. The *Catalogue of Western Manuscripts in the Old Royal and King's Collections in the British Museum* (1921) suggests that it may have been *gules* a fess between six crosses crosslet *or*, the arms of Beauchamp, Earl of Warwick. As Matthew Gurney married (after 1362) Alice Beauchamp, daughter of Thomas, Earl of Warwick, this would be a convenient supposition. However, even the eye of faith cannot now discern the six crosses crosslet, or identify any other charge. We are on safer ground with a fourteenth-century manuscript *Prisciani Caesariensis Commentariorum grammaticorum libri* [and other works], that belonged first to Pope Gregory XI and later to Jean Duc de Berry (BL Burney MS 275). It has been rebound in twentieth-century blue morocco, but the edges were gilt and painted either when the book was presented to the Duc de Berry or when he had it bound, as each displays in the centre his coat of arms as it occurs in many manuscripts that were made for him: *azure* a semis of fleurs-de-lis *or*, within a bordure *gules*. A manuscript that is extremely well documented is the Litlyngton Missal at Westminster Abbey (MS 37). It was written for the Abbey by Thomas Preston in 1383–1384 on the command of Abbot Nicholas Litlyngton (1362–1386). It is lavishly and very beautifully illuminated and has the initials and arms of the Abbot, as well as those of the Abbey in several places in the text. The original account for the 'new Missal' survives among the Abbey muniments.[18] There are separate entries for the vellum, the illumination of the large initials, the painting of the Crucifixion page, the writing of the musical notation, as well as for the scribe and the cloth for his livery. The binding cost 21 shillings; there was apparently also a loose embroidered cover that came to 8s.4d for the cover and 6s.10d for the embroidery thereof. Unfortunately, the Missal was rebound in the early nineteenth century by John Bohn[19] who split it into two volumes. The edges are gilt and painted in red and blue, possibly green, to a design of elaborate scrollwork with leaves in a black outline, surrounding the coat of arms of Abbot Litlyngton, quarterly *argent* and *gules*, on the 2nd and 3rd quarters a fret *or*, over all a bend *azure* charged with three fleurs-de-lis *or*. The fact that no mention is made in the account of the edge painting, though there is no doubt that it was done at the time the manuscript was finished and first bound, may indicate that this was understood to be included in the work of the illuminators as a matter of course.

Six more examples date from the fifteenth century. Aegidius de Columna, *De regimine principum*, an English manuscript *c.* 1400 in a contemporary binding of pink-dyed sheepskin over wooden boards with traces of two pairs of clasps hinging on the upper cover and with two holes for pins near the centre of the lower board, has in the lower margin of fol. 1 the coat of arms of Thorp, *gules* a fess between six fleurs-de-lis *argent* (MS Bodley 234). The individual charges of this coat can be found on the edges, painted in black outline on a red ground. A fifteenth-century English manuscript from the Cottonian Library (BL MS Cotton, Cleopatra A.XIII) contains a *Tractatus de regimine principum, etc.*, dedicated to King Henry VI [and] *Variae matutinae et orationes ad B. Virginem* by John, Prior of Bridlington. It was rebound in the nineteenth century and the edges shifted in the process, but the decoration of the tail-edge is still quite clearly visible. The edges are gilt and the English royal arms as used by Henry VI (quarterly, 1st and 4th *azure* three fleurs-de-lis *or*; 2nd and 3rd *gules* three lions passant guardant *or*) are painted in the centre. The identity of the owner of a fifteenth-century Book of Hours of Sarum use (BL MS Harley 2900) has been well established.[20] On fol. 55 we find an initial G containing a coat of arms, *gules* a rampant lion *ermine*. They are the arms of Sir William Oldhall of Narford (d.1460); a miniature on the same folio depicts him dressed in a tabard patterned with his arms, kneeling before St George. On fol. 200 his wife Margaret is depicted kneeling before her patron saint. She holds a scroll with the opening words of the office 'o intemerata et in eternum' and at her feet is her own family's coat of arms, quarterly 1st and 4th *sable* a cross engrailed *or*; 2nd and 3rd *gules* a cross moline *argent*. She was a daughter of William, 5th Lord Willoughby of Eresby. The manuscript has been rebound in modern red velvet. Though the edges have moved, there are traces of gilding and of painted scrollwork in black, blue and green. The fore-edge has the arms of Sir William Oldhall impaling those of his wife. The *Catalogue of Manuscripts in the Harleian Collection in the British Museum* (1808) states that the kneeling figure on fol. 55 portrays John Duke of Bedford, but his arms are quarterly France modern and England with a label of five points, the two on the dexter side *ermine* and each of the other three charged with three fleurs-de-lis. The heraldic evidence therefore does not bear out this attribution. He was the third son of Henry IV and he married in 1423 Anne, sister of Philip the Good, Duke of Burgundy.

Philip the Good's illegitimate son by Jeanne de Presler was Anthony, great bastard of Burgundy for whom a fifteenth-century *Missale ad usum Romanae ecclesiae* was written and illuminated (BL MS Harley 2967). His arms and emblems decorate the borders and initials. The manuscript was rebound in the nineteenth century. The edges are gilt and have been painted with the arms of Anthony of Burgundy surrounded by leaves and flowers in red, green, blue and yellow. Among the foliage we also find Anthony's crest, an owl, and a scroll with his emblem of a barbican conjoined. The motto 'Nul ne s'y frotte' that occurs on a similar scroll and barbican in the text (e.g. on fol. 9) is no longer visible on the edge. A late fifteenth-century manuscript Jean Boutiller, *La Somme rurale*, written on paper in eastern France, bound in blind-tooled reversed calf over wooden boards was sold at Sotheby's in Monte-Carlo on 28 February 1987 (lot 88). The edges are painted in black and red with curving branches surrounding on the fore-edge the arms of Claude de Neufchatel sieur de Fay, governor of the Duchy of Luxembourg (*gules*, a bend *argent* with a label).

My last heraldic example comes from the Netherlands. A three-volume Bible in Latin, written at Utrecht, probably for Herman van Lochorst (or Lockhorst), dean of the Cathedral there (d. 1438), was originally bound in brown calf over wooden boards with an alum tawed leather chemise held to the boards by five large brass bosses on each cover. Each volume has remnants of two pairs of clasps fastening on the upper cover and traces of a chain ring at the top of the lower cover (Fitzwilliam Museum Cambridge, MS 289). The binding was repaired by Sydney Cockerell in March 1987. Though he took obvious care to disturb the original structure as little as possible, the edges have shifted slightly. The painting on the edges is still visible and shows on a gilt ground a kneeling angel outlined in black and painted in orange and green, holding a large shield with the arms of the Lochorst family. This example, being both heraldic and pictorial, brings me to my last category which consists of the most splendid edges of all: those on the lives of St Cuthbert, St Aidan and St Oswald by Bede, a late twelfth-century manuscript in Latin in Durham Cathedral Library (A.IV.35).[21] The manuscript has been rebound at least twice. It is presently in a binding by W. H. Smith & Son, but the sixteenth-century blind-tooled brown calf binding over wooden boards has been preserved separately and so have fragments of the original twelfth-century binding. The sixteenth-century binding was made in Oxford and is decorated with a roll signed GK;[22] it is probable that the bevelled boards also date from the sixteenth century. Originally the manuscript was bound in alum tawed leather of which the spine with a semi-circular tab, sewn round with a whip stitch in yellow, red and green silk, was retained to reinforce the spine in the sixteenth century. There is a fragment of red silk tab lining, while the tab also has a linen or canvas lining. Two double alum tawed thongs and the original tailband, an alum tawed core oversewn with green, red and yellow silk, have also been preserved. The only cropping of the manuscript is of original catchwords, a marginal rubric and some of the fore-edge pricking; the edges were most probably painted when the manuscript was first bound. The top edge shows on a green background St Oswald, crowned and bearing a sceptre, beneath an architectural arch. He is dressed in green and orange vestments with a little gold and white rim; his shoes are gold and his hands and face are drawn in black outline. The tail edge has, also on a green ground, an arch with, against a red background, the figure of St Aidan, wearing a bishop's mitre and raising one hand in blessing. He is dressed in white, green and gold and is wearing golden shoes. The fore-edge has a green ground with white and gold clouds near the top. An arch frames on a red background St Cuthbert wearing a mitre with a large cross in gold, green, white and gold vestments and golden shoes. He too raises one hand in blessing and stands on three green hillocks.

Edge paintings of this kind are obviously exceptional, both in their execution and in the elaboration of their subject, though religious scenes become much less rare on edges of the Restoration period and are fairly common in the eighteenth century. Before 1500 most painted edges display abstract, floral or heraldic designs. My impression is that they were painted by illuminators rather than by binders, the—alas fairly rare—connections between the illumination of the manuscript and its edges supports this. Their artistic value is possibly peripheral though not negligible, and one can only urge restorers of the future to treat them with more respect than they have received in the past.

1. Gilt and gauffered edges can also clearly be seen in a number of paintings, e.g. by Hans Memling, Petrus Christus and Gerard David. Unless indicated otherwise, all paintings referred to are on view in the National Gallery, London.
2. Fourteenth-century paintings showing books with striped edges were painted by e.g. Giovanni del Ponte, Nardo di Cione, Masolino and Carlo Crivelli.
3. I am most grateful to my colleague, Miss Janet Backhouse and to Professor Albinia de la Mare of King's College, London, (formerly of the Bodleian Library) for all their help. I also owe much to O. Pächt and J. J. G. Alexander, *Illuminated Manuscripts in the Bodleian Library, Oxford*, Oxford, 1973; N. Morgan, *Early Gothic Manuscripts, Vol.I, 1190–1250*, London, 1982; Lucy Freeman Sandler, *Gothic Manuscripts, 1285–1385*, London, 1986; and to the various printed catalogues of manuscript collections in the British Library.
4. The manuscript is too lavish to have remained unbound for any length of time.

5. According to W. Y. Fletcher, *Foreign Bookbindings in the British Museum*, London, 1896, pl. 3, the binding dates from the twelfth century. C. Davenport, 'Decoration of book-edges', *Bibliographica*, II (1896), p. 387 suggests that the edge decoration may date from the fourteenth century. No reason for this suggestion is given.

6. [D. Miner], *The History of Bookbinding, 525–1950 A.D. An Exhibition held at the Baltimore Museum of Art*, Baltimore, 1957, no. 103 refers to an eleventh-century Byzantine manuscript, bound possibly in the sixteenth century, which has edges painted with a design of circles. Another sixteenth-century example is Ludwig MS XV.2 in the Getty Museum at Malibu.

7. J. Alexander and P. Binski (eds.), *Age of Chivalry*, London, 1987, no. 564.

8. According to J. B. Oldham, *English Blind-stamped Bindings*, Cambridge, 1952, p. 8, clasps on German and Dutch bindings have their hinges on the lower cover and fasten on the upper cover. The presence of two kinds of fastenings suggests that the earlier clasps (which fastened on pins) were replaced at a later date with a type that fastened with catches.

9. The Sotheby's catalogue records a number of examples of painted edges, not all of which I have seen.

10. I am very grateful to Dr A. I. Doyle who has drawn my attention to this and to the two other manuscripts at Durham mentioned below.

11. A thirteenth-century French manuscript Bible (Bodley, MS Canon. Bibl. Lat. 15), rebound in late eighteenth- or early nineteenth-century russia, also has painted edges. The top edge shows two large curls, the tail edge has a fleuron and floral shapes, and the fore-edge has traces of red and green paint. The shape of the fleuron on the tail edge suggests that the painting may date from the sixteenth century.

12. W. H. J. Weale and L. Taylor, *Early Stamped Bookbindings in the British Museum*, London, 1922, no. 20.

13. This example shows that the use of tabs is not limited to the late twelfth and early thirteenth centuries; see G. Pollard, 'The construction of English twelfth-century bindings', *The Library*, fifth series, XVII (1962), pp. 1–22, esp. pp. 12, 16.

14. W. H. J. Weale and L. Taylor, *op. cit.*, (see note 12), no. 152. A. Horodisch, 'Die Buchbinderei zu Freiburg (Schweiz) im 15. Jahrhundert', *Zeitschrift für Schweizerische Archaeologie und Kunstgeschichte*, Band 6 (1944), pp. 207–43.

15. *Age of Chivalry, op. cit.*, (see note 7), no. 150.

16. M. M. Foot, *Pictorial Bookbindings*, London, 1986, no. 50. P. Wallis, 'The embroidered binding of the Felbrigge Psalter', *British Library Journal*, XIII (1987), pp. 71–8. See also Fig. 53.1 above.

17. *Age of Chivalry, op. cit.*, (see note 7), no. 573.

18. J. Wickham Legg, *Missale ad usum ecclesie Westmonasteriensis*, London, 1891. J. A. Robinson and M. R. James, *The Manuscripts of Westminster Abbey*, Cambridge, 1909, pp. 7–8.

19. H. M. Nixon, *Five Centuries of English Bookbinding*, London, 1978, no. 82.

20. C. E. Wright, *English Heraldic Manuscripts in the British Museum*, London, 1973, pp. 5, 20, pl. 9. R. Marks and A. Payne, *British Heraldry from its origins to c. 1800*, London, 1978, no. 32. I am very grateful to Mrs Jenny Stratford for her help.

21. R. Mynors, *Durham Cathedral Manuscripts to the End of the Twelfth Century*, Durham, 1939, no. 131. B. Colgrave, 'The New Bede MS.', *The Durham University Journal*, XXX, no. 1 (1936), pp. 1–5 suggests that the edge

painting is contemporary with the sixteenth-century binding. The 'paint' he has noticed occurs on the twelfth-century tab and is in fact a bit of red wax. The colour of the paint on the top edge closest to the headband is green.

22. J. B. Oldham, *English Blind-stamped Bindings*, Cambridge, 1952, MW.a(1)857.

Index of Binders

(including binding designers) and paper decorators (pd)

Index of Owners

Institutions and libraries have been indexed under place name